HE Church THROUGH History

Rev. Maurice O'Connell | **Joseph Stoutzenberger**

Harcourt
Religion Publishers

Harcourt Religion Publishers

Our Mission

The primary mission of Harcourt Religion Publishers is to
provide the Catholic and Christian educational markets with the
highest quality catechetical print and media resources.
The content of these resources reflects the best insights of current
theology, methodology, and pedagogical research. The resources are
practical and easy to use, designed to meet expressed market needs,
and written to reflect the teachings of the Catholic Church.

Nihil Obstat

Rev. Dennis J. Colter

Imprimatur

✠ Most Rev. Jerome Hanus OSB
Archbishop of Dubuque
January 2, 2002
Feast day of SS Basil the Great Gregory Nazianzen, Bishops and Doctors

For permission to reprint copyrighted material, grateful acknowledgement is made to the
following sources:

New Revised Standard Version Bible: Catholic Edition copyright © 1993 and 1989 by the
Division of Christian Education of the National Council of the Churches of Christ in the
U.S.A. Used by permission. All rights reserved.

Excerpts from the English translation of the *Catechism of the Catholic Church* for use in the
United States of America copyright © 1994, United States Catholic Conference, Inc.—
Libreria Editrice Vaticana. English translation of the *Catechism of the Catholic Church:
Modifications from the Editio Typica* copyright © 1997, United States catholic Conference,
Inc.—Libreria Editrice Vaticana. Used with Permission.

Photo credits appear on page 340.

Printed in the United States of America

ISBN 0-15-901094-2

10 9 8 7 6 5 4 3 2 1

CONTENTS

Bostonian Classics
9½

ALLOWING THE PAST TO SPEAK

INTRODUCTION OVERVIEW

- History is more than an accumulation of facts.

- Church history traces the impact of Christ in the lives of people over the past two thousand years.

- Studying history involves learning the facts while delving into the stories of those affected by the events.

- The Catholic Church has adapted to the historical and cultural circumstances in which it has found itself.

- Numerous tools are available to us in our study of the past.

THE PRESENT BEGAN IN THE PAST

Why do you have your last name? What is your cultural and ethnic background? Why do you live in your current neighborhood? Where do or did your great-grandparents live? How does your family traditionally celebrate special occasions? Are there certain phrases that are unique to your family or group of friends? These are questions that we may seldom ask ourselves but actually say a lot about who we are. The answers to these questions are to be found in our family history. The present always has its beginnings in the past, but we have to know how to look at our past, our history. The same questions can be asked of communities, states, countries, and even institutions like governments and Churches. The very best way to learn about this history is to find a good storyteller.

Storytellers: Bringing the Past to Life

Every family should have a Nellie O'Brien. She was my grandfather's first cousin and my godmother. She attended school only through the sixth grade; and although she could read and write, it was her memory that was her greatest asset. She was the best storyteller I ever met. She was born in 1897 and knew all our family stories. From the time I was able to drive, it was my job to get her to and from family gatherings. I loved those times together when she would tell me the stories of my family, beginning with my great-grandparents. Without her, I would have known only their names. Nellie made them real for me. She told me about the times they lived in and about what they thought and did. She was the family historian.

History is not just about what, when, and where. More importantly, it is about who, how, and why. One way to view history is through the study of names, dates, and events that occurred in the past. This type of chronological studying of history deals in the "just the facts" approach to looking at the past. While that may make for interesting trivia, it doesn't have the fascination of real history. History involves passing on stories and describing the personalities involved in those stories, all the while seeking to make sense of why people did what they did.

History opens up new worlds to us. In so doing, it also sheds new light on our own world. Because of Nellie, the historian, the past came alive for me and took on personal meaning. It involved learning about the people whose actions, whether I like it or not, shaped me and my present situation and would also influence my future. The who, why, and how of events in our family give them color, personality, and meaning. When the people of our past cease to be merely pictures in a family album, and we try to allow them to speak to us, then we truly appreciate and understand our family history (Father Maury O'Connell).

HISTORY VERSUS CHRONOLOGY

All of us know about the tragedy of the Holocaust that occurred prior to and during World War II. Six million Jews and three million others were killed ruthlessly and senselessly at the hands of the Nazi regime in Germany. Those are the bare facts of the Holocaust. Chronology is helpful here—listing concentration camps, trying to number how many people died in each one, identifying victims by nationality and religion, and so forth. However, many people have also tried various ways to get to the heart of this monumental tragedy—that is to say, to tell the history of it. To do so they recount the stories of those who have died, describe what life had been like for victims and victimizers, identify possible causes of the tragedy, tell about how different people responded to the same events. This approach to studying history allows the people of the era of the Holocaust to speak to us today.

During the Holocaust, Maximilian Kolbe was imprisoned in a concentration camp. When another prisoner was chosen at random to be executed, Kolbe—a Franciscan priest—offered to take his place. Those in charge at the camp accepted his offer. Maximilian endured many days of starvation and finally was put to death.

Today the Catholic Church proclaims Maximilian Kolbe to be a saint because, besides recognizing the saintliness of the man, it wants his story and the stories of others who responded with heroism in those dark and desperate circumstances to inspire us and guide us today.

Understanding the past better, as the study of history attempts to do, can help us appreciate where and who we have come from, how our world today fits into the bigger picture of the past and present, why we are who we are, and how we might react to upcoming challenges.

Pope John Paul II enters the gates of Auschwitz concentration camp in 1979. He visited the cell in block 11 where Fr. Kolbe died giving his life in exchange for one of the other prisoners.

Maximilian Kolbe (below).

The Dynamics of History at Work

People in our world today have come to take seriously the need to preserve our natural resources and to cut down on the amount of waste we produce. If we are to understand our attitude toward the use of things and toward what we should do with things when we're through with them, then it is necessary to look to the past. How have people in different times and in different places viewed their place in nature? Have there been giants who rose above the crowd to alert us to be more sensitive to the environment? Have Christians historically been in the forefront of nature-consciousness? As these questions indicate, the past has much to say to us even about this one issue facing us today. At the same time, aren't we who are alive today taking recycling so seriously because it is part of our legacy for the future? Our children and grandchildren will suffer or benefit by the actions we take today. Such is the dynamic nature of history.

Activity

Recall an event you have heard about from your family's history. (If possible, ask your family storyteller about the details of the event.)

1. Write about the event in short story form.

2. Describe how this story might speak to you in some way—to understand yourself and your family members better, to appreciate how today is similar to or different from yesterday, or to offer guidance about things you might do in the future.

HISTORY AND CHURCH HISTORY

Christianity is essentially a historical religion. God reveals himself to his people, not in doctrinal statements nor in theoretical studies, but in action, in the outworking of a story of relationships.

John Briggs, *"God, Time and History,"* quoted in *Introduction to the History of Christianity,* Tim Dowley, ed. (Minneapolis: Fortress Press, 1995), 15.

History has many elements, such as names, dates, and places. It recounts stories of individuals with varied personalities and relationships. As it traces the development of thoughts and ideas, it is anything but impersonal or boring. Indeed, it is a record of the human condition itself. You will see that all of these elements come into play in studying the history of the Church, plus an additional element—Church history has Jesus the Christ.

The study of Church history looks at what transpired in the last 2000 years in the unfolding and continuing story of Christ's presence in the world. Church history is an ongoing story, one of a living family. It contains important messages for today in the history of Catholics who are members of that family. Those of us presently living are making our own stories, creating our own history, and shaping the world for future generations. In this ongoing process it is helpful—indeed, essential—that we learn from the past. More particularly, if we want Christ to be a part of today and the future then we need to learn from people of the past who called themselves Christians. This is where our study of Church history comes in.

Discussion

Imagine what the future might be like if everyone forgot about Christ and his message. Then imagine a future in which most people seek to know and follow Christ. Describe the differences in these two visions of the future. How could the study of Church history help you better understand your vision of the future?

Allowing the Past to Speak

The Church—Ageless and Always Changing

The following statement is from a document of Vatican Council II (1962–1965), the largest gathering of Catholic bishops in the history of the Catholic Church:

> Henceforward the Church, endowed with the gifts of her founder and faithfully observing his precepts of charity, humility and self-denial, receives the mission of proclaiming and establishing among all peoples the kingdom of Christ and of God, and she is, on earth, the seed and the beginning of that Kingdom ("Constitution on the Church" *Lumen Gentium*, 1:5).

This statement indicates that the dual nature of the Church is to manifest the person of Jesus to people, and to be a community who proclaims Jesus as Lord and Savior through word and action. These two dimensions of Church can never be separated: Jesus Christ is present *to* people so that he can be present *through* people.

While the Church must always remain true to its connection with Christ, it is also an institution that has existed in different societies and cultures over the last twenty centuries. While its center—Jesus Christ—and the continuing of his mission of proclaiming God's reign has not changed, the Church's role in the world has developed over time. Learning about various ways people choose to be Church helps us to ask how we can best do so in our time and culture, making thoughtful choices that truly demonstrate our relationship to Jesus and his teachings.

The Catechism Describes the Church

The most recent compilation of official Catholic teaching can be found in the *Catechism of the Catholic Church* published in English in 1994. The Catechism tries to communicate the dual nature of the Church. It says that the Church is in history, and also transcends history. "With the eyes of faith," we can see the Church as a visible reality and a spiritual reality that brings divine life (#770). When we look at all the people who make up the Church today and who have been the Church of the past, we see humans struggling to make it through life. However, behind this visible reality lies another reality, for the Church is the people of God. We might wish that Christ were present in some other form than in the motley collection of people who have made up the Church past and present, but that is not the case. Its humanity is part of the mystery of the Church. The Catechism explains the past and present make-up of the Church as a hierarchical society that is the body of Christ, a visible and spiritual community, and an earthly Church and a Church with spiritual gifts (#771).

Church history seeks to look at history with "the eyes of faith," believing that the hand of God is at work even when we have difficulty understanding how.

Activity

List five specific ways that you think the Church could meaningfully live out its mission to proclaim Christ in the world today. Explain your list.

Tools that Help Us in Our Study of History

Physicians who study the human body make use of certain tools that help them know better how the body functions. What tools are available to us that can make our journey into the past more fruitful? Here are some tools used in this textbook.

Time Lines. At the beginning of each chapter, there is a time line that places the events of Church history in chronological order. These time lines are meant to help us keep focused on the ongoing flow of world history and the Church's place in that story.

Vocabulary. Knowing the original meanings of words and how they were used at particular times can help us make important connections with our past. Key words will surface during our study, and these help us develop a Church history vocabulary.

People. Just as there are various people who were particularly important in the history of a family, many different men and women have left their imprint on the Church. In each chapter, individuals are singled out who have made unique contributions to the Church in a particular period of history. While it is misleading to reduce history to the story of "great men and women of the past," at the same time certain people encapsulate the spirit of their age so strongly that it is worthwhile to hear their story.

Pivotal Events. Certain events in a family's history lead people to move to another place, to begin different jobs, or even to change the family name. Such pivotal events also occurred in the Church. Looking at them helps us understand how the Church of the twenty-first century came to be what it is.

Family Stories and Traditions. The story *Roots,* made into a popular TV miniseries in 1976, illustrates the difference between chronology (the listing of names and dates in a family) and family history (the stories and traditions, as well as the names and dates). People began to see that their family stories were rooted in historical reality. We will trace the development of certain Church traditions that may be taken for granted today. Church leadership, celebrating sacraments, and the ways we honor Mary are just a few examples of such traditions.

Maps. In studying Church history, maps are like old photographs that offer a visual of something we've only heard about. They help us know the physical setting in which events occurred. Comparisons of maps from one time period to another help us visualize changes that occurred in the geography of a land or city.

Let's Get Started

Now we have some idea of what we will be studying, why we are studying it, and how we will approach the study. Let us begin. The story starts with a small group of friends who followed Jesus and whose descendants became one of the most important communities in world history, the Catholic Church.

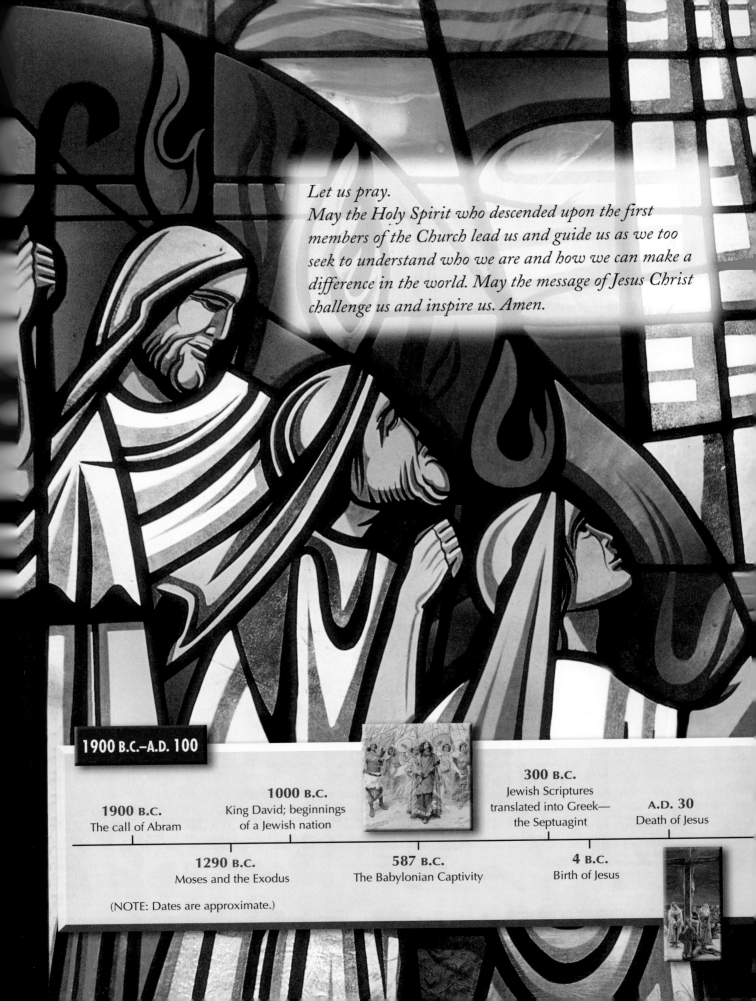

Let us pray.
May the Holy Spirit who descended upon the first
members of the Church lead us and guide us as we too
seek to understand who we are and how we can make a
difference in the world. May the message of Jesus Christ
challenge us and inspire us. Amen.

1900 B.C.–A.D. 100

1900 B.C.
The call of Abram

1290 B.C.
Moses and the Exodus

1000 B.C.
King David; beginnings
of a Jewish nation

587 B.C.
The Babylonian Captivity

300 B.C.
Jewish Scriptures
translated into Greek—
the Septuagint

4 B.C.
Birth of Jesus

A.D. 30
Death of Jesus

(NOTE: Dates are approximate.)

CHAPTER ONE
A.D. 30–100

BEGINNINGS
The Church of the Apostles

CHAPTER OVERVIEW

■ At Pentecost the followers of Jesus begin to understand their role as Christ's presence in the world.

■ The early Church builds a new identity based on its Jewish roots.

■ Key themes inspiring people to join the Church were trust in God, liberation through God's intervention, and personal and social conversion.

■ The growth of a diverse, hopefilled Christian community unified in Christ.

A.D. 34
Death of Stephen,
first Christian martyr

A.D. 50
Council of
Jerusalem

A.D. 70
Destruction of the
temple in Jerusalem

A.D. 100
Death of Saint John, end
of the Apostolic Age

A.D. 35–67
Saint Paul's conversion and
mission to the Gentiles

A.D. 64–67
Martyrdom of Peter and Paul during the
first Roman persecution under Nero

A.D. 81
Domitian persecution begins

Have you ever had an experience that completely turned your life around? Did you ever experience an event that filled you with great joy or that helped you make sense out of life? Are there people you have known who were able to forget their own problems and be genuinely concerned about others? Have you ever been part of a group where you felt accepted and cared for?

During his lifetime Jesus built a community in which people had experiences such as these. Within decades after his death, the followers of Jesus grew in number and took on a new and distinctive identity. By the end of the first century, the community, initially made up of country folk and people from small towns, believed strongly enough in their Lord's message to spread it throughout the civilized world. Even before the death of the last apostle, the basic framework that Jesus established for this community had been firmly implanted. Through the power of the Father, Son, and Holy Spirit, the Church was born.

Before We Begin . . .

Think about at least three possible images that could symbolize *Church* for you. Draw a symbolic representation of *Church* centered on one or more of these images. After you have completed your drawing, answer the following questions:

- If someone else looked at your drawing, what understanding of *Church* do you think that person would find there?

- What aspects of the *Church* does your drawing emphasize? What aspects of *Church* can you think of that are not represented in your drawing?

- Why do you think that your drawing would be an accurate representation of the *Church* in its beginning stages?

- What other symbols for *Church* did you consider? Why did you choose the one you did and not others?

- Now that you've thought about it more, what other images might you have used to symbolize *Church*?

PENTECOST

The Followers of Jesus before Pentecost

fyi!

The Greek name for *Shavu'ot* was *Pentecost,* a word that means "fiftieth day."

Paraphrase

ascension *vocab*
the entry of Jesus' humanity into divine glory in God's heavenly domain, forty days after his resurrection

Pope John Paul II at a World Youth Day gathering.

A most astonishing event occurred around the year A.D. 30 during *Shavu'ot,* the Jewish harvest *Festival of Weeks,* so called because it took place fifty days—or a week of weeks—after Passover. Many Jewish people gathered in Jerusalem for this feast. A small group of Jews, meeting in an upper room, were followers of a Jewish man named Jesus. They had received an almost unbelievable message of hope when Jesus performed miraculous deeds of healing and power while proclaiming the reign of God.

However, just as the number of Jesus' followers was beginning to grow, Roman soldiers had arrested Jesus. Some religious leaders and a number of other people—perhaps even some of Jesus' former followers—called for his crucifixion (the cruelest form of execution then practiced in the Roman Empire). Most of his followers abandoned him during or shortly after his death.

Youth News

Imagine a dynamic speaker in front of a crowd of thousands of people from a number of different countries. He speaks of hope, faith, love, and living a life directed toward building God's kingdom. You could be standing in the crowd with Peter at the first Christian Pentecost or you may be numbered among the youth at World Youth Day with the pope. WYD is held every other year, at different places throughout the world. Find out where and when the next World Youth Day will be held and consider attending.

However, on the Sunday after Jesus' crucifixion, some of his women followers visited his tomb to anoint the body. They reported that the tomb was empty. On a few occasions thereafter, Jesus appeared to a number of his followers. They were overjoyed as they remembered that he had prophesied that he would rise from the dead. (See Mark 8:31 and Luke 24:6.) Eventually, Jesus left them once again in his **ascension** to the Father. (See Luke 24:51.)

As these followers gathered in the upper room, they tried to make sense of this series of events. We can hardly imagine their confused states of mind after the topsy-turvy experiences they had had with Jesus. They had been filled with wonder at miraculous deeds one day, only to be baffled by puzzling statements the next. The crowd of followers had grown daily and then were left in despair by Jesus' torture and death. To be sure, his resurrection comforted them, but they were soon left alone again by his sudden departure. They were left with the question, "Now what?"

The Holy Spirit Stirs Jesus' Followers into Action

Acts of the Apostles
the book of the New Testament that depicts the actions of the early Church community

We can read about what happened next in the second chapter of the **Acts of the Apostles,** a book contained in the New Testament. *"And suddenly from heaven there came a sound like the rush of a violent wind, and it filled the entire house where they were sitting. Divided tongues, as of fire, appeared among them, and a tongue rested on each of them. All of them were filled with the Holy Sprit and began to speak in other languages, as the Spirit gave them ability"* (Acts 2:2–4). According to this recorded account, traditional Jewish symbols for the Spirit of God (fire and wind) were seen and heard. The Holy Spirit filled the apostles, and they spoke in other languages. Suddenly, the disciples began to understand their new role—*they* were being empowered by the Holy Spirit to manifest the Lord Jesus to their world.

The disciples in the upper room were not a gathering of community leaders. Most of them were more comfortable with manual labor than with public speaking. However, filled with the Holy Spirit, they were able to do things which had previously been impossible. The leader of the group, a fisherman named Peter who had denied the Lord before his crucifixion, now stood his ground and proceeded to preach to the crowd of pilgrims gathered from all parts of the empire. He preached with such conviction, while inspired by the Holy Spirit, three thousand new members were added in a single day to the newborn Church (Acts 2:41).

Pentecost
for Christians, the day the Holy Spirit was manifested, given, and communicated as a divine Person to the Church, fulfilling the Paschal mystery of Christ according to his promise

No wonder **Pentecost** is often called the "birthday of the Church"! Before the first Christian Pentecost, the gospel was the mission of a single person. Jesus preached, healed, and gathered people together through his own personal presence. He told people about God the Father, about what he wanted of them, and about what he had in store for them. Now, thanks to the miraculous gift of the Holy Spirit, Jesus' followers were about to embark on a new journey. They were now Christ present in the world. They invited everyone to be baptized and to join them in proclaiming and living the gospel.

Activity

1. Write an essay describing a situation that would be a challenge to your courage and to your convictions. Describe what you think the experience would be like if you were not true to your convictions and then what it would be like if you *were* true to your convictions.

2. The Church proclaims that Pentecost was not a one-time event. Even today people continue to be filled with the Holy Spirit. Write a poem or essay that tells how the Holy Spirit has been present in your life or in the world today, or draw your own representation of the presence of the Holy Spirit in your own life.

Review

1. What accounted for the attitude of uncertainty among the followers of Jesus who gathered at Pentecost?

2. Which book of the Bible tells about the actions of the early Church community?

3. What two images indicated the presence of the Holy Spirit at Pentecost?

4. What new understanding came to the followers of Jesus as a result of the first Christian Pentecost?

PETER THE FISHERMAN

We know little about Peter, the man identified in the Gospels as the original leader of Jesus' followers. Scripture indicates he made his living as a fisherman along with his brother Andrew, and the two brothers, James and John, known as the "sons of Zebedee." All would later become apostles of Jesus. These business partners worked hard, fishing and caring for their small fleet of boats. We know that Peter was married since the Gospels mention his mother-in-law. The Gospels also portray him as having a fiery and strong personality.

His given name was not Peter but Shim'on or, in Greek, Simōn. We know him as Peter because Jesus gives him this name, which means "rock" in Aramaic. Why does Jesus call Peter the "rock" upon which the Church will be built? The answer is found in Matthew 16:13–17:

"Now when Jesus came into the district of Caesarea Philippi, he asked his disciples, 'Who do people say that the Son of Man is?' And they said, 'Some say John the Baptist, but others Elijah, and still others Jeremiah or one of the prophets.' He said to them, 'But who do you say that I am?' Simon Peter answered, 'You are the Messiah, the Son of the living God.' And Jesus answered him, 'Blessed are you, Simon, son of Jonah. For flesh and blood has not revealed this to you, but my Father in heaven.' " After this inspired response Jesus identifies Peter as the foundation stone of the Church and the model for all later Christians.

The Gospels also portray a very human side to Peter, perhaps the most famous account of which takes place during Jesus' trial, when the same Peter who earlier had proclaimed Jesus "Son of the living God" denied that he even knew him. Nonetheless, after Pentecost, Peter was clearly the head of the Christian community. He performed miracles, and Scripture says that even people standing in his shadow were healed.

After years of travel Peter ended up in Rome, where, according to tradition, he was put to death in A.D. 64 during the persecutions under Nero. Considering himself unworthy to die as Jesus did, Peter asked to be crucified upside down. Buried on Vatican Hill, one of the seven hills of Rome, his tomb has become a place of pilgrimage. In the fourth century a large church was built on the spot. Today Saint Peter's Basilica is the central church for all Catholics. In 1950, excavations uncovered a tomb in the basilica believed to be that of Peter. The bones from this tomb now rest directly under the main altar of the basilica. Catholics · consider the pope, the bishop of Rome, to be Peter's successor and therefore head of the Church.

JEWISH ROOTS OF THE CHURCH

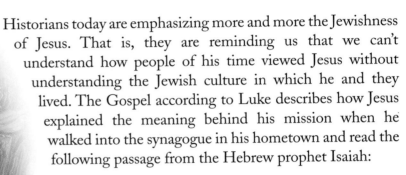

The Church is closely linked with the Jewish people, who first heard the word of God. Judaism is a response to the revelation of God and to the covenant. God's covenant with the Jews has never been revoked.

See *Catechism of the Catholic Church*, #839.

"Jesus in the Synogogue"
by James J. Tissot

Historians today are emphasizing more and more the Jewishness of Jesus. That is, they are reminding us that we can't understand how people of his time viewed Jesus without understanding the Jewish culture in which he and they lived. The Gospel according to Luke describes how Jesus explained the meaning behind his mission when he walked into the synagogue in his hometown and read the following passage from the Hebrew prophet Isaiah:

> *"The Spirit of the Lord is upon me,*
> *because he has anointed me to bring good news to*
> *the poor.*
> *He has sent me to proclaim release to the captives*
> *and recovery of sight to the blind, to let the*
> *oppressed go free,*
> *to proclaim the year of the Lord's favor."*
>
> *Luke 4:18–19*

Christianity finds its roots in Judaism. In the Old Testament stories, we find themes that become important ones for the Christian Church as well. Without knowing that these themes were adopted from Jewish roots, we cannot understand how members of the early Church perceived themselves. You might already have studied the Bible, where much of our knowledge of early Jewish history comes from, but let us do a little remembering.

Activity

Read each of the following Scripture verses. Explain how the messages contained in each might help us understand what the Church is, or is meant to be.

Genesis 12:1–4	Exodus 14:5–14	Jeremiah 1:4–10
Genesis 32:22–32	Isaiah 9:2–7	Ezekiel 37:1–14

"The Offering of Abraham" by James J. Tissot.

How great a sacrifice would you be willing to make? For whom?

Abraham: Father in Faith of the Christian Church

According to Genesis, long before Jesus a man named Abram (later renamed Abraham) and his wife Sarai (later renamed Sarah) lived in Ur, in what is today the country of Iraq. Abram had a religious experience in which he came to believe in only one God, rather than the many gods of his people. Belief in one God, called *monotheism,* is the central belief of the Jewish faith. Judaism, Christianity, and Islam all practice monotheism and recognize Abraham as their father in faith.

In response to God's direction, Abraham left Ur and settled near the Dead Sea in the land of modern-day Israel. He had a son, Isaac, whom he loved. However, when Abraham believed that God wanted him to kill his son as a sacrifice, he immediately began preparations to follow God's will. God did not require him to make this ultimate sacrifice, but, because Abraham passed such a great test of faith, God promised him that he would be the father of many nations.

In harmony with its Jewish roots, the Christian Church insists on monotheism, not only as an article of faith, but also as a teaching that has implications about how we should live our life. The Church also continues to share the good news that all people are children of one God. Furthermore, the Church recognizes that the sacrifice, which Abraham thought God was asking him to make, prefigured Jesus' sacrifice on the cross. Jesus' ultimate sacrifice makes a powerful statement about how much God loves people and inspires members of the Church to carry on the self-sacrificing work of Jesus. Thus, knowing the story of Abraham helps us understand how early followers of Jesus understood who he was and what it means to be Church.

Discussion

1. List and discuss some elements from the Jewish faith that we use in Christianity today.

2. Debate the following statements: In terms of how they actually live their lives, it makes no difference whether or not people
   - believe in God.
   - believe in many gods or one god.
   - believe that every tribe, nation, or ethnic group has its own god.

The Exodus Reveals a Loving God

Exodus
God's saving intervention in history, as narrated in the Book of Exodus, by which he liberated the Hebrew people from slavery in Egypt, made a covenant with them, and brought them into the Promised Land

Passover
Jewish feast commemorating the deliverance of the Jewish people from death by the blood of the lamb sprinkled on the doorposts in Egypt, which the angel of death saw and "passed over"

www. The Sedar Meal is the most important event in the Passover celebration. Visit **www.holidays.net/ passover/sedar.html** for an explanation of the special foods, utensils, and dishware that are used.

Babylonian Captivity period from 587 to 539 B.C. when the Jewish nation did not exist and Jewish leaders were exiled to Babylon

Another event that Christians link directly to Jesus is the **Exodus.** Abraham's descendants settled in Egypt as a result of the movement of family tribes. There they were eventually enslaved. In their misery, the Israelites cried out to their God for freedom from bondage. According to history, God sent them Moses who led them out of slavery, through the desert, and into the Promised Land, the land where Abraham had once lived.

Jews celebrate the Exodus each year at **Passover.** Pious Jews do not simply recall the historical event but also enter into it as participants. In other words, God didn't just free the ancient Israelites' ancestors from slavery; he also frees their descendents from spiritual slavery today. Christians link the Exodus story to the story of Jesus' death and resurrection. Throughout history the community of people who make up the Church proclaims that they have been set free from the slavery of sin through Jesus, as God set free the Israelites in the Exodus. As an ongoing Exodus event, Church history is the story of liberation. As you read about the Church in different times and in different cultural contexts, pay attention to how Church members understood what freedom meant for them and what freedom inspired by Jesus means for us today.

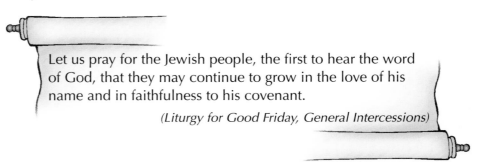

Let us pray for the Jewish people, the first to hear the word of God, that they may continue to grow in the love of his name and in faithfulness to his covenant.

(Liturgy for Good Friday, General Intercessions)

The Jews of Israel Versus the Hellenistic Jews

To understand conflicts that arose within Christianity in its earliest stages, we also need to look back into Jewish history. In the Hellenistic and Roman periods, the region around Jerusalem became known as Judea. Judea and the nearby regions of Samaria and Galilee were also called Palestine. This is the region that today is called Israel or Palestine.

In 587 B.C. the forces of Babylon destroyed the kingdom of Judah and took many of the Jewish elite, the educated, and craftsmen back to Babylon in chains. The Babylonians destroyed the temple and took its treasures. In so doing they destroyed the center of Jewish life and worship as well. Many of the Jewish prisoners held onto their faith during their captivity, a period that lasted about fifty years and is known in Jewish history as the **Babylonian Captivity.** In time, these Jews became members of Babylonian society. Because they could not worship at their temple, they developed a system of synagogues, which were initially informal meeting rooms where they would pray together and discuss the beliefs of their faith.

The Kingdom of Judah
from the time of
the divided kingdom
until the Babylonian
Captivity, 950–587 B.C.

Judea at the time
of Jesus

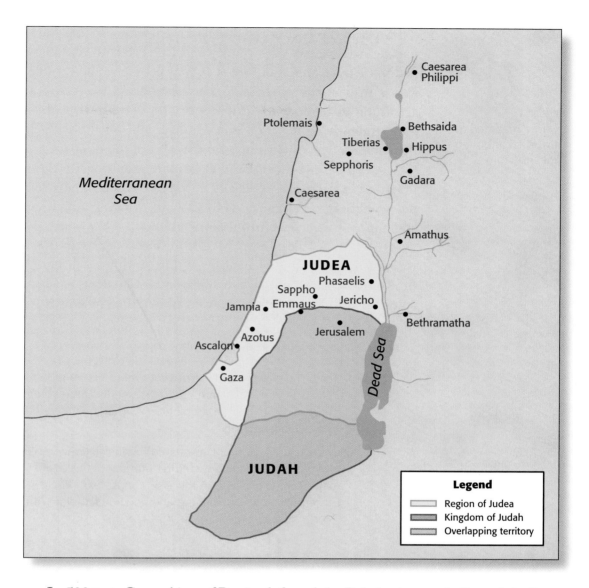

In 539 B.C. Cyrus, king of Persia, defeated the Babylonians and allowed the Jews to return to their homeland. Many returned to Judah, but some stayed in Babylon or went to other parts of the world. The Jews who continued to live outside of Judah became known as the Jews of the **diaspora.** There were probably about four million Jews in the diaspora, while only about a million lived in Palestine.

In 331 B.C., Alexander the Great conquered the Persian Empire. Alexander was from Macedonia, and his empire was centered in Macedonia and Greece. Greek culture became the dominant culture throughout the eastern Mediterranean area. Greek culture greatly influenced the Jews of the diaspora, some of whom even took Greek names. The term for the spread of Greek culture is *Hellenization.* Jews who adapted their Judaism to Greek culture are known as "Hellenistic Jews" or Hellenists.

By the time of Jesus, there were large Hellenistic communities in Rome, Alexandria, and Antioch. The Hellenistic Jews were frequently urban and wealthy, while those in Palestine were primarily rural and often poor. Those in Israel were isolated or "protected" from their non-Jewish neighbors. The Jews of the diaspora interacted in commerce and in social situations with their neighbors.

diaspora
scattering of the
Israelites, Jewish
people, from their
homeland

fyi!
Israel was a
collective name
for the twelve
tribes of people
who were
descendents of
Jacob.

Most of the Jews of the diaspora read, wrote, spoke, and thought in Greek. They had so little contact with the Jews of Israel that around 200 B.C. the Hebrew Bible had to be translated into Greek so that people would be able to understand it when it was read at the synagogue. This translation was called the *Septuagint* because, according to **legend**, seventy scholars (or seventy-two in some accounts) worked independently on the translation and yet all came up with the same text. It became the commonly used Scripture for the Jews of the diaspora.

The Judaism of the diaspora became intentionally different from the Judaism practiced in Palestine, especially in Jerusalem. Eventually some Jews of the diaspora moved back into Palestine and lived there, bringing with them the synagogue system and a more tolerant view of their neighbors.

In 63 B.C. Palestine came under Roman rule, as the Roman Empire spread throughout the region. Hellenistic culture continued during the Roman period. By the time of Jesus, most Jews of the diaspora were Hellenists. Many of the first converts to "the Way" of Christianity came from among the Hellenistic Jews in Palestine.

Discussion

1. Describe what you believe is your religion's attitude toward other religions. Are you aware of disagreements among members of your religion about how other religions should be viewed? If so, what are these disagreements?

2. Make a case for or against the following statement: North American culture is the dominant culture throughout the world today. Those who want to succeed in this world must learn English, wear North American styles of clothing, and become familiar with aspects of North American culture, such as U.S. television and music.

Activity

1. The stories of Abraham and the Exodus are journey stories; the Church consists of "pilgrim people." In response to this image, answer the following questions:
   - From what would you say members of the Church community are journeying?
   - Toward what are they journeying?
   - What are some of the tasks in which they should be engaged if they are to reach their destination?

2. Write an essay or use another medium to report on the Babylonian Captivity, Jews of the diaspora, or the Septuagint.

3. Write a report on classical Greek culture, Hellenization, or differences between Greek culture and traditional Jewish culture.

Review

1. Why is it important that historians today are emphasizing more and more the Jewishness of Jesus?

2. What three religions recognize Abraham as their father in faith?

3. What great test of faith did God lay before Abraham?

4. Name two Christian beliefs that reflect themes found in the story of Abraham.

5. Describe the major events that encompass the Exodus story.

6. How do modern Jews view the Exodus as it relates to their own lives?

7. What Exodus theme runs through Church history?

8. What was the Babylonian Captivity?

9. What distinguished Jews in Israel from Jews of the diaspora?

10. What is Hellenization?

11. What was the Septuagint? Why was it written?

BUILT ON THE GOOD NEWS

If time stood still, we wouldn't need a Church history course. We would live in an eternal present. We could simply spend time with Jesus, and through him and in him, we would meet God. However, time has not stood still, and we have both past and present to consider. Therefore, we look to people who have made up the Church over the past two thousand years to help us understand who Jesus was and is. Of course, we need always to keep the person of Jesus fully human, fully divine, fresh in our minds when we consider what the Church is and should be. The primary sources of our knowledge about Jesus are the New Testament and the Tradition of the Church. Over the past century or so, discoveries in the areas of language and archaeology have also given us a better understanding of the life and ministry of Jesus.

To understand the message of Jesus for the Church, we need to grapple with some concepts that have been examined and reexamined for centuries. Jesus called for a **conversion** of heart and mind. He spoke of both a personal and a societal conversion. This new way of being, the **reign of God,** included a radical transformation in the way people viewed themselves, their God, and one another. Jesus actually proclaimed that the reign of God was already at work in the world wherever people saw themselves as beloved daughters and sons of God and treated one another as such. Therefore, he taught a style of life that was filled with love and forgiveness. The prayer that Jesus taught his disciples begins by addressing God as "our Father," proclaiming that God is a loving parent of all people. While this notion was not new to the Jews of his day, the tone of intimacy, familiarity, and informality with which Jesus addressed God was.

What does Jesus have to say about the situation in this photo?

Telling people that God loves them and wants them to love one another doesn't sound particularly radical or upsetting until we start describing specific implications of the message. Then people begin to get angry. For instance, the reign of God is a very challenging concept when some people consider themselves to be separate from and superior to others, or when they possess excessive wealth while others are starving to death or barely scraping by.

We have already described the result of Jesus' teachings and behavior for himself: he was condemned by the authorities and crucified. His death was not the end, however. Instead, he was raised from the tomb and appeared to his disciples in his glorified body on a number of occasions. When Jesus finally left them, he told them to pray and to wait for the coming of the Spirit. The Spirit came during the first Christian Pentecost, and those who believe in Jesus have proclaimed and embodied his message ever since.

Activity

1. Compose a poem or story illustrating one of the following themes:
   - "Love is a challenge."
   - "Love can upset people."
   - "Believing in a God of love is not easy."

2. Complete each of the following sentences:
   - Jesus' message is challenging because . . .
   - Jesus' message gives hope because . . .
   - Jesus' message is radical because . . .
   - Jesus' message has lived on because . . .

3. A central message of Jesus was personal and societal conversion.
   - If you were to "turn your life around" based on Jesus' teaching, how would you be different?
   - If our society were to be turned around based on Jesus' teaching, how would it be different?

The Beginning of the Church

Christ accomplished God the Father's plan of salvation, which was the reason he was sent into the world. By preaching the good news of the reign of God, which had been promised in the Scriptures, Jesus inaugurated the Church.

See *Catechism of the Catholic Church, #763*

Messiah
In traditional Jewish belief, someone who will become king and restore Israel to peace and prosperity; Jesus radically challenged this definition with his divine mission of priest, prophet, and king.

The Church was formed through the power of the Holy Spirit by those who believed in Jesus as **Messiah** and Son of God. Jesus wanted his followers to continue to believe in him and to follow in his work. He did not intend his message to die with him on Good Friday, the day of his death—otherwise what was the point of the resurrection? He affirmed his desire to have his followers carry on his message after his ascension into heaven by sending the Holy Spirit at Pentecost.

As was explained earlier in this chapter, after Pentecost the disciples of Jesus understood their role to be proclaiming the reign of God and calling upon people to join them in living as Jesus intended them to. The Acts of the Apostles inseparably links Jesus and the Church. This book of the Bible is generally thought to be written by the same author who wrote the Gospel according to Luke. The author considers the Spirit at work in Jesus to be the same Holy Spirit at work in the ongoing drama of the Church.

Scripture scholars now tell us that many early Christians believed that the "coming of the reign of God" would happen in their own lifetimes and that the world as they knew it would end. That is, Jesus would come again and take all believers with him to heaven. As time passed, however, Jesus' followers came to see that this was not going to happen immediately. They needed to constantly reform their lives and convince others to change as well. In this way the reign of God would develop on earth and someday be perfected in heaven.

Once the followers of Jesus realized that the task ahead of them was going to be long-term, they had to make a number of practical decisions. They divided up work, chose leaders, clarified teachings, and resolved inevitable conflicts. These decisions led to the Church as we know it today.

Discussion

Describe a situation in which you participated in a group project that you felt strongly about. How did people get along? What were some of the conflicts that arose? How were they handled? What sustained you during your work on the project? If you were to participate in this activity again, what would you do differently?

Architects of the Early Church

Thus far, we have identified key themes indicating the work of the Holy Spirit in inspiring people to join the Church:

- Radical trust in God
- Freedom through God's intervention
- Personal and social conversion—viewing oneself and others as daughters and sons of one God, caring for and sharing with one another
- The reign of God—composed of people from all social, ethnic, and economic backgrounds; already in existence but also a work in progress to which the Christian community commits itself through Christ Jesus
- A community inspired by the Holy Spirit to proclaim Christ's message and carry on his work

People joined the Christian community and worked to embody these themes. (Isn't this as true today as it was then? People respond to Christianity largely because of how they see its message embodied in those who call themselves Christian.) Now it is time to find out who became the Church, what challenges they faced, and what became of them.

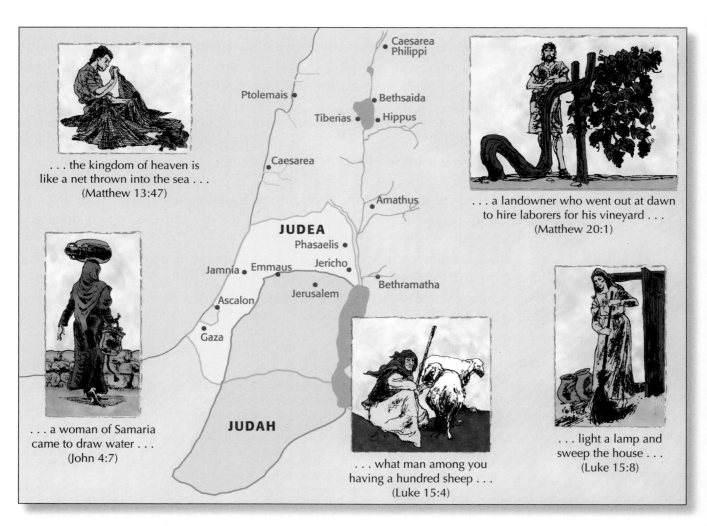

. . . the kingdom of heaven is like a net thrown into the sea . . . (Matthew 13:47)

. . . a woman of Samaria came to draw water . . . (John 4:7)

. . . a landowner who went out at dawn to hire laborers for his vineyard . . . (Matthew 20:1)

. . . what man among you having a hundred sheep . . . (Luke 15:4)

. . . light a lamp and sweep the house . . . (Luke 15:8)

Caesarea Philippi

Ptolemais

Bethsaida

Tiberias

Hippus

Caesarea

Amathus

JUDEA

Phasaelis

Jamnia

Emmaus

Jericho

Ascalon

Jerusalem

Bethramatha

Gaza

JUDAH

Gamaliel's Words of Wisdom

Sanhedrin
in Jesus' time, a group of seventy-one men made up of the chief priest, scribes, and elders who made decisions regarding actions of the people of the Jewish community

We have already alluded to the Acts of the Apostles, the book of the Bible that contains the account of Pentecost. This book gives us some idea about activities engaged in by the early Church. For instance, we know from Acts that tensions between the followers of Jesus and some of the Jewish authorities grew stronger after Jesus' death. We read that on one occasion Peter and John were arrested, imprisoned, and brought before the **Sanhedrin,** the Jewish high court. Before being released, Peter and John were threatened and told not to preach about Jesus ever again. They continued to preach even though it meant risking their lives (Acts 4:1–22).

On another occasion, the apostles were arrested and put in jail. During the night, however, an angel opened the gates and told them to go out into the temple area and preach to the people about the new life offered by Jesus. They did so. When the Sanhedrin became aware of the apostles' escape from prison and of their preaching in the temple again, they wanted to kill them. But Gamaliel, a wise and respected member of the court, spoke up and saved their lives. He suggested waiting and letting the apostles alone saying, ". . . if this plan or this undertaking is of human origin, it will fail; but if it is of God, you will not be able to overthrow them—in that case you may be found fighting against God." The Sanhedrin followed his advice. They had the apostles flogged and then released (Acts 5:17–42). Gamaliel's practical suggestion is an excellent model for the testing of religious experience. If an experience is truly the gift of God, it will stand the test of time.

Discussion

Debate the following statement: The great and continuing success in drawing large numbers to itself indicates that Christianity is indeed the work of God.

Activity

It is sometimes difficult to "get inside Scripture," to appreciate that the events recorded happened to real people in a real world. Scripture is rich, however, in names of people who have had only bit parts in the great drama of God. Taking these names and imagining ourselves in each person's acts and life can help us to remember that the Bible is about God's gracious power working through real people.

Listed below are three such people. Imagine your way into their lives and write a brief story about each of them.

- Lydia, the lady of purple cloth (Acts 16:14–15, 40)
- Eutychus, a young man who fell for the gospel in a big way (Acts 20:7–12)
- Onesimus, the useless useful one whom Paul made useful again (Letter to Philemon)

Review

1. Name the two traditional sources of information we have about Jesus and two more recent sources.

2. Why was Jesus' reference to God as "our Father" radical for his time?

3. Give two indications that Jesus intended his community to continue his work.

4. How did the early Christians view the coming of the reign of God?

5. What types of activities were required once the followers of Jesus realized that their earthly task would be a long-term one?

6. What position did Gamaliel take on the treatment of Jewish Christians?

CHRISTIANS INSPIRE HOPE

If we were to read the Gospels and the Acts of the Apostles uncritically, we might conclude that Christians were a clearly identifiable group from the beginning. In other words, there were "the Christians" as opposed to "the Jews," and neither group was kind to the other. In reality, the first followers of Jesus continued to see themselves as Jews. Being faithful Jews, they worshiped in the temple, attended synagogue services, and followed the Mosaic Law. They also met in each others' homes to share meals.

The Christian Jews, however, always considered the sharing of meals—the "breaking of bread"—to be a part of their life together with Jesus. Jesus, Lord and Savior, remained present to them in the Bread and Wine they shared. The early Jewish Christians were held together by a dual bond, their Judaism and their belief in Jesus. They didn't specify where their Judaism left off and their Christianity began. That was the work of later generations.

The Acts of the Apostles presents the image of Christians living closely together, awaiting Jesus, and growing in number. Chapter 2 of Acts tells us that "signs and wonders" accompanied the preaching of the apostles, which led to a daily increase in the number of believers. Accounts of these signs and wonders describe miraculous, supernatural events, such as healing at the touch of a hand. Acts also reports that the early Christians sold their possessions and gave the proceeds to the apostles for equal distribution. Food and goods were shared in common and distributed according to need. This was an excellent means of evangelization. When a person is on the brink of starvation, the gift of food can seem as miraculous as the healing touch of an apostolic hand.

Discussion

According to the Acts of the Apostles, the early Christians "shared all things in common." It's easy to understand how those who where destitute would find this practice appealing. However, people joined Christianity from all social and economic levels. Why do you think people of modest means and people of wealth became Christian in those early days? What appeal do you think Christianity holds today for people?

"St. Peter Healing with His Shade" be Masaccio, early fifteenth century. See Acts 5:12–16.

Mary—Model of the Church

During this time of initial growth in the Church, Mary plays a special role. On Calvary, she is at the foot of the cross, accepting from her Son a new relationship in love. She will care for, as well as be cared for by, the beloved disciple. Thus, Mary becomes the mystical mother of all Christ's beloved disciples in time and eternity.

We see Mary for the last time in Scripture in Acts 1:14, which relates the events that happened between the ascension and Pentecost: "All [the disciples] were constantly devoting themselves to prayer, together with certain women, including Mary the mother of Jesus, as well as his brothers." What incredible joy, pain, and sorrow must have been mingled together in her prayers as she reflected on her life. Jesus' and Mary's life stories are memorized in the cycle of prayers known as the Mysteries of the Rosary. The Joyful Mysteries remember the angel's appearance, Mary's visit to Elizabeth, the birth of Jesus, his presentation at the temple, and his being lost in Jerusalem when only a youth.

Mary's thoughts and prayers in that upper room must have been filled with the anguish of the events we know as the Sorrowful Mysteries: the anguish of her son's agony, the pain of his scourging,

the mockery of the crowning with thorns, his bearing of the cross, and finally his crucifixion.

These events led to those recognized in the third set of mysteries, known as the Glorious Mysteries. The resurrection, the ascension, the descent of the Holy Spirit, the assumption, and the coronation of the Blessed Virgin in heaven are all eternal events reverberating in the temporal events which established Christ's Church on earth—"Thy kingdom come, thy will be done, on earth as it is in heaven."

Activity

It is often very difficult to share deep emotions with other people. On a day when you are feeling great joy, share your joy with Mary in the recitation of the Joyful Mysteries; on a day of great sorrow, share your pain with her in the recitation of the Sorrowful Mysteries. Her love and receptivity to our joy and to our sorrow have sustained Christians throughout the history of our Church.

Early Christian Communities: Unity out of Diversity

Gentile
a person of non-Jewish faith or origin

God-fearers
Gentiles attracted to Judaism who maintained some association with local Jewish communities without becoming Jews

Jesus, the majority of his original disciples, and most of the earliest followers of Jesus were Jews born and raised in Palestine. Their Scriptures were written in traditional Hebrew, even though they spoke Aramaic. By A.D. 100, however, most Jews lived in other parts of the Roman Empire.

Alongside the Jewish communities there were also some **Gentiles** who were drawn to the monotheism and the strong sense of morality that Judaism possessed. These Gentiles often attached themselves to the synagogues and the Jewish communities in their particular cities without actually converting to Judaism; they were known as **"God-fearers."** Since Christianity was a Jewish sect at this time, many of these "God-fearers" found Christianity appealing.

This time period was one of great religious searching. The official religion of the empire, a mixture of emperor worship and worship of many gods, did not meet the spiritual needs of many people. Christianity was one of many new religions that intrigued serious religious searchers. Gentiles in this group sometimes also became "fellow travelers" with the growing Christian Church.

This tapestry of Saint Paul preaching in Athens is Raphael and is now in the Vatican museums.

Activity

1. Jesus and some of his closest followers would have been viewed as landless peasants in a culture where owning land was one of the primary marks of wealth and power. Think about a group of people who tend to lack power and wealth and who demonstrate characteristics that might be labeled "lower class" in today's society. What spiritual insights could some members of this group offer as a result of their unique experience?

2. Write or use another medium to describe a time when you have experienced one group of people criticizing another for the way they talk or dress or act. What lesson can be learned from such an experience?

Review

1. How can the relationship between Christians and Jews during the first decades after Jesus be misunderstood if the New Testament is read uncritically?

2. What were some of the characteristics of the lifestyle of the early Christians?

3. Name two groups from which the Christian community formed.

PAUL—THE APOSTLE TO THE GENTILES

SAINT PAUL THE APOSTLE

THE JUST SHALL LIVE BY FAITH

A young Jewish man named Saul concurred when a mob stoned to death Stephen, a fellow Jew who became the first known martyr for the Christian faith. Who was this Saul? He was a member of the Pharisees, a group of Jews known for their attempts to perfectly embody the Law in their lives. Saul studied in Jerusalem under the great rabbi Gamaliel. Many Pharisees and some of the people associated with them considered Christianity to be a threat to the Mosaic Law. Another significant fact about Saul is that he was born and raised in Tarsus, a city in modern-day Turkey. Therefore, while he was Jewish, he was also familiar with the culture of the Gentile world. In fact, Saul was a Roman citizen, which accorded him privileges that most people in the empire didn't possess.

After the death of Stephen, Saul addressed the high priest in Jerusalem to obtain letters to the synagogues in Damascus empowering him to arrest and to bring to trial any followers of Jesus. *"Now as he was going along and approaching Damascus, suddenly a light from heaven flashed around him. He fell to the ground and heard a voice saying to him, 'Saul, Saul, why do you persecute me?' He asked, 'Who are you, Lord?' The reply came, 'I am Jesus, whom you are persecuting. But get up and enter the city, and you will be told what you are to do' "* (Acts 9:3–6). After this encounter with Jesus, Saul became an enthusiastic follower of the Christian way. He preached the gospel throughout the Roman Empire. He is known to us more by his Greek and Roman name, Paul. During his travels he also wrote letters to the young church communities that sprang up in various cities. Some of these letters, also called epistles, are an essential part of the New Testament.

After almost a decade of spreading the Christian message, Paul returned to Jerusalem in A.D. 58. While he was there, the Jews with whom he had sided when he was persecuting Christians attempted to kill him. He was taken into protective custody by Roman authorities and sent for trial to the Roman procurator Felix in Caesarea. He spent two years in prison until the new procurator Porcius Feshis, wanting to please the Jewish leaders, asked Paul if he would be willing to go to trial in Jerusalem on the charge of misrepresenting the true Jewish faith. Paul realized that he would be found guilty in Jerusalem. As a Roman citizen, he appealed to the emperor for a judgment and thus was taken to Rome in the year A.D. 61.

Under house arrest in Rome for about two years, Paul met with other Christians there and wrote several important letters to young churches. He may even have made a fourth missionary journey to Spain after his incarceration ended. During Nero's persecution of Christians, somewhere between 64 and 67, Paul was beheaded, a more honorable form of execution due to his Roman citizenship.

Through his missionary journeys Paul added greatly to the numbers of Christians, especially from among the Gentile population. Therefore he is called "the Apostle to the Gentiles." In his writings, he reflected theologically about the place of Jesus in the divine plan and about what it means to believe in Jesus. Paul of Tarsus was indeed one of the most influential figures in the development of the Church at its beginning stages.

GENTILE CONVERTS

While the Acts of the Apostles sometimes makes it sound like the various factions within the Christian community got along well, this was not always the case. Even deciding who could join the community caused conflict. Early on, Christians debated whether—and if so, under what conditions—Gentiles could join the Christian community. Gentile beliefs and practices simply were not compatible with Judaism, and vice versa. Pious Jews couldn't sit down and share a meal with Gentiles because of strict dietary rules. An interesting story in Acts 10 speaks about this tension. But with the help of the Holy Spirit, Peter arrived at an important decision regarding Gentiles seeking to join the community.

In the story two men have a vision. A man named Cornelius, a Roman centurion who is a God-fearer, is told by an angel to send for the apostle Peter. Meanwhile, Peter is having a vision of his own. In a trance, he sees a sheet filled with all kinds of animals, including animals considered "unclean" by traditional Jewish standards. A voice says to him, "Take and eat." Peter replies that he has never eaten unclean food. He doesn't understand what the vision means.

When the messengers from Cornelius find Peter, Peter accompanies them back to their master's house. After hearing about the intense desire on the part of Cornelius to learn about the Lord, Peter realizes that his vision was telling him to offer God's word to people such as Roman centurions whom many other Jews would consider "unclean." Those who are gathered during this meeting feel the presence of the Holy Spirit, and Peter orders the Gentiles to be baptized. Since people joined the Christian community through baptism, it also meant that they could now join in the community's meals during a time when sharing meals by Jews and Gentiles was taboo. Incidents such as this one led Christianity to accept Gentiles, but they also led to the distinct separation between Christianity and Judaism that exists today.

Jerusalem today is a holy place for Judaism, Christianity, and Islam.

The issue of Gentiles seeking baptism was not resolved simply by a vision from God. The Acts of the Apostles describes an ongoing conflict about this issue, and Peter, as head of the community, seems caught in the middle of the debate. Some Jewish Christians even refused to participate in the communal meal when Gentiles were present. Leaders of the Church addressed the issue directly during a meeting that took place in Jerusalem around the year 50.

Council of Jerusalem
the first Church council which was called to resolve the growing controversy over whether or not Gentile Christians would have to observe Jewish law

An account of this meeting, called the **Council of Jerusalem,** is found in Acts 15. This meeting was occasioned when some Christian Jews taught at Antioch that Gentile converts had to be circumcised. Paul, Baranabas, and others traveled to Jerusalem to consider this matter with the apostles and presbyters there. Peter, speaking on behalf of the Church, announced the decision to free the Gentiles from this and other dietary proscriptions of the Lord.

As a result of this meeting the Gentiles were welcomed as full and active members of the Christian community, and they soon became the majority in the community. No longer was the Christian way strictly a Jewish way.

Activity

At the Council of Jerusalem, Paul was the leading advocate for accepting Gentiles into the Christian community. Some of the elders associated with the Church of Jerusalem disagreed. The community listened to arguments put forth from both sides. In the end, they made a decision. Recreate the debate about the "Gentile question" as it might have taken place. Describe arguments for both positions and the decision that Peter and the elders finalized. Compare your debate with the one described in Acts 15.

Review

1. What issue is illustrated in the story of Peter and Cornelius?

2. What resolution resulted from the Council of Jerusalem?

Conclusion

What do these first Christians have to say to us today? The early Church exemplifies the spark of excitement and enthusiasm that a new way of being can bring. Pentecost marked the beginning of this Spirit-filled community, not simply as an event in time but as an event for all time. The early Church consisted of members who walked and talked with Jesus. Thus the Church today, whose ancestors were these early apostles and disciples who directly touched and were touched by Jesus, remains anapostolic Church, one that looks always to Jesus as model, guide, and more—God in the flesh. Through the Church people today can still touch and be touched by Jesus.

O Lord, we praise you for your holy martyrs. Inspired by their sacrifices, we are people of hope, knowing that beyond suffering and death lies new life with you and all the saints. Grant us hope and faith in you as we, too, face the difficulties that come our way. Amen.

100–300

200
Church leaders begin deciding
on canon of New Testament

203
Martyrdom of
Perpetua and Felicity

248
Cyprian is bishop
of Carthage

249
Decius begins empire-
wide persecutions

251
Problem of the
lapsed begins

SPREADING THE MESSAGE

The Church Enters the Empire

CHAPTER OVERVIEW

- For their first three hundred years Christians endure persecution or the threat of persecution.

- As it grows the Church develops institutional structures and statements of belief in response to challenges from without (persecutions) and from within (heresies).

- During its first three hundred years, leaders emerge who guide and shape the Church.

- In the fourth century, the Church emerges as the dominant religion of the Roman Empire.

- Through development in its theology, liturgy, and initiation, the Church takes shape.

257	260	284
Valerian persecution begins	Era of Peace	Diocletian becomes emperor

258	264
Martyrdom of Saint Laurence	Council of Antioch

Do you know anything about the most distant ancestors of your family—those who lived hundreds or even thousands of years ago? Many faced great hardships to make life better for those who came after them. The way they handled the challenges and the joys they shared are a legacy handed down to you. More recently, did certain members of your family ever have a disagreement that led to months or years of no contact among them? Do some members of your family have a different spelling or pronunciation of the family's last name? How did that happen? Does one faction claim to have the "correct" spelling or pronunciation?

Such issues faced the followers of Jesus in the first three hundred years of the Church's history. During that time they went from being a small group of believers in a crucified and risen leader, to being a community encompassing a significant percentage of the empire that tried every possible means to crush them. These early Christians endured persecutions and internal dissension but included in their number some of the most courageous people and greatest minds of the time. They attracted to their movement slaves, peasants, artisans, philosophers, and politicians. These people formed the basis of a Church that profoundly affected the history of the world for the next two thousand years.

Before We Begin . . .

The period of Church history covered in this chapter is filled with martyrs—that is, people who witnessed so strongly to their beliefs that they accepted torture and death rather than renounce their beliefs. Describe a situation in which you, or someone you know, witnessed on behalf of a person or belief in which you or they believed. Explain what happened as a result of this witness.

MARTYRS

Inter-Jewish Conflicts Lead to Christian Persecutions

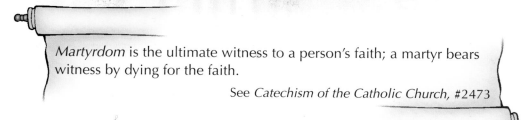

Martyrdom is the ultimate witness to a person's faith; a martyr bears witness by dying for the faith.

See *Catechism of the Catholic Church, #2473*

deacon
third degree of the Sacrament of Holy Orders; an assistant to a bishop or a priest; in the early Church, someone appointed to serve those who were poor or otherwise needy in the community

martyr
a witness to the truth of the faith, in which the martyr endures even death to be faithful to Christ

As early as the first century, Christian Jews were caught up in the conflicts among the various Jewish factions. For instance, Hellenistic converts to Christianity complained that their widows were not being given their fair share of food. The apostles decided that there needed to be servants, or **deacons,** who were Greek-speaking and could answer the needs of the Hellenistic converts. (See Acts 6:1–7.)

One of the first deacons was named Stephen. In addition to his duties of serving the needs of those who were poor and preaching, he also worked wonders and great signs among the people. He was seen as "a man full of grace and power," and he engaged in debates with other Greek-speaking Jews in their synagogues. Because Stephen "did great wonders and signs among the people," he was denounced as a blasphemer and brought before the Sanhedrin. During the debate that followed, Stephen traced for his listeners the history of Israel and showed how Jesus was the Messiah. He reproached them for their part in putting Jesus to death. The crowd that was gathered was furious. Some of them grabbed him, took him outside, and stoned him to death. He is considered the first Christian **martyr.** (See Acts 6–7.)

The first persecution of Christians, therefore, centered mostly on the Hellenistic Jewish Christians. Before Stephen's death, the Hebrew-speaking followers of Jesus thought of themselves as Jews. They came to the temple and followed Jewish dietary laws. They saw themselves as continuing in the line of Abraham and Moses along with other Jews. They believed that Jesus was the long-awaited Messiah and preached this message primarily to their fellow Jews. With the death of Stephen, many of the Hellenistic followers fled Jerusalem to avoid the persecutions led by Saul of Tarsus. Some went to Antioch, the capital of Syria, where they began preaching to non-Jews, an audience eager to hear the message. Gentile converts grew in number. Jesus' followers were first called *Christians* in Antioch. (See Acts 11:26.).

Discussion

The Church follows a liturgical calendar that contains major and minor feast days throughout the year. The feast of Saint Stephen follows immediately after Christmas, the feast of the birth of Christ into the world. What symbolic significance does the juxtaposition of these two feasts have for Christianity?

The Roman Persecutions

The persecutions that most profoundly affected Christianity were the Roman persecutions. In the early days of the Church, leaders of the Roman Empire took little notice of the Christian community. The group seemed to be a small splinter group of Judaism. The Romans found the Jews difficult to conquer and to control. Usually when they occupied a country, the Romans added the religious practices of the people onto their own. Because of monotheism, this kind of peaceful transition was not possible with the Jews. After many failed attempts at inclusion, the Romans decided to allow the Jewish people to practice their own religion. As Christianity was at first seen as a sect of Judaism, this attitude was extended to it also. Later, Christianity's beliefs and practices came into direct conflict with the purposes of the emperor and the persecutions began.

Nero burned Christians as torches in his "Golden House." This painting is by the Polish artist Henry de Siemieradzki (1843–1904).

FACTORS THAT MADE CHRISTIANITY SUSCEPTIBLE TO PERSECUTION

- Once Christianity separated from Judaism, it was an illegal religion.

- Christianity spread quickly throughout the empire.

- Christianity rejected the worship of the emperor and the gods of the Romans.

- At an early date (Council of Jerusalem in 50), Christianity began to accept Gentiles as full members of the Church.

- All parties came to view Christianity as distinct from Judaism.

- Its members met in secret assemblies.

Activity

Between 1900 and 1990, 26 million Christians were killed for their faith; thousands more have been martyred since 1990. Research a modern-day martyr and report your findings to the class. (Examples of modern-day martyrs are the Filipino Jesuit Richie Fernando; the martyrs of El Salvador–Archbishop Oscar Romero, Jean Donovan, Sister Dorothy Kazel, Sister Maura Clarke, Sister Ita Ford; the Jesuit Martyrs and their women workers; and Charles Lwanga of Uganda and his twenty-one companions.)

An Age of Persecutions

Historians often speak of the ten major persecutions of the Church, but actually there was only one persecution. It spanned two hundred and fifty years, from about 50 to 300, and varied in locale. Active persecutions alternated with periods of tranquility and benign neglect. The emperor-appointed ruler of Palestine, Herod Agrippa I, initiated persecution of Christians in Jerusalem. He did so to strengthen his relationship with the local Jewish leaders. During this time of persecution, the apostle James, head of the Jerusalem Christian community, was beheaded, and many Christians (including Peter) were imprisoned. (See Acts 12:1–3.)

A TIME OF PEACE AND PERSECUTIONS	
64	Nero persecution begins
81	Domitian persecution begins
98	Trajan persecution begins
138	Antonius Pius persecution begins
161	Marcus Aurelius persecution begins
193	Septimus Severus persecution begins
211	First era of peace begins
250	Decius begins empire-wide persecution
257	Valerian persecution begins
260	Second era of peace begins
303	The Great Persecution begins under Diocletian
313	Edict of Milan

Nero initiated the first Roman persecution in Rome. On the nineteenth of July in 64, there was a tremendous fire in Rome that gutted entire districts of the city. Some fifty years later, the Roman historian Tacitus wrote that the emperor himself had started the fire because he wanted to rebuild Rome. However, when he realized how angry the citizens were, Nero blamed the Christians and their God for the blaze. Whatever the cause of the fire, it began a full-scale persecution of Christians. Both Peter and Paul are believed to have died as a result of this period of persecution that lasted from 64 to 67.

The Emperor Domitian began the first empire-wide persecution (81 to 96). During persecutions some Christians hid or left the area to avoid being captured or imprisoned. Only when the danger was over did they return to their regular lives. Even while taking these precautions, however, many Christians suffered torture and death during these periods.

We have a letter from the early second century sent by a Roman governor named Pliny to his emperor Trajan asking what to do about Christians. The emperor replied that Christians should not be sought out but if reported and convicted were to be punished. If they repented and worshiped the gods, they should be set free. Later, Emperor Decius decreed that every citizen had to publicly worship the Roman gods, in which case they would receive a certificate indicating that they were loyal citizens. Anyone found not carrying this certificate could be tortured until agreeing to offer public worship.

Activity

Pliny's letter suggests that many Roman officials were seeking sensible ways to deal with the subversive group of Christians. Reenact a mock trial of a group of Christians in the Roman Empire. Lawyers from each side should explain why Christians should or should not be punished.

The Legend of Deacon Laurence

During persecutions in 258, soldiers in Rome barged in upon Pope Sixtus II as he was celebrating Mass and killed him and all those present. The local deacon, Laurence, was absent at the time, but a few days later he was also killed. Because of their martyrdom, Pope Sixtus and Deacon Laurence were venerated by Christians, and legends developed about them.

According to one legend, Sixtus was imprisoned before being killed. Laurence went to see the pope and pleaded to be jailed with him. Instead Sixtus directed him to go, give away all the money the church had available, sell whatever possessions they had, and give the money to those in need. A government official overheard this request and ordered Laurence to return in three days with the treasury of the church. When Laurence returned at the appointed time, he brought with him all those who were supported by the church—widows, maidens, lepers, orphans, and persons who were disabled. He said to the official, "Behold the treasure of the church."

The official was furious. He shouted that the empire would not be mocked. He assured Laurence that he would indeed get his request to die, but his death would be a slow and painful one. He ordered a large gridiron to be prepared and placed over hot coals. Deacon Laurence was stripped and slowly roasted on it. After a while Laurence cheerfully announced, "You may turn me now, this side is done." Laurence's story was told often after this and served as a source of encouragement to those still facing the possibility of torture and death. The Christian writer Tertullian said in reference to Laurence, "Crucify us; torture us; send us to death; wipe us out! Your injustice is the proof of our innocence! . . . The blood of Christians is a seed!"

Perpetua and Felicity

A document from the early Church illustrates the faith and courage of other Christian martyrs. A twenty-two-year-old married woman named Perpetua lived during the third century in North Africa. She kept a diary. A later writer completed her story. She was of noble birth and had a slave named Felicity who served as her companion. When they were arrested, Perpetua and Felicity were catechumens participating in the two-or three-year program in preparation for Baptism. Since they were kept under house arrest, they were able to continue studying the faith and were baptized. Along with their instructor in the faith, Saturus, they were then moved to a prison in the city of Carthage.

In her diary, Perpetua details what it was like waiting for their deaths. Perpetua had an infant son whom she was breastfeeding. Her father, who was not a Christian, pleaded with her to think of her child and to "throw a little incense" over the statues of the non-Christian gods. Perpetua refused. Felicity was eight months pregnant when arrested. She feared that she would not be put to death with the other prisoners since Roman law forbade executing pregnant women. Three days before they were to be sent to the arena, she gave birth to a baby girl and gave it to a Christian woman to raise.

Christian prisoners were to be fed to wild animals as part of the emperor's birthday celebration. Perpetua and Felicity were told to dress in the robes of non-Christian priestesses but refused. Therefore they were tossed into the arena naked except for nets thrown over them. The animals attacked but did not kill them. Gladiators were called upon to execute them. The two women stood next to each other and exchanged the Christian sign of peace as they met their deaths. These two women so well represented the strength and courage of the martyrs that their names are included in the first Eucharistic Prayer often recited at liturgies.

From Outsiders to Insiders

The middle decades of the third century proved to be a particularly corrupt period in Roman history. From 235 to 284 there were twenty-three different emperors—some holding the title for only a month—leaving the empire on the brink of destruction. Diocletian came to the throne in 284 and, unlike his predecessors, demonstrated good management skills. He divided the empire into East and West and then further divided it into twelve areas that he called "dioceses," named after himself. He felt that by not allowing people so much freedom, he could better keep things under control. One area he wanted control of was the gods the people worshiped. In 303, he began what later came to be called the *Great Persecution* by reinstating mandatory emperor worship for all citizens. He intended his new system to result in a peaceful transition of power instead of the conflicts that had been taking place before him.

However, when Diocletian stepped down, a power struggle again occurred. In 312 the armies of two generals met to determine who would be emperor of the West. One of these generals, Constantine, claimed to have had a vision of a cross in which he was told that in this sign he would conquer. He placed a Chi-Rho on his standards and during battle on the Milvian Bridge, he indeed was victorious. Constantine became the undisputed emperor in the West.

The next year Constantine met with Licinius, the ruler of the Eastern Empire, and together they signed the **Edict of Milan** that instituted tolerance for all religions. Thus the year 313 marks the end of an era for the Christian Church. Persecutions did not entirely cease for Christians. For instance, to spite Constantine, Licinius later persecuted Christians. Constantine responded by defeating him in 324 and he became the master of the entire Roman world. On his deathbed, Constantine himself became a Christian. Thus the few hundred people who considered themselves Jesus' followers in A.D. 30, now, even after all the years of persecutions, had grown to number about five million, one of whom was the emperor himself.

Edict of Milan
declaration allowing religious freedom in the Roman Empire

Youth News

"Profess your faith in the emperor." "Deny Jesus or die!" This type of martyrdom no longer exists in our country. Modern times have given birth to other ways of expressing our belief in Jesus in everyday activities, such as going to work or to school. At this point in your life, how willing are you to stand up for what you believe? Today's Christians, just like those of the early Church, are still being challenged to take a stand for Jesus. Check out NET Ministries or the Jesuit Volunteer Corps for two examples of organizations who help young adults profess their faith in Jesus in their work environments.

The Colosseum in Rome became the stage for the martyrdom of many Christians. Up to 50,000 people could gather there to witness such events.

Art: "Christian Martyr: The Last Prayer" by Jean-Leon Gerome (1824–1904).

Martyrs—Heroes of the Church

What do the gruesome tales of martyrs tell us about the early Christians? For one thing, we learn from such accounts that Christians were an increasingly irritating thorn in the side of the Roman emperors. From a Christian point of view, however, we discover that a great number of people felt strongly enough about their faith that they were willing to undergo horrible suffering and even death rather than renounce their faith. For Christians from that time on, these early martyrs serve as a reminder of how precious faith is. There was no special desire on the part of Christians to die, but many found the courage to stand and proclaim their faith even at the cost of their lives.

These martyrs came to hold a special place of honor and respect in the community. Accounts of their deaths circulated; describing the extent of their tortures showed how forcefully they held to their faith. Throughout the year, the Church celebrates the deaths of martyrs as their "birthdays" into eternal life. Their graves and tombs became places where Christians gathered to celebrate the Eucharist. Even today some altars in Catholic churches still contain stones with relics of martyrs—often small pieces of bones—to continue the custom of gathering around the martyrs' tombs to celebrate the Mass. The early martyrs are the great heroes of the Church.

 Research more of the lives of the martyrs of this time period at **www.ucc.ie/milmart/shortlist.html**

Review

1. Who is the first known Christian martyr?

2. Which group of Christians was the primary target of Jewish persecutions?

3. In what city were the followers of Jesus first called *Christians?*

4. List three reasons why Christians were particularly susceptible to Roman persecution.

5. Who was the Roman emperor who first persecuted Christians? Why did he do so?

6. What did Diocletian do to try to restore order to the empire?

7. What did the Edict of Milan grant?

8. Who was the first emperor to become Christian?

THE CHURCH TAKES SHAPE

Three areas of Church life that the Christian community needed to address were the way it expressed its beliefs, the way it celebrated and ritualized its beliefs, and the way it structured itself. In other words, the Church during this time period took major steps toward establishing its creed (essential beliefs), its rites (sacramental system), and its community organization (roles performed by various Church members).

Then, as now, the Christian faith was a lived experience. Beliefs and practices formed as people reflected on what was being said and done. For instance, if a particular bishop during celebration of the Eucharist used a prayer that people found to be especially meaningful, other bishops often copied it. Eventually, only those prayers deemed most meaningful and most appropriate were used during liturgies. The same can be said of the Church's beliefs and organizational structures. Inspired by the Holy Spirit, the Christian community gained a greater understanding of the wonderful mystery of Jesus Christ that they were experiencing.

This deeper understanding did not always come easily or quickly. As we will see, great thinkers battled, sometimes for centuries, to determine what was "right thinking" in Christianity. Also, disagreements about leadership among the various Christian communities played an important role in divisions that occurred in the Church later on. Following is a description of some of the most important thinking that occurred regarding creed, rites, and community in the early Church.

From the beginning Church practices took on the flavor of the surrounding cultures.

Apologists Explain and Defend the Faith

The early Christians obviously had a powerful and wonderful sense that God was at work among them. They struggled to understand exactly what knowledge and insights set them apart from their Jewish brothers and sisters, as well as from the wider community. In response to this challenge, there emerged in the Church great thinkers who explained and defended the Christian faith in clear and convincing terms.

Christianity had begun in Jewish culture but it soon moved into the Greek culture that dominated the Roman Empire of the time. This move profoundly affected how Christians viewed God and Jesus. Jews accepted that God exists and lovingly cares for his people. So they concentrated on how people should act in response to God. In other words, the primary focus in Judaism was on the people's part of the covenant—right behavior as expressed in the Torah, or "the Law." Greek thought focused more on "being" than on "doing." Therefore, it examined the nature of God and human nature, philosophical questions rather than the practical questions of Judaism. In other words, the primary focus of Greek thought was philosophy—right thinking. As a result, when Christianity began to make its mark in the world beyond Judaism, it had to explain in philosophical terms God the Father, Jesus, and the Holy Spirit, and the relationship among the three.

The rational, intellectual study of religious matters is called *theology*. Bishops and other Christian thinkers discussed and debated theological questions among themselves. By Constantine's time, Church leaders were able to agree on a statement of core Christian beliefs. That agreement did not come easily, however. Along the way intellectual battles raged. When someone proposed an interpretation of Christ that did not ring true to the growing consensus of thought, then he or she was branded a **heretic.** Those who most clearly and most successfully explained and defended Christian beliefs were called **apologists.**

When not faced with the immediate threat of persecutions, great thinkers of the Church dealt with issues of theology. For instance, Alexandria in Egypt had long been a center of learning for both Jewish and Gentile scholars. Great scholars of Christianity were able to form their own school in Alexandria by reflecting on Jesus and his message and by writing tracts or pamphlets that answered some of the criticisms being made against Christianity. Christian apologists addressed criticisms against the Church and in so doing formulated a Christian theology.

heretic
one who holds a position on an article of faith that conflicts with officially defined teachings

apologist
a Christian thinker who defended and explained Christian beliefs

Atheism	Christians were accused of atheism because they refused to worship the gods of the empire.
Incarnation	The idea of a god who would lower himself to become human made no sense! As a result, some heresies said that Jesus was God and not human; while others said that Jesus was human but not God.
Christian practices	Christianity, which linked the human and the divine in a mysterious fashion, seemed unnatural and caused suspicion.
Social structure	The Christian community itself was seen as disruptive and antisocial. Christians called one another "brothers and sisters" and downplayed long-established social structures upon which the society of the time was based.

Important controversies

atheism
the denial that God exists

incarnation
the fact that the Son of God assumed human nature and became man in order to accomplish our salvation

Orthodoxy and Heresy

Since "official Christian teaching" was just developing, it is understandable that disagreements would be plentiful. It took time, discussion, debate, and the sheer power of persuasion to arrive at **orthodoxy** or "right thinking" as opposed to **heresy** or "wrong thinking" about Christian beliefs. Most importantly, Church leaders throughout history point out that it took the guidance of the Holy Spirit for anyone to come to a true understanding of God, Jesus, and the human condition. Apologists, such as Justin Martyr, Tatian, and Tertullian to name a few, were those who helped the early Church arrive at the formulation of essential Christian teachings that has sustained it ever since.

orthodoxy
correct teachings about basic Christian beliefs

heresy
a position on an article of faith that conflicts with officially defined teachings

The Debate about Church Practices

Early Christianity was faced not only with hammering out its theology but also with what constituted "right practice." For instance, one urgent issue concerned Christians who gave in to pressure under persecution and offered worship to non-Christian gods. Could these people rejoin Christian communities when others had given their lives for refusing to worship other gods? Those who gave in were called *lapsi* in Latin, because they had lapsed in the practice of their faith.

In 251, Novatian and Cornelius were rival candidates for Bishop of Rome. Novatian preached that the worship of non-Christian gods by baptized Christians was an unforgivable sin and that accepting *lapsi* back into the Church was being "soft on sin." Cornelius declared that lapsi should be welcomed back into the community after a reinitiation. The controversy ended when Cyprian, Bishop of Carthage, accepted communion with Cornelius rather than with Novatian.

Discussion

Defend and explain to an imaginary person of another faith an important issue on which the Catholic Church takes a stand today.

A related controversy considered the validity of baptisms performed by a lapsed minister. Stephen, the new Bishop of Rome (254–256), declared that the sacraments belong to Christ and not to the Church. Therefore, the validity of the sacrament depends upon the correctness of the form and not upon that of the minister. As we will see, this determination became a part of the controversy about sacraments that led to the Protestant Reformation.

Discussion

Offer arguments to explain why you agree or disagree with the following statements:

1. Christians should aim for a higher standard of behavior than other people.

2. The Church should impose stricter punishments when a member does something morally wrong.

The sacraments are efficacious—they have spiritual effects and bring about what they signify. Christ works in the sacraments, baptizing, giving grace. The power of God is at work in the sacraments, rather than the righteousness of the celebrant or the person participating in the sacrament.

See *Catechism of the Catholic Church,* #s 1127–1128.

Another disagreement was called the "Easter controversy." This controversy centered on the date on which Easter should be celebrated. Essentially, churches in the western part of the empire celebrated Easter on a different day than those in the eastern part. This variation in practice suggests the type of differences that led eventually to a split between the Eastern and the Western Churches.

Christian beliefs are lived out day to day.

Setting the Canon—The Church Identifies Its Scriptures

The decision of which books to include in the Bible was made through the discernment of the Church's apostolic Tradition. The complete canon or list includes the Old Testament with forty-six books and the New Testament with twenty-seven books.

See *Catechism of the Catholic Church,* #120.

At Pentecost, the Holy Spirit inspired Jesus' first followers. However, they did not immediately sit down to write the books of the New Testament. Instead, the New Testament took shape as the Church did. Scholars tell us that the Gospels developed in three stages.

STAGES OF GOSPEL DEVELOPMENT

The life and teaching of Jesus

Jesus, a Jew from Galilee, lived in what is now known as the beginning of the first century. He preached a message of love and taught others about the kingdom of God while offering healing and forgiveness. Some of those who saw and heard became his followers—apostles and disciples.

The Oral Tradition

This stage began as the apostles and disciples who witnessed the life, death, and resurrection of Jesus shared with others what they had heard and seen, but with the fuller understanding provided through the enlightenment of the Holy Spirit. Eventually, others who had not witnessed the words and deeds of Jesus came to believe in him and share the good news. Preaching was then carried out by means of a combination of eyewitnesses and non-eyewitnesses and was adapted to the needs of different audiences.

The written Gospels

The four Gospel writers combined both the oral stories with those that were already in written form. They chose to include stories that would be important to each author's particular audience while maintaining the authenticity of the events.

We know that a number of Gospels were circulating in the Christian community of the first century. Four of these were accepted as part of the New Testament. The process by which this happened is called "setting the canon." **Canon** is a Greek word for "measuring rod," like a ruler or a yardstick used to measure length. Early Church leaders had to choose from among all the writings of the time and decide which ones should be accepted for inclusion into the canon of the New Testament. They made this decision based on the answers to the following questions:

- Was a particular work written by an eyewitness to events, by someone who actually knew Jesus, or by an apostle?
- Did the writing accurately reflect the teachings of Jesus as the apostles remembered them?
- Had the piece of writing been consistently used in liturgical settings by Church communities for some time?
- Was there a general consensus that a particular writing was sacred and special?

Two infancy Gospels that were not included in the canon of the New Testament are known as the *Infancy Story of Thomas* and the *Gospel of the Birth of Mary*.

While these Gospels were popular, they were not judged to be accurate readings of the life and message of Jesus, so Church leaders excluded them from the canon. A similar process was followed to determine which letters and other books were to be a part of the canon of the New Testament.

It is important to realize that the Bible is not the only source available to us for the transmission of the beliefs, doctrines, rituals, and life of the Church. We also have available to us the **Tradition** of the Church. Both the living Tradition and written Scriptures have their common source in the revelation of God in Christ. The content of Tradition communicates the whole life and activity of the Church. The process of Tradition is the passing on to future generations the truth and reality of Christ's mission and the message of the Church.

Scripture and Tradition have the same source—God. They are bound together so closely that they are in some way one thing moving toward the same goal, making "present and fruitful in the Church the mystery of Christ."

See *Catechism of the Catholic Church,* #80.

Beginnings of a Sacramental Life

sacrament

an efficacious sign of grace, instituted by Christ and entrusted to the Church, by which divine life is dispensed to us through the work of the Holy Spirit

The **sacraments** have their origin and foundation in Christ. Through the sacraments Christians experience life in Christ. In Christ, Christians experience God. The Catholic Church recognizes seven sacraments that touch some of the important stages and moments of Christian life. Anyone familiar with Catholicism knows that the sacraments have a fundamental role in the life of faith. Each of the sacraments celebrates, in some way, the Paschal mystery of Jesus' dying and rising to new life. Each offers the opportunity of experiencing the Paschal mystery in one's own life. The sacraments are also said to be *efficacious,* meaning that their effectiveness results not from anything wonderful that the people receiving them do but from God's love and power that is made manifest through Christ and works through the Holy Spirit in the Church. In other words, through the grace of the sacraments, God's life is celebrated by the person fortunate enough to experience it.

Did first-century Christians know that there were to be seven sacraments? In those exact terms they did not—not even Peter himself! Instead we need to look at what early Christians did that today we would consider sacramental. What were the first stages in the understanding of the seven sacraments that have become so essential to the Catholic Church?

To begin with, the word *sacrament* has pre-Christian origins. It first meant the initiation rite by which someone became a member of the great Roman army. Latin-speaking Christians decided upon the term *sacramentum* to translate the visible aspect of the Greek term *mysterion.* (See #774, *Catechism of the Catholic Church.*) The word sacrament, then, refers to the ways that Christians enter into and celebrate the mystery of their life in Christ. There is evidence that early Christians performed a number of rituals or ceremonies that they believed initiated them into this mystery. Over time these rituals became increasingly more formal and spiritual.

How does a sacrament become more formal and spiritual? Here are a few examples. Evidence indicates that in the beginning the Eucharist took place at a real meal with real food and drink. Paul even criticizes one of the Christian communities for overeating and excessive drinking rather than making sure that everyone at the meal is fed adequately. (See 1 Corinthians 11.) Over time one group performed Eucharist in a way that other groups found particularly inspiring and so that particular formula for the ceremony spread—the Eucharist became more formalized, that is, took on a specific form. At the same time, partially because of abuses such as those Paul mentions, the Eucharist became a more formalized ritualistic meal. That is, the only thing people attending actually ate was a small piece of sacred Bread and they drank a sip of sacred Wine. In this way the Eucharist, which originally happened during the celebration of a meal, became a separate eucharistic ritual with deep spiritual meaning. Paul's complaint that people were leaving the Eucharist physically overstuffed and drunk would not be made against Christians from the second century onward.

"The Disciples of Jesus Baptizing" by James J. Tissot.

Similarly, Baptism began as a real bath. (The Greek word from which Baptism comes means to plunge or immerse.) The earliest Christians baptized by immersion into a river or other body of water. Later, Christians built separate buildings for their baptisms—modeled after the Roman baths—where new members would be stripped naked and totally immersed in water. In time, new members to the community had water poured only over their heads to celebrate their Baptism.

Changes in the form used to celebrate these rituals did not diminish their essential significance. We find that early Christian communities were filled with a sense of the mystery of Christ's life-giving presence among them. They engaged in many activities that were particularly effective in making that mystery real for them. In the Greek-speaking churches, *mysterion* referred to a person's entire life with Christ as well as to the specific ways he or she lived out that mystery. Latin-speaking churches adopted the terms *mysterium* and *sacramentum* for these Christian mysteries. While certain actions, in particular the Eucharist and Baptism, clearly fall into the category of mystery and sacrament, there was no set number of sacraments in the beginning. These Christians found Christ in all aspects of their lives. As time went by, certain actions were recognized as having special significance, and today Catholics celebrate them as the seven sacraments: Baptism, Confirmation, Eucharist, Penance or Reconciliation, Anointing of the Sick, Holy Orders, and Matrimony.

Activity

1. List what you consider to be the important stages or moments of Christian life. Identify the sacrament that celebrates each stage or moment.

2. Look through the Gospels for Jesus' words and actions that relate to each of the sacraments. For example, look for an instance where Jesus healed someone by touching him or her.

Initiation into the Church

fyi!

The Second Vatican Council mandated the restoration of an adult catechumenate. The Rite of Christian Initiation for Adults (RCIA) was revised and restored in 1972 and mandated for use in the U.S. in 1988. The RCIA process models the initiation process for those received into the early Christian community.

catechumen
an unbaptized person preparing for membership in the Church

assimilation
members of minority groups adopting the values and characteristics of the dominant culture in which they live

Because of the frequent need for secrecy amid persecution and the far-flung nature of the early Church, preparation for Baptism and membership in the Church differed from place to place. However, there were common elements, such as hearing and responding to the good news, a process of learning the essentials of the faith, mentoring, and a gradual welcoming into the community of faith.

Within every local Church community, there were people preparing for initiation. Over time, a generally accepted procedure developed. The **catechumens** went through a process of formation that helped them move from their previous faith communities into that of the Christians communities. Often this meant giving up associations and even occupations that were contrary to the Christian message. Mentors (also called sponsors) and teachers (catechists) helped these individuals discern the changes they had to make and supported them with prayer and the teachings of Jesus. Generally the catechumens joined the community worship on Sunday for the reading of Scripture and the initial prayers (what today we call the Liturgy of the Word). They were then dismissed, along with a catechist who guided them through a reflection on the Scriptures read that day and helped them apply the readings to their lives and decisions.

Before their initiation the catechumens (now called the *elect*, the chosen ones) participated in a lengthy retreat-type experience. This eventually became what we now know as the Season of Lent. When the community gathered for the all-night Easter vigil, the elect were welcomed into the Christian community with great joy. They were immersed in the waters of Baptism, anointed with the oil of chrism, and welcomed at the table of the Lord. They were new Christians with a new family and a new home.

The formation of the neophytes (new Christians) continued for some time after their initiation. This mystagogy time included more learning, a great deal of reflection, and an **assimilation** into the community and into its worship and works of charity. In time, the new Christians were able to help guide other catechumens on their journey into the Christian community.

Today the elect celebrate the Sacraments of Initiation at the Easter Vigil.

An Institutional Structure Emerges: One Body, Different Functions

For as in one body we have many members, and not all members have the same function, so we, who are many, are one body in Christ, and individually we are members one of another.

Romans 12:4–5

Discussion

Describe the various ministries that people in your parish perform.

Did Jesus intend Christianity as it exists today? Did Jesus intend his Church to be structured as a hierarchical institution with the apostles and their successors as leaders? Let's try to answer this question in light of developments that took place in the early centuries of Church history.

The previously quoted words from Paul point out that different members of Christ's body, the Church, have different functions. However, elsewhere Paul emphasizes that Christ alone is head of the body. If we take the Church to be the Body of Christ, then are popes and bishops—in fact, anyone who claims leadership in the Christian community—in violation of this principle? A first point to be made related to this question is that Jesus left us no exact blueprint for Church organization. Nowhere in the Gospels did Jesus say, "You twelve and your successors are bishops, and you will have the following job description: . . . Others of you are to be ordained priests, and you will be responsible for the following duties: . . . Some others of you will be called deacons, and you are to serve those who are poor. The rest of you will be called the laity. Your duties will be . . ."

However, as already mentioned, the case can clearly be made, based on Gospel accounts, that Jesus selected twelve apostles for a leadership role among his followers. He identified Peter as the leader of this group. We see Peter immediately accept this position, as followers of Jesus—a group of about 120 men and women—gathered together to choose a man named Matthias to take the place of Judas, the apostle who betrayed Jesus and then died (Acts 1:15–26). Therefore, we see that the apostles stepped into leadership positions in the Christian community from its earliest existence.

Those in the ordained ministry continue to lead the Christian community in worship and service.

UNDERSTANDING THE DEVELOPMENT OF CHURCH STRUCTURES

1. Leadership positions did exist in the earliest Christian community.

2. A variety of forms of organization existed in the earliest days of the Church.

3. As the Church grew, clearly defined structures of authority grew with it.

4. The model that exists in the Catholic Church today became standard—that is, bishops, priests, deacons, and laypeople have different functions serving a common purpose.

bishop

means "overseer"; in the Catholic faith the word refers to one who has received the fullness of the Sacrament of Holy Orders; the shepherd of a particular church entrusted to him

presbyter

another name for elder or priest; in the early Church presbyters served in leadership positions in some faith communities; one who has received the second order in Holy Orders

If we read further in Acts, we also discover that a variety of forms of organization existed in the earliest days of the Church. Some local churches had an overseer, like a bishop, who served as its leader. Other churches had a group of elders who exercised a group leadership. Such differences in organizational structure didn't cause those who followed one style to reject those who followed another. In Acts we read that the apostles prayed, laid hands on those chosen for service and ministry, and sent them out. (See Acts 6:6, 13:3.)

However, as the Church grew, clearly defined structures of authority grew with it. At an early stage, the model that exists in the Catholic Church today became the standard model of Church governance. Individuals were appointed or elected to lead local communities, just as today **bishops** are regional leaders under the authority of the pope. Deacons assisted these local leaders, especially in the important work of caring for people with special needs in the community. Eventually **presbyters** became exclusive representatives of the bishops as local communities expanded farther and farther. In summary, the early Christian community recognized that it was to be "of one heart and soul" in embodying the Holy Spirit and in carrying out the message of Jesus (Acts 4:32). It formed particular structures to help it in its task. Through its institutional structure, today's Catholic Church remains faithful to the model first developed as early as apostolic times.

Women in the Early Church

Determining what roles women had in the early Church requires a kind of detective work. We know from the Gospels, for instance, that Jesus treated women as equal to men. This was not typical in the culture of his time. Although Jesus chose twelve men as apostles, there were a number of women among his regular followers—for example, Mary his mother; Mary of Magdala; Susanna; and Joanna, the wife of Herod's steward, Chuza.

Paul also had a number of women who helped him in his ministry. Although Paul seems ultra-conservative in his view of women by today's standards, it is important to judge Paul by the standards of his own time. Paul would have been considered a radical champion of women in his day. At a time when a woman could be divorced for over-salting the stew, Paul's instructions about marital relations found in Colossians 3 would have been most welcomed!

Discussion

Read Ephesians 5:21–33 and Colossians 3:18–25. What might have been the reaction of women and children in Paul's time to these writings? How are they interpreted today?

fyi!

In the early centuries of the Church, women deacons were mainly engaged in ministry to widows, women, and children. The role of women deacons diminished around the sixth century in the Western Church and the eleventh century in the Eastern Church.

In his letter to Christians in Rome, Paul mentions several women who served the Christian community in leadership roles:

I commend to you our sister Phoebe, a deacon of the church at Cenchreae, so that you may welcome her in the Lord as is fitting for the saints, and help her in whatever she may require from you, for she has been a benefactor of many and of myself as well. Greet Prisca and Aquila, who work with me in Christ Jesus, and who risked their necks for my life, to whom not only I give thanks, but also all the churches of the Gentiles. Greet also the church in their house. Greet my beloved Epaenetus, who was the first convert in Asia for Christ. Greet Mary, who has worked very hard among you. Greet Andronicus and Junia, my relatives who were in prison with me; they are prominent among the apostles, and they were in Christ before I was.

Romans 16:1–7

Contemporary Church leaders admit that historically within the Church community, women have at times been unjustly left out or harmed because of patriarchal attitudes prevalent in the cultures in which the Church found itself. Church leaders have concluded that while women cannot be ordained, they are and should be full and active members of the community just as they were from the beginning.

In 1995 Pope John Paul II said the following about women and Church history:

Unfortunately, a certain way of writing history has paid greater attention to extraordinary and sensational events than to the daily rhythm of life, and the resulting history is almost only concerned with the achievements of men. This tendency should be reversed. "How much still needs to be said and written about man's enormous debt to woman in every other realm of social and cultural progress!" (*L'Osservatore Romano,* English edition, 31 May 1995, #6.)

"History Needs to Include Women's Contributions," #1.

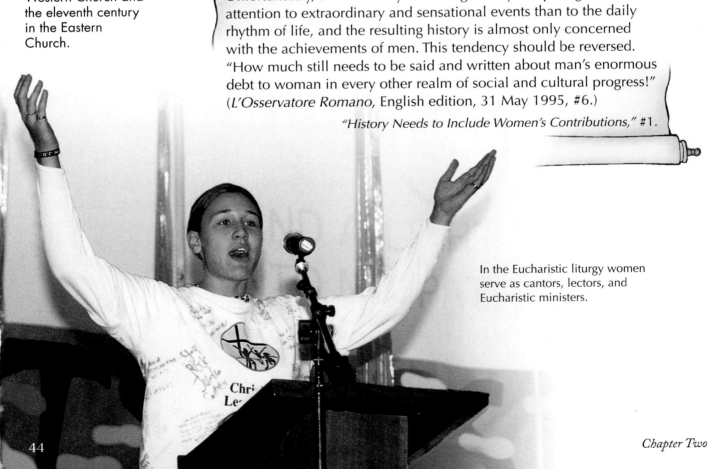

In the Eucharistic liturgy women serve as cantors, lectors, and Eucharistic ministers.

List the roles each of the following women played in the early Church:

Phoebe (Romans 16:1–2)
Priscilla [also called Prisca] (Acts18:2, 18, 26; Romans 16:3; and 1 Corinthians 16:19)
Euodia and Syntyche (Philippians 4:2–3)
Nympha (Colossians 4:15)
Lydia of Philippi (Acts 16:14–15, 40)
Tabitha (Acts 9:36–42)

1. As applied to the Church, what do *creed, rite,* and *community* mean?

2. Describe a major difference between Jewish and Greek thought.

3. What is theology?

4. What function did apologists serve in the early Church?

5. What is the difference between orthodoxy and heresy?

6. What was the debate about people who were called *lapsi?*

7. What does "setting the canon" mean in regard to Scripture?

8. What principles did Church leaders use in setting the canon?

9. What two sources does the Church use to determine Christian teachings? What is their common source?

10. What is the pre-Christian meaning of the term *sacramentum?*

11. How did Greek-speaking churches refer to what Latin churches called sacraments?

12. What does it mean to say that sacraments became more formalized and spiritualized?

13. Outline the basic transformation that took place in the early Church's institutional structure.

14. Who were Junia and Phoebe?

Conclusion

It wasn't long before members of the early Church encountered attacks and persecutions. They had the story of Jesus, who also suffered and died but was raised from the dead, to sustain them during these difficult first centuries. The witness given by these martyrs can't help but inspire anyone who wonders whether there is anything worth living—and dying—for. The Church also had its internal conflicts and controversies. Even people who share a common vision and purpose can disagree about what exactly the vision means and about how to achieve their goals. When people feel very strongly about something, as the early Christians sometimes did, then disagreements become even more heated. Today's world is not the first to address multiculturalism and various forms of diversity. Now, as then, Christians have Jesus to remind them that sharing of resources and caring especially for people in particular need make God's presence real. Finally, the Church gradually took on a definite shape. While differences remained from place to place, essentials of belief and practice became standard over these early centuries. Members of the Church today have inspiring stories, statements of beliefs that great thinkers hammered out, established rituals for sacraments by which to encounter Christ, and an organization that connects them to fellow Church members down the street and around the globe. The early Christians gave their lives to be Church and to create a Church through which Christ can continue to be present. Their legacy remains with us today.

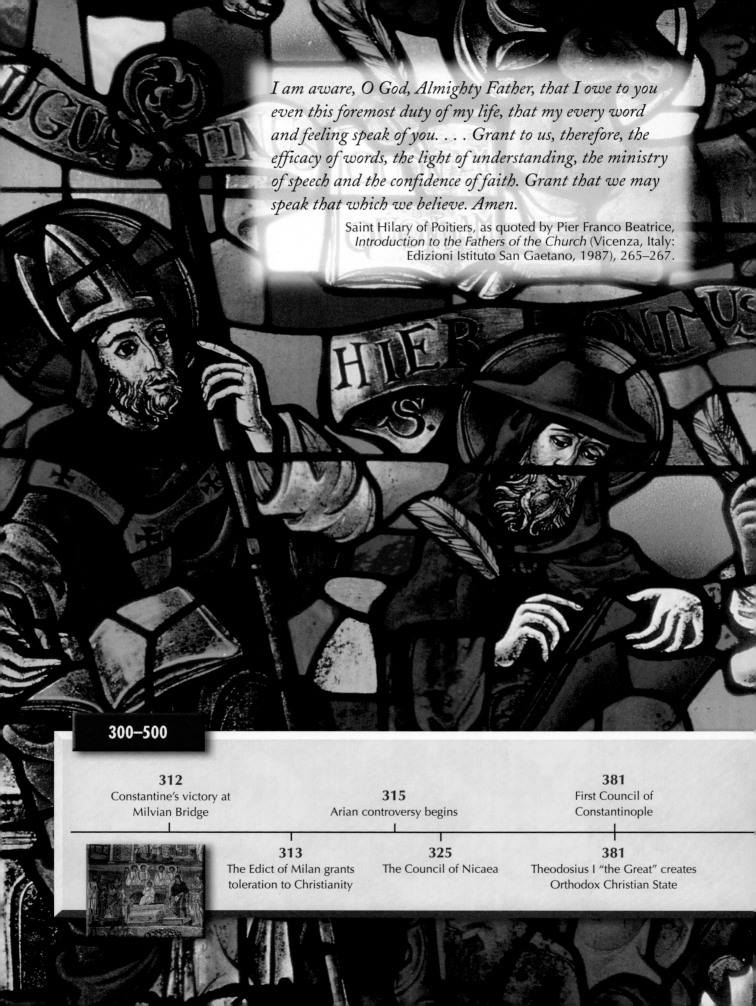

I am aware, O God, Almighty Father, that I owe to you even this foremost duty of my life, that my every word and feeling speak of you. . . . Grant to us, therefore, the efficacy of words, the light of understanding, the ministry of speech and the confidence of faith. Grant that we may speak that which we believe. Amen.

Saint Hilary of Poitiers, as quoted by Pier Franco Beatrice, *Introduction to the Fathers of the Church* (Vicenza, Italy: Edizioni Istituto San Gaetano, 1987), 265–267.

300–500

312
Constantine's victory at
Milvian Bridge

315
Arian controversy begins

381
First Council of
Constantinople

313
The Edict of Milan grants
toleration to Christianity

325
The Council of Nicaea

381
Theodosius I "the Great" creates
Orthodox Christian State

CHURCH VICTORIOUS

The Age of the Fathers

CHAPTER OVERVIEW

- With Constantine as emperor, Christianity becomes the religion of the Roman Empire.

- Christian leaders, called the Fathers of the Church, guide the community through controversies and identify beliefs and practices that have sustained the Church ever since.

- Following the age of martyrs and persecutions, much of Christian spirituality centers on the monastic life.

387
The conversion of Augustine

398
John Chrysostom becomes
patriarch of Constantinople

405
Jerome completes
the Vulgate

432
Patrick returns to
Ireland as bishop

451
The Council of
Chalcedon

452
Pope Leo the Great turns
back Attila from Rome

Have you ever been on a team that went from last place one year to first place the next? Do you have a sense of what it sometimes feels like to be freshmen—outsiders, picked on, and considered unimportant, and then to be seniors—the people in leadership positions who set the standards for everyone else to follow? A drastic turnabout such as this happened to Christianity. The Church begun by Jesus went from its humble origins to being the official religion of the mighty Roman Empire three hundred years later. The wave of enthusiasm that had sustained the Christian Church during its time of persecutions led to great expansion and growth when it found itself guiding Roman power rather than being under its attack. Church leaders provided leadership and kept civilization alive at a time when emperors were often weak, corrupt, or inept.

Debates about the true meaning of the Christian faith didn't end when Christianity rose to power. Emperors themselves offered opinions about the relationship between God the Father and God the Son. To sustain the spiritual vitality of the Church, a new form of living the Christian life emerged—monasticism. During the period covered in this chapter, shifts in political and economic fortunes had a lasting impact on the Church. Civilization and Christianity flourished in the eastern part of the empire, leading to many remarkable developments in the Eastern or Byzantine branches of the Church. Western Europe during this period experienced both destruction and development. The one light flickering during these dark times was the light of Christ kept burning by the members of his Church.

Before We Begin . . .

Read through the list below. Then rank the factors in terms of why you think Christianity gained such popularity during its first five centuries. Explain how your top three choices may have contributed to Christian expansion and growth.

___9___ the beauty and mystery of the liturgy and sacraments

___8___ the sense of community and mutual concern among Church members

___7___ the image of Christ crucified as savior of the world

___3___ the spirit of morality and justice advocated by the Church

___2___ the profound depth of Christian beliefs and teachings

___1___ the promise of eternal life that fills Church members with hope

___4___ the inspiration of the many holy men and women living out their Christian faith

___5___ the Christian spirituality that leads people to a deeper level of human experience

___6___ the joy and peace emanating from members of the Church

THE RELIGION OF THE EMPIRE

The Edict of Milan Changes Christianity

Truly one of the most significant events in Church history—indeed, one of the most important events in all of history—was the Roman Empire's embracing of Christianity during the reign of Constantine. Being Christian is one experience when those in power fear, distrust, and hate Christians; it is a totally different experience when the rulers and the lawmakers are Christian themselves. To put it in today's perspective, the difference would be much greater than sitting with your own student body or the rival's student body during a hotly contested basketball game.

As mentioned in the last chapter, under Constantine Christianity went from being a religion of outsiders to being a religion of insiders. After Constantine issued the Edict of Milan, Christians could sit amid the rich and powerful as one of their own.

The rise to power did not dampen the spirit within the Christian community. It did, however, cause that spirit to be channeled in different directions. For instance, Church leaders no longer guided only isolated groups of Christians, providing safe haven from outsiders and keeping them on the right track. Now, Church leaders were called upon to provide guidance in secular affairs as well. The empire's leaders no longer persecuted or ignored Christianity. Instead they looked to Christianity to maintain and foster the well-being of the empire. Divisions within the empire led to divisions within the Christian community. Similarly, divisions within the Christian community caused divisions within the empire. Christians who wanted to give their all for Christ no longer lived under the threat of martyrdom. Now, those who wanted to sacrifice all the comforts of life in Christ's name had to make their way out to deserts or other isolated spots. Christian worship became a public ceremony, and places of worship openly represented Christ triumphant. Christian missionaries spread not only the Christian faith but also Roman civilization.

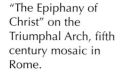

"The Epiphany of Christ" on the Triumphal Arch, fifth century mosaic in Rome.

Constantine—From Roman General to Christian Ruler

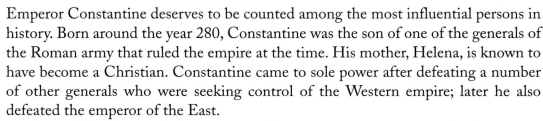

www. To graphically view the universality of the christian faith visit **www. adherent.com**

Emperor Constantine deserves to be counted among the most influential persons in history. Born around the year 280, Constantine was the son of one of the generals of the Roman army that ruled the empire at the time. His mother, Helena, is known to have become a Christian. Constantine came to sole power after defeating a number of other generals who were seeking control of the Western empire; later he also defeated the emperor of the East.

One of Constantine's first acts upon becoming emperor was to abandon Rome and build a new capital city along the straits of the Bosporus, the waters that divide Europe from Asia Minor. Formerly a small trading post called *Byzantium*, the city was renamed New Rome by Constantine. Most people, however, simply called it *Constantinople* Constantine's city. Today the city is known as Istanbul, Turkey.

The central and eastern Mediterranean world today.

Because he moved the empire's capital to Asia Minor, the center of civilization also moved from West to East. For the most part, from this time on emperors and government leaders abandoned Rome and allowed the Romans to deal with the city's rising decay. They also had to deal with the steadily increasing threats from nomadic Germanic tribes from outside the Roman Empire who pillaged Roman communities living on the frontiers of the empire and eventually controlled the Western half of the empire. With civil power centered in the East, only Church leaders remained to care for the crumbling empire in the West.

Constantine favored Christianity, but he also allowed non-Christian customs to continue. He kept the image of the sun god on the official coins of the empire and retained for himself the title **Pontifex Maximus.** As during non-Christian times, emperors saw themselves in the priestly role of bridging the gap between the human and the divine. This title, held by the Roman emperors before Constantine, was later adopted by Christian popes. (The title today has been adapted to "pontiff.") Even though Constantine turned to Christianity in 312, he was not baptized until just before his death in 337. The Byzantine Church considers Constantine to be a saint.

Pontifex Maximus the term means "the greatest bridge-builder"; title for emperors and, eventually, the pope

Activity

Constantine's turn to Christianity followed the Battle of the Milvian Bridge in the year 312. Research the life of Constantine, highlighting the Christian standards he legislated during his reign.

Review

1. Name three changes in the Church's role and practice that came about after Christianity gained power in the Roman Empire.

2. How did Constantine's decision to move his capital from Rome to Constantinople affect the Eastern and Western sections of the empire?

3. Give an example illustrating how Constantine continued to hold onto non-Christian ways.

THE COUNCIL OF NICAEA

Arianism
a heresy denying that Jesus is truly God

No sooner had peace and freedom come to the Church than a conflict arose that had been festering for some time. A new heresy begun by an Alexandrian priest Arius—**Ariansim**—caused much discord. Christian teaching described God as being of one substance but three persons. This teaching is known as the mystery of the Trinity. However, early in the fourth century a priest in Egypt named Arius wrote a book of popular songs entitled *Thaleia* (*The Banquet*), in which he proclaimed that Jesus was not of the same substance as the Father. He proposed that only God the Father could be immortal. Arius's teaching stated, "There was once when he [the Son] was not." Therefore, Jesus must have been created, and while Jesus is like the Father, he is not truly God.

> God is one in substance (essence, nature). The words *person* and *hypostasis* refer to the Father, Son, and Holy Spirit as they are distinct. The word *relation* refers to the fact that they are distinct in relation to each other.
>
> See *Catechism of the Catholic Church*, #252.

"Portrait of Arius" by Andrea di Buonaioto, fourteenth century.

Many newly baptized Christians accepted this view as it was more in line with their pre-Christian concepts. They could accept God as the perfection of all things, as described in Greek thought and Jesus as the superhero found in Greek and Roman mythology. Having previously believed these myths, new Christians saw no problem in viewing Jesus this way. Arius's bishop, Alexander of Alexandria, however, saw this perspective as a rejection of the belief that Jesus was divine in the full sense of the word. He gathered together local Church leaders who discussed the matter and condemned Arius and his teachings. This condemnation did not settle the conflict, however. Arius was a very popular pastor who was skilled at composing catchy tunes that people loved to sing and through which he spread his teachings. Members of the Church joined one side or the other in the dispute. Riots even broke out in Egypt, where the debates were most intense. Eventually, the controversy began to affect the security of the empire itself.

Emperor Constantine was so concerned about the Arian controversy that in 325 he called for a meeting of all Church leaders to take place at a palace he had in the town of Nicaea, about fifty miles southeast of Constantinople. The meeting is considered to be the first **ecumenical council**, or worldwide gathering of Christian bishops. (Although in fact, almost all who attended the **Council of Nicaea** were from the Eastern Church, and the bishop of Rome did not attend.) The emperor himself opened the council with great pomp and insisted that the over three hundred bishops in attendance must resolve this issue because he wanted a Church that had beliefs that would be **catholic**. "Division in the Church is worse than war," he declared, "because it involves souls." Arius was called upon to present his teachings. The bishops rejected the teachings and decided that they needed to formulate a creed that would describe clearly the relationship between God the Father and Jesus the Son. All but two bishops signed the creed, and these two were condemned and exiled along with Arius.

The creed the bishops created is called the **Nicene Creed,** or Niceno-Constantinopolitan Creed since a later council at Constantinople added to it. Catholic Churches all over the world proclaim this creed during Sunday Mass. In the creed, Jesus is described as "true God from true God, begotten not made, one in Being with the Father." The key phrase is "one in Being." Arius called for wording that would mean "of similar being." The difference may seem minor. In the end, however, Arianism split the Church of the time.

Even with the council's decree, the Arian heresy was not stamped out for another sixty years. Disagreement about the relationship among the three Persons of the Blessed Trinity—God the Father, Son, and Holy Spirit—continued to be debated and eventually figured into the split between the Eastern Orthodox and Western Churches.

LESSONS TO LEARN FROM THE ARIAN CONTROVERSY AND THE COUNCIL OF NICAEA

- Controversies over Christian teaching have been part of Church history for a long time.

- Councils provide a procedure for the Church to settle matters of conflict.

- In the midst of conflicts and adversity, wise leaders will emerge who clarify and keep alive the Christian message.

- The Christian message is not just about eternal life but is also concerned about temporal affairs in light of eternity.

Activity

Write a report on the life of Saint Athanasius to learn the story of someone who suffered greatly to hold the line against Arianism.

Councils Further Clarify Christian Beliefs

The Council of Nicaea and the Nicene Creed did not resolve all disputes about the place of Jesus in the Christian perspective on reality. A series of councils took place over the next century or so. The last council recognized as official by all Christian Churches was the Council of Chalcedon in 451. It challenged another way of viewing Jesus that once again watered down the subtlety of Christian teaching about him.

Eutyches, the head of a monastery near Constantinople, was a leading advocate of what came to be known as the heresy of **Monophysitism.** (*Mono* means "one," and *physis* means "nature.") According to Eutyches, the human nature of Jesus was lost in the divine, just as "a drop of honey, which falls into the sea, dissolves in it." This teaching gained such support that it was endorsed at a council at Ephesus in 449. However, Pope Leo declared this council to be invalid. The emperor Marcias called for another council. Four hundred bishops attended the Council of Chalcedon and condemned monophysitism. Mainstream Christian teaching declares that Jesus is one person who possesses two natures—human and divine.

Monophysitism
belief that Jesus has only a divine nature, instead of the traditional Christian teaching that Jesus has two natures—human and divine

Faced with this heresy [Monophysitism], the fourth ecumenical council, at Chalcedon in 451, confessed:

. . . We confess that one and the same Christ, Lord, and only-begotten Son, is to be acknowledged in two natures without confusion, change, division, or separation. The distinction between the natures was never abolished by their union, but rather the character proper to each of the two natures was preserved as they came together in one person (*prosopon*) and one hypostasis [Council of Chalcedon: DS 302].

See *Catechism of the Catholic Church,* #467.

Interestingly, Monophysite communities continue to exist today. People who believed that Jesus possessed only a divine nature made their way eastward and established strongholds in what is today Iran and Iraq. They traveled as far as India, and evidence indicates that in the eighth century descendants of these Monophysites even entered the capital of China.

We may think of theological controversies as debates between scholars that have little impact on ordinary people. Obviously, that was not the case with the debates over theological questions that took place in the early centuries of the Church. Today, if a Christian said, "I don't believe that Jesus is God," other Christians would probably look puzzled because Christians have been taught for centuries that Jesus is human and divine. However, during these earlier times, people struggled to come to an accurate and precise understanding of core Christian beliefs.

THE ECUMENICAL COUNCILS OF THE EARLY CHURCH

Location	Date	Emperor	Major Outcomes
Nicaea	325	Constantine	• declared Jesus, the Son of God, *homoousios* (coequal, consubstantial, and coeternal) with the Father • condemned Arius — *condemned + denied Christ's divinity* • drafted original form of Nicene Creed • *Declared that Christ was fully divine*
Constantinople	381	Theodosius *said that official rel. of Roman empire was Christianity*	• confirmed results of Council of Nicaea • affirmed deity *God* of the Holy Spirit — *led to Trinity* • condemned Apollinarianism — *had human body but didn't suffer any pain* • *Christ is fully human*
Ephesus	431	Theodosius II	• declared Nestorianism a heresy *rejected Mary being mother of God* • condemned Pelagianism *Can get to heaven w/ grace (God's help) AKA - just faith*
Chalcedon	451	Marcian	• declared Christ's two natures unmixed, unchanged, undivided, inseparable • condemned monophysitism *Denied Christ's humanity* • *Said Christ both human + divine*

Chi Rho

Robert C. Walton, *Chronological and Background Charts of Church History* (Grand Rapids, Mich.: Academie Books/Zondervan Publishing House, 1986), #18.

Activity

Research and report on one of these heresies: Apollinarianism, Nestorianism, Pelagianism.

Review

1. Who was Arius, and what is the principal teaching of Arianism?

2. Who called for the Council of Nicaea? What does it mean to say that it was the first ecumenical council?

3. What is the Nicene Creed, and how does it describe the relationship between God the Father and Jesus?

4. What is Monophysitism, and what response did the Council of Chalcedon make to it?

WESTERN ROMAN EMPIRE FALLS

The time between the classical era and the Middle Ages was in many ways a dark period for Western Europe. This period was marked by marauding tribes from the North and East who fought against the people of the empire and among themselves, diminishing many of the accomplishments that marked earlier periods. These tribes, referred to collectively as barbarians, inhabited the territory beyond the western and northern frontiers of the Roman Empire.

For the most part the tribes from the North and East had no established cities or communities and instead moved about so that their flocks could pasture. As Rome's control spread into their territory, the various groups attacked those who lived on the edges of the empire. Eventually Roman soldiers could no longer control these invasions into the empire, and by the fifth century Rome itself was under attack. In 410 one of these invading groups, the **Visigoths**, actually overtook Rome.

With a depleted army and no effective defense against the invaders, authorities in the empire decided that one solution to the problem was to welcome the invaders as citizens. First to accept the offer were the Visigoths, the inhabitants of modern-day Spain, who had attacked and taken control of Rome. The **Vandals** were next. They gained control over much of the empire. Both groups adopted Christianity. However, they both also chose Arianism and ended up persecuting mainstream Christians in territories controlled by them.

Visigoths
a Germanic tribe who settled primarily in Spain; the first such group to lay siege to Rome

Vandals
one of the most destructive nomadic tribes; adopted Arianism when they converted to Christianity

fyi!

The word *barbarian* has come to have a variety of negative connotations. Originally the term simply referred to people who couldn't speak Greek properly.

These marauding tribes were viewed by Roman citizens as rowdy and uncultured. If you are of European descent, some of these so-called barbarians are probably your ancestors.

The **Huns** came from the East, originally from the steppes of China. Their leader, Attila, received the nickname "the scourge of God" because of the havoc he wrought on the civilized towns and people that lay in his path. One group fleeing the Huns found themselves stopped by the sea in what is now northern Italy. To protect themselves from the Huns, they built islands on pilings and an elaborate series of canals that were separate from solid land. That watery settlement still exists as the city of Venice.

By the end of the fifth century, the empire in the West ceased to exist. It was now a collection of lands ruled by various barbarian tribes. As they settled into domestic life, leaders of the tribes saw Christianity as a unifying force that would allow their people to live peacefully with their neighbors. Although Arianism was the dominant religion in most of the West during the early stages of the Christian tribal period, the steadfast fidelity of the bishops of Rome and others kept Catholic Christianity alive so that it eventually came to dominate in Europe.

The Bishop of Rome as Emperor of the West

Looking back on history, we know that empires rise and fall. However, people who lived in the Roman Empire during the first four hundred years thought of Rome as more than a city or an empire. Rome meant civilization, order, the way things are meant to be. This period of widespread and orderly Roman rule is known as *Pax Romana.* When Constantine moved the capital to Constantinople, it must have been quite a shock to citizens of the empire—even though he did name the new capital New Rome.

Very early in Christian history the bishop of Rome came to be viewed as the leader of Christianity. During the time of the invasions, the position of the pope—as the bishop of Rome came to be called—grew in importance. While the rulers of the empire were living in Constantinople safely away from the fray, the bishop of Rome became, in effect, the emperor of the West. In the East, emperors and patriarchs divided secular and spiritual rule, even though the one at times interfered with matters of concern to the other. In the

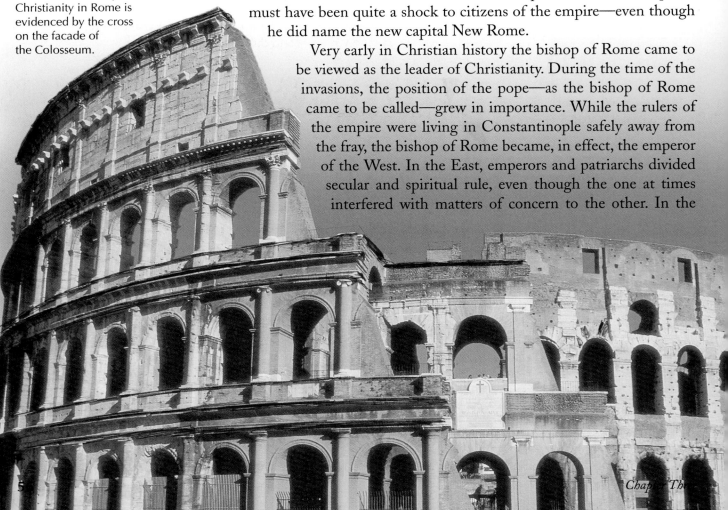

The eventual triumph of Christianity in Rome is evidenced by the cross on the facade of the Colosseum.

Apostolic See
a term used for the papacy, identifying papal power with that of the apostles; also called the "Holy See"

fyi!

The word *see* is an abbreviation for the word *seat*—the chair designating an office of authority such as the chairperson of a committee or a county seat. Every bishop has a chair symbolizing his authority in a diocese.

West, the popes were the sole power overseeing the material and spiritual welfare of Western Europe. Popes had to rely on faith and conviction to battle invaders intent on pillaging the city and the western territories.

Since the empire relied on a strong papacy, as the diocese of Rome came to be called, the popes of the time often acted as autocratic rulers. Saint Damasus I, who was pope from 366–384, first used the term **Apostolic See** to refer to his office in order to strengthen in people's minds the connection between the papacy and the apostles.

Pope Damasus claimed that the East sent Peter and Paul, leaders among the apostles, to Rome. Since they died in the city, Rome could claim them as citizens. Because of his personal holiness and his willingness to challenge heresy, Emperor Theodosius ordered all inhabitants of the empire to follow the form of religion advocated by Pope Damasus. Damasus also asked Saint Jerome to translate the standard Bible from Greek into Latin and changed the language of the liturgy from Greek to Latin so that more people could understand it. These changes strengthened the position of the papacy even more and also added to the growing separation between the Western, Latin Church and the Eastern, Greek Church.

Discussion

The first four centuries of Roman rule are considered the glory days for Rome, similiar to the way some people refer to the twentieth century as the *American century* because North American ideals and culture so dominated at least the second half of that century. Discuss what North American ways of thinking and living have become common to the world during the past fifty years.

Below: The interior of the Colosseum with the underground system exposed.

Right: The Arch of Constantine near the Colosseum.

Saint Leo the Great

Because of his strong defense of the role of the papacy, Pope Leo I, who served as pope from 440–461, is one of only two popes referred to as "the Great" (the other being Gregory I). With no army behind him, Leo I was the sole authority representing Roman interests to the Huns, and then later to the Vandals. Leo I negotiated with Attila the Hun to spare the city and actually convinced Attila to do so. He also strengthened the papacy by stating that each pope succeeds Saint Peter rather than the previous pope. Each pope, therefore, inherits the powers of Peter. This teaching implies that individual failings or vices of particular popes do not diminish the role of the papacy itself. Two hundred years after his death, Leo's body was exhumed and reburied near the tomb of Saint Peter in Saint Peter's Basilica; he was the first pope so honored. Leo's strengthening of the power of the papacy was particularly important because the expectation at the time was that the emperor needed to approve whoever was to become pope. The distance between Rome and the East naturally limited the influence and control of the emperor over the papacy, and popes such as Leo the Great helped make the papacy a powerful and independent force overseeing the Western Church. (The emperor continued to appoint, at least to all appearances, the patriarch of Constantinople for some time after this.)

Review

1. Who were considered barbarians by citizens of the Roman Empire?

2. Which invading group first took control of Rome?

3. What type of Christianity did the tribes from the North and East usually adopt when they became citizens of the Roman Empire?

4. Who was Attila, and what did Pope Leo the Great convince him not to do?

5. What does it mean to say that *Rome* meant more than a city or an empire?

6. What did Leo the Great do to shape the papacy?

THE FATHERS OF THE CHURCH

What is the right way to think about God the Father, the role of Jesus, and the function that the Holy Spirit plays in the workings of the Church? What is the best way for Christians to practice their faith? During the heady days following Christianity's spread throughout the empire, such topics were discussed at all levels of social life in many parts of the empire. One writer of the time reported that when he went to the market, people were talking more about the nature of the Trinity than about the price of meat!

The writings and exemplary lives of many outstanding Christian leaders of the time assisted Church members then and now in deciding matters of Christian beliefs and practice. These great thinkers are known collectively as the **Fathers of the Church.** Though the complete list numbers thirty-nine men from the Western Church and fifty-one from the Eastern Church, during this formative period a number of impressive women also made important contributions to Christian thought and practice. Because of social restrictions in existence at the time, the writings of the women are few.

Fathers of the Church
a designation for Church leaders during the early centuries of Christianity whose teachings collectively formulated Christian doctrine and practices

THE FATHERS OF THE CHURCH

West or Latin Church	East or Greek Church
Saint Ambrose, bishop of Milan	Saint Athanasius, archbishop of Alexandria Gregory of Nyssa, bishop of Sebaste
Saint Augustine, bishop of Hippo	Saint Basil, archbishop of Caesarea
Saint Gregory (I) the Great, pope	Saint Gregory of Nazianzus, bishop of Sasima; patriarch of Constantinople
Saint Jerome, priest; translated the Scriptures into Latin (the Vulgate)	Saint John Chrysostom, patriarch of Constantinople

St. Gregory (I) the Great

Saint John Chrysostom

The Patristic Period

The Church Fathers were people of courage, conviction, wisdom, and faith who sustained the Church during difficult times and fashioned the Church as it has existed down through the ages. Because of the large number of men given the honor of being called a Father of the Church, our discussion here will be limited to three of the most prominent ones.

Saint Ambrose (339–397)

The son of an important Roman official, Ambrose used his family connections to become governor of northern Italy with its headquarters in Milan. This was a time when Arians were fighting mainstream Christians for control of territory. When Milan's bishop died in 374, Arians and Catholics gathered in the cathedral to battle over who would become the next bishop. When Ambrose heard about the commotion going on, he went to the cathedral to calm things down. Eventually someone shouted, "Ambrose for bishop." Soon the rest of the crowd joined in. Ambrose, who was not even baptized at the time, fled the building but was surrounded by the people and finally agreed to their wishes. Within a week he was baptized, confirmed, ordained a priest, and then bishop.

As bishop, Ambrose applied his skills as a civil servant to being a servant of the Church. He trained his clergy and strengthened the program for those preparing for Baptism. He made sure that those in Milan who were poor were taken care of, even giving away all of his own personal possessions.

He studied the Bible so that he could deliver a thoughtful and inspiring sermon every Sunday. He wrote books on theology and commentaries on Scripture. Ambrose also needed his skills as a politician to address the Arian controversy, as he had to defend the Church's doctrine against the Emperor Valentinian who favored the Arians. When the emperor ordered that one of Ambrose's churches was to be given to the Arians, Ambrose refused. Troops arrived to take control of the church, but Ambrose stood in front of it and said, "The emperor is in the Church, not over it." The emperor backed down.

Of all the contributions that Ambrose made to the Church, however, his greatest perhaps was his role in inspiring Saint Augustine to become a Christian.

Saint Augustine of Hippo (354–430)

Saint Augustine is best known for his monumental work, *City of God*. Augustine also wrote what is the first true autobiography, *Confessions*. He was born in northern Africa of a non-Christian father and a Christian mother, Monica. Augustine was very bright but he also engaged in a life of pleasure-seeking and self-indulgence. After he fathered a child out of wedlock, he turned to a religious cult known as the **Manicheans**, who believed that matter, which is evil, was in a constant struggle with God, the source of all good. Around the age of thirty Augustine went first to Rome and then to Milan. In Milan he met Ambrose, under whose influence Augustine turned toward Christianity.

In *Confessions*, Augustine states he had a religious experience when a voice said to him, "Take and read." He began reading the Bible and found the answers that he was seeking. Ambrose baptized Augustine in 387, and Augustine decided to return to

Manicheism
a religious movement that viewed reality as a constant struggle between the forces of spiritual good and physical evil; the physical world is entirely evil

Africa and live the remainder of his life as a monk. Four years later, however, the people of his local church asked him to be their priest and then their bishop. He served as bishop of Hippo for thirty-five years. Augustine's writings are numerous, and he is recognized by many as the greatest theologian of the Western Church.

Saint Jerome (331–420)

A contemporary of Ambrose and Augustine, Jerome was from northern Italy but educated in Rome. He was particularly skilled in languages, being one of the few people in the West who knew Hebrew and Greek. One night in a dream he heard God ask him how he saw himself. Jerome answered, "I am a Christian." God responded, "You are not a Christian. You are a Ciceronian. Where your treasure is, there is your heart." (Cicero was one of the greatest pre-Christian Latin writers.) As so many people of the time did in response to a powerful religious experience, Jerome left the world and became a monk. Henceforth, he dedicated himself to the study of the Scriptures. When Jerome was fifty years old, Pope Damasus asked him to return to Rome to become his secretary, which he did. Jerome made many enemies in Rome because he spoke out forcefully against the luxurious living and corruption that he found there. He had verbal skills to belittle the best opponent, and he didn't hesitate to use them.

Pope Damasus decided that he could use Jerome's skills with language to undertake an important task. The Greek translation of the Bible was in common use at the time. However, Latin was now the language of the people in the West. Some Latin translations had been made, but were not of good quality. Damasus asked Jerome to make a new Latin translation of the Bible, from the original Hebrew and Greek. Jerome left Rome for Bethlehem and spent most of the remainder of his life working on a Latin translation. His translation of the Bible, known as the **Vulgate** because it is in the language of the common people, served as the official Bible of the Church for over fifteen hundred years.

Besides his Latin translation of the Bible, Jerome performed another service for the Church. He taught the Bible to women. Jerome found the wisdom and depth of understanding in his women companions to be of great assistance as he himself struggled to make sense of the Scriptures. Although he lived alone in a cave near the site of the birth of Jesus in Bethlehem, he and one of his women students established a number of monasteries in the area. These monasteries provided refuge for people who left their homes and came to the Holy Lands while Italy was under attack from the nomadic tribes.

Vulgate
Saint Jerome's Latin translation of the Bible; the word *vulgate* is derived from the same Latin root as *vulgar*, which originally simply meant "of the common people"

Activity

Research the life and teachings of one of the Fathers of the Church. Report one of the teachings to the class, written as a homily that this person might give.

This statue of Saint Jerome is on the exterior of St. Catherine's Church in Bethlehem.

S. HIERONYMUS

Literal and Spiritual Worldviews

The Fathers of the Church often disagreed. However, one theme found throughout their teachings is the insight that Christians should view everything on two levels. If we concentrate only on the surface of things, we miss the more important truth that lies below the surface. Reading Scripture merely on a literal level, for instance, is inadequate. For example, to say that the first humans' sin led to human suffering and death makes sense only in light of the Christian story which provides a deeper, spiritual meaning—namely that Jesus, Savior of the world, died and was raised, and thus conquered the power of sin, suffering, and everlasting death. We need to recognize the deeper, spiritual significance of even the most commonplace things surrounding us if we are to appreciate the Christian message. For instance, water quenches thirst and preserves the health and life of the body. On a deeper level, the waters of Baptism satisfy the human thirst for ultimate peace, bring spiritual health, initiate the baptized person into a new relationship with God, and provide eternal life that "purifies, justifies, and sanctifies." Similarly, in the Eucharist the bread tastes and smells like bread. However, on a deeper, much more significant level, Eucharistic bread is the Body of Christ.

"Rifle Raigo" by David Griffin; one of the submissions for the Jesus 2000 contest.

The Fathers of the Church asked Christians to see a deeper, spiritual meaning to everything. In *The City of God,* Saint Augustine applied this theme to the major crisis of his time—the conquest of Rome and the fall of the empire in the West. In this book, which Saint Augustine spent thirteen years writing, he reassured his readers that, while earthly kingdoms rise and fall, the City of God lasts forever. The history of nations is merely a ripple on the surface of reality. True history lies much deeper. It is the story of human souls that came from God making their way back to God. This perspective on reality, that the eternal is more important than the temporal and that everything should be looked at in light of eternity, became the dominant worldview of the medieval period.

Activity

Create an art piece, write a poem or story, or create a video that has both a surface-level meaning and a deeper, spiritual meaning.

Review

1. What role did the Fathers of the Church perform?

2. What view of reality did Manicheans have?

3. What is the *Vulgate?*

4. What role did Saint Jerome play in helping Christians understand the Bible?

5. What was a central theme found in the teachings of the Fathers of the Church?

6. What crisis did Saint Augustine address in his *City of God?*

7. What was the dominant worldview of the medieval period?

MONASTICISM

Beginning in the third century, quite a few people went to great extremes to live a solitary life. As society became increasingly Christian, more and more people felt the need to leave society. Christian men and women who lived apart from the mainstream realized that while Christianity was transforming Roman society, Roman values and lifestyles were also transforming Christianity—and not always for the better. Therefore, they determined that the best way to pursue life with Christ was to separate themselves from the corrupting influences of society.

> Let us not look back upon the world and fancy we have given up great things. For the whole of earth is a very little thing compared with the whole of heaven.
>
> *Saint Anthony of Egypt,* quoted in Robert Ellsberg, *All Saints* (New York: Crossroad, 1997), 34.

monastic movement
living alone or in community apart from the rest of society in order to experience God's presence, especially through regular prayer and self-denial, marked by the profession of religious vows

monk
a person who lives the monastic life

desert fathers
Christian men who lived alone in desert territories of northern Africa and the Middle East in order to sacrifice their lives to Christ

A precursor to the later **monastic movement** may be seen in the early Christian tradition of widows who were cared for by the Church. These women lived together and were responsible for intercessory prayer and service. (See 1 Timothy 5:3–16.) By the end of the third century, in Syria there were people who lived celibate lives and practiced simple living in their own homes.

Most major religions in the world have some form of monasticism. For Christians, monasticism means living alone and giving the highest priority to experiencing a relationship with Christ. The Greek root of this term, *mono,* means "one."

The first known **monk** was Saint Anthony of Egypt (250–355). According to a biography written by Saint Athanasius, Saint Anthony of Egypt spent over eighty years living in the desert, providing for his needs with whatever food and shelter he could find there. He practiced great self-sacrifice, which became a characteristic of the monastic life. So many people imitated his lifestyle that he is known as the first of the **desert fathers.** He attracted a number of followers who wanted to live under his guidance. Although it might appear to be contrary to the meaning of the word "monk," Anthony established a rule for monks who wished to live together.

The Greek Orthodox Monastery of St. George at Wadi Qilt, west on Jericho in Israel, is typical of the many monasteries built in the deserts of the Holy Land.

Saint Anthony of Egypt

We know about the founder of monasticism from the biography *Life of Saint Anthony* written by Athanasius, bishop of Alexandria in Egypt. Two passages from Scripture inspired Anthony to begin his life as a monk. His parents died and left him a large farm and care of a younger sister. One day he heard the words from the Gospels: "Go, sell all that you have and give it to the poor." Taking the passage to heart, he gave away all of his wealth except for enough to care for his sister. Later he heard another passage: "Be not concerned for tomorrow." In response to this message, he gave his sister into the care of religious women (the first time we have a recorded mention of convent life). He himself began to live as a hermit in the desert of what is today Libya—in an abandoned tomb carved out of a mountain.

Saint Anthony possessed a brilliant mind, committing to memory much of Scripture. When his reputation for wisdom and holiness drew people to him, he moved farther and farther into the desert. After living alone in an abandoned fort for twenty years, he was persuaded to come out and begin a community of monks. He started the monks in their monastic life, left them, and then came back on occasion to see that they were living out his suggestions. He himself preferred the solitary life. Athanasius reports that Anthony lived without any illness or bad health until his peaceful death at the age of 105.

Teaching and Living the Faith

Many Christian women during this period also studied the Scriptures, and established and ran monasteries for women and men. In addition, some women made their mark through their influence on sons and husbands.

Saint Nonna (374) deserves double recognition. First she converted her Jewish husband to Christianity. He later became a bishop and is also recognized as a saint—Saint Gregory Nazianzen the Elder. Nonna and her husband had three children, all of whom lived such exemplary lives that they too are counted among the saints.

The eldest child, Saint Gregory Nazianzen the Divine, became Patriarch of Constantinople and is known for his sermons explaining Christian beliefs in clear and precise terms. The other two children are Saint Gargonia and Saint Caesarius.

Emperor Constantine's mother, Saint Helena, visited the Holy Land where, according to legendary tradition, she found the cross on which Christ was crucified.

Saint Monica, the mother of Augustine of Hippo, was a holy Christian and prayed constantly for her son's conversion. He too became a saint.

The widowed mother of Saint John Chrysostom oversaw his education and training. He became perhaps the greatest preacher of the time.

Clovis, leader of the Franks, the last major Germanic tribe to become Christian, married Saint Clotilde. Soon after, she joined the Catholic faith. As other tribes invading the empire were converted to Arianism, Clovis received help from Catholic and Roman friends in establishing the foundation of the modern French nation.

These women and others influenced the Catholic Church tremendously.

Eastern Monasticism

In the East in 353, Saint Basil the Great receives credit for creating an effective system for monastic life. During the same time his sister, Saint Macrina, organized monasteries, or **convents,** for women. In the Western Church, credit is given to Saint Benedict during the middle of the sixth century for shaping a style of monastic life that balanced work and prayer. His sister, Saint Scholastica, founded a convent directly across from Benedict's monastery on Monte Cassino in Italy.

In the fourth and fifth centuries, an amazing number of men and women chose to live as monks—the population of some monasteries numbered in the thousands. One study found that in the seventh century over thirty percent of monasteries were communities of women. Often these communities were known as double monasteries—communities of women and men near each other under common leadership. Monasteries following Saint Benedict's model came to be one of the most important social institutions of the Middle Ages in Europe.

convent

the residence of religious women who are bound together by vows to a religious life

fyi!

In Ireland Christianity was spread by the monks. Unlike the enclosed monasteries where the monks rarely left the grounds, the monastic life introduced by Saint Patrick emphasized evangelization—going out to spread the good news. This explains why Irish monasticism had outposts in Scotland, England, and on the continent as far south as Italy.

> ### Youth News
>
> After Constantine's edict for religious tolerance was issued, finding a time to be alone in prayer meant for some seeking a quiet place and setting aside specific time to grow spiritually. Many of the early Christians went to the desert; today, many go on retreat. In a world where teens use daily planners and cell phones, taking time to look at our relationship with Jesus and others, away from the hustle and bustle of daily living, is more important than ever. Seek out an opportunity through your church or school to participate in a retreat that is offered in your area, such as TEC (Teens Encounter Christ) for seniors or *Search* for younger students; or plan on attending a larger gathering of the teen Church, such as the National Catholic Teen Conference.

Evangelization by Christian missionaries eventually resulted in a worldwide Church and native clergy and religious communities.

Imagine that Saint Basil writes a letter to you containing the following message. Write a letter to Saint Basil in response.

Things that merely improve this life have no true value for us; they are not what we call "the real thing." Good family, athletic valor, a handsome face, tall stature, men's esteem, dominion over others—none of these are important in our eyes or a petition fit for prayer; it is not our way to pay court to those who can boast them. Our ideals soar far above all that.

Basil the Great, quoted by Jill Haak Adels, ed.
The Wisdom of the Saints *(Oxford, UK: Oxford University Press, 1987), 26.*

1. Who was the first known Christian monk?

2. What contribution to Christianity was made by Saints Basil and Macrina in the East and Saints Benedict and Scholastica in the West?

3. How were the monasteries in Ireland different from those in the East and the West?

Conclusion

After Constantine came to power, Church leaders became leaders in the broader community. During the era of the Fathers of the Church, Christian men and women clarified Christian teaching and practice so well that a uniform set of beliefs was established. Many of those who were involved in examining and clarifying Christian teachings reached an unprecedented level of intellectual achievement. Christianity also gave birth to a phenomenon that for centuries nourished the spiritual life of the Church—monasticism.

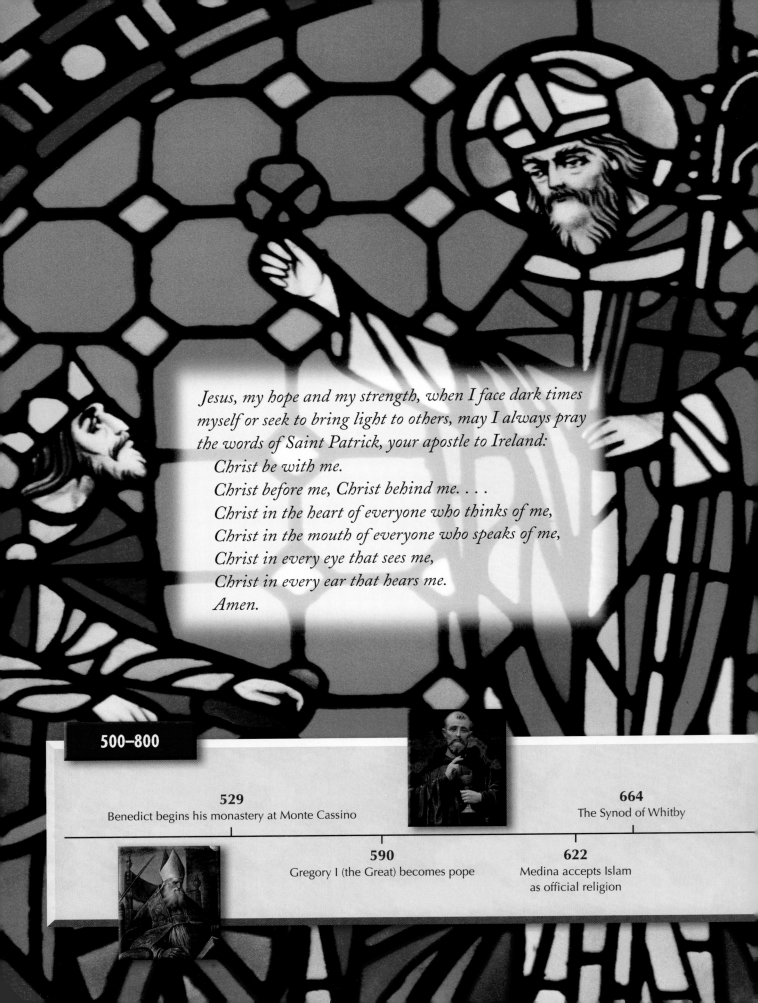

Jesus, my hope and my strength, when I face dark times
myself or seek to bring light to others, may I always pray
the words of Saint Patrick, your apostle to Ireland:
    Christ be with me.
    Christ before me, Christ behind me. . . .
    Christ in the heart of everyone who thinks of me,
    Christ in the mouth of everyone who speaks of me,
    Christ in every eye that sees me,
    Christ in every ear that hears me.
    Amen.

500–800

529
Benedict begins his monastery at Monte Cassino

664
The Synod of Whitby

590
Gregory I (the Great) becomes pope

622
Medina accepts Islam
as official religion

CHAPTER FOUR

500–800

EXPANSION AND GROWTH

Creating a Christian European World

CHAPTER OVERVIEW

■ The separation of the empire into East and West led to differences between Eastern Churches and the Western Church.

■ As more and more people join Christianity, all aspects of life become increasingly Christianized.

■ Through the efforts of courageous missionaries and determined popes, Europe becomes a predominantly Christian continent.

716
Boniface begins his
missionary work

732
The Battle of Tours

756
Pepin gives Pope
Stephen the Papal States

731
The Venerable Bede writes *Ecclesiastical
History of the English People*

800
Pope Leo III crowns Charlemagne
as Holy Roman Emperor

Have you ever felt God's presence in your life? If so, did this experience take place during some kind of religious ceremony? Did the experience occur privately or in a community? What kind of community ceremonies would best celebrate God's presence? By the year 500 large numbers of people in an expanding Christian world were experiencing God as manifested through Jesus Christ and witnessed to by Mary and an ever-growing community of saints. Christianity was firmly entrenched in the empire, both East and West. Churches in the East flourished under relative stability during this period until the new religious movement, Islam, emerged out of the Arabian Desert in the seventh century. The Eastern Churches held on to their distinctive styles of church design and worship and became increasingly isolated from the struggles and developments occurring in the Western Church. In the West, there remained many groups of people who were not Christian and who were not part of Roman society. Christian missionaries often sacrificed their lives to introduce these people from distant lands to Christ's love for them. The courage, conviction, and sheer energy of these missionaries are a testament to the power of the Christian message. As the Christian faith spread, the Church shaped each new culture, and the various cultures where it spread helped shape the Church. Those bent upon destroying the Church became its faithful sons and daughters. By the year 800 the transformation that had earlier occurred in the Roman Empire was being repeated in outlying lands.

Before We Begin . . .

Imagine that some young people come to you and make the following comments: "We're stuck. On the one hand, we feel a strong desire to experience God more in our lives. On the other hand, we also feel great spiritual emptiness. What do you suggest we do?"

■ If you were to design a set of practices that might help them develop their spiritual lives, what might it involve?

■ How are these practices similar to and different from the sacraments and other religious activities that are available through the Catholic Church?

CHRISTIANITY EAST AND WEST

Discussion

1. If you received a million dollars, would you give a substantial portion of it to build a beautiful church building? Why or why not?

2. Have you ever spent time in an ornate and artistically designed church? Is there value for people to have available such churches? Explain.

Hagia Sophia
Church of the Holy Wisdom built in Constantinople and currently serving as a museum in Istanbul, Turkey

The thousands of Christians who chose to live simple, austere lives in deserts, on remote mountaintops, or along rocky coasts of sea-swept islands represent only one portrait of the Church from the fourth to the ninth century. In Constantinople, the emperor continued to rule, and Church and state worked together as twin forces of authority. In 537 Emperor Justinian consecrated a great church lined with polished marble and modeled after the finest public buildings in the empire at the time. He is reported to have said about this building, "Solomon, I have surpassed you." (King Solomon built the temple in Jerusalem.) Justinian named the church in honor of Holy Wisdom—**Hagia Sophia.** Its grandeur makes a striking contrast with the simplicity of the monasteries that sprouted up from Ireland in the West to the Holy Land in the East. Hagia Sophia served as the central church of Eastern Christianity for over nine hundred years, after which it became a Muslim mosque. It still stands as a testament to those early days of imperial Christianity when people, including emperors, wanted to offer praise to the Christian God in whatever way they could.

When the persecutions ceased in the fourth century, Christians built churches both as gathering places and as monuments representing their faith in God. Church buildings carried over decorative styles from the non-Christian past. In some cases, Christians merely transformed temples into Christian churches. As best they could, Christians used church architecture to convey what Christianity at the time stood for—protection and stability, a Christian vision of reality, the dominance of eternal over temporal concerns, and the Church as the center of life.

Discussion

Imagine that you are a Christian missionary sent to a remote tribe of two hundred people who have had minimal contact with the rest of the world. The leader of the tribe tells you that he or she is ready to accept Baptism and that the rest of the tribe would therefore also accept Christianity. What would you do?

As leaders of tribes from the North and East became Christian, their followers typically joined Christianity as well. Just as earlier Jewish Christians and Christians steeped in Greco-Roman culture added to Christian thought and practice from their own heritage, so also converts from these groups brought with them their perspectives about what it means to be Christian. In other words, the Irish added to the Christian worldview, as did people from what is present-day France, Germany, and other places where Christianity spread. However, often these new Christians accepted Baptism just because their ruler did. Christian leaders might have been pleased when entire groups were baptized all at once, but these mass conversions contained seeds for later problems. That is, the faith of the people often had little depth; their traditional beliefs lay just below the surface ready to reappear at the smallest encouragement.

It is not surprising, therefore, that Church leaders felt the need to formalize beliefs and practices for Western Europe. The Church was to be not just catholic (universal), but a Church of Rome—following the rules set down by the bishop of Rome, who represented Peter. The Church recognized the need to be united and uniform. Only a united Church could claim to be the Body of Christ—one, holy, catholic, and apostolic. These attributes came to be known as the **marks of the Church.**

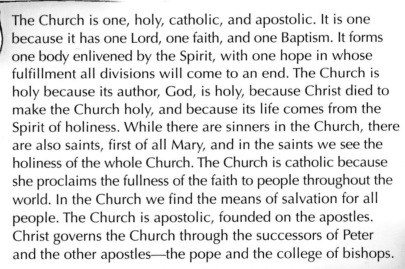

The Church is one, holy, catholic, and apostolic. It is one because it has one Lord, one faith, and one Baptism. It forms one body enlivened by the Spirit, with one hope in whose fulfillment all divisions will come to an end. The Church is holy because its author, God, is holy, because Christ died to make the Church holy, and because its life comes from the Spirit of holiness. While there are sinners in the Church, there are also saints, first of all Mary, and in the saints we see the holiness of the whole Church. The Church is catholic because she proclaims the fullness of the faith to people throughout the world. In the Church we find the means of salvation for all people. The Church is apostolic, founded on the apostles. Christ governs the Church through the successors of Peter and the other apostles—the pope and the college of bishops.

See *Catechism of the Catholic Church,* #s 866–869.

Review

1. What is Hagia Sophia?

2. Why did Christians build magnificent church buildings?

3. What are the four marks of the Church?

MAJOR CHRISTIAN CENTERS

patriarch
leader of the Christian community in major cities of the Roman Empire

fyi!
The Eastern Church is sometimes called the "Greek Church" and the Western Church the "Latin Church."

Major population centers arose in the vast stretches of the Roman Empire. The largest cities became major Christian centers and greatly influenced the communities surrounding them. The leaders of the Christian communities in these cities were given the title **patriarch.** One early list names the following patriarchates, or cities with patriarchs: Rome in Europe, Alexandria in Egypt, Constantinople in Asia Minor, Antioch in Asia Minor, and Jerusalem in the Middle East.

Even though the head of the Church in Rome continued to be viewed as head of the Western Church, the patriarch of Constantinople held a place of prominence in the East, since Constantinople was the center of power in the empire. Sometimes the other patriarchs recognized the patriarch of Rome as having a "primacy of honor" but did not believe he had the power to make decisions without consulting them. For one thing, Christian communities existed in Jerusalem, Antioch, and Alexandria at least as early as in Rome. Remember also that while Rome struggled under the threat of invasion, the Eastern Churches enjoyed a few centuries of peace and prosperity. That left Rome as the sole center of Christian authority in the West, often fighting for its life and travelling a course of development more and more distinct from that of the Eastern Churches.

From the fifth century on, the gap between East and West continued to grow. Eastern Churches used Greek, which was the common language of the people living in the eastern part of the empire. The Western Church used its common language, Latin. As time went by, both civil and Church leaders from these two sections of the empire no longer even understood each other's language. Thus language contributed to the crisis that eventually resulted in an official split between the two Churches.

Keep in mind that after Constantine became emperor, the Eastern Churches flourished while the West focused primarily on keeping damage from invasions to a minimum. The emperor played an active role in Church matters through his power to install or remove the patriarch of Constantinople. The leaders of the various Christian Churches in the East gathered together to address common concerns. However, each patriarch or leader of a particular Church had an autonomy greater than that of individual Churches in the West. After Constantine abandoned Rome, the pope served as both the spiritual and secular leader of Christian communities in the West.

Differences in Church practices and spirituality also created tension between East and West. For instance, there were differences in rules about fasting, about the kind of bread to be used for the Eucharist, about priests marrying, and even about whether or not priests should have beards.

Solemnity and mystery are evident in liturgies of the East.

Discussion

Name things that people might do before, during, and after participating in Mass that would help them enter into the Paschal mystery more fully.

Paschal mystery
Christ's work of redemption accomplished principally by his passion, death, resurrection, and glorious ascension

Then as now, the Eastern and Western liturgies followed the same basic structure but could appear to be very different. Eastern spirituality underlying the liturgy tended to be more mystical. That is, when Eastern Christians spoke about *mystery*, they tended to mean an experience of God's presence. *Mystery* in Western Christianity tended to mean a belief beyond normal comprehension, such as the mystery of the Blessed Trinity. For Eastern Christians, for example, the liturgy was the time when the union of humans and God was most evident and when humans especially shared in the divine life. " 'God's holy gifts for God's holy people' is proclaimed by the celebrant in most Eastern liturgies during the elevation of the holy Gifts before the distribution of communion" (*Catechism of the Catholic Church*, #948). Liturgy in the West was above all a celebration of the **Paschal mystery** by which Christ accomplished the work of our salvation. Both Eastern and Western perspectives and practices reflected valid ways of encountering Christ, but the differences led to tensions between the two.

Review

1. What role did patriarchs play in the early Church?

2. How did other patriarchs view the pope of Rome?

3. Name two ways that Eastern and Western Churches' understanding of liturgy differed.

CHRISTIANITY MEETS ISLAM

Muhammad
(560–632) founder of the Islamic religion

Muslim
a member of the religion of Islam

hijrah
the flight of Muslims from Mecca to Medina in 622; event marks the beginning of the Muslim calendar

Islam
a religion based on submission to God's will as it was revealed to Muhammad

Early in the seventh century, a new religious movement began in Arabia that would have an impact on both Eastern and Western Christianity. At the time, Arabian society was tribal. Jews, Christians, other monotheists, and polytheistic tribes interacted with one another. Sometimes their exchanges were peaceful; at other times they battled over resources that were scarce in the harsh desert territory of Arabia. Beginning in 610, a caravan driver from the centrally located town of Mecca told his wife, his acquaintances, and then anyone who would listen that in caves outside of town the one, true God was speaking to him. The messages from God that the man, **Muhammad,** shared with his listeners were so compelling that large numbers of the townspeople of Mecca took them to heart. So many joined the group known as **Muslims**—people who submit to God's will—that non-Muslims felt threatened. In a migration called the *hijrah* (an Arabic word meaning "flight"), the Muslims secretly left Mecca and made their way to the city of Yathrib, which they renamed Medina. The citizens of Medina welcomed them and accepted **Islam,** the religion and way of life of the Muslims, as the law of the land. The *hijrah* occurred in 622, but, because this was the first year a Muslim community existed, Muslims identify it as year one of the Islamic calendar. Within one hundred years, Muslims controlled lands stretching from the Atlantic Ocean in the West to portions of India in the East.

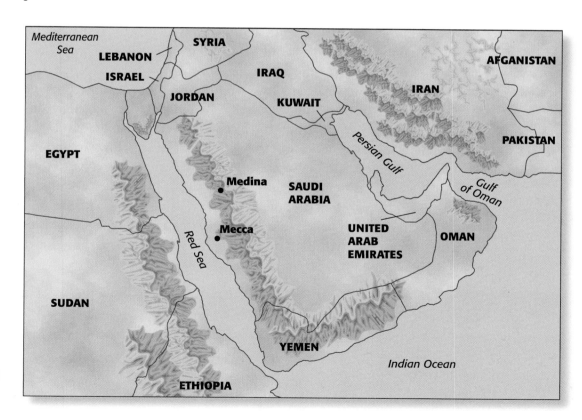

The Islamic holy cities of Mecca and Medina are in Saudi Arabia today.

Avove: A mosque in Mecca.

Right: Muslims at prayer in India.

fyi!

God's plan of salvation also includes the Muslims. The followers of Islam claim the faith of Abraham. With Jews and Christians, they worship the one, merciful God who will judge all humankind on the last day.

See *Catechism of the Catholic Church,* #841.

Muslims placed the Jewish and Christian people in a category different from infidels, or nonbelievers. In the Islamic worldview, people who were Jewish and people who were Christian believed in the one, true God in whom Muslims also believed. Muslims considered Jews and Christians to be "people of the book"—that is, people who had prophets who spoke for God and Scriptures that contained God's word. But they believed that Judaism and Christianity had corrupted the original message of the prophets.

Many Christians converted to Islam in Muslim-controlled areas. For one thing, non-Muslims were required to pay taxes that Muslims did not have to pay. The majority of Christian converts, however, probably found Islam appealing because of its message, because of the enthusiasm of its followers, and because it was the religion of a spreading empire. Just before the year 700, Muslims began a siege of Constantinople that lasted five years, but the city withstood the attacks. By the middle of the 700s, much of Spain came under Muslim rule and remained so until the late 1400s. At the *Battle of Tours* in 731, the Christian prince Charles Martel defeated a Muslim army that had invaded France. If not for this defeat, all of Europe might have fallen to the Muslim forces.

Activity

Write a report on one of the following topics and share it with your class.

- Early Muslim conquests
- Islamic beliefs
- Islamic perspectives on Jesus and Christianity
- The Battle of Tours

Review

1. Who was the founder of the Muslim faith?

2. What significance does the *hijrah* have for Muslims?

3. How did Muslims view Jews and Christians in territories they conquered?

4. Name two reasons why many Christians converted to Islam.

5. Why is the Battle of Tours important?

THE CHRISTIAN EXPERIENCE

The movie "Gladiator" portrays a pre-Christian Roman general named Maximus praying devoutly before stone figures of his household gods. A few centuries later this same imaginary general would probably have offered his prayers to the Christian God. Is that the extent of the difference between pre-Christian Roman society and the experience of religion that most people had upon becoming Christian—the substitution of one image of god for another? In other words, what difference did Jesus and his Church make between the years 300 and 800?

A World of Grace

grace
participation in the life of God and the free and undeserved gift that God gives us to respond to our vocation to become his adopted children

liturgical calendar
division of the year to mark events in the life of Christ

The most influential thinker in the Western Church during this period was Saint Augustine of Hippo. Augustine, and a number of theologians following him, wrote extensively about the concept of **grace.** According to the *Catechism of the Catholic Church,* "Grace is a *participation in the life of God*" (#1997). Christians could believe that they participated in the life of God because, in Jesus Christ, God participated in human life. As Christianity spread, therefore, Christians of the time found grace everywhere. Their lives were sacramentalized from birth to death. The seasons of the year were Christianized into a **liturgical calendar.** This calendar was divided into the Seasons of Advent, Christmas, Lent, the Triduum, Easter, and Ordinary Time.

Near the end of the fifth century, some farmers in present-day France approached their local bishop with concerns about their harvest.

Earthquake, fire, and inclement weather combined to cause crop failure and widespread hunger. Mamertus, the bishop of Vienne, called for penance and prayer on the three days preceding Ascension Thursday. The people responded to the call, and the Lord responded to the prayer.

Throughout France, and ultimately beyond, word of this litany, this rogation, spread, finding a readiness in the hearts of believers. As the years went by, the same three days of penitential prayer were observed annually, and by the eighth century, universally.

Rev. Peter Klein, *The Catholic Source Book,* (Dubuque, IA.: BROWN-ROA, 2000), 18).

Rogation Days
three days of prayer and penance before the Solemnity of the Ascension to ask God's blessing on the harvest

These days are known as **Rogation Days.** Thus, no aspects of life were beyond God's concern. Such practices helped Christians experience themselves as being awash in a sea of God's grace.

According to Saint Augustine, Roman religion was a legalistic and superstitious affair. That is, performing rituals regularly and properly was the Roman way to appease the gods and avoid their anger. Certain aspects of the Roman view of the gods entered Christianity. Even though the image of Jesus on the cross represented a complete reversal of the image of the mighty and vengeful Roman gods, Christians frequently continued to view God as a fearsome and threatening judge. Safer intercessors were Mary and the saints who became the advocates before God for many, especially in the Eastern Church.

The Christian Calendar

During this era the designation of years was Christianized. In an attempt to establish the date for Easter, a Russian monk named Dionysius Exiguus decided that designating years starting with the founding of the city of Rome or in terms of the beginning of a particular emperor's reign was improper. He calculated as best he could when Jesus was born and designated years after that as A.D. (*anno Domini,* "the year of our Lord") and A.C. (*ante Christum,* "before Christ"), which later became B.C. "before Christ." Within a few centuries this new, Christian calendar was adopted throughout Europe and eventually the world.

Activity

Grace is a participation in the life of God. Make a day-long list of activities in which you shared in grace.

fyi!

Often today, in order to be sensitive to non-Christians the neutral designation B.C.E. (before the common era) and C.E. (common era) are used for the calendar commonly in use without referring to Christ.

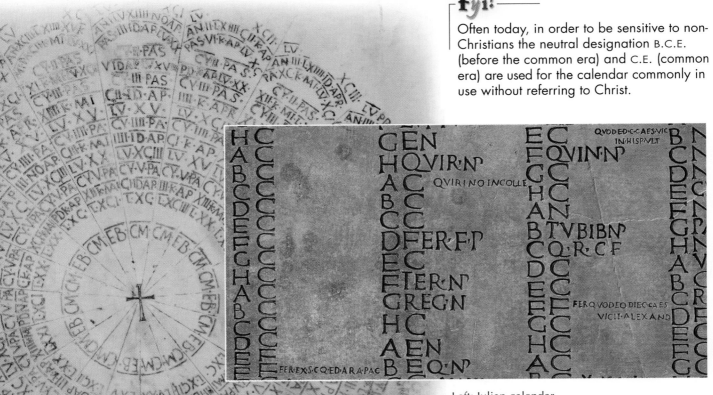

Left: Julian calendar.

Above: Roman Calendar.

Developments in Church Practice

baptistry
the place where Baptisms are celebrated; originally a separate building and now typically a section of a church

basilica
a Greek word meaning "king's hall"; currently the term is used to designate a certain church of historical significance that continues to play an important part in the religious life of a particular region

Gregorian chant
type of song in which one vocal part predominates and no instruments are used; mainly uses chords D, E, F, and G

Not until the Second Council of Lyons in 1274 did a Church council officially identify the seven sacraments. Even if an official listing of seven sacraments did not exist before this time, nonetheless the various sacramental celebrations performed by members of the Church were definitely viewed as means of grace. For a period of time, each of the two principal sacraments—Baptism and Eucharist—had buildings designed exclusively for them. A **baptistry** was a smaller building located next to a church where Baptisms were held. Baptistries were modeled after the Roman public baths. As infant Baptism became the norm, Baptisms were performed in the churches themselves.

As in the case of Hagia Sophia, church design typically imitated that of public buildings popular at the time. **Basilicas** were rectangular in shape with one rounded end. A bishop would sit at the rounded end. An altar would separate him from the people. Thus, the bishop and the rest of the congregation at least symbolically gathered around the altar. As the clergy became a more distinct group, during liturgy they were separated from the rest of the people by an altar rail in the West and a screen in the East. This separation of priest from people during liturgies led to a sense that the priest was offering the Eucharist *for* the people rather than together *with* them.

Another development that took place within the liturgy of the Western Church happened around the year 600. This was the introduction of a particular form of chant. **Gregorian chant,** named after Pope Gregory the Great, was probably modeled after an earlier form of Jewish chant. It came to be used at all solemn liturgies and in monasteries where monks and nuns regularly filled monastery chapels with the chanting of the psalms. Even though Gregorian chant is no longer used regularly during church services, you probably have heard it at some time. When a news program does a piece about Catholicism or a television commercial features a Catholic monk, invariably Gregorian chant is playing in the background. The music evokes the image of a majestic medieval cathedral and light shining through stained-glass windows. For almost fifteen hundred years Gregorian chant has been intimately associated with Catholic worship. To hear live Gregorian chant today you probably would need to go to a monastery where monks or nuns continue to use it for singing their daily prayers.

Activity

1. Write a report about life in the Christian West during the sixth to the eighth centuries. Include in your report the answers to the following questions:
   - What role did religion play in people's lives?
   - What aspects of the Christian message would be most helpful to the people of the time?

2. Listen to a recording of a Gregorian chant. Use a creative media besides music to describe the feelings and images that the music evokes in you as you listen.

celibacy
the state or condition of those who have chosen to remain unmarried for the sake of the kingdom of heaven in order to give themselves entirely to God and to the service of his people

Even though as early as the fourth century Church leaders were calling on priests to be celibate so that they would place spiritual fatherhood over physical fatherhood, as late as the tenth century some bishops and priests were still marrying. **Celibacy** became a standard practice for clergy in the West when an official policy was declared in 1123 at the First Lateran Council. This canon was renewed in 1139 at the Second Lateran Council. In the Eastern Churches this policy took a different turn. Bishops must remain single, while priests, deacons, and other clerics may be married if they marry prior to ordination. If single when ordained, they must remain single.

During this time period the manner in which sinners were offered forgiveness by the Church underwent a major change. Up until the seventh century, baptized Christians who had committed such a serious misdeed that they separated themselves from the Church underwent a reinitiation process. This process was public, overseen by the local bishop, and lasted for a period of years. Since being a public penitent meant performing acts of penance, many people put off requesting reconciliation until they felt they were near death. Reportedly, an Irish monk named Saint Columban (543–615) began in the West a practice of spiritual direction during which sins were privately confessed and the need for change was discussed. It was rooted in the process of spiritual direction engaged in by monks in Egypt and the Holy Land. He and other Irish monks spread private penance to mainland Europe where it became popular and eventually the officially recognized form of the **Sacrament of Reconciliation** or Penance.

Sacrament of Reconciliation
one of the Sacraments of Healing; the sacrament in which one is forgiven and healed of sin and reunited with God and the Christian community

During this time no specifically Christian wedding ceremony existed. Again, this does not mean that Christians did not view marriage as a sacramental experience, a means of grace. However, the Fathers of the Church say little about marriage, and the early Church leaders left the regulations regarding marriages to civil authorities. As Church leadership became more stable than civil government, bishops and priests became more actively involved in performing wedding ceremonies and regulating marriages. Beginning in the fourth century, Christian couples were asking for a priest's blessing as part of their wedding ceremony. By the eighth century a priest's blessing of a marriage was accepted practice, and soon afterward it became the standard practice for Catholics.

Review

1. What purpose did the liturgical calendar play during the expansion of Christianity?

2. When did the Church officially recognize the existence of seven sacraments?

3. What was a baptistry? What led to the standard practice of performing Baptisms in a church?

4. What was the standard design of a basilica?

5. What effect did the use of altar rails and screens have on the way the Eucharist was experienced?

6. When did celibacy become officially required of priests in the Western Church?

7. How did Reconciliation change after the 700s?

8. What development resulted in Church leaders becoming involved in performing weddings and in regulating marriages?

THE WORK OF MISSIONARIES

In every century God's love has motivated the Church to respond with enthusiasm to its responsibility to be missionary. "God wills the salvation of everyone through the knowledge of truth." God has entrusted this truth to the Church, and the Church must bring this truth to people everywhere. Because the Church firmly believes that God wants all people to be saved, it has no choice but to be missionary.

See *Catechism of the Catholic Church,* #851.

missionaries
people who spread the Christian message to other people, usually in other lands

The mission of the Church is to further God's reign in the world by sharing the good news with those who have not heard it. Missionary activity goes back to the time of Jesus, who sent out his followers two by two to tell others of God's kingdom (see Luke 10:1–3). Were it not for courageous **missionaries,** places such as Ireland, England, and Germany would not have become the strongholds of Christianity that they did.

Youth News

Besides missionaries, there are many individuals and groups who bring the good news of Jesus Christ to those who have not yet heard it. As members of the Church, we have a responsibility to evangelize, to share the good news of God's love with others. We can do this by our willingness to talk about our faith and to stand up for our belief in Jesus. We can also think about spending time as a member of a lay missionary or volunteer group. For more information, check out **www.maryknoll.org/mmaf** and **www.salesianmissions.org/ salesians/who/lay.htm**

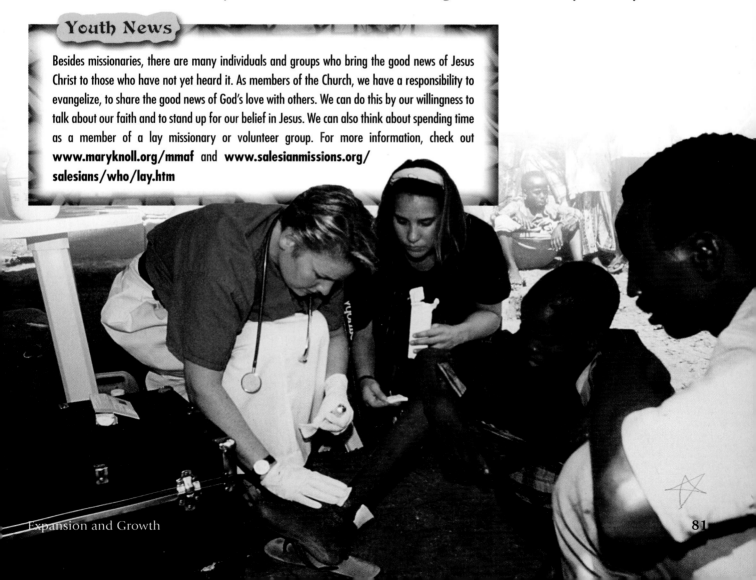

The Conversion of Ireland

Saint Patrick, Apostle of Ireland, is one of the best known missionaries. He wrote an autobiography that provides some personal information. He tells us that he was the grandson of a priest and the son of a deacon. He lived in Britain (probably England, or it might have been northern France), but at the age of sixteen he was captured by Irish pirates and lived as a slave in Ireland for six years. While spending his time as a shepherd, he came to a greater appreciation of the faith that his parents had tried to impart to him. He managed to escape from Ireland to France where he became a priest. Although he had wanted desperately to escape from Ireland and risked his life to do so, he found that he kept dreaming that the voices of Ireland were constantly calling to him, "We beseech thee, holy youth, to come and walk among us again."

After being made a bishop, Patrick returned to Ireland in 432. He spent his remaining thirty years crossing the length and breadth of the island. He met with great success, virtually converting all of Ireland to Christianity by the time of his death. He personally baptized tens of thousands of converts. One of the keys to his success was his blending of Irish-Celtic culture with Christianity. He ordained hundreds of Irish priests and bishops and founded many monasteries. From these monasteries and religious communities would go forth many missionaries to the farthest parts of the world. The Irish monks also copied whatever writings they could get their hands on and even wrote down many of their own pre-Christian legends. Because of the zeal for Christianity among the Irish and their influence on Christianity in other lands, Ireland has gained the title, "Isle of Saints."

Ireland is sometimes called the Emerald Island.

Those involved in the missionary work of the Church must carry on a respectful dialogue with those to whom they introduce the gospel. This dialogue benefits members of the Church because it helps them appreciate the elements of truth and grace found among other groups which point to the presence of God.

See *Catechism of the Catholic Church*, #856.

Chapter Four

The Conversion of England

Pope Gregory the Great was one of the most remarkable figures to serve as a bridge between ancient times and the Middle Ages. Although he counted two popes among his ancestors, Gregory began his public life in civil, not religious, service. He served as prefect of Rome, meaning that he was a combination mayor, police chief, and treasurer. Rome at the time was in great need of repair, and Gregory restored the city. When his father died, Gregory sold his possessions and made his family home into a monastery. For four years he lived the simple life of a monk and established six monastic communities. Then the pope asked him to serve as the papal ambassador to Constantinople at a time when tensions between East and West were heating up. When the pope died in 590, the people of Rome called for Gregory to take his place. Gregory asked the emperor not to approve their choice, but the emperor knew of Gregory's talents. Thus, Gregory became the first monk to become pope.

In addition, Gregory sent missionaries to numerous countries, spreading monastic spirituality throughout the Church. He did a great deal to reform the Church from within. For instance, he wrote guidelines for bishops to follow and took steps to straighten out the moral life of the clergy. He signed the many documents he wrote by referring to himself in a way that popes ever since have used: "Servant of the servants of God." For instance, Gregory asked a Roman monk named Augustine, known to history as Saint Augustine of Canterbury, to go to England with a group of forty monks to convert the English to Christianity.

Soon after Augustine's time, however, England returned to its pre-Christian ways. Christianity was reintroduced into the country through a Celtic priest, Saint Aidan, who followed some practices that were different from Roman practices. This caused tension and confusion until Celtic and Roman clergy met in 664 to resolve the issues between them. During this meeting, called the **Synod of Whitby,** the question was asked: Is the pope, the successor of Peter, appointed to head the Church? All agreed that he was. The king then decreed that England would follow Roman Church customs in all matters, such as the date when Easter is to be celebrated. This opened the way for the organization of the whole English Church to be united in doctrine and practice under one head. The Church in England flourished, and monks from Rome brought many famous manuscripts from Rome to English monasteries, where they were copied and made available to many. One product of these monasteries is a work which some consider to be the first true book of history, the *Ecclesiastical History of the English People* (731), by a monk known as the Venerable Bede.

fyi!

A legend about Saint Gregory asserts that he passed a slave auction in Rome one day and noticed a group of boys on the auction block. When he asked what manner of boys these were, he was told that they were Angles, that is, English. Gregory responded, I will call them not *Angli* (Angles) but *angeli* (angels). This experience inspired him to seek the conversion of the people of Angle-land, or England.

Synod of Whitby
A meeting of Roman and Celtic Christians to determine which style of Christianity would be followed in England

Saint Hilda, Abbess of Whitby

The struggle between the Celtic and Roman strains of Christianity points up interesting differences in the two societies. While Roman society was primarily male-dominated, such was not necessarily the case in the Celtic realms. In Ireland, a free woman held near-equality from earliest times: retaining her own property in marriage and sharing in joint property; enjoying equal educational and professional opportunities; holding equal status before the law; and, occasionally, being accepted as a warrior.

Saint Hilda (614–680) is a case in point. Descended from the Northumbrian line, she was the pupil of Saint Aidan who restored Christianity to Northumbria after its brief lapse into a non-Christian religion. Aidan put Hilda in charge of a religious house at Hartlepool. She later founded a double monastery for men and women at Whitby in 657. At the time the country was divided between followers of Roman and Celtic rites. In 663, the matter became more serious when King Oswy of the Celtic Rite realized that he would be celebrating Easter while his wife, who belonged to the Roman Rite, would be in the midst of Lent. Clearly, a solution was needed.

A synod was called in 664 at Whitby, under the supervision of the great Abbess Hilda. She was of the Celtic persuasion and sided with Colman, Bishop of Lindisfarne; they traced their tradition back to Saint Columban and Saint John. The opposition was represented by Saint Wilfred who looked to Rome and Saint Peter. After some discussion, the king gave judgment in favor of the Roman Rite, saying that he would rather be on good terms with the Keeper of Heaven's gate than with Saint Columban. The decision was a triumph for Rome and a bitter blow to the Celts.

Characteristically, Saint Hilda loyally accepted the decision for Rome, thus ending what might have been a serious Church crisis.

The Conversion of Europe

Saint Patrick made use of some of the pre-Christian spirit of the Irish to spread the Christian message. Apparently some druid holy men became Christian priests during the early stages of the conversion of Ireland. In England, Pope Gregory advised Augustine of Canterbury to let the older temples remain standing and to transform them into Christian churches. "Thus the people, seeing that their places of worship have not been destroyed, will forget their errors and, having attained knowledge of the true God, will come to worship him in the very places where their ancestors assembled" (Saint Gregory the Great, quoted in Jean Comby, *How to Read Church History*, Vol. 1 [New York: Crossroad, 1995], 123).

www. For news about the current work of missionaries in the U.S., visit **www.catholic-extension.org**

fyi!

As happened previously in Christianity, pre-Christian German practices entered into Christian practices. For example, many Christians today bring a tree into their houses during the Christmas Season.

Saint Boniface, known as the Apostle to Germany, used a much less accommodating approach, at least according to a longstanding legend. Boniface heard about a sacred tree, one dedicated to the god Thor. He went to the tree and immediately chopped it down and used the wood to build a chapel. When the people who observed this spectacle realized that Boniface wasn't struck dead as a result of this assault on their god, they accepted Christianity.

The incident with the tree is thought to have happened in 723, which means that he didn't simply set foot on the continent and bring people to Christianity without a struggle. One historian describes the message by which missionaries gained success in attracting new members:

> The arguments which the missionaries used to combat pagan beliefs were simplistic but, given the limited literacy of many of the converts, compelling. God created the universe. There is only one God. The pagan gods and goddesses are mere sticks and stones. God sent his son Jesus Christ to offer salvation to all those who believe in his name; and for those who do not, there awaits the vivid pains of hell. Those who believe will receive their due reward, possibly in this life and certainly in the next.
>
> Vivian Green, *A New History of Christianity* (Leicester, UK: Sutton Publishing, 1996), 51–52.

Saint Boniface chopped down the tree dedicated to Thor.

In other words, missionaries such as Boniface engaged in a contest: the Christian God versus the other gods. According to this view, in Europe between the years 300 to 800, the Christian God won.

One of the last of the independent Germanic tribes were the Franks. Even before they embraced Christianity, however, they enjoyed a relationship with the empire that was known as *foederati*, which means that they were recognized as partners and not enemies of Rome. King Clovis was the first leader of the Franks to become Christian. In 492 he married a Christian woman named Clotilde. Four years later Clovis won a critical battle and proclaimed that he gained victory through the intercession of the Christian God. He was baptized by Saint Remy, for whom Reims, France, is named. Clovis announced that "those who do not present themselves with me at the river tomorrow for baptism will incur my displeasure." Thus began a Christian kingdom that would rule Europe into the modern era.

This painting of Charles Martel in the Battle of Tours dates from the seventh or eighth century.

Donation of Pepin
King Pepin's designation of the central part of Italy to be governed by the pope

Papal States
section of Italy ruled by the pope until 1870

Charlemagne
King of the Franks who was crowned Roman Emperor by the pope in 800

Clovis's sons and heirs were generally weak rulers. Some two hundred years after Clovis, the Merovingian dynasty came to an end when a palace official who was strong enough to unite the kingdom again rose to power. The official, Charles Martel, defeated the forces of Islam in 732 at the *Battle of Tours*. Charles Martel's son and grandson figure strongly in the fortunes of the Church. His son, Pepin the Short, was crowned King of the Franks in 751 by Saint Boniface, the same Boniface who had converted the Germans. Thus began the Carolingian dynasty. Since Boniface was acting as the pope's representative, Pepin rewarded the pope five years later by declaring him to be ruler of the middle section of Italy. This **Donation of Pepin** created the **Papal States** and made the pope a secular as well as a spiritual leader. It may be hard for us to imagine the pope as both the head of a nation and the head of the Church, but in fact the Papal States continued to exist until 1870. (Actually Vatican City is still a city-state separate from Italy. For that reason, countries such as the United States have ambassadors to the Vatican.) On Christmas day in the year 800, Pepin's son Charles was crowned Holy Roman Emperor by Pope Leo III. He is known to history as **Charlemagne**—Charles the Great.

Christianization of Europe meant not only getting people to accept Christianity. It also meant making sure that people understood that Jesus Christ was not just another god, even though one more powerful than their previous gods. That task continued, and still continues. During the Middle Ages, Church leaders and secular leaders would design a Christian worldview that would sustain Europe until the Renaissance.

Entanglements of Church and State

The series of events that took place during the second half of the eighth century needs to be examined in light of circumstances at the time. When Pepin gave the pope control over a large portion of Italy, he was essentially making official what already existed. The Roman emperor was supposed to protect the Church and citizens of the empire wherever they were. Instead, the pope was trying to do what he could to hold off attacks on Rome by the Lombards from Germany and from the Muslims known as Saracens.

When the pope crowned Charlemagne emperor, it was a slap in the face to the emperor in Constantinople. However, the pope was again formalizing what already existed. The Frankish kings, not the emperors in Constantinople, really held power in Europe. The pope could communicate with and work with the Frankish kings much more readily that he could with the emperor. Once Charlemagne was crowned emperor, he was committed to protecting the Church and making sure that Church laws and practices were enforced throughout his empire. However, he also would oversee the appointment of various Church leaders, as the emperor had been doing in the Eastern Church. These entanglements of Church and state would create problems throughout the Middle Ages and into the modern era.

Discussion

Do you support the following statement? Why or why not?

It would be good to have a Christian nation, that is, one governed by leaders who publicly espouse the beliefs and values of Christianity.

The Papal States cut through the center of present-day Italy.

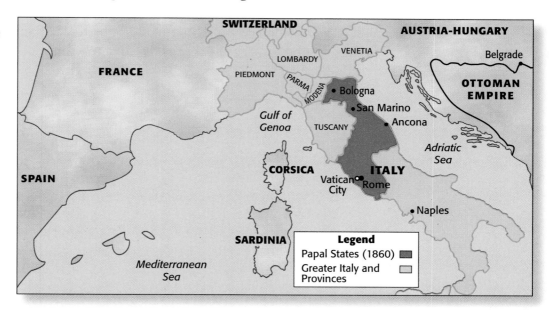

Review

1. What did missionaries do for Christianity?

2. Briefly sketch the outline of Saint Patrick's life.

3. What Roman monk headed the missionary activities in England?

4. What controversy did the Synod of Whitby solve?

5. What is Saint Boniface reported to have done to convince the Germans of the power of the Christian God?

6. Who were Clovis and Clotilde?

7. What did Saint Boniface do for Pepin the Short, and what gift did Pepin give the pope in return?

8. What took place on Christmas day in the year 800?

9. Give reasons why popes during the later years of the eighth century felt compelled to side with the Frankish kings rather than with the emperor in Constantinople.

THE JEWISH PEOPLE

How did Church leaders view the Jewish people during this period? Remember that according to Roman law, Jews were free to practice their religion. At the time of Christ, the Jewish people made up ten percent of the population of the empire, and synagogues occupied prominent positions in many of the major towns and cities. When Christianity came to power, some Church Fathers had harsh words to say about the Jewish people and Judaism, but the words were generally not accompanied by persecutions of the Jewish people. Saint Augustine of Hippo spoke out against persecution of the Jewish people and gave the following two reasons: First, the Old Testament, to which Jews continue to witness, demonstrates that Christianity has deep and ancient roots. Second, the demise of Judaism illustrates what happens when a people denies Jesus Christ as the Messiah. In other words, Augustine's position was both good news and bad news for the Jewish people. That is, he advocated that the Jewish people should be left alone but that they should not prosper as compared to Christians.

In 591 Pope Gregory I had to deal with a situation in southern France where Christians were forcing Baptism upon the Jewish people living there. Pope Gregory admonished the Christians in France that people should be brought to conversion through "the sweetness of preaching" and not by force. A Jewish historian gives the following overall summary of Jewish-Christian relations during these early centuries of the Middle Ages:

> A recent study has concluded that of several hundred European rulers and sixty-seven popes over a period of four centuries in the early Middle Ages, only a dozen appear to have had an anti-Jewish policy. Many of them, recognizing the value of Jewish communities, followed a policy that was vigorously and consistently pro-Jewish. In their realms, Jews prospered, enjoying a legal status not materially different from that of their Christian neighbors.
>
> Marc Saperstein, *Moments of Crisis in Jewish-Christian Relations* (London: SCM Press, 1989), 16.

As we will see in the next chapter, this overall atmosphere of tolerance for the Jewish people by the dominant Christian community would change drastically in a few centuries, in particular during a series of military actions known as the *Crusades*.

Review

1. What two reasons did Saint Augustine give for not harming Jews?

2. What was the overall atmosphere in Jewish-Christian relations in the early Middle Ages?

Conclusion

The Church that became entwined with the Roman Empire under Constantine faced external challenges from Germanic tribes in the West and, later, Muslims in the East. Gradually Christianity won over the tribes, but Christianity's relations with Islam remained a significant concern of the Church throughout the Middle Ages. By the time of Charlemagne, political boundaries in Europe, northern Africa, and western Asia were established and they would remain in place until the modern era. During this period of great expansion and growth, the Church drew in many people from a wide variety of cultures. Some members of the Church were leaders in the great political and economic transformations taking place, especially in Europe. Others separated themselves from worldly affairs altogether. When the frightened disciples of a Jewish teacher started preaching his message at the first Christian Pentecost—the beginning of the Church—few could have predicted that eight hundred years later, most of Europe and portions of the Middle East would be dominated by their spiritual descendants.

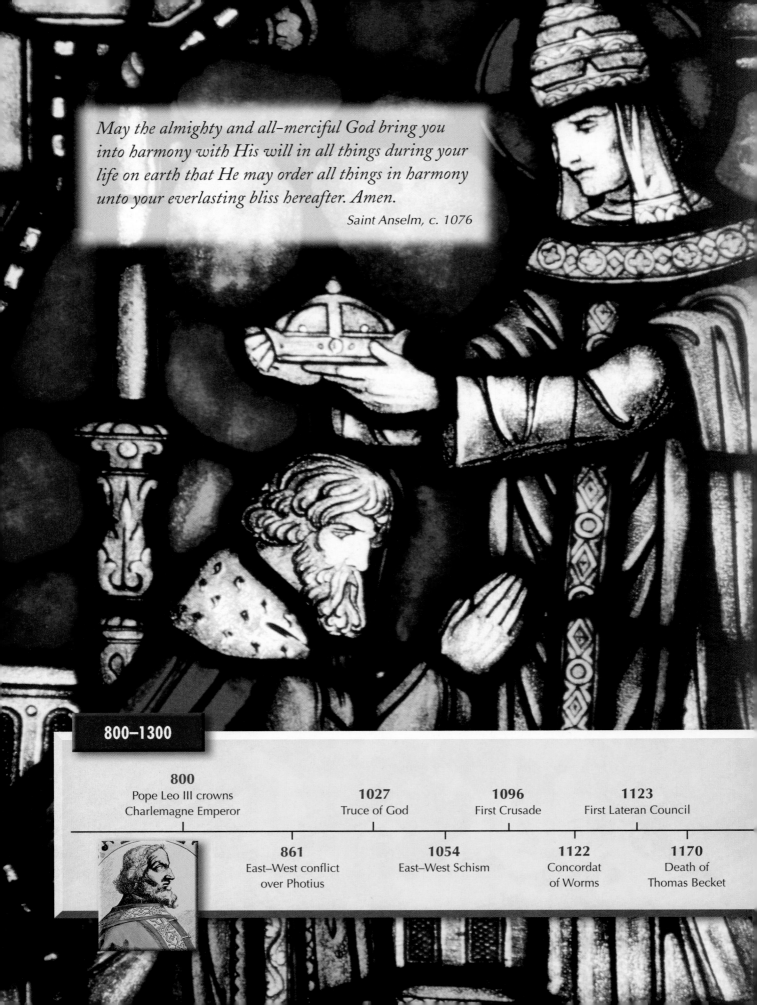

May the almighty and all–merciful God bring you into harmony with His will in all things during your life on earth that He may order all things in harmony unto your everlasting bliss hereafter. Amen.

Saint Anselm, c. 1076

800–1300

800
Pope Leo III crowns
Charlemagne Emperor

861
East–West conflict
over Photius

1027
Truce of God

1054
East–West Schism

1096
First Crusade

1122
Concordat
of Worms

1123
First Lateran Council

1170
Death of
Thomas Becket

THE CHURCH AND WORLD UNITED

Toward the High Middle Ages

CHAPTER OVERVIEW

- Feudalism provides a pyramid-shaped structure for society and Church to meet the needs of Western Europe.

- Church leaders and other Church members initiate reforms to counteract certain corrupting practices.

- The Western and Eastern Churches officially split in 1054.

- A variety of practices and lifestyles nourish the spiritual life of people during the Middle Ages.

- Christian-Muslim tensions and renewed heresies lead to a series of crusades and an inquisition.

| **1226**
Death of Francis of Assisi | | **1253**
Death of Clare of Assisi | **1274**
Death of
Thomas Aquinas |

| **1221**
Death of Dominic | **1232**
Pope Gregory IX
appoints inquisitors | **1270**
Eighth and last Crusade |

Do you believe in an afterlife? Do you find profound truth in the stories of Adam and Eve, Moses and the Ten Commandments, Jesus' death and resurrection? If you were to have a child, would you want your child baptized? If you were near death, would you want a priest by your side?

By the time we arrive at the height of the Middle Ages, a Christian worldview is taken for granted. It marks the seasons and cycles of people's lives. Springtime is not just the time for planting; it is the season of Lent and then Easter. Death may be the end of earthly life, but it is also the entrance into eternal life. Rulers who make laws or make war must appeal to Christian teachings to explain their decisions. Education is done by and for the Church. During the Middle Ages, it is impossible to separate the Church from everything else. Although the pope, bishops, priests, monks, and nuns were most directly identified with the Church, all Christians measured their lives in terms of its beliefs and practices.

Western Europe united as Christendom—a Holy Roman Empire—adopts a system of organization called feudalism that becomes the accepted way that people view both Church and society. During this period, the tension between Eastern and Western Christianity finally results in an official split between the two. Christian Europe attempts to contend with those who do not fit under the umbrella called Christianity—Muslims and Jews. Holy men and women emerge to revitalize the spirit of Christ for their time.

Before We Begin . . .

Before reading this chapter, find a book or access a website on the period of European history called the Middle Ages. Name at least five things associated with the period. Then respond to the following questions:

■ What do you think would have been the advantages and disadvantages about living during the Middle Ages?

■ How could the Church have best served the people of the Middle Ages?

THE MEDIEVAL WORLD

Saints and Sinners

fyi!

This is not the first time that the Church was composed of a combination of saints and sinners. Remember that Saint Peter had denied knowing Jesus and Saint Jerome used his biting wit to put down those who dared disagree with him. Constantine used ruthless measures to secure his power over the empire but is counted among the saints in the Eastern Church.

You may already have formed some impressions about the **medieval** world. Knights rode about on horseback, dressed in heavy armor, while ladies in flowing gowns waited for them back at the castle. Kings and queens lived in splendor and ruled with an iron hand. Lower-class people worked away in surrounding fields all day, barely ever looking up to notice what the lords, ladies, and knights were doing. Monks or friars were harmless, even comical characters who lived on the fringes of the social world of the Middle Ages. Bishops dressed like princes and lived princely lifestyles, paying little attention to the sufferings of the lowly people surrounding their grand cathedrals.

As is true with any stereotype of the past, these images are partial truths at best. Since through the ages the Church and society have never been so closely united, it is important for us to look more attentively at the images that make up the myth of the Middle Ages. In response to circumstances at the time, unique religious, political, social, and economic structures developed during this period. We will see that the message of Jesus, and the Church conveying that message, blended into the medieval world of warring knights, overworked serfs, ladies of the manor, and wandering monks.

Be forewarned. We will discover in our study of this period that the Church was made up of both saints and sinners, and even at times of people who were a combination of both. The first dominant figure of the Middle Ages—Charlemagne—is one such complex Christian. His dedication to the Church and to his Christian faith cannot be doubted. However, his ways of expressing his fidelity to the faith can certainly be questioned.

In this illustration from a manuscript, Heart, Desire, and Melancholy are represented by allegorical figures approaching a dangerous bridge guarded by a knight.

When Were the "Middle Ages"?

Discussion

Using specific examples, respond to the statement: Religion should guide and direct all aspects of one's life.

The crowning of Charlemagne marks an important turning point for Western Europe and the Church. Before looking more closely at Charlemagne and the Europe that emerged after his coronation, we need to analyze the very concept of the "Middle Ages." When exactly were the Middle Ages? The broadest time span is 476 to 1600. In 476 the classical Roman Empire in the West ended. By the year 1600, radically new viewpoints dominated the European scene. So the Middle Ages, broadly speaking, lasted from the sixth to the sixteenth century. However, the central period of the Middle Ages lasted from around 800 to 1300. This period is often called the High Middle Ages and will be the focus in this chapter.

The Middle Ages are sometimes viewed in a negative light. In fact, the Middle Ages saw thriving intellectual life, set standards for church architecture, and established political and economic arrangements that complimented the classical Roman system with influences from other sources. In particular, the Middle Ages were a time when people believed that Christianity provided guiding principles governing all aspects of life. In other words, Europe of the Middle Ages was **Christendom,** where Christian rulers and Church leaders attempted to create the world as they thought God intended it to be and in a way that dominated the culture. Medieval Christendom had to respond to the breakdown of centralized power and continuing attacks from outside the Christian world. The Church itself continued to be intertwined with the political, social, economic, and even military activity of the day. We may question how some people of the time understood Christianity, but we cannot deny that Christianity provided the primary lens through which all of reality was viewed.

Christendom
the Christian world as dominated by Christianity; used during the Middle Ages to denote Western Europe

By 800 Islam had overtaken large land masses belonging to the Church in the West and to the Church in the East.

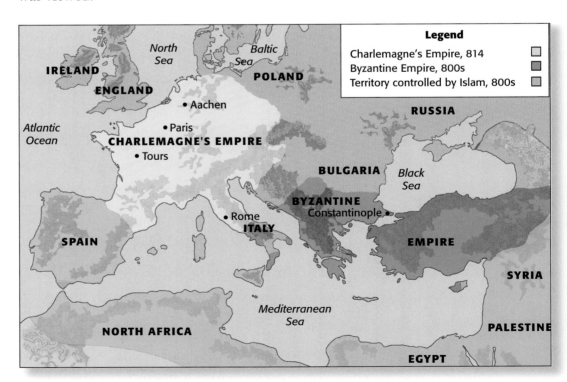

The coronation of
Charlemagne by
Pope Leo III marked
to union of Church
and state in Western
Europe.

Charlemagne and the Holy Roman Empire

History reports that when Pope Leo III crowned Charlemagne "Emperor of the Western Empire," it was a spontaneous gesture. Planned or not, the pope's action that Christmas in the year 800 was an attempt to bring back the peace and stability of the earlier glory days of the Roman Empire in the West.

Pope Leo saw in Charlemagne a man who could make life better for Europe. By crowning him, the pope was asserting that this emperor was to be a holy emperor; Charlemagne's empire was to be a holy empire. From that day on, Charlemagne signed all his official documents, "Charles, by the will of God, Roman Emperor." He took the Christian nature of his position seriously.

Charlemagne, therefore, is often called the "second Constantine" because he formed all of Europe into one family of faith. In 771 he began a thirty-year project to enlarge his kingdom by getting all the various Christian tribes to accept him as their leader. And by 800 Charlemagne, King of the Franks, was accepted as ruler by all the peoples of Western Europe from the Baltic to the Mediterranean Sea. With a strong military force behind him, he secured the borders surrounding these lands. Therefore, Pope Leo was merely making official what already existed in fact—Charlemagne *was* emperor of the West. The pope's crowning of an emperor symbolized the union of Church and state in Western Europe, a union which would remain strong but tense throughout the medieval period.

The emperor in the East was furious when he heard about this crowning of Charlemagne. In his mind, he alone was emperor of all the lands that were the Roman Empire. However, he was powerless to challenge Charlemagne's claim. The crowning of Charlemagne added to the growing breach between Rome and Constantinople. In time the political division between East and West would also lead to a split between Eastern and Western Christianity.

Charlemagne, the Christian Emperor

Who was this Emperor Charlemagne? A biographer describes him as strong and athletic, a skilled hunter and an avid swimmer. Of course, like all the competing princes of his day, he was a warrior. Although he himself could barely read, he recognized the importance of learning and education. He decreed that every monastery must have a school where young men could be educated. He brought the most learned monk of the time, Alcuin, to his capital and commissioned him to establish the finest school in the empire. He arranged for manuscripts to be brought to the school from all over the empire to be copied by the monks. A new form of writing called *script* was developed so that manuscripts would be transcribed in a uniform fashion. Some of the greatest written treasures of the ancient world were saved because of the monastery libraries of Charlemagne's time.

Charlemagne believed that he ruled the empire in God's name. Although he was crowned by the pope, he was determined not to be subservient to the pope. Charlemagne felt that it was his responsibility as Christian emperor to promote the welfare of the Church. As a result he established a policy of involvement in Church affairs by lay rulers that would cause problems later on. He arranged for the manner of worship used in Rome to be followed throughout the empire. As a result, Western Christianity took on a uniformity that never existed in the Eastern Churches.

Charlemagne also attempted to establish a procedure by which the canons (priests) of a cathedral would choose the bishop, and monks or nuns of an abbey (monastery) would select its leader, called the *abbot* or *abbess*. In this way he hoped to insure that holy and worthy people would hold positions of power in the Church. Charlemagne also instituted a set of rules for members of the clergy designed to make sure that they were living a religious life. Finally, he enacted laws against heresy and fought against the Saxons who were not yet Christian, offering them either Baptism or death.

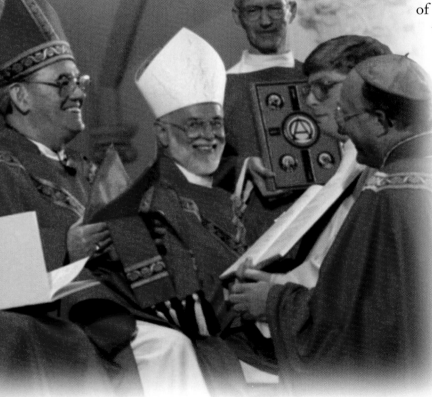

Today some of the rituals of coronations are carried on in the ordination rite for bishops.

Activity

Historically, the United States has had laws, called "blue laws," based solely on religious beliefs, such as restricting the sale of alcohol on Sundays. Research "blue laws" of the U.S. and then explain how these laws relate to Charlemagne and his understanding of Christian principles as the basis for laws in his empire.

Chapter Five

The Book of Kells, a finely illustrated manuscript of the Four Gospels in Latin, demonstrates both the exquisite work that monks of the early Middle Ages produced and the importance they placed on the written word. The Book of Kells is on display at Trinity College in Dublin, Ireland. For more information: **www.tcd.ie/Library/kells.html**

Chaos Overtakes Charlemagne's Empire

The period of time in Western European history between the end of Charlemagne's reign in 814 and the beginning of Otto I's reign as Holy Roman Emperor in 962 is sometimes referred to as the Dark Ages. The beginning and end of the period are not well defined. Some people apply the term to the entire Middle Ages. In this view, the era of classical Rome was a period of light, darkened by the conquest of nomadic tribes and then medieval superstition. Not until the Enlightenment, when people appealed to reason and science to arrive at truth, did the "darkness" over Europe disperse. Most historians reject the term "Dark Ages" completely.

The one hundred and fifty years or so between Charlemagne and Otto were a time of much chaos in Western Europe. Charlemagne's successors—Louis the Pious, Louis the Stammerer, Louis the Child, Charles the Bald, Charles the Fat, and Charles the Simple—couldn't hold the empire together. The empire disintegrated into small territories with semi-independent rulers who often fought one another. Until Otto was crowned by the pope, there was no emperor in Europe during most of these years. Also at this time, armies of nomadic Muslims, called **Saracens,** took advantage of the weakened empire to attack southern Italy. Since there was little to prevent them, Saracens even succeeded in overtaking Rome. The pope had to build a wall around Rome and provide for its protection as best he could. Another group, called the **Magyars,** raided throughout Western Europe before eventually settling in modern-day Hungary.

Most destructive of all during this period were the **Vikings,** who met little resistance as they raided seacoast villages and sailed up rivers to take whatever they wanted. They soon discovered that monasteries were particularly defenseless and contained some of the best riches and stores of food supplies available.

Irish monasteries, which had assembled fine libraries containing manuscripts of both Christian and pre-Christian writings, were constantly attacked and ravaged by Vikings. At first the monks built towers without ground-level entrances to try to hide their precious objects. This did not deter Vikings who wanted, not the manuscripts, but the fine jewels that often adorned them. The *Book of Kells,* one of the few manuscripts we still have from this time, survived because it was sent inland and hidden away.

Saracens
nomadic Muslim people who raided Mediterranean coastal areas, especially around southern Italy

Magyars
nomadic people from the Eastern frontier

Vikings
a seafaring people who originated in Denmark

Feudalism: The Medieval Way of Life

As previously mentioned, during the Middle Ages religious matters were not separate from the rest of life. When nomadic groups became Christian, they replaced their gods with the Christian God and they adapted their style of life to fit the Roman system. The nomads were accustomed to living off the land and to moving about from place to place in order to supply their needs. Fighting among themselves and against Roman settlers was simply a part of their lifestyle. The move to Christianity and to Roman civilization led to a different economic, social, and political arrangement for the nomadic tribes and the people they encountered. The new structure for society came to be known as **feudalism.**

The division of society that existed under feudalism has been summed up in these words: Some pray, some fight, some work, and a few rule. Feudalism was a system of contracts among groups of people designed to make productive use of the land while offering protection for those who worked it. (With the collapse of the empire, the army was no longer available for protection.) To be able to provide this service, the lord forced or paid soldiers and knights to fight for him if needed. The lord in turn would offer himself as a **vassal** to a stronger lord or king. He would promise respect and obedience to this overlord and would pay him taxes in return for his protection.

In Western Europe the king was the landowner of his entire kingdom. Portions of land were rented to succeeding levels of underlings, from king down to **serf.** The lowest class of people, the serfs, tilled the fields, planted and harvested crops, and tended the livestock. As determined by those in power above them, they retained a portion of the produce for themselves and the rest went to the lord of the land. Until late in the medieval period, over ninety percent of the people in Western Europe were serfs.

While medieval kings theoretically held absolute power, in reality they were dependent on those below them for peace and prosperity. Feudalism, therefore, represented a pyramid of power and responsibilities, most of which were based on force and necessity.

Feudalism and the Church

The feudal system had an impact on Church life in three ways. First, bishops and monasteries were collectively the largest group of landowners. A bishop or an abbot of a monastery would have serfs work the land and would receive the profits. For protection of the property, the bishop or abbot would become the vassal of a strong lord or king. Once again, taxes would go to the overlord. These properties provided a healthy financial return, and so when a bishop or abbot died, the king would appoint to take his place someone who would ensure that the profits would continue. One historian describes the close link between Church leaders and the feudal system in these words:

feudalism
a social form of interlocking relationships based on the use of land in payment for military services

vassal
in the feudal system, someone who is subject to and under the protection of another person

serf
one who tilled soil in the feudal system and was bound to the will of the landowner

Bishops and abbots acquired purely secular titles such as duke or count, minted their own coin, judged civil lawsuits and rode about dressed in armor as they went off to war like any other lord. By the 11th century no one in medieval Europe knew a bishop or an abbot who was not also a powerful secular lord.

Anthony E. Gilles, *The People of the Faith* (Cincinnati, Ohio: St. Anthony Messenger Press, 1986), 34.

The second impact of feudalism was that the pyramid structure of Church governance, which was already in place, became more firmly established. Like the emperor, the pope was lord over all Christendom, at least in the West. A bishop had to answer to the pope and align with the local lord; often he was a member of the lord's family. Priests, who had to answer to the bishops, ministered to those on the lower levels of society. Laypeople were next in line in the Church pyramid.

Great Chain of Being perception of reality as a pyramid from God at the top to inanimate objects at the bottom

Third and most important, people of the Middle Ages viewed all reality, beginning with the spiritual realm, in terms of levels of authority and importance. God presides over all reality. Angels, pure spirits, occupy the next level. Humans, creatures of body and spirit, are one step below angels, but also share their physical existence with lower creatures. Animals, plants, and nonliving things complete the levels of the pyramid. This structuring of reality is known as the **Great Chain of Being** or, for created beings, the hierarchy of creatures. Medieval cathedrals often reflected this pyramidal view of Church and reality. At the base of a cathedral's front façade would be many images, often of common people going about their daily work. Middle levels would be much less busy, with depictions of saints such as the four evangelists. These saints might be shown adorned in the garb of a medieval lord. The top of a cathedral would rise gradually to one simple but majestic point.

Activity

The "Great Chain of Being" pyramid is one way of viewing reality. Draw a picture that would illustrate another view of reality. Then answer these questions:

- What does your illustration of reality imply about values and relationships and your place in the universe? How is it similar to and different from the Great Chain of Being?

- Is the Great Chain of Being still the dominant view of reality in the world today? Explain.

Review

1. Which centuries encompass the Middle Ages?

2. Why can the term *the Middle Ages* carry a negative meaning?

3. Why are the Middle Ages in Europe also known as the time of Christendom?

4. What does it mean to say that Charlemagne was a "holy emperor" and the "second Constantine"?

5. Name two ways that Charlemagne attempted to serve the Church as Holy Roman Emperor.

6. Who were the Vikings, Saracens, and Magyars?

7. What kind of work did serfs do?

8. How did the feudal system function?

9. Name three ways that feudalism affected the Church of the Middle Ages.

TROUBLES AND TRIUMPHS

lay investiture
the practice of lay persons (such as kings) appointing bishops, priests, abbots, and abbesses

simony
the payment of money to be appointed to a Church office

Who ultimately ruled the Medieval Church—pope or emperor? Charlemagne believed that as emperor he ruled the Church and that the pope's role was to pray for the Church. However, when Charlemagne's descendants proved to be weak rulers, the popes grew in temporal power. Sixty years later Pope Nicholas I (858–867) stated that the pope governed the Church; the emperor's role was to protect it.

When Pope Leo III, who had crowned Charlemagne emperor, died in 816, the wealthy families of Rome began to consider the papacy to be a personal prize passed among them. By law, only clergy elected the pope. In fact, the most powerful Roman families decided who would be chosen. Most of the popes over the next two hundred years were good men but weak rulers. This period of "weak popes" is one more example of the challenge that exists in the Church as it struggles to be both human and holy.

Three Problems That Plagued the Medieval Church

Besides being spiritual leaders, bishops and abbots were also vassals to a king in the feudal system. The practice of kings or lords naming Church leaders is known as **lay investiture.** Of course, lay rulers who invested authority in bishops and abbots expected favors in return. Lay investiture was one of the main causes of Church-related problems during the Middle Ages. The pope, bishops, and abbots found it difficult to differentiate their roles as secular rulers and spiritual leaders.

A second problem that plagued the Church was **simony**. A wealthy lord could purchase for one of his sons the position of bishop of an important diocese or abbot of a local monastery. The son might or might not carry out his duties responsibly.

A third practice that caused problems was disregard for *celibacy* among the clergy. That is, a larger number of priests and bishops lived with women without being married. Sons commonly entered their father's profession, but the son of a priest or bishop did not necessarily qualify to become a priest. Also, being a priest with unofficial family entanglements created conflicts for both the priest and his family. The ownership of Church property became a major issue. If the Church of the Middle Ages was to restore its spiritual leadership in Europe, it had to address these three problems.

Activity

How effective do you think the following strategies would have been in reforming the medieval Church? Rank and explain each of the following from one (no effect) to ten (very effective).

1. Church leaders should have divested themselves of all lands and property except for church buildings and monasteries.

2. Church leaders should have forbidden any members of noble families from becoming pope, bishops, or abbots.

3. Church leaders should have excommunicated all bishops and priests known to have disobeyed the rule of celibacy.

4. The pope should have appointed all bishops.

5. Monks of a monastery should have elected their abbot.

Cluny and the Reform of Monastic Life

In 909 in France, a local duke and a holy monk teamed up to set in motion an instrument of reform that would transform the whole Church. Duke William of Aquitaine gave a tract of land in Cluny, in southeastern France, to a monk named Berno so that he could establish a monastery there. Actually, William deeded it directly "to Saint Peter and Saint Paul." The pope was to act on behalf of the apostles but not to possess that which belonged only to the apostles. Therefore William placed the monastery directly under the authority of the pope, but the monks themselves were to select their abbot.

William wanted this monastery to provide an example of spiritual life to counteract the immorality that he saw around him. He was concerned that many monastic communities had become corrupt after the destruction they underwent at the hands of Vikings and other groups and as a result of the appointment of immoral men to positions of leadership by power-hungry lords. William intended this monastery to be a place of authentic prayer and spiritual life. Abbot Berno used the Rule of Saint Benedict, who had introduced monasticism to the West, to set up strict guidelines for the monastery. Monks at Cluny lived simply. Instead of the emphasis on prayer and work that marked the monastic system of the time, the monks of Cluny emphasized prayer. They recited together five or six times a day the Divine Office, or Liturgy of the Hours.

The monks renewed the spiritual life of others in a number of ways. They were artists who contributed to the inspiring art of the Middle Ages. They joined local diocesan councils to bring about change in the moral life of the clergy, particularly in terms of celibacy. They were instrumental in a movement called the **Truce of God,** which called on Christian warriors to abstain from doing battle during Christmas, Lent, special saints' feast days, and so on. In time other monasteries followed in the footsteps of Cluny. Monks from the Cluny system became advisors to kings, bishops, and even the pope. Abuses, such as simony, were greatly diminished.

Truce of God
a rule enacted by the medieval Church forbidding warfare during certain holy days of the year

The abbey church at Cluny gives an indication of the importance of the monastery to the region.

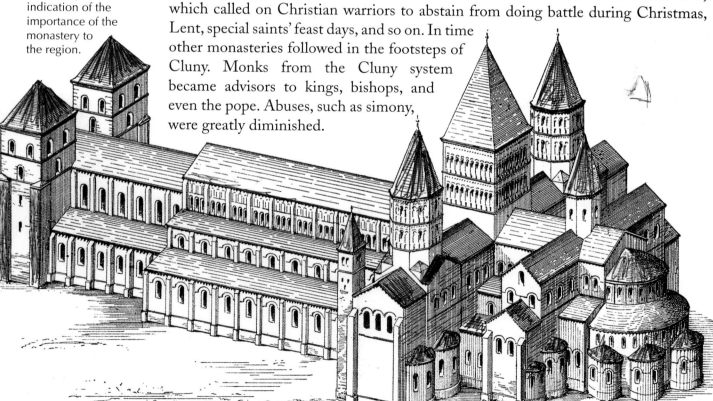

Hildebrand—The Reforming Pope

Despite its political involvement, the Church was viewed as greater than politics. Although the papacy sometimes suffered from poor leadership, people nevertheless continued to be concerned about salvation and the Church as a spiritual force in their lives. A holy pope or bishop was capable of doing more good for people than were the civil authorities. In 1057 Pope Nicholas II took steps to stop the election of popes by the emperor or families of Rome. On the death of a pope, the cardinals who resided in Rome or who could come to Rome within nine days would go into a secret meeting called a **conclave** (con = with; clave = key). Only cardinals, who were locked behind closed doors during this time, could vote for the pope. Election of the pope by a conclave of cardinals continues to this day. Reforms such as these helped the Church regain its stature as the wellspring nourishing the spiritual life of Christians of the Middle Ages.

A number of popes following Nicholas II continued to reform the papacy and the Church. The most noted was Hildebrand, who in 1073 became Pope Gregory VII. Hildebrand had worked for a number of popes before being chosen himself. In fact, he was instrumental in designing the procedure of electing the pope in conclave. During his twelve years as pope, Hildebrand initiated so many measures to eliminate corruption that these changes came to be known as the **Gregorian reforms.** Each Lent he would gather together Church leaders and invoke new legislation.

conclave
a meeting of cardinals to elect a pope

Gregorian reforms
a series of reforms under Pope Gregory VII that addressed major problems in the Church

A group of cardinals enter the Sistine Chapel to begin the conclave to elect a new pope.

Pope Gregory fiercely attacked two of the serious problems already mentioned—simony and lay investiture. He wanted no secular powers to have control or influence over the Church. The emperor at the time, Henry IV, did not want to hand over power to the pope. When the emperor refused to accept the pope's reforms, Pope Gregory excommunicated him. Fearing that other German princes would use the situation to wrest control from him, Henry went to the palace where the pope was staying to ask his forgiveness. The pope supposedly left Henry standing outside in the snow for three days until he finally forgave him and welcomed him back into the Church. However, the emperor soon felt confident enough in his power that he attacked Rome and forced Pope Gregory to leave.

Gregory lived in exile until his death in 1085. As he lay dying Gregory said, "I have loved justice and therefore die in exile." The reforms that he began would continue with succeeding popes.

Gregory's successor, Callistus II, arrived at an agreement with Emperor Henry V, son of Henry IV. The pope would have the power to choose bishops and abbots and invest them with spiritual power, while the emperor would invest them with symbols of their temporal power. This compromise agreement is known as the *Concordat of Worms*.

Thanks in large part to the Gregorian reforms, the papacy would soon come to the height of its power.

Gregorian Reforms

- election of the pope by a conclave of cardinals
- celibacy for priests
- papal power to choose bishops and abbots

Activity

Role-play a debate between Emperor Henry IV and Pope Gregory VII over who should decide the appointment of bishops and abbots. Include in the debate the history of this practice during Constantine's and Charlemagne's time. Also, describe how the issue might be addressed today.

Further Christian Expansion

In the early Middle Ages, not all of Europe was Christian. Part of Spain remained under Muslim control until the end of the fifteenth century. However, the Scandinavian countries and Eastern Europe turned to Christianity during these early centuries of the Middle Ages. Early missionary attempts to convert the "dreaded Norsemen"—the Vikings of Northern Europe—ended in martyrdom for the missionaries. Even after a monk named Anskar succeeded in getting permission from the Swedish king to build a church, his success was short-lived—at his death, the people of the area returned to their previous religious practices.

Interestingly, Christianity came to Scandinavia not through missionaries but through the kings. In 1015 Olaf I became king of Norway. He had been educated in England, where he became a Christian. On becoming king he forced his subjects to accept Christianity and sent missionaries to Iceland and Greenland. Two other kings, Eric IX of Sweden and Canute of Denmark, were instrumental in bringing Christianity to their countries. They may have done so partially in order to have good relations with the rest of Europe and to make trade easier. Whatever the reasons, by the twelfth century northern Europe had joined the Christian world.

The expansion of Christianity in Europe

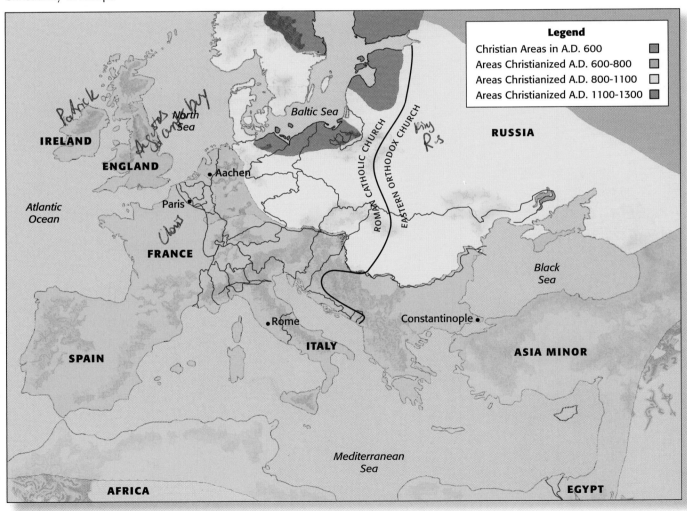

Legend
Christian Areas in A.D. 600
Areas Christianized A.D. 600-800
Areas Christianized A.D. 800-1100
Areas Christianized A.D. 1100-1300

Margaret of Scotland

An English princess is credited with bringing Christianity to Scotland in the British Isles. Margaret and her mother sailed to Scotland to escape from the king who had conquered their land. King Malcolm of Scotland welcomed them and before long asked for Margaret's hand in marriage. As queen, Margaret changed her husband and the country for the better. Prominent among Margaret's activities was religious reform. She encouraged abstaining from work on Sunday, observance of the seasons of Advent and Lent, and the reception of Eucharist on Easter. She was the founder of several missions and frequently visited and cared for those who were sick. In sddition, she had hostels constructed for those who were poor.

Margaret was declared a saint in 1250, particularly for her work for religious reform and her charitable works. In 1673 she was declared patroness of Scotland.

Cyril and Methodius

A move toward Christianity was also taking place in eastern Europe. Two brothers, Cyril and Methodius, figure prominently in the conversion of the Slavic people of the area. Methodius had been a governor in a Slavic territory, and both he and his brother knew the Slavic language. The Byzantine Emperor commissioned them to spread Christianity to the Khazars in Russia and then to the Slavic people. To assist them in their work, the brothers wrote an alphabet for the Slavic language, known as the *Cyrillic alphabet.* Thanks to Cyril and Methodius, Slavic became a written as well as a spoken language. The brothers also used the Slavic language in the liturgy.

Many Church leaders, especially German bishops, questioned this practice. The Eastern Church used Greek in its liturgy; in the West, Latin was standard. Cyril and Methodius had to go to Rome to defend their teachings and their practices. In 878, after the death of his brother, Methodius received the pope's permission to use Slavic in the liturgy. In 1980 Pope John Paul II proclaimed Cyril and Methodius copatron saints (along with Saint Benedict) of Europe.

Cubans in the United States, like other cultural and ethnic groups, celebrate the liturgy with their own traditions and customs.

Discussion

1. Should liturgies incorporate different languages, styles, and practices to reflect those who are participating in the services?

2. If you wanted to introduce someone from a different religion to the beauty and meaningfulness of Catholic worship, to what type of service would you bring him or her? Why?

In 899 King Stephen of Hungary became Christian and brought with him the Magyars who had wrought such havoc on Rome and northern Italy in previous years. Around 992 the people of Poland converted to Latin Christianity as well. The conversion of Ukraine and Russia to Christianity had a unique twist to it. In 988, Prince Vladimir of Rus, whose capital city was Kiev in modern-day Ukraine, decided that it was time to join one of the major religions bordering his territory. He sent envoys to Western Christianity, Byzantine Christianity, Islam, and Judaism. When the envoys to Constantinople came back with reports of the beauty and majesty of Hagia Sophia and of the lavish liturgies celebrated there, Prince Vladimir adopted Eastern Christianity for himself and his people. Vladimir cemented the relationship between the people of Rus and the Eastern Empire when he married the sister of the Byzantine emperor the next year. With the conversion of Russia, Poland, and the Slavic people of Eastern Europe, the Christian world now extended from the northwest tip of Spain to the Baltic Sea in the West and to Russia and Constantinople in the East.

Review

1. What was the difference between the positions of Charlemagne and Pope Nicholas I on Church governance?

2. Name three problems that the Church had to face during the early Middle Ages.

3. How did the Cluny movement help reform Church practices?

4. What is a conclave of cardinals?

5. Who was Hildebrand? What action did he take against Emperor Henry IV, and why did he do so?

6. What are the changes called that Pope Gregory VII introduced into the Church?

7. How did the Concordat of Worms strengthen the position of the pope?

8. What contributions to Slavic culture did Saints Cyril and Methodius make?

9. What form of Christianity did Prince Vladimir of Rus adopt?

THE EAST–WEST SCHISM

The tenth and eleventh centuries should be known as the time when Christianity welcomed into the fold many European peoples. However, in 1054 a problem that had been brewing for some time cast a shadow over these advances. Even before Christianity had become the religion of the Roman Empire, differences between East and West caused problems. As the Eastern and Western sections of the Empire grew apart, so did the Eastern and Western Churches. For instance, many in the Eastern Church saw the role of bishop as that of a father to his particular community but as a brother to all his fellow bishops. Bishops in the East viewed the patriarch of Constantinople as the eldest brother. Even though they accepted that the bishop of Rome held a special place of honor because of that city's relationship to the apostles Peter and Paul, they viewed the pope as a distant and foreign figure. On the other hand, Christians in the West saw the pope as the head of the entire Church, the successor of Saint Peter, the patriarch or "Holy Father" of the whole Christian community.

For a thousand years the Eastern Church held on to its Hellenistic tradition and Greek language. Little had changed in Eastern Church practice, and few people saw the need for dramatic change. The Western Church, on the other hand, had faced different challenges that required adaptation. For instance, Romans, Irish, English, French, and Germans made their mark on the Western Church. The need for the pope to be a strong secular as well as religious leader influenced the role of the papacy in a way unknown to the Eastern Church. Thus two sections of the one Church—East and West—had grown apart. The distance and differences between them led to tensions and mutual suspicion as well.

The **East–West Schism** officially happened in 1054. A schism is a breaking of a relationship between two groups who still hold essential beliefs in common. As we will see, the leader of each section of the Church excommunicated the other. This mutual **excommunication,** however, was merely the culmination of a series of problems and misunderstandings between leaders of the Eastern and Western Churches. Here are highlights of events leading up to and following the East-West Schism.

When Pope John Paul II visited Romania, he met with the Orthodox Romanian patriarch, who presides over the majority of Christians in that country.

The *Filioque* and Iconoclast Controversies

We read about the Nicene Creed in chapter 3. The bishops at the Council of Nicaea (A.D. 325) wrote that the Holy Spirit proceeds "from the Father." Later, in order to make the teaching clearer and to counteract some heretical views then popular in the West, some churches in the West changed the wording to "from the Father *and the Son.*" The emperor Charlemagne, who as you recall desired uniformity in worship, allowed the change to be used by the entire Western Church. This is known as the *filioque* controversy.

Church leaders in the East were angry, not only because they disagreed with the change in wording, but also because it was imposed by secular rather than Church authority, and because they were not consulted about the change. This controversy illustrates the type of problems that consistently plagued relations between Eastern and Western Churches. Conflicts were not only about theology and teachings but also about governance and the two groups getting along.

The **iconoclast controversy** is another example of how the way in which issues were dealt with caused problems. **Icon,** or *ikon,* is a Greek word meaning "image." While Judaism and Islam either discourage or even condemn the use of images for the sacred, Christianity encouraged the use of pictures to portray parts of the liturgy and stories from the Bible, the life of Christ, and the lives of the saints. These paintings inspired the faithful and helped a largely illiterate community to better understand their faith. The Church Father, Gregory of Nyssa, explained the use of icons by saying that, "The silent painting speaks on the walls and does much good."

While both the Eastern and Western Churches made use of sacred images, icons held special significance for Eastern Christians, where an icon artist created a painting according to very specific guidelines.

In 726 the Eastern Emperor Leo the Isaurian forbade the use of icons because he felt it was **idolatry.** Supported by the patriarch of Constantinople, Leo had thousands of icons destroyed. The common people, supported by monks, held an uprising in support of icons. The pope, Gregory II, supported the use of icons in liturgy. The pope may not have understood exactly how icons were viewed by Eastern Christians. Rather, he was upholding the principle that civil authority—Leo the Isaurian—had no right to intervene in Church matters. The iconoclast controversy continued for over fifty years and caused many bloody confrontations. In 787 the Second Council of Nicaea upheld the use of icons and condemned as heresy the calling of their use "worshiping false idols." Questions for East-West relations during this controversy were: Does the pope have jurisdiction over the patriarch of Constantinople, and does the emperor have jurisdiction over the Church?

filioque
Latin term meaning "and the Son"

iconoclast controversy
disagreement caused by the Eastern emperor's decision to condemn the use of icons in worship

icon
a highly stylized painting venerated in Eastern Christianity

idolatry
worship of false gods or of an image of God

Activity

For an introduction to icons and an explanation as to how they are painted, visit www.pallasart.com/ikons/ Write a report on one aspect of this art or try your own hand at painting an icon using the directions given.

Sicily—East or West?

fyi!

In 1965 Pope Paul VI and Patriarch Athenagoras of Constantinople rescinded the mutual excommunication. However, at the present time the Eastern Orthodox Churches remain officially separate from the Catholic Church centered in Rome.

Events such as the *filioque* and iconoclast controversies demonstrated that relations between the Eastern and Western Churches needed only a spark to ignite the embers of distrust between them into a roaring fire. This spark occurred in 1043 and started the two sides on the road to the schism that remains in effect today. Sicily, an island off the coast of southwest Italy, had for a long time been under the control of the Eastern Empire. The patriarch of Constantinople had responsibility for the Church there, which followed Eastern practices.

In 1043 Normans captured Sicily, and the Eastern emperor was powerless to try to regain control of it. With Sicily now ruled by Europeans, who was to oversee the Church there? The patriarch of Constantinople, Michael Cerularius, declared that he had jurisdiction over Sicily, and the Eastern Emperor supported him. The pope, however, appointed a new archbishop of Sicily to bring Western practices to the churches there.

Patriarch Michael Cerularius called together Eastern bishops and condemned the pope for not supporting the patriarch's responsibility for Sicily. The patriarch also brought up charges that Eastern Church leaders had made before against the Western Church. In retaliation for the pope's actions in Sicily, the patriarch closed all Western Christian churches in his jurisdiction and removed the name of the pope from prayers said during the liturgy. Although attempts were made to resolve the dispute, it dragged on. As mentioned earlier, part of the problem at this time was that leaders on both sides did not really understand the language or culture of the other. Finally, in 1053 Pope Leo IX sent a special envoy to attempt a reconciliation.

Pope Paul VI and Patriarch Athenagoras exchanged a sign of peace during their meeting at the Vatican.

The envoy, Cardinal Humbert, was a man of high moral character, but he could be unbending and uncompromising. Although well educated, he knew little of the Greek culture and none of the language. In his mind, he was going to Constantinople to have the Greek Church submit to the authority of the pope. For a period of time Patriarch Michael Cerularius refused to meet with Cardinal Humbert. Incensed at this inhospitable treatment, Humbert placed on the altar of Hagia Sophia a proclamation, signed by Pope Leo, which declared that the patriarch and the entire Greek Church were excommunicated. In retaliation, the patriarch excommunicated the pope and all the Latin Church.

At first, leaders of other Eastern Churches didn't take seriously this mutual excommunication. They viewed it as a squabble between two feuding brothers, such as had happened before in the life of the Church. However, this time those involved in the split would resist efforts at reconciliation, especially as the animosity between the Eastern and Western Church was fueled by the fires of the Crusades.

Eastern Orthodox and Eastern Rite Catholics

The Eastern Churches no longer in union with Rome came to be known as the Orthodox Churches. To complicate things even further, however, some of the Eastern Churches decided that they wished to stay in union with Rome by accepting the supremacy of the pope over the entire Church. Therefore, today there are **Eastern Orthodox Churches** and **Eastern Rite Catholic Churches**. Eastern Catholics accept the pope as head of the Church but continue to follow the styles of worship and Church practices of the Eastern Churches. Although different from Western Catholics in this way, they are nonetheless fully Catholic. The vast majority of Eastern Christians, however, are Orthodox and are not officially in union with the Church centered in Rome.

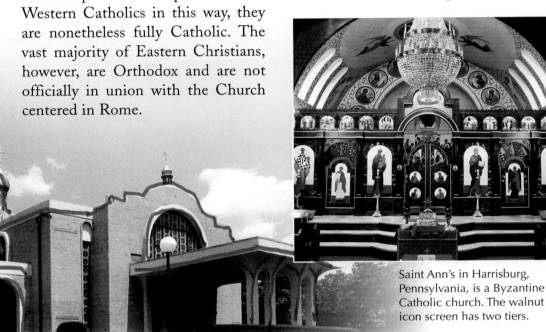

Saint Ann's in Harrisburg, Pennsylvania, is a Byzantine Catholic church. The walnut icon screen has two tiers.

Activity

If you are a Western Catholic or a member of another Western Christian Church, under the direction of your teacher and pastor attend a service at an Eastern Rite Catholic or an Eastern Orthodox Church. Describe in writing how the experience differs from Mass as you know it.

Review

1. Describe the difference in how Eastern Christians and Western Christians viewed their bishops.

2. Explain the *filioque* controversy.

3. What are icons? What function do they play in the Churches in the East?

4. Explain the iconoclast controversy.

5. What roles did Patriarch Michael Cerularius and Cardinal Humbert play in the break between the Eastern and Western Churches?

6. What is the difference between Eastern Orthodox and Eastern Rite Catholic Churches?

MEDIEVAL CHRISTIAN EXPERIENCE

The people of the Middle Ages found a variety of ways to express their faith. In fact, they viewed all that they did as an expression of their faith, whether it was farming or fighting, ruling or praying. In this section, we will look at some of the ways that medieval people experienced and expressed their Christianity.

The Pilgrim

A pilgrimage is a religiously motivated journey to a sacred shrine or holy place. The medieval pilgrimage became a metaphor for the journey of the human person searching for salvation and eternal life with God in the next world while traveling through this world.

Thomas D. McGonigle and James F. Quigley, *A History of the Christian Tradition.* (New York: Paulist Press, 1988), 148.

Over 70,000 Catholic pilgrims gathered for a sunrise Mass in La Vang, Vietnam. The three-day festival commemorates an apparition of Mary in 1798.

According to the Christian worldview, we are all on a journey from God, seeking to make our way back to God. That is, whether we ever leave our hometown or not, we are all pilgrims. As a religious experience, pilgrimage is not simply about the destination. The journey itself is meant to have religious significance. Christians went on pilgrimage fairly early in Church history, usually to the Holy Land to visit the spots where Jesus lived. History indicates that for many people during the Middle Ages, going on a pilgrimage was a major expression of their religious faith. Pilgrimages were highly regulated. Pilgrims received special papers from their local religious leaders, wore special clothing identifying them as pilgrims, and generally visited specific holy sites.

The most important destinations for pilgrims were the Holy Land, Rome, and the tombs of the early martyrs—such as Compostela in Spain, where the apostle James the Greater is said to be buried, and Canterbury in England, where Saint Thomas Becket was martyred.

Of course, going on pilgrimage was also an adventure, just as traveling is today. And as you can imagine, maintaining a popular pilgrimage spot was also good business. However, none of this takes away from pilgrimage as a deeply religious experience. Later in the medieval period, in his work *The Canterbury Tales* Geoffrey Chaucer catalogued the pilgrimage experiences of some traveler. Although Chaucer's Wife of Bath is a fictional character, she mentions the most popular pilgrimage destinations during the Middle Ages:

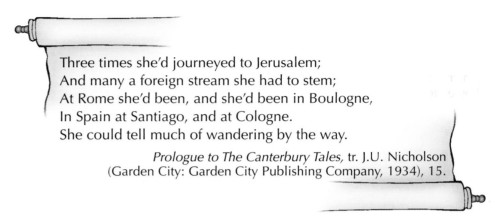

Three times she'd journeyed to Jerusalem;
And many a foreign stream she had to stem;
At Rome she'd been, and she'd been in Boulogne,
In Spain at Santiago, and at Cologne.
She could tell much of wandering by the way.

Prologue to The Canterbury Tales, tr. J.U. Nicholson
(Garden City: Garden City Publishing Company, 1934), 15.

But the bawdy Wife of Bath herself provides a good clue to the minds of some medieval pilgrims. Having had five lawful husbands—and perhaps others as well—she enjoys the "good life" and intends to do so for a long time to come, as manifested in her ribald tale. But she also goes on pilgrimage, thus exhibiting the medieval awareness and acceptance of the intimate connection between body and soul, heaven and earth, human and divine.

Pilgrimage provides a window into the Christian mind-set of the Middle Ages. Jesus is both God and a human who was born, lived, and died in actual places that one could visit. In the medieval mind-set these places were the "Holy Land." The apostles and the saints, especially the martyrs, were also flesh-and-blood persons. Their physical remains and objects associated with them (relics), their graves, and the places where they spent time were sacred. The medieval pilgrim went on pilgrimage to absorb the special aura that surrounded the holy places. Both the journey and the destination had symbolic, spiritual significance.

We get a glimpse into a more modern perspective on pilgrimages from two prominent figures of the Reformation era (sixteenth century). Erasmus criticized people for going on pilgrimage in these words: "You could run off to Rome or Compostela and buy up a million indulgences, but in the last analysis there is no better way of reconciling yourself with God than reconciling yourself with your brother" (Lawrence Cunningham, *The Catholic Heritage* [New York: Crossroad, 1986], 58). Martin Luther gave this advice to someone who planned to go on a pilgrimage: " . . . apply the money and effort required for the pilgrimage to fulfilling God's commandments, and to doing works a thousand times better than a pilgrimage, namely, meeting the needs of his family and his poor neighbors" (Cunningham, *The Catholic Heritage,* 59).

www.

Become a virtual pilgrim by taking a virtual tour of the Holy Land at **www.jesus2000.com**

The Cathedral

The Catholic tradition has always been sympathetic to, and supportive of, artistic activity. Catholicism as a historical tradition is unthinkable apart from its churches, paintings, sculptures, works of literature, musical compositions, and finely crafted items of religious and liturgical usage.

Lawrence Cunningham, *The Catholic Heritage,* 128.

Gothic
a style of architecture developed in northern France that allowed for higher walls and expanded space for windows

Romanesque
style of architecture developed in Italy characterized by decorative use of arcades and profuse ornamentation

If you walk into a museum that features art of the Middle Ages, you can't help but notice that religious themes are part of practically every art piece. The art form in which medieval Europe excelled was architecture. While the Greek Church had its icons, the Western Church of the Middle Ages had its great **Gothic** cathedrals to uplift the faithful to an experience of God. A *cathedral,* from the Latin word *cathedra* meaning "chair," is officially the church of the bishop of a diocese. In popular usage, a cathedral has come to mean a particularly large church. Before the twelfth century the style of large churches was **Romanesque.** This style mimicked ancient Roman architecture. In a Romanesque church, walls were thick and openings for light were small, creating a dark, fortress-like atmosphere.

In 1124 Abbot Suger wanted to rebuild his abbey church in Paris in a way that would introduce more light into the building. He came up with a combination of innovations that would allow walls to be higher and lighter, allowing much more space for windows. The larger window spaces resulted in an interior bathed in light. Abbot Suger used stained glass to depict scenes of the Christian story while creating a rainbow of light within the church. This style became known as Gothic architecture.

Above: The Romanesque Notre Dame la Grande in Poitiers, France.
Left: The Gothic Cathedral of Notre Dame in Chartres, France.

WWW. Go to GATEWAY TO ART HISTORY compiled for use with Gardner's *Art through the Ages,* Harcourt College Publishers' Art History Resources on the Web to find slide examples of Gothic and Romanesque architecture and cathedrals of the Middle Ages.

Summma Theologica
Saint Thomas Aquinas's comprehensive systematic examination of Christian theology

Just as the medieval pilgrimage had symbolic as well as physical meaning, so also the shape and design of Gothic cathedrals had symbolic, spiritual significance. Both from the outside and the inside, the lines of a cathedral seem to be pointing ever upward. By design, they uplift the gaze to the awesome mystery of God. The medieval pilgrim who stepped inside a cathedral and was bathed in the light from the stained glass windows would naturally relate that light to Christ, the Light of the World. To emphasize the connection between the light and Christ, artisans typically built cathedrals facing east so that the congregation, facing the altar on which the Son of God was made present, was also facing the rising sun. To be inside one of the great Gothic cathedrals was to have a foretaste of heaven.

The Theologian

After the appearance of a translation of Aristotle (from Greek to Latin), Aristotle's philosophy and that of his teacher Plato became the philosophical basis for much of medieval theology. Theologians of the day placed great emphasis on using reason to investigate the teachings of Christianity.

The first medieval theologian to attempt a rigorous study of Christian thought was Saint Anselm, who defined theology as "faith seeking understanding." This approach to theology, using the philosophical tools of the Greek philosophy of Aristotle to understand and organize Christian teaching, came to be known as scholasticism. The schools of theology flowered into great medieval universities. The university system of education that exists throughout the world today can trace its origins back to this movement during the Middle Ages.

The most renowned of the medieval theologians was Saint Thomas Aquinas (1225–1274). A Dominican priest, Aquinas succeeded in writing a complete and rigorous investigation of Christian thought. He used Aristolelian and Platonic philosophy as the philosophical basis of his thought. His monumental ***Summa Theologica*** makes a strong case for the reasonableness of Christian teaching. After Aquinas, if any thinker attempted to dispute that Christianity rests on solid philosophical foundations, he or she would need to confront the logical presentation of Christian teachings in Aquinas's summary of theology. While Protestantism moved away from Aquinas as being unbiblical, Catholic theology emphasized the scholastic approach well into the modern era. Thus Catholicism sees faith and reason as complementary and never contradictory. In 1880 Aquinas was named patron saint of Catholic schools, colleges, and universities.

Argument	Observations	Implications	Conclusion
From motion	Motion cannot start itself but must be started by something already in motion.	An infinite chain of movers is impossible, for then there would be no first mover and therefore no motion at all. The chain must have a beginning.	The unmoved mover is the one whom we call God.
From causation of existence	Certain events are caused by other events, which are themselves caused by prior events, and so on.	As above, the causal chain cannot be inifinite.	The uncaused first cause is the one whom we call God.
From possibility	Certain things are temporary, their existence unoriginal. Their existence is possible rather than necessary.	The chain of unoriginal existence cannot be infinite but must find its source in a self-existent necessary being.	This self-existent necessary being is the one whom we call God.
From imperfection	We judge certain things to have a lesser degree of perfection than others.	Relative assessments require an absolute standard of perfection.	This absolute standard, God, must exist.
From design	Inanimate things function together to accomplish an ordered purpose.	This cannot occur by chance but requires an intelligent designer.	This designer is the one whom we call God.

Adapted from Robert C. Walton, *Chronological and Background Charts of Church History* (Grand Rapids, Mich.: Academie Books/Zondervan Publishing House).

Activity

Describe what you think is the relationship between reason and faith. As part of your description, state whether you see reason as a help or a hindrance to an experience of faith.

This illustration depicts the symbolic story of Saint George slaying the dragon.

The Knight

Saint George is usually depicted as a medieval knight on horseback, slaying a dragon. The true Saint George died as a martyr around 300. Beyond that, we know very little about him. However, we do know that devotion to Saint George was very popular during the Middle Ages. He was a model for Christian knights because he selflessly went out to do battle against evil, symbolized by the dragon, and protected women and others who needed him. His symbol, a red cross on a white background, became the banner for the knights who fought in the Crusades. Saint George is the patron saint of a number of countries, including England which incorporates his red cross on white background as part of its flag.

During the Middle Ages, knighthood came to be viewed as an ideal expression of the Christian life. The European groups who joined Christianity had a history of engaging in warfare. Rather than eradicating this instinct, Christian leaders of the Middle Ages channeled it into a form of service: Knights were to uphold morality and fight for the good. The ceremony by which someone received the title of knight reveals that the profession had religious significance. Before becoming a knight, a young man spent a night in prayer in a chapel. In the morning he took a ritual bath, had his weapons blessed by a priest, and received his knight's garb in a religious ceremony. Becoming a knight had as much religious significance as becoming a monk or a priest. Knights were expected to be persons of strong moral character, ready to give their lives for others. In the eyes of the Church, the greatest act of heroism that a knight could perform was to fight in defense of the faith. This brings us to the Crusades.

Activity

1. Stories about medieval knighthood can be found in the stories about King Arthur and the knights of the Round Table and the search for the Holy Grail. Read one of the stories. Describe possible religious symbolism or meaning that it might have.

2. How can these models of medieval life deepen your faith and help you grow spiritually?

Review

1. What does it mean to say that a pilgrimage symbolizes the Christian experience?

2. Name two popular destinations for medieval pilgrims.

3. What position did Erasmus and Martin Luther hold regarding pilgrimage?

4. Describe the difference between Romanesque and Gothic architecture.

5. What is scholasticism?

6. Whose *Summa Theologica* examined Christian beliefs in light of Greek philosophy?

7. How did Christian leaders of the Middle Ages christianize the profession of knighthood?

CRUSADERS AND REFORMERS

Let us pray that each one of us, looking to the Lord Jesus, meek and humble of heart, will recognize that even men of the church, in the name of faith and morals, have sometimes used methods not in keeping with the Gospel in the solemn duty of defending the truth.

Pope John Paul II, "Service Requesting Pardon," *Origins 29:40* (March 23, 2000): 647.

In this section we will discuss one of the low points and one of the high points of the Middle Ages. In hindsight, we can say that the results of the Crusades were shameful. Yet even while Christian knights were killing Jews, Muslims, and other Christians, a young Italian man from Assisi chose to reject war and to live instead a life of simplicity. His story continues to inspire Christians and people of other religions to this day. Also in this time period another type of religious community emerged, and its members were instrumental in addressing new heresies confronting the Church.

The Christian Attempt to Win Back the Holy Land

The followers of Muhammand gained control of most of the Middle East, including the Christian holy lands, in the seventh century. Christian leaders were never comfortable knowing that the places where Jesus lived were controlled by non-Christians. From the time of Charlemagne, an uneasy peace prevailed between Muslims and Christians who lived in this area. Christians did travel to the Holy Land on pilgrimage, and some settled there and lived as neighbors to Muslims.

The peace came to an end in 1071 when Seljuk Turks conquered Jerusalem and prevented Christians from living in or coming in pilgrimage to the Holy Land. When, a few years later, Muslims began to attack Constantinople, the Eastern Emperor sent an urgent message to the pope asking that Western Christians come to the aid of their fellow Christians. Pope Urban II convened a council in Clermont in 1095. At the council the pope called on the nobility of Europe to take up the sword and to free the Holy Land. The cry went up, *"Deus vult"*—"God wills it!" Those who accepted this mission wore on their chests a cross of red fabric called *crociati* and thus became known as *crusaders*.

The First Crusade lasted from 1096 to 1099. It resulted in the recapturing of Jerusalem and the setting up of western principalities at Edessa and Antioch, where some of the crusaders remained and established feudal-estates. After the Turks recaptured some of the conquered territory, the Second Crusade commenced in 1147.

The monk Saint Bernard of Clairvaux preached strongly in favor of it, but, because of conflicts between the German and French kings who were leading it, the Second Crusade was a dismal failure. The Third Crusade, in 1190, also encountered difficulty but, thanks to the leadership of Richard the Lionhearted of England, managed to take the city of Jaffa and to arrange for safe passage for Christian pilgrims to Jerusalem. The Fourth Crusade (1200–1204) marked a turning point in the crusades as the recovery of the Holy Land for spiritual reasons became a secondary motive to the economic advantages of having control of the Holy Land. The crusaders attacked and plundered Constantinople. Thousands of Eastern Christians were massacred, and many important religious artifacts were taken.

Two unofficial crusades took place, which also resulted in disaster. Even before the actual armies of the First Crusade arrived in the Holy Land, a *People's Crusade* set out. An eccentric but eloquent preacher named Peter the Hermit called on the simple folk of Europe to go on a crusade of their own. He gathered together a poorly armed and disorganized band who intended to make their way to Jerusalem and set it free. Peter led the people through Asia Minor and into Constantinople. From there, those who had survived the arduous journey went to the Holy Land, where most of them were massacred. Later on in 1212, there was a *Children's Crusade.* Caught up in crusader fever, some people called on children to mount their own crusade. Thousands of youth from all over Western Europe gathered together, believing that with God's help they would simply walk to Jerusalem without resistance. Many children died of starvation and disease as they marched to the sea. Before reaching the Holy Land, many were sold into slavery and were never seen again.

In total, there were eight crusades between 1096 and 1270. They did little to achieve their original objective, which was the return of Christian control of the Holy Land. In fact, the wanton killing that took place during the crusades—of Muslims, Jews, and Eastern Christians alike—caused many people from those traditions to distrust Western Christians and the Latin Church. The popes and other Church leaders who called for crusades never intended the crusaders to massacre people as they did, and they certainly didn't want the churches and religious objects of their fellow Christians to be destroyed. The human weakness, indiscriminate violence, and greed exhibited by many of the crusaders mark the crusades as a regrettable episode in the Christian story.

In May of 2001 while visiting Greece, Pope John Paul II apologized to Orthodox Christians for the "sins of action and omission" by Catholics, including the sacking of Constantinople by crusaders in 1204 that contributed to the collapse of the Byzantine Empire about three centuries later.

Activity

Research the Just War Principles regulating when warfare is justified. Based on each of these principles, evaluate the Crusades.

The Mendicant Orders—Franciscans and Dominicans

In 1219 during the time of the Fifth Crusade, a young man asked the cardinal overseeing the crusading forces in Egypt for permission for he and his companion to go to the Muslim leader Sultan Malik-al-Kamil to seek his conversion to Christianity. The cardinal said that Muslims understood the sword. The only thing to do was nothing but to kill them. Nonetheless, due to the young man's persistence, the cardinal gave in and allowed the two to set out for enemy territory. The two men, Francis of Assisi and Brother Illuminato, were members of a new kind of religious order. They were soon captured and tortured by Muslim forces; but their strange appearance—unarmed, unafraid, and dressed in beggar's robes—peaked the curiosity of the sultan. Francis and the sultan met daily for a month, discussing religion. Neither converted the other, but the sultan was so impressed with Francis that he granted Francis and Illuminato a passport to travel safely to the Holy Land. Francis and the sultan departed from each other as brothers.

"Saint Francis" by Giovanni Bellini, late 1470s. The scene is Mount Alvernia, where Francis received the stigmata.

Who was this Francis who approached the so-called enemies of Christianity in a spirit so different from that of the Crusaders? For centuries, living the religious life meant living as a monk in a specially designated community within a monastery. As we have seen, during the Middle Ages most monasteries functioned within the feudal system in existence at the time.

However, several religious orders emerged that challenged this system. Instead of living apart from the rest of people, the members of these orders lived among the people in towns and cities. Instead of being independent, they attempted to be totally dependent on God's providence. Instead of being self-sufficient like monasteries were, these groups lived on whatever people chose to give them. Therefore, these new religious orders are called *mendicant,* a word that means "to beg." The two men who founded the largest of the mendicant orders were Saint Francis of Assisi and Saint Dominic.

mendicant
religious communities whose members live among people and rely on the charity of others or work at the lowest-paying jobs available

Saint Francis of Assisi

Francis was born in 1182, the son of a wealthy Italian cloth merchant. Francis grew up spoiled and self-indulgent. He was carefree and popular with the other youth of the city, always ready to spend his family's wealth. Then in his twenties, he took part in a battle against a rival city and was captured and imprisoned. On his return to Assisi, he remained ill for about a year and then had what he called his "conversion."

Friars Minor
the community of "little brothers" founded by Saint Francis of Assisi

Later, praying in the rundown chapel of San Damiano outside of Assisi, Francis heard a command from the chapel's crucifix, "Repair my church, which has fallen into disrepair." Francis took the command literally, and set about restoring the little chapel, stone by stone. To get supplies, he sold material and clothing from his father's storehouse. His father was furious and beat him and locked him in a room. Francis escaped and went to the local bishop. When his father came to demand repayment, Francis stripped himself and gave back to his father everything that his father had given him, including his name. The bishop covered Francis in a coarse cloth. He continued to wear this robe as a sign of his new life and his new commitment to living free of all earthly possessions.

As Francis continued his rebuilding of San Damiano, other young men from the town joined him in the project. They formed a community called the **Friars Minor.** A young woman friend, Clare, following Francis's spirit and teachings, and with his help, founded a convent of women. Francis wanted his community to be totally dependent upon God's providence, living in complete poverty and simplicity. By doing so, he radically challenged the growing materialism of his time. For instance, on one occasion he and some of the members of his community were living in an abandoned monastery. A young member of the community came to Francis and said, "I looked for you in your

cell, and you were not there." Francis replied, "I have no cell of my own," and never returned to that room again.

Francis and his followers owned nothing and found food and shelter by begging from the people in the towns through which they traveled. In 1210 Francis appealed in person to the pope, who approved the rule of the group that has come to be called the Franciscans.

One of the messages that Francis taught was the unity of all creation. He referred to the sun as "Brother Sun" and the moon as "Sister Moon." Therefore, people in the ecology movement look to Francis for inspiration.

In 1224 Francis received the *stigmata,* visible wounds on his body similar to those of Jesus on the cross. Francis died in 1226, requesting to be laid on the earthen floor, dressed in the habit his bishop had given him. Two years after his death Francis was declared a saint. The pope said of him that in Francis we find the most perfect example of a true follower of Jesus. His feast day is October 4th.

Youth News

Saint Francis took seriously the common vocation we all have to be caretakers of God's creation. To be made in God's image and likeness means, among other things, being called to cooperate with God in the care of his creation. This means to appreciate the beauty and wonder of nature, to protect and preserve the environment, and to respect human life, to work in partnership with God in building up not only our world but the kingdom of God. One way to do this is to make an effort, especially on Earth Day (April 22), to make a special commitment to help the environment. Another way is to work with Right to Life organizations.

Saint Clare of Assisi

Clare was born at Assisi on July 16, 1194. She was the cofoundress of the Order of Poor Ladies, or Poor Clares. She was from a wealthy family who owned a large castle in Assisi. Even as a young girl she was known for her devotion to prayer and for her desire to grow spiritually. She was eighteen when she heard Francis preach. Inspired by his message, she set out to follow his simple way of life.

Believing God was calling her to be a nun, she ran away from home and, with Francis's help, entered a Benedictine convent. Eventually Francis established a convent for Clare and others who had chosen to join her. Within a few years monasteries of Clare's followers were located in Italy, France, and Germany. The order adopted Francis's way of life—sleeping on the ground, eating only vegetables, and not speaking unless an act of charity necessitated it.

The story is told that in 1234 as the army of Frederick II was attacking Assisi, Clare arose from her sickbed and carried the ciborium containing the Blessed Sacrament to the window of the abbey. She raised the ciborium just as the soldiers were ready to attack the monastary, and the soldiers retreated. It is with reference to this incident that Saint Clare is often portrayed in art bearing a ciborium.

Claire died in 1253, twenty-seven years after the death of the man who had inspired her. Her feast day is August 11.

Saint Dominic

Albigensianism
heresy that believes the physical to be evil and only the spiritual to be good, similar to the beliefs of Manicheism

Domingo de Guzman, now known as Dominic, was born in Spain in 1170. He became a priest and served as a canon of the cathedral in the town of Osma. Well-liked by the community, Dominic was asked to assume many leadership roles. At the time, a major problem facing the Church in Spain and around the city of Albi in southern France was the resurgence of an old heresy that saw matter as evil and spirit as good. The group who held this belief came to be known as Albigensians. The most adamant of the followers of **Albigensianism** were called the *perfects*. They practiced severe mortification, even to the point of starvation and suicide. The less extreme members, called *believers*, did not engage in these practices but sometimes would help the perfects to accomplish the state they sought by murdering them.

Pope Innocent III asked Dominic's bishop to preach to the Albigensians. Dominic, known for his preaching, accompanied the bishop and had some success. However, when the pope's representative was murdered, a crusade against the Albigensians took place and much bloodshed resulted. Dominic attempted to restore peace but eventually withdrew.

With the help of a wealthy benefactor, Dominic received a castle to which he invited those who wanted to join a community dedicated to the conversion of heretics. Like Francis, he wanted his followers to be out on the road, but Dominic's primary objective was to have his followers preach against heresy. After much opposition, Dominic received permission to found the **Order of Preachers**—the Dominicans. Dominic died in 1221 and was canonized in 1234. His feast day is August 8.

As part of the campaign against the Albigensians, the pope called for trials during which the beliefs of the heresy were to be examined and shown to be in error. If heretics persisted in error, they were to be excommunicated from the Church. This process was known as the **Inquisition.** At the time, heresy was seen as an attack against both the state and the Church, and any remedy was considered acceptable. In 1252, in keeping with civil and Church standards of time, Pope Innocent IV permitted the use of torture to seek out truth. Punishment could include public penance and imprisonment. Those who were unyielding were handed over to civil authorities who tortured and killed the supposed heretics. By the end of the fourteenth century, the use of inquisition against heretics declined. We will encounter the term *inquisition* again in the late fifteenth century, after Christian rule was restored in Spain.

Order of Preachers
the religious community founded by Saint Dominic

Inquisition
Church trials established to help curb the spread of heretical doctrines

---

fyi!

During a special Mass at the Vatican on March 12, 2000, designated the *Day of Pardon*, Pope John Paul II took an unprecedented step. As the leader of the Catholic faith he publicly asked God's forgiveness for the sins committed by Catholics over the past 2000 years—including their treatment of Jews, heretics, women, and native peoples.

Activity

1. Use the Internet or another source to research Earth Day. Describe three actions you could take to further the ecology movement and the spirit of Saint Francis.

2. Read about Saints Francis of Assisi and Dominic. Name three themes associated with their movements. Describe ways that you could reflect these themes in your own life.

Review

1. What two actions by the Seljuk Turks helped spark the crusades?

2. What was the intended outcome of the crusades? How successful were the crusades in meeting their objective?

3. What two unofficial crusades took place during the period of the crusades?

4. How were the mendicant religious communities different from monastic communities?

5. How did Saint Francis of Assisi initially interpret the message, "Repair my church"?

6. What is the name of the religious community founded by Saint Francis?

7. Against what heresy did Saint Dominic preach? What were the beliefs of this heresy?

8. What is the name of the religious community founded by Saint Dominic?

Conclusion

During the Middle Ages in Europe, Christianity touched every aspect of life. The Church was intimately connected with society and political decision making. The period saw practices that opened the door to corruption in the Church. It also saw exceptional saintliness. The beautiful and the holy blended together during the Middle Ages, and great cathedrals and great works of art resulted. Christianity expanded to include almost all of Europe, but for the first time we find an official large-scale division within Christianity as Churches of the East and the West severed their ties. Life was hard for the medieval Christian, but the Church continued to carry the message of hope offered by Jesus. Because of the Church, people saw that beyond their temporal trials, eternal life awaited them.

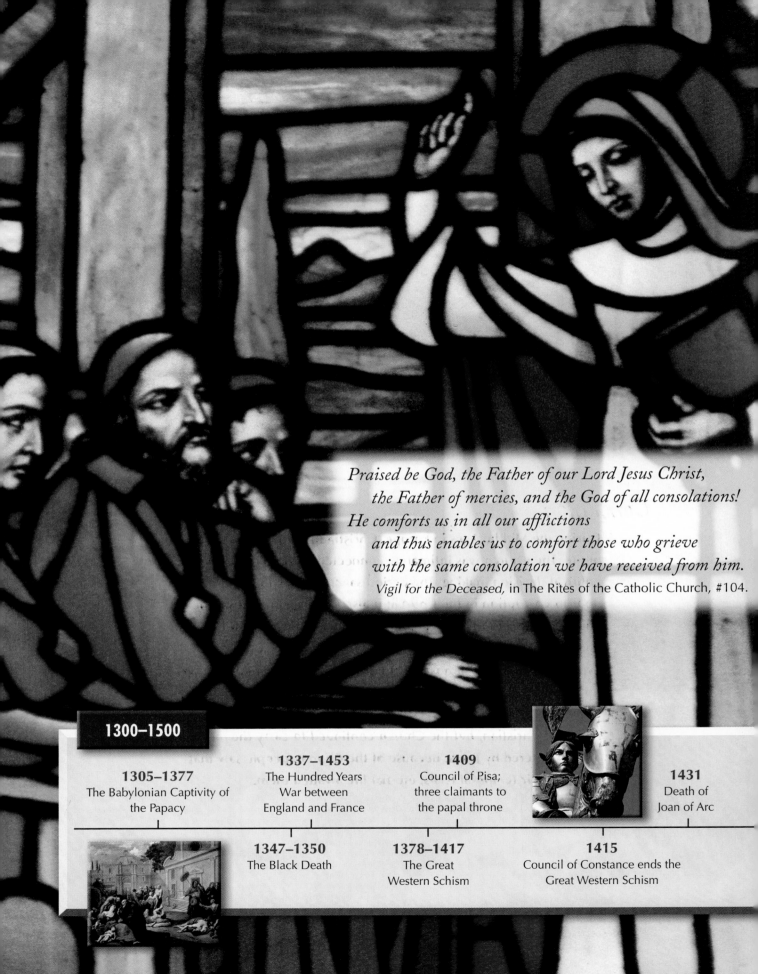

Praised be God, the Father of our Lord Jesus Christ,
the Father of mercies, and the God of all consolations!
He comforts us in all our afflictions
and thus enables us to comfort those who grieve
with the same consolation we have received from him.

Vigil for the Deceased, in The Rites of the Catholic Church, #104.

1300–1500

1305–1377
The Babylonian Captivity of
the Papacy

1337–1453
The Hundred Years
War between
England and France

1409
Council of Pisa;
three claimants to
the papal throne

1431
Death of
Joan of Arc

1347–1350
The Black Death

1378–1417
The Great
Western Schism

1415
Council of Constance ends the
Great Western Schism

FROM DISORDER TO BEAUTY AND HOPE

The Road to the Renaissance

CHAPTER OVERVIEW

- The power of the papacy is weakened during the period of the Avignon popes and the Great Western Schism.

- The Black Death devastates Europe and the Church.

- Medieval mystics foster spirituality based on their experiences of God's love.

- The fall of Constantinople leads to a power shift in the Eastern Church.

- Spanish rulers reclaim their country for Christianity and introduce the religion to new lands.

- The Renaissance ushers in a period of renewed creative and artistic activity.

1453
Fall of Constantinople

1469
Queen Isabella and King Ferdinand of Spain unite their kingdoms

1492
Expulsion of Muslims and Jews from Spain

1498
Death of Savonarola

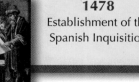

1455
Invention of the printing press

1478
Establishment of the Spanish Inquisition

1492
Columbus discovers America

1498
Missionaries arrive in India

Have you ever had a day when everything seemed to go wrong? Europe and the Church went through such a period beginning in the fourteenth century. Certainly the Church has always faced conflicts and crises. However, during the late Middle Ages, the pope went from being perhaps the strongest person in all of Europe to being challenged by a new generation of rulers and populations who placed loyalty to nation over loyalty to Church. Thus the ideal of a unified Christendom, in which the pope would preside over all the people of Europe and would guide them in living the Christian life, disintegrated into nation fighting nation, or one city fighting another. One war, between England and France, actually lasted nearly a hundred years. The papacy itself was caught up in conflicts resulting from pursuing political self-interests. (Imagine if one of your teachers got on the intercom, condemned the principal as a fraud, and claimed to be running the school from now on!)

Even more devastating than the power struggles of this century was the "Black Death"—the bubonic plague—which ravaged Europe. One-third of the population of the continent died because of it. (Imagine what your school would be like if a third of everyone, including teachers and staff, were suddenly gone.) Nonetheless, during this period, a number of women and men attained levels of spiritual experience that have helped shape Catholic spirituality ever since. Also toward the end of this period, a flowering of artistic creativity emerged from which we have some of the finest religious works of art ever produced.

Before We Begin . . .

Do you identify more with your nation or with your religion? What possible conflicts might there be between the values and interests of your nation and those of your religion? How would you address such conflicts?

DECLINE OF UNITY

Church-State Conflicts

jubilee year
a special year of prayer and pilgrimage in the Catholic Church that takes place every fifty years; also called a holy year

If you would ever be fortunate enough to travel to Rome, you would marvel at the magnificent churches and works of art found there. Some of that artwork was created for a special celebration held in 1300 when Pope Boniface VIII called for the first **jubilee year.** All during 1300, thousands of pilgrims went to Rome to receive the special graces associated with the celebration and also to enjoy the beauty and grandeur that the city had to offer. Even in the midst of this display of Rome's glory and papal power, forces were at work aimed at diminishing the authority of the pope, at least in secular matters.

We may presume that the world has always been divided into various nations. Actually, the division of the world into separate nation-states is a fairly recent occurrence. Recall that under Constantine, and later under Charlemagne, there was an empire which spread across many ethnic and language groups. Although often in tension, leaders of Church and state ruled the empire together, following their understanding of Christian principles.

Late in the thirteenth century, however, rulers of specific nations started to see themselves as solely responsible for what happened in their respective countries. For instance, the kings of France and England decided that members of the clergy were obligated to pay taxes to the crown. The English king said the clergy would have no protection of law until they paid taxes. The pope responded that secular princes could not tax members of the clergy. In 1302 Pope Boniface VIII issued a **papal bull** called *Unam Sanctam* (literally "one holy"), stating that all rulers are subject to the pope and that it was "necessary for salvation" for every human to be subject to the pope. The two kings were not pleased with the pope's pronouncement. King Philip IV of France sent soldiers to arrest him. Although some people from his hometown in Anagni rescued Pope Boniface, he died a month later. Boniface's successor served as pope for only eight months, and then no one was chosen for almost a year. Of the sixteen cardinals at the time, none of them wanted to elect someone who would continue the conflict with the French and English kings.

papal bull
a formal decree by a pope sealed with a round leaden seal (in Latin, *bulla*)

fyi!

A jubilee year is a biblical concept. The Sabbath, the "seventh day," is a day of prayer. The fiftieth year is the year after seven times seven years.

> Of the one and only church there is one body and one head, not two heads, like a monster—namely Christ, and Christ's vicar is Peter, and Peter's successor. . . . The temporal authority must be subject to spiritual authority. . . . For this authority, although given to a man and exercised by a man, is not human, but rather divine, given at God's mouth to Peter and established on a rock for him . . . furthermore we declare, state, define and pronounce that it is altogether necessary for every human creature to be subject to the Roman pontiff.
>
> From "Unam Sanctam" in *How to Read Church History,* Vol. 1, (New York: Crossroad, 1995), 173.

View of Avignon, France, seat of the papacy from 1309 to 1377.

The Avignon Papacy

Finally, the cardinals reached a compromise that they hoped would appease both the English and the French. They chose an English archbishop—archbishop of Bordeaux—who agreed to be crowned at Lyons in France. However, the archbishop did not want to settle in French territory. Suffering from cancer at the time, he accepted the hospitality of Dominican friars in the town of Avignon in the kingdom of Naples. His decision had an important effect on the Church because his successors also decided to stay in Avignon. For the next seventy years the pope, the bishop of Rome, would not live in Rome. Instead, a series of seven popes lived in Avignon. Rome, which had been the physical and spiritual center of the Church, lost its political and moral clout.

The Italian poet Petrarch referred to the period from 1309 to 1377 as the **Babylonian Captivity of the Papacy,** equating it to the years, described in the Bible, when the Israelites had been forced to live in exile in Babylon. In time, one of the Avignon popes purchased a stretch of land in Avignon and built a papal palace. Most of the popes during this period did good works and continued reforming Church structures. For instance, Pope Benedict XII ordered all bishops and priests who were "hangers on" at the papal court to go home and serve their people. He called for religious communities to meet every three years to examine their lifestyle. Some popes made major improvements to the city of Rome, even though they never went there.

Babylonian Captivity of the Papacy
period during which the pope resided in Avignon, (France), in the Kingdom of Naples

Although most people of the time believed that the pope belonged in Rome, having the pope residing in Avignon was not such a crazy idea. For one thing, Avignon was a more peaceful place than the bustling city of Rome. Second, Avignon was, or at least became, papal territory. Third, it was closer than Rome was to many of the major centers of Christianity in Western Europe. And finally, the popes of the time and the majority of cardinals were French. On occasion, the issue of the pope's returning to Rome was discussed, but nothing permanent came of it. Two women of the time who were recognized for their holiness, Saints Bridget of Sweden and Catherine of Siena, implored the pope to return to Rome. Perhaps due to their influence, in 1377 the newly elected Pope Gregory XI did move to Rome. He died three months later.

Popes and Anti-Popes

Of the sixteen cardinals who gathered in Rome to elect the pope after the brief reign of Gregory XI, nine were French. The people of Rome were incensed by the French dominance. Marching around the building where the cardinals were meeting, the people demanded a Roman or at least an Italian pope. The cardinals chose an Italian archbishop who lived in Bari, which was a distance from Rome. Since he couldn't get to the city quickly, the cardinals dressed one of their own as pope and presented him to the people to calm the crowd. Then the cardinals fled the city.

When the elected pope arrived in Rome in April 1378, he took the name Urban VI. The people of Rome accepted him, and in time the cardinals of the Church returned to Rome and pledged their obedience to him. At first, the new pope seemed to be a good choice. He had a great deal of experience in Church and state affairs, was a capable administrator, and was recognized as an honest man. However, in a few weeks another side of his character surfaced, disturbing some of the cardinals. That is, he made quick decisions and would not listen to advice. He criticized the decisions of others, especially those of the cardinals. Historians suggest that he was mentally unstable, volatile, and abusive.

All the cardinals except one left Rome and met in northern Italy. They announced that, since they were under duress when they chose Urban as pope, his election was unlawful. The cardinals "elected" another man, a French cardinal named Roger of Geneva, to be "pope." He attempted to take the papal throne by force but was repelled by the people of Rome. Roger then took up residence in Avignon and claimed to be the rightful pope.

Many people, including Saint Catherine of Siena, pointed out that the cardinals had accepted Urban VI as pope, had celebrated Holy Week liturgy with him as pope, and had pledged their obedience to him. Therefore, there was no question that he was the validly elected pope. However, the cardinals would not back down. Pope Urban named new cardinals and excommunicated the old ones, including the cardinal claiming to be pope and living in Avignon. The Avignon "pope" in turn excommunicated Pope Urban and his followers. Thus the world found itself with two claimants to the papal throne. Secular leaders and the common people began to take sides with one or the other. This situation, in which two people claimed to be pope at the same time, lasted thirty-eight years and is called the **Great Western Schism.**

Great Western Schism
the period from 1378 to 1417 during which two and then three rival people claimed papal authority

Pope Celestine V

Just before the period of the Avignon papacy and the Great Western Schism, something happened that caused Church leaders to be cautious about papal elections. Beginning in 1292, cardinals spent twenty-six months unable to decide upon a pope. Then a cardinal shared a communication he received from a hermit monk named Peter Marone, warning the cardinals that God would punish them unless they elected a pope immediately. The cardinal suggested that perhaps this was God's way of telling them to choose the hermit himself. Peter had a reputation for holiness, and he founded a community that worked with those who were poor and sick. The cardinals elected Peter to be pope. When he heard the news, Peter was stunned but was prevailed upon to accept the position. As Pope Celestine V, Peter was a disaster since he knew nothing of administration and decision making. Instead, he took whatever advice was given him. Being a holy and righteous man, Peter knew that he was not a good pope. Praying for guidance, after only five months he abdicated the papacy.

Resolving the Schism

The first attempt to end the Great Western Schism took place in 1409 when leaders of both Church and state called for a council to be held at Pisa, Italy. The council deposed both claimants to the papal throne and elected Peter of Candia to be pope. He lived only a short time thereafter, but the cardinals he had named chose the next "pope," who took the name John XXIII. Neither of the two previous claimants to the papacy recognized the right of a council to be convened without papal approval, and so they did not resign. Now the Church had *three* people claiming to be pope: Gregory XII in Rome, Benedict XIII in Avignon, and John XXIII.

Finally, in 1414 the Holy Roman Emperor at the time forced John XXIII to convene a council at Constance, Italy. This council was well attended and lasted for over three years. During this time, the legitimate pope, Gregory XII in Rome, offered his resignation but soon after died. Benedict XIII in Avignon refused to resign. He was denounced by the council, accused of heresy and schism, and went into exile still believing he was pope. The man who went by "Pope John XXIII" tried to flee but was stopped and forced to resign. He then retired quietly and served as a bishop in Italy. In November of 1417, the council declared the papal throne to be empty. Cardinals met and elected one of their own, who took the name Pope Martin V. For the first time in forty years, one person was universally recognized as the pope and as the rightful successor to Peter. The Great Western Schism was over.

The popes who served at Rome continued as the true popes during the thirty-eight years of the schism. Those who called themselves pope but resided in Avignon during this period are not recognized as valid popes and are therefore known as anti-popes. However, into the modern era it was not completely clear whether the two popes selected by the Council of Pisa were valid. As you recall, one of those two men took the name "Pope John XXIII." Then, in 1958 when Cardinal Giuseppe Roncalli was elected pope, he announced that he would take the name John. The cardinal-deacon said to him, "You will be John XXIV." The pope-elect corrected him, "No, I will be John XXIII." Thus ended any question about the status of the fifteenth-century John XXIII.

CHURCH-RECOGNIZED POPES DURING THE GREAT WESTERN SCHISM	
Urban VI	April 8, 1378–October 15, 1389
Boniface IX	November 2, 1389–October 1, 1404
Innocent VII	October 17, 1404–November 6, 1406
Gregory XII	November 30, 1406–July 4, 1415
Martin V	November 11, 1417–February 20, 1431

Pope or Council—Who Has the Greater Authority?

conciliarism
belief that Church councils have greater authority than the pope

It took two Church councils to straighten out the Great Western Schism. Some of the leaders gathered at these meetings proposed that councils therefore had more authority in the Church than the pope and that councils be held on a regular basis. This position is known as **conciliarism.** A council did meet a number of years after the schism ended, but it dragged on without settling anything. Conciliarism proved to be so chaotic that after this period, Church leaders hesitated to call another council. In the next century, the Reformation progressed beyond any hope of reconciliation before Church leaders called for a full council—the Council of Trent—to address the issues.

Discussion

The Catholic Church continues to be a community that transcends national loyalties. Apart from its religious value, why is it beneficial to belong to an organization that spans the globe?

Saint Catherine of Siena

We know that after a thirty-year-old Italian woman met with the pope in Avignon, he returned the papacy to Rome. Who was this person who could convince a pope to move from the place that had been home to the papacy for seventy years? Catherine of Siena was one of twenty-five children of the Benincasa family. As early as five years old, she had profound spiritual experiences. Such experiences continued throughout her life. The road to holiness, however, was not an easy one for Catherine. For three years she struggled with doubts and demonic visions. This dry spell ended with the help of, in her words, laughter. She experienced a profound sense of union with Christ.

Catherine worked with those who were sick, including plague victims and condemned prisoners. She also gave her attention to broader affairs. She wrote hundreds of letters to the pope and other religious and secular leaders offering them advice. Given her reputation for holiness, her advice was not easily dismissed. At one point in her life, she experienced a profound sense of union with Christ. Toward the end of her life, she wrote about her religious experiences. Because of the impact that her writings have had on the Church, Catherine was declared a Doctor of the Church in 1970. She is also the patroness of Italy.

Review

1. What is a jubilee year? When was the first jubilee year held?

2. What action by the English and French kings created a conflict with Pope Boniface VIII? What was the pope's response?

3. To what does the term *Babylonian Captivity of the Papacy* refer?

4. What two saints were instrumental in convincing the pope to return to Rome?

5. What action by the majority of cardinals at the time brought on the Great Western Schism?

6. How was the Great Western Schism resolved?

7. How did the pope elected in 1958 resolve the question of the status of the earlier so-called Pope John XXIII?

8. What position on Church authority is held by conciliarism?

THE BLACK DEATH

During the time of the Avignon papacy, a disaster struck Europe that would leave its mark for years to come. The bubonic plague, known as the **Black Death,** began in 1347. The first outbreak lasted for three years. During that time, one-third of Europe's population died. The plague, probably carried by rats aboard ships, first appeared in the Italian seaport of Genoa. Fleas on the rats carried the plague to humans. When it spread to Venice and Florence, 100,000 people died in each city. Siena lost 80,000 people, four-fifths of its population. The French city of Marseilles lost 57,000 people, including its bishop and most of its clergy. In Paris, 80,000 people died in less than four months.

Although the plague abated during the winter of 1350, it surfaced again in England and France between 1361 and 1400. Each time, large portions of the population died. European life was never the same.

Besides the unbelievable number of deaths, the bubonic plague caused immeasurable suffering. It caused the organs of infected persons, including their tongues, to swell. Since they could not swallow, people often died slowly of starvation. So many died that burial was impossible. Entire towns and villages fell into ruin as nobles and townsfolk alike died and left no structures for organization, government, or service. In many towns, people with no experience in leadership were called upon to oversee community life under extremely trying circumstances.

WWW. To follow the route of the Black Death with text, maps, visuals, and an audio tour, visit **www.discovery. com/stories/history /blackdeath/ blackdeath.html**

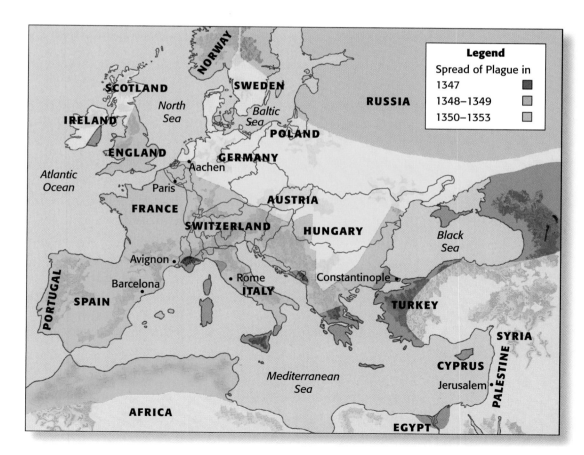

"Cardinal Chige Caring for Plaque Victims," eighteenth century painting

The Impact on the Church and Religious Life

Church leaders attempted to mandate sanitation policies, and many religious communities took charge of tending those who were sick and burying those who died. However, so many towns were left without any priests that large numbers of people received no consolation of the sacraments in their time of greatest need.

Even before the plague, there had been no buildings or formal processes set aside for the training of priests. If a priest knew someone he thought would make a good priest, he invited the young man to come and reside with him. The young man might be his son, a student, or just a member of the village. The priest taught the younger man some Latin, whatever other academic subjects he thought would be helpful, and how to say Mass and celebrate the sacraments. When the older priest became ill or died, the younger priest took his place.

With the sudden death of so many clergy during the time of the plague, many students of the priesthood who knew only the basic parts of the Mass and sacraments were left without mentors. Because the people wanted the Mass and sacraments to be available to them, they didn't care if the priest was poorly trained. The young priest might perform the Mass with a combination of poor Latin and superstitious gestures. Sacramental events were at times little more than pre-Christian rituals. And the people received little theology that dealt with a loving God and the heart of the Christian message.

When the plague spread to England, many abbeys and monasteries lost large numbers of monks. Because they needed many people to function, monasteries fell into disrepair. Monasticism never again returned to the level it had reached during the earlier Middle Ages.

Two responses to the plague were a search for scapegoats and a search for miracle cures. All kinds of explanations were put forward for the plague, from claims that the end of the world was coming to claims that enemies were poisoning the well water. As has happened a number of times in history, some people blamed Jews for the plague. Prior to this time, laws had been enacted that required Jews to wear distinctive clothing, and restricted them from working the land. Jews, therefore, generally lived apart from their Christian neighbors as a separate and distinct group. When Jewish people in the Avignon area were accused of spreading the plague and were being persecuted, the pope opened up safe havens for Jews living in the area. The pope also extended sanctuary in Germany to Jews blamed for the plague there. Nonetheless, hundreds of Jewish communities were destroyed by people who suspected Jews of spreading the plague.

Many people tried all kinds of superstitious practices in an attempt to ward off the disease. Some superstitions had no relationship to Christianity whatsoever; some were even appeals to witchcraft. Other people began to say that the plague was a punishment from God for human sinfulness. As a result, Christian practices or sacred objects themselves, such as relics, were treated in a superstitious manner.

During the plague, religion focused on death and the afterlife. Frightening images of hell and purgatory abounded. Many people wanted to ensure that Masses and prayers would be offered for them after they died so that they would be spared the torments of purgatory and enter heaven quickly.

Even today we do not know why the plague stopped, but we do know that it caused great disruption to Church life and European society. That disruption also helped set the stage for the Reformation, which we will study in our next chapter.

Activity

1. During the time of the plague, death was often depicted as a leering skeleton holding an hourglass that has almost run out of sand or as a tall figure dressed in black hood and cape with a sickle in his hand. Create a cast of characters and descriptions for a play or movie on the plagues. Include Death, the Church, and Church members.

2. People of the Middle Ages saw power in the holiness exhibited by the saints, and they wanted to tap into that holiness. Anything associated with a saint was treated with great reverence and was also viewed as possessing special power. These items are called relics and have played a role in Christianity from the time of the martyrs. Write a report on the use of relics in Catholic spirituality. As part of your report, address the following questions:

   • What would you describe as an appropriate attitude toward relics?

   • What would you consider to be a misuse of relics?

   • Is there still a place for relics in today's spirituality?

Review

1. As a result of the plague, what was the death toll in Europe?

2. What effect did the plague have on the quality of the celebration of the Mass and sacraments in Europe?

3. What group underwent persecution because they were blamed for the plague?

From Disorder to Beauty and Hope

MEDIEVAL MYSTICISM

This icon presents God as Sophia (Wisdom) with the virtues of faith, hope, and charity.

Even in the midst of the horrible devastation caused by the plague, some Christians were certain that in the end all would be well. Where did their confidence come from? The answer was **mysticism**—the strong, tangible experiences of communion with God. Mysticism plays a role in most religious traditions. Often it emerges during particularly desperate times when some people reach unusually deep levels of communion with God. According to Saint Thomas Aquinas, "Mysticism is the knowledge of God through experience." That is, while theology attempts to *know about* God, mysticism seeks an *experience of* God. By way of analogy, mysticism is like directly experiencing a beautiful sunset as opposed to understanding a scientific explanation of a sunset.

The late Middle Ages produced a number of Christian mystics. Some of them wrote about their experiences in a way that gives us a hint of how they perceived God. One popular preacher of the time who also wrote about mysticism was the German Dominican friar Meister Eckhart (1260–1328). One of the most important contributions that Eckhart made to our understanding of God is sometimes called **negative theology.** Eckhart reminds us that God completely surpasses any image or concept that we might have of God. For instance, the Bible says that "God is love." Eckhart would point out that God's love actually goes beyond any notion of love that we might have. While we may constantly attempt a description of God, Eckhart wants us to remember that the mystery of God cannot be confined to or contained by our limited capacity to comprehend the mystery. Eckhart challenges us not to settle for a God that we can "know about" and pushes us to be open to an "experience of" God who is indescribable Mystery.

Eckhart's ideas certainly stretched the Christian imagination. Some people questioned whether Eckhart's ideas were heresy. Eckhart denied that any of his teachings were heresy, but he was summoned to the papal court in Avignon to explain his ideas. He died before he had a chance to state his case. Even so, the papal court did rule that some of his teachings were in fact heretical. A number of Dominicans, in good standing with the Church, followed Eckhart and continued to advocate the importance of experiencing God's presence within them and around them.

A Mystic Describes God's Love

Mysticism is open to everyone, not just monks, nuns, or people who are educated. One mystic, an Englishwoman who lived alone in a room attached to her parish church, had mystical experiences that she called simply **showings.** We know her as Julian of Norwich (1342–1424). As is typical of mystics, she speaks of being overwhelmed by God's love. The language she uses is not intellectual but rather emotional; it is the language of love. She refers to God in feminine terms and even calls Jesus our true mother who carries us in the womb and nourishes us like a mother. Here is her account of a "showing" that she received during one of her mystical experiences.

I saw that he [Jesus] is to us everything which is good and comforting for our help. He is our clothing, who wraps and enfolds us for love, embraces us and shelters us, surrounds us for his love, which is so tender that he may never desert us. And so in this sight I saw that he is everything which is good, as I understood. And in this he showed me something small, no bigger than a hazelnut, lying in the palm of my hand, as it seemed to me, and it was round like a ball. I looked at it with the eye of my understanding and thought: What can this be? I was amazed that it could last, for I thought that because of its littleness it would suddenly have fallen into nothing. And I was answered in my understanding: It lasts and always will, because God loves it; and thus everything has being through the love of God.

In this little thing I saw three properties. The first is that God made it, the second is that God loves it, the third is that God preserves it. But what did I see in it? It is that God is the Creator and the protector and the lover.

Patrick V. Reid, *Readings in Western Religious Thought,* Vol. II (New York: Paulist Press, 1995), 270–71.

The words that Julian uses for her encounter with Christ are words of love: He wraps around us, enfolds us, embraces us, and shelters us tenderly. She sees herself as very small and insignificant, practically nothing—like a hazelnut. And yet, even in her littleness, she experiences herself as created and loved by God. She sees that she will also be preserved forever by God. The message expressed in this passage is basic Christian theology. However, actually to *experience* the message is a special gift from God. Such is the gift of the mystics.

Activity

1. Describe activities offered by Catholicism that are aimed at helping you experience God's presence in your life. What do these experiences tell us about God?

2. Have you ever felt God's presence in your life in a particularly strong way? If so, using a creative form of your choice, describe something of the experience.

Review

1. What role does mysticism play in religion?

2. Describe Meister Eckhart's negative theology.

3. How did Julian use the image of a hazelnut to describe her relationship with God?

Joan of Arc—Maid of Orleans

A person from this time period who fascinates Catholics and others is Saint Joan of Arc. Born in the small village of Domremy in 1412, Joan worked on her family's farm. Although she could neither read nor write, Joan knew all her prayers by heart. As a child she loved to hear stories of the saints.

One day, at the age of thirteen, she heard bells ringing and saw a bright light descend upon her in the garden. She knelt down, and a voice told her not to be afraid. The voice identified itself as that of the archangel Michael. The angel told her that soon Saint Catherine of Alexandria and Saint Margaret of Antioch would visit her and guide her on what she was to do. Over the next five years, these saints appeared to Joan about three times a week and encouraged her in her spiritual life. Joan vowed to be like them—to remain a virgin and to be open to whatever God wanted her to do. The local priests, with whom she shared these visions, encouraged her in her spiritual development.

In time Joan came to learn that three tasks were being entrusted to her: She was to save the city of Orleans from its siege by the English; she was to arrange for the crowning of the dauphin, Charles, as king of France at the cathedral in Reims; and she was to drive the English from French soil.

Just a teenager at the time, Joan went to Chinon where the dauphin lived and said simply, "I have been sent from God to bring help to the kingdom and to yourself." After many delays and examinations, Charles gave Joan permission to lead his troops in an attempt to seize Orleans back for the French. When she was successful, Charles agreed to go to Reims and be crowned as king. On the way Joan led the troops in a series of victories. She then asked Charles to allow her to drive out the English, but Charles was hesitant. Instead of going to Paris, the capital, he took his court to Gien. There Joan was forced to await the king's pleasure. While waiting she was told by her voices that the enemy would capture her. On May 23, 1430, she fell into the hands of the Burgundians, who later sold her to the English.

Joan's captors wanted to kill her but were afraid to do so. Instead, they turned her over to an ecclesiastical (Church) court. Here she could be tried as a heretic for claiming to hear saints speaking to her. Joan resisted all manner of abuse and torture for several months. At last, exhausted and abandoned by her friends, she "submitted to the Church" and denied her voices. She was condemned to life in prison. Within days, she retracted her submission, whereupon she was handed over to the secular leaders as a relapsed heretic. On May 30, 1431, she was burned at the stake in Rouen. Almost immediately, many people began to question the validity of the trial, and in 1456 the trial and its verdict were annulled. In 1920 Joan was declared Saint Joan of Arc, the Maid of Orleans and patroness of France.

EVER-CHANGING GEOGRAPHY

The fifteenth century saw the beginning of more transformations in the geography of Christianity. One event, the discovery of the Americas by Europeans, introduced whole new continents to Christianity. During this time the fate of Christianity in many areas was linked to the fortunes of Islam. In the East, Muslim Turks brought an end to the Roman Empire. In the West, Christian rulers regained control over all of Spain after nearly eight hundred years of an Islamic presence there.

The Fall of Constantinople

One issue that arose again after the Great Western Schism ended was the relationship between the Western and Eastern Churches. By 1386 Ottoman Turks had encircled and conquered all but a small area around Constantinople in the Eastern Roman Empire. Finally, in 1439 a delegation from the East, including the emperor himself, came to Florence to meet with the pope and other Church leaders. The emperor believed that the pope was still in a position to call for a crusade and to come to his aid against the Turks. Desperate for help, the Eastern delegates agreed to all matters that had been in dispute between the two groups, including the *filioque* clause in the creed and the supremacy of the pope. All participants signed a statement called the **Union of Florence,** which would have officially ended the split between Eastern and Western Christianity.

However, when the Eastern delegates returned home, their members condemned their giving in to the Latins. A mob attacked Hagia Sophia, the great church in Constantinople, and rejected the clergy who had signed the Union. When the head of the Russian Church arrived home wearing a Roman cross, he was imprisoned. His fellow bishops condemned his action as treason and elected a new patriarch. This was the beginning of a separate Russian Orthodox Church.

Thus, the union between East and West failed, and the Eastern Empire was left to its own resources in combating the Turks. In 1453 the final siege of Constantinople began. There were only 7,000 defenders against an army of 80,000. The siege lasted eight weeks. On May 29 the city fell, marking the end of the Roman Empire. Soon after the fall of Constantinople, Russian rulers began to look upon their capital, Moscow, as the Third Rome. The rulers even began to refer to themselves as *czar,* meaning Caesar. From 1500 on, the Russian Orthodox Church became a leading voice in the world for Eastern or Orthodox Christianity. The rich tradition of Eastern Christian spirituality remained strong in Russia until the communist takeover of the country in the twentieth century.

Union of Florence
a short-lived agreement between leaders of Eastern and Western Christianity on certain doctrines of faith

The Restoration of Christianity to Spain and Its Introduction to the New World

Spain had been a divided country ever since Muslims took control of it in the eighth century. In the fifteenth century that control was limited and growing weaker. In 1469 two Christian rulers of sections of Christian-controlled Spain were married—Isabella and Ferdinand. They determined to rid Spain of heretics and of anyone who was not a Christian. Leaders of Church and state viewed being Christian and being a loyal subject as one and the same. In 1478 Queen Isabella and King Ferdinand asked the pope to reinstitute the Inquisition in order to investigate the sincerity of people who had converted to Christianity from Judaism or Islam.

Although the pope issued strict guidelines about how to conduct these trials, many abuses occurred and many people were tortured and killed in Spain in the late fifteenth century. This was the **Spanish Inquisition.** To correct abuses, in 1483 the pope appointed the Dominican Tomas de Torquemada as Grand Inquisitor to oversee all inquisitions in Spain. It is estimated that under Torquemada at least two thousand Jews were burnt as unrepentant sinners. Frequently, their property was confiscated by their accusers.

Spanish Inquisition
the process in Spain for identifying and punishing non-Christians and those said to be heretics

In 1492 Isabella and Ferdinand gained control of all of Spain, ending Muslim rule in the southern part of the country. In the same year, they expelled all Jews from Spain. Actually, Jews had a choice: they could either convert to Christianity or leave the country. Dangers and suffering accompanied either option. Of those who left the country, many died en route to Morocco or elsewhere. Some ended up being sold into slavery.

conversos
Jews and Muslims who converted to Christianity, either willingly or unwillingly, following the Christian takeover of Spain

Jews and Muslims who converted to Christianity were called *conversos*. According to traditional Christian teaching, once people are baptized and become members of the Church, they should be welcomed into the fold and treated as brothers and sisters in Christ. However, in the atmosphere of distrust that existed in Spain at the time, some older Christians suspected that the new converts were not sincere in their motives for entering the Church. Some newly converted Jews were accused of "Judaizing" Christianity and of trying to subvert the Church, now from within. Thus, some of the *conversos* were subject to the trials and tortures of the Inquisition. Although in time its implementation subsided, the Spanish Inquisition did not officially end until 1834.

As you know, 1492 is significant for another reason. The Spanish rulers commissioned an Italian sailor to seek a western passage to India and the East. When Christopher Columbus arrived instead in the Americas, a whole new chapter in the story of Christianity began. We will look at that story in depth in chapter nine.

As part of Jubilee Year 2000 activities, Pope John Paul II asked forgiveness for mistreatment of Jews throughout history:

God of our fathers, you chose Abraham and his descendants to bring your name to the nations: We are deeply saddened by the behavior of those who in the course of history have caused these children of yours to suffer, and asking your forgiveness, we wish to commit ourselves to genuine brotherhood with the people of the covenant. We ask this through Christ our Lord. Amen.

Pope John Paul II during *"Service Requesting Pardon"* as part of Jubilee Year 2000 (Origins 29:40): 647.

Activity

The Spanish Inquisition resembles something of the spirit behind the anti-communist U.S. congressional hearings of the 1950s and the later movement in the United States to make flag burning a crime. Research the tensions that existed in fifteenth-century Spain that led to the strong measures undertaken by the Inquisition. Are there groups in the United States today who might be considered dangerous and subversive either by government leaders or by other people? If so, explain why they might be viewed in a negative light.

Review

1. What crisis led Eastern leaders to seek union with the Western Church?

2. What was the Union of Florence? Why did it fail to hold?

3. How and when did the Roman Empire end?

4. Which country saw itself as inheriting the legacy of Rome after the fall of Constantinople?

5. How did the Isabella and Ferdinand go about insuring the Christianization of their nation?

6. What discovery in 1492 opened new lands to Christianity?

THE RENAISSANCE

The Renaissance was more than a movement; it was a happening. From the birth of the poet Petrarch in 1304 to the death of Titian in 1576, Italy experienced a flowering of artistic expression that left an indelible mark on that country and the world. That the Renaissance began in present-day Italy is understandable because the area had relative political stability. There was no nation of Italy until 1870; instead, it was a collection of city-states. These city-states vied with each other for economic superiority, but at the time of the Renaissance each was having great success. For this reason they had the resources to endow the arts. Scholars, poets, craftsmen, and artists were supported by patrons such as the Medici family of Florence, the doges (mayors) of Venice, the Storza family of Milan, and the popes of Rome.

The word *renaissance* means "rebirth" or "revival." It has come to mean the humanistic revival of classical art, architecture, literature, and learning that originated in Italy in the fourteenth century and spread from there to the rest of Europe.

While the spiritual was the point of focus in the earlier Middle Ages, the Renaissance emphasized broader human endeavors. For this reason the Renaissance is known as a time of **humanism.** Sculpture and art glorified the human form, much as classical Greek art had done. However, the Renaissance did not reject the spiritual dimension of human life. Just as Aquinas had used Greek thought to help people understand Christianity better, so Renaissance artists and thinkers used styles inspired by the classical period to bring people closer to God. Renaissance poets and artists recognized that the source of all beauty was God, and they used their talents to create beauty that evoked a sense of the sacred. Nonetheless, the Renaissance focused on humanity and fostered an overall sense of human creativity and ingenuity.

humanism
during the Renaissance, an emphasis on the human in intellectual and artistic activity

fyi!

A few days after the completion of *La Pietà*, Michelangelo moved among the visitors to hear their comments. He overheard one person saying that the sculpture was the work of a rival of Michelangelo's. Later that night, Michelangelo returned and chiseled his name on the statue. It is the only work that he ever signed.

La Pietà
Michelangelo's statue of Mary holding the crucified Jesus

Leonardo da Vinci (1452–1519) was a model "Renaissance man"—an artist, scientist, inventor, and all-around scholar. For instance, da Vinci envisioned flying machines long before the invention of the airplane. Michelangelo (1475–1564), who was also a fine poet, showed his great abilities as a sculptor in the statue of young David that he did for the city of Florence. Later, in 1499 he signed a contract in which he promised to create "the most beautiful work in marble that exists today in Rome." The result was *La Pietà*—a magnificent and moving statue of the dead Jesus lying in the arms of his mother. This beautiful work stands today inside Saint Peter's Basilica in Rome.

Pope Julius II also called upon Michelangelo to paint his private chapel, the Sistine Chapel, in the Vatican. At first Michelangelo refused because he saw himself as a sculptor, not a painter. However, he finally agreed and spent almost four years seventy feet above the chapel floor painting the ceiling. The painting he did remains even today the most magnificent fresco ever produced.

Activity

1. Design your own work of art or choose the work of another that you believe conveys a sense of the sacred. In writing, explain why.

2. Find a book by Sister Wendy Beckett or watch a PBS portion of one of her videos. Write about a work of art that she believes conveys a sense of the sacred. Explain her reasons.

3. Choose one of the depictions of Jesus from *Jesus 2000* and tell why it has special meaning for you.

Dissenting Opinions during the Renaissance

The controversies over the papacy and the flourishing of artistic expression that took place during the Renaissance influenced people's attitudes toward Christianity and the Church as well. For instance, some people began to question structures and beliefs that had been at the center of European society. This questioning reached a high point during the period of the Reformation. However, over one hundred years before the Reformation certain thinkers posed viewpoints that would take hold among Protestants. John Wyclif, an English theologian (1324–1384), proposed that Scripture is more important than Tradition for Christian teaching. Perhaps in response to the battles going on among Church leaders, Wyclif also taught that all Christians together were the Church and that the Church has no head except Christ. Therefore, the Church and state do not have the right to rule others.

Later a theologian from Prague followed along the same line of thinking. John Hus (1369–1415) criticized conditions in the Church and called on it to return to the poverty and simplicity of the Gospels. His sermons were passionate and well received by many, but some—for instance, wealthy clergy in his native Czechoslovakia—attacked him. Hus was called upon to defend his ideas before the Council of Constance, the same council that settled the Great Western Schism. The council condemned his ideas. Hus was executed, but for decades this action sparked dissension in his native country.

A third person who anticipated the controversies that would erupt in the Reformation was Girolamo Savonarola (1452–1498). Savonarola was a fiery Dominican preacher who succeeded in bringing great moral reform to the city of Florence. However, when he ended up attacking the pope of the time, the pope responded by placing an **interdict** on Florence. An interdict meant that no Masses would be offered, no sacraments would be performed, and people would be refused a Christian burial. The people of Florence turned against Savonarola, and he was tortured and burned at the stake as a heretic in 1498.

Girolamo Savonarola

interdict
prohibition against celebrating sacraments in a particular area

Review

1. What and when was the Renaissance?

2. Where did the Renaissance begin?

3. Who is the model for the "Renaissance man"?

4. Name two creations of Michelangelo.

5. What two positions did John Wyclif hold that would later be advocated by Protestants?

6. What was the focus of the sermons of John Hus?

7. What happened that turned the people of Florence against Savonarola?

Conclusion

As the Church moved out of the Middle Ages, it faced many political challenges—including challenges to the papacy itself. The center of power in Eastern Christianity shifted northward to Russia. In the West, people were coming more and more to identify with their particular national group. Meanwhile, Church leaders and many of its members did what they could to help the people of Europe as they suffered through the onslaught of the plague. Some Christians provided solace to others by conveying a message of God's loving concern, which they received during mystical encounters with Christ. Finally, Europe underwent a Renaissance that combined Christian themes with classical Greek concepts in a marriage that gave birth to some of the greatest artistic masterpieces ever produced. The Renaissance offered a vision of beauty and hope. The Church was a major advocate of that vision. However, Christianity in the West was entering another phase. As has always been the case, new situations call for new responses. The question now before the Church was: Would the response be reform or revolt?

As God's chosen ones, holy and beloved, clothe yourselves with compassion, kindness, humility, meekness, and patience. Bear with one another and, if anyone has a complaint against another, forgive each other; just as the Lord has forgiven you, so you also must forgive. Above all, clothe yourselves with love, which binds everything together in perfect harmony.

Colossians 3:12–14

1500–1600

1509
Henry VIII becomes king of England

1521
Pope Leo X excommunicates Luther

1529
Second Diet of Speyer reverses earlier concessions

1517
Martin Luther issues his *Ninety-Five Theses*

1521
Emperor Charles V and Diet of Worms find Luther guilty of heresy

1525–26
Peasants' Revolt takes place

1533
English parliament declares King Henry VIII head of the Church in England

CHALLENGE AND RESPONSE

The Church in Disunity

CHAPTER OVERVIEW

- A controversy over selling indulgences leads to a split within the Western Church.

- Multiple factors create an atmosphere that makes the Reformation both possible and likely.

- A Protestant theology emerges that contains fundamental differences from traditional Catholic theology.

- The Council of Trent initiates reform of the Catholic Church.

- New religious orders and the saintly dedication of many Catholics set new directions for the Catholic Church.

1541
John Calvin institutes Presbyterian theocracy in Geneva, Switzerland

1555
Peace of Augsburg

1598
Edict of Nantes grants Protestants some rights in France

1540
Pope approves Society of Jesus (the Jesuits)

1545–63
Council of Trent brings reform

1562
Saint Teresa of Ávila establishes Carmelite order

Have you ever been in a relationship in which tensions were left to simmer for a long time? If your bad feelings toward someone lingered and then you actually confronted the person, you might have ended up saying things and doing things that went far beyond your original intent. Your words most likely caused the two of you to harbor anger and distrust afterward. Sometimes others got involved in the disagreement and made matters even worse.

The sixteenth century brought this type of severing of relationships within the Church. A number of conditions existed that caused the Protestant Reformation. Once sparks were ignited, the fire spread throughout Western Europe. By mid-century, a united Christianity no longer existed. At this time being Catholic meant not being Protestant. Even though people who left the Catholic Church preached a powerful message and gained ardent followers, the majority of Europeans remained with the Catholic Church. In response to the Protestant Reformation, the Catholic Church clarified its own principles of belief and established its own agenda for reform. By the end of the century, Catholicism was transformed into a renewed and vibrant Church. However, the anguish of a divided Christianity remains to this day.

Before We Begin . . .

If you disagreed strongly with certain policies and practices of your school or an organization or team to which you belong, what type of action would you take? Can you imagine feeling so strongly about policies that you would take actions that could lead to your being expelled or dismissed? Explain why you would or would not take such actions.

THE PROTESTANT REFORMATION

Protestantism Develops

Reformation
political and religious event beginning in the sixteenth century that resulted in the division of Western Christianity into Catholic and Protestant faiths

The **Reformation** refers to a series of events that took place primarily during the first half of the sixteenth century. The outcome of these events was, in fact, more than a reform. It was a total transformation of the political and religious landscape of Western Europe. At the beginning of the century, all people in Western Europe who called themselves Christian belonged to the same Church. Indeed, they couldn't imagine things being otherwise. By mid-century there were traditional Catholic Christians and Christians clamoring for so many changes that they could no longer call themselves Catholic. (In time, the latter were named Protestants and their religious practices, Protestantism). At the beginning of the century, an emperor—at least in name—ruled much of Western Europe. By mid-century, Europe had become deeply divided politically and religiously. At the beginning of the century, Church-affiliated groups owned over half of the land on the continent. By mid-century most of that land had been taken over by non-religious leaders. What precipitated this remarkable transformation? It began innocently enough with a debate over indulgences, but also included dissent over the Church's teachings on the nature of justification and whether Baptism truly removed original sin, as well as the nature of Christ's presence in the sacraments, especially the Eucharist.

Luther's Ninety-Five Theses—The Reformation Begins

On October 31, 1517, a German Augustinian friar wrote a local archbishop outlining his position on a number of theological issues. He never envisioned that his action would lead to a division in Christianity that has yet to be healed. Father Martin Luther included **ninety-five theses** in his letter to Archbishop Albrecht of Mainz. Luther sent copies to a number of other bishops, hoping to spark debate and discussion in a scholarly fashion.

ninety-five theses
Martin Luther's statement of principles regarding penance and the abuse of indulgences

indulgences
the remission before God of the temporal punishment due to sin the guilt of which has already been forgiven

Luther was a university professor, a priest, and a loyal son of the Church. His immediate concern was a practice then occurring in his area that he found to be scandalous—the selling of **indulgences.** Archbishop Albrecht owed the pope a good deal of money. (Albrecht, who was also a secular prince, already "owned" two dioceses. As was customary at the time, his appointment to a third diocese would cost money, since he stood to gain from revenues collected in the diocese.) The pope granted the archbishop's representatives permission to collect money in exchange for a certificate granting indulgences, with the understanding that half of the money collected would be used for the construction of Saint Peter's Basilica in Rome.

The belief was that indulgences reduce or eliminate time spent in purgatory after death. One way to gain an indulgence was by contributing money to a good cause—in this case building the great basilica in Rome. People received certification from the pope himself that they gained a plenary (full) indulgence, that is, removal of all punishment due to sin.

Luther was not the first person to recognize that the theology behind indulgences was being misinterpreted and misunderstood. However, in this particular incident the preachers overseeing the sale of indulgences got carried away in their enthusiasm for raising money for the Church. One of the preachers, a Dominican named John Tetzel, seemed to offer those who purchased a certificate, or members of their families who had died, guilt-free sinning and an automatic ticket to heaven. All this could be accomplished for the right amount of money.

A number of factors enflamed the controversy instigated by this campaign. The selling of indulgences affected money and taxation when money (as opposed to land) was growing in importance. It meant taking money out of Germany and sending it to Rome at a time when people were beginning to identify more and more with their own nation. Many people were irritated that the money was going to what they perceived to be corrupt and decadent Church leadership. And thanks to the printing press, Luther's message spread throughout Europe where it resonated with the angry feelings that many people had toward a number of Church abuses.

Archbishop Albrecht wrote the pope accusing Luther of "new teachings." In August of 1518, Luther was to appear in Rome to answer for his teachings. However, Luther asked Duke Frederick of Saxony to move the hearing to Augsburg, Germany. The pope's representative, not interested in debating Luther on the indulgence issue, simply condemned Luther for questioning the pope's authority.

fyi!

Popular legend has it that Luther posted his theses on the door of his church in Wittenberg. Although no solid historical evidence exists that he actually did this, today the doors of the church have Martin Luther's theses permanently inscribed in them.

Luther on Indulgences

Luther believed that if the pope knew how the selling of indulgences was being manipulated and abused, the pope would condemn the practice. Here are some of the ninety-five theses that explain Luther's position.

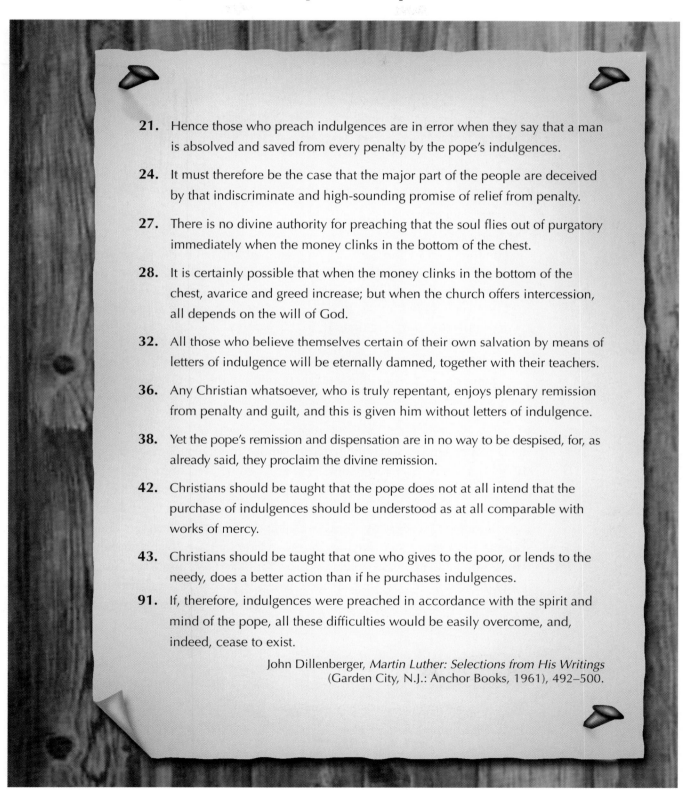

21. Hence those who preach indulgences are in error when they say that a man is absolved and saved from every penalty by the pope's indulgences.

24. It must therefore be the case that the major part of the people are deceived by that indiscriminate and high-sounding promise of relief from penalty.

27. There is no divine authority for preaching that the soul flies out of purgatory immediately when the money clinks in the bottom of the chest.

28. It is certainly possible that when the money clinks in the bottom of the chest, avarice and greed increase; but when the church offers intercession, all depends on the will of God.

32. All those who believe themselves certain of their own salvation by means of letters of indulgence will be eternally damned, together with their teachers.

36. Any Christian whatsoever, who is truly repentant, enjoys plenary remission from penalty and guilt, and this is given him without letters of indulgence.

38. Yet the pope's remission and dispensation are in no way to be despised, for, as already said, they proclaim the divine remission.

42. Christians should be taught that the pope does not at all intend that the purchase of indulgences should be understood as at all comparable with works of mercy.

43. Christians should be taught that one who gives to the poor, or lends to the needy, does a better action than if he purchases indulgences.

91. If, therefore, indulgences were preached in accordance with the spirit and mind of the pope, all these difficulties would be easily overcome, and, indeed, cease to exist.

John Dillenberger, *Martin Luther: Selections from His Writings* (Garden City, N.J.: Anchor Books, 1961), 492–500.

A detail of saints, the Church triumphant, from a larger piece on the Spanish Chapel in Florence, Italy.

Church Teaching on Indulgences

Church teaching on indulgences makes sense only in light of another Catholic teaching—the *communion of saints*. According to the *Catechism of the Catholic Church*:

In the communion of saints, "a perennial link of charity exists between the faithful who have already reached their heavenly home, those who are expiating their sins in purgatory and those who are still pilgrims on earth. Between them there is, too, an abundant exchange of all good things" [*Indulgentiarum doctrina,* 5]. In this wonderful exchange, the holiness of one profits others, well beyond the harm that the sin of one could cause others. Thus recourse to the communion of saints lets the contrite sinner be more promptly and efficaciously purified of the punishments of sin (#1475).

In other words, Catholic teaching about indulgences rests upon the belief that connections exist between people past and people present and that these connections are dynamic and useful. We might wonder: How can we ever make amends for harm we have done? The concept of indulgences points out that Christ, Mary, and the saints have built up a "treasury of merit" available through the Church to those of us who are seeking to make good, having in the Sacrament of Reconciliation admitted our wrongdoing and expressed sincere sorrow for our sins. Church teaching on indulgences is not meant to let us off the hook when it comes to straightening out our lives. However, it does remind us that we are not alone in our quest to turn our lives around. The holiness of Christ, Mary, and the saints brings us untold benefits.

Review

1. How was Western Christianity changed as a result of the Reformation?

2. What action by Martin Luther led the way to the Reformation? What was he protesting?

3. Name three factors that helped enflame Luther's protest.

4. How did the papal representative initially respond to charges against Luther?

THE BREAK WITH CATHOLICISM

**Exsurge Domine and
Decet Romanum
Pontificem**
papal decrees
excommunicating
Martin Luther

While the pope and Church leaders concerned themselves with other matters after this initial condemnation of his ideas, Luther spent the next few years refining his theological position. His ideas grew in popularity. Generally, Vatican officials saw the matter as a debate between two religious orders—the Augustinians (Luther) and the Dominicans (Tetzel). Some German princes saw Luther as a local hero standing up to the Italians in Rome. Many German peasants believed that Luther and his ideas supported their cause against oppressive landowners. Finally, in 1520 Pope Leo X issued a papal bull *Exsurge Domine,* excommunicating Luther unless he retracted his beliefs. However, when the pope's representatives attempted to post the decree in German villages, they met with much resistance. On December 10, 1520, Luther gathered together students from the University of Wittenberg where he taught, built a bonfire outside of the town, and tossed the papal letter into the flames. On January 3, 1521, in the papal bull *Decet Romanum Pontificem,* Pope Leo formally excommunicated Luther.

The next step after excommunication was for secular authorities, in this case Emperor Charles V, to deal with Luther as an outlaw. Luther appeared before the emperor at a gathering called the **Diet of Worms.** When asked if he recanted his heretical teachings, Luther responded:

Diet of Worms
meeting of the
leadership of the
Holy Roman
Empire during
which Luther
refused to recant
his beliefs

> Since then your serene majesty and your lordships seek a simple answer, I will give it. . . . Unless I am convinced by the testimony of the Scriptures or by clear reason (for I do not trust either in the pope or in councils alone, since it is well known that they have often erred and contradicted themselves), I am bound by the Scriptures I have quoted, and my conscience is captive to the Word of God. I cannot and I will not retract anything, since it is neither safe nor right to go against conscience. May God help me. Amen.
>
> Quoted in Mark Edwards and George Tavard, *Luther: A Reformer for the Churches* (Philadelphia: Fortress Press, 1983), 12.

The emperor signed the Edict of Worms in May 1521, declaring Luther a heretic who could be punished by death. However, before Luther could be arrested, Duke Frederick had Luther "kidnapped" and taken to his castle in Wartburg to protect him from harm. Luther stayed there for over a year, working on a translation of the Bible into German and refining his theology. Meanwhile, other people were using Luther's ideas to back up their grievances, taking his ideas in directions that Luther himself would consider heretical.

Peasants' Revolt

There had been a number of revolts by peasants before Luther's time, but now German peasants saw an opportunity to use religious backing in their call for justice. At first Luther supported the peasants. But after the German princes' killed thousands of their number, peasants retaliated by murdering and plundering in indiscriminate fashion. Luther rejected these actions of the peasants and encouraged the princes to use whatever means necessary to restore order. In all, over 130,000 German peasants were killed during this period of the **Peasants' Revolt.** After this rejection by Luther, most peasants either rejoined the Catholic Church or joined one of the more radical Protestant groups. On the other hand, many princes began to see Luther and Lutheranism as an ally to their cause.

The first Diet of Speyer, in 1526, allowed each prince of the Holy Roman Empire to determine the religion of his territory. Some German princes ended up aligning themselves with Luther, while others aligned themselves with Catholicism. Under renewed Catholic pressure, in 1529 the emperor called the second Diet of Speyer, which led to the reversal of earlier concessions. Some of the Catholic representatives also called for carrying out the earlier prosecution of Luther as a heretic. Lutheran princes "protested" these decisions, thus receiving the name *Protestants.* This name became the popular designation for those groups in Europe who rejected Catholicism, though often non-Lutherans are called Reformed Churches.

Over the next few decades, a number of attempts at reunion were made and failed. Finally, in 1555 the emperor reluctantly approved a decision made by the imperial assembly, a decision called the **Peace of Augsburg.** According to this decree, the prince or king of each state could select either Catholicism or Lutheranism as the official religion for his territory. It forbade all sects of Protestantism other than Lutheranism and ordered all Catholic bishops to give up their property if they turned Lutheran. This agreement is known in Latin as *cuius regio, eius religio.* That is, the region in which people live determines their religion. People who didn't want to join the local official religion could move to a state where their religion was approved. In less than forty years, Luther's call for scholarly debate had become the basis for a state-supported religion separate from Catholicism.

Peasants' Revolt
a series of uprisings by German peasants against their landowners

Peace of Augsburg
allowed each prince to decide the religion of his subjects

Activity

Luther initially wanted to debate teachings *within the Church*—not to *dissent from* Church teachings. Name three teachings or practices that are currently being debated within the Catholic Church. Write a report about one of these arguments—giving the pros and cons.

Review

1. What happened at the Diet of Worms?
2. What was the Peasants' Revolt? How did Luther respond to it?
3. When did *Protestant* become the popular term for those who rejected Catholicism?
4. What decision was reached at the Peace of Augsburg assembly?

SPREAD OF PROTESTANTISM

Protestantism is best viewed as a movement. Essentially, Protestantism was a movement away from certain beliefs and practices associated with Catholicism of the time. To appreciate conflicts that the Church will face later, we need to understand the Reformation, the spread of Protestantism, and the differences and similarities between Protestantism and Catholicism.

The Reformation in France and Spain

France was having the same problems among its Church leaders that other countries were having. However, Protestantism never made the inroads into France that it made in the northern European countries. For one thing, ever since the Avignon papacy in 1378, France had maintained greater control over internal Church affairs than other countries had. Another reason for the weak Protestant stance was that Catholic scholars at France's great universities negated Protestant ideas early on. French Protestants, known as **Huguenots** (meaning "oath comrades" asserting their independence from the Church), did gather strength over the course of the sixteenth century. And even the first Bourbon king of France, Henry IV (1589–1619), flirted with Protestantism for a while until he realized that

Huguenots
members of the French Reformed community

Edict of Nantes
document granting some rights to Huguenots

the lower classes had remained stau[nchly] Catholic and that he needed their supp[ort]. Henry then reconverted to Catholicis[m] saying, "Paris is worth a Mass." In 1598 Henry promulgated the **Edict of Nantes,** by which Huguenots were allowed to build churches and hold religious services in specified villages in France. This edict ended a series of religious wars between Catholics and Protestants that ravaged France from 1562 to 1598. Although the Protestant movement diminished greatly in Franc[e] the Protestant-Catholic conflicts crea[ted] among many French people a critical at[titude] toward Church leaders, an attitude [that] remained strong into modern times.

Queen Isabella

For the most part, Spain also avoided Protestant influence. This was due largely to three factors. First, in the late 1400s, Queen Isabella herself instigated reforms in the Church. These reforms were not related to Church teaching but to corruption and abuses by Church leaders. Second, the Inquisition held heresy in check with the threat of force. Third, a number of exceptional figures who emerged in Spain and Portugal during the Reformation helped restore the Church to a more intense spiritual life.

King Henry VIII and the Anglican Church

The position of king of England fell to Henry VIII only after his older brother died. Barely a teenager, Henry was betrothed to his brother's eighteen-year-old widow, Catherine of Aragon. They were married a few years later. Henry became king in 1509 at the age of eighteen. A devoted Catholic, in 1521 Henry wrote a pamphlet against Luther and Protestantism. In response the pope gave Henry the special title, "Defender of the Faith."

Although Henry and Catherine had a number of children, only one, a daughter named Mary, lived past infancy. Mary became betrothed to the heir to the French throne. Therefore, if Henry had no other children, the king of France (Mary's husband) might become king of England as well. Such a state of affairs would be totally unacceptable to the English. Henry petitioned the pope to have his marriage to Catherine annulled so that he could, hopefully, have male children with another wife. For a number of reasons, some of them certainly political, the pope's representative refused to grant the annulment. In 1533 Henry called upon the English parliament to declare that he was not responsible to any foreign powers. In effect, parliament was proclaiming the king as the head of the Church in England. This constituted a break with the pope and the Catholic Church.

Initially, therefore, the English Reformation was based largely upon a disagreement with the pope and Catholicism. That is, Henry did not see this separation from Rome as a move in the direction of Protestantism. For the most part he wanted to keep Church practices as they had been.

As head of the Church in England, Henry VIII took over all monastery lands and divided the lands up among his most loyal subjects. During the reign of Henry VIII's daughter, Queen Elizabeth I, the Church of England became more Protestant. Many English people who remained Catholic were killed or persecuted during Elizabeth's reign. One group of English Protestants wanted to "purify" the English Church even further by ridding the Church of all Catholic trappings and to return to biblical simplicity. However, they, too, were suppressed and eventually made their way to America where we know them as the Puritans.

Review

1. Give two reasons why Protestantism did not become strong in France.

2. Name three factors that helped keep Spain Catholic.

3. What title did the pope give King Henry VIII of England? Why?

4. Why did Henry VIII want to divorce Catherine of Aragon?

5. Who were the Puritans?

TWO PROTESTANT REFORMERS

theocracy
form of government in which religious leaders are the secular leaders as well

In many ways Luther had more in common theologically with Catholicism than with many of the other Protestant leaders during the Reformation period. Ulrich Zwingli (1484–1531) introduced Reformation ideas into Switzerland even before Luther issued his ninety-five theses in Germany. Zwingli advocated Scripture as the sole source of truth and denied that Church leaders had special authority to interpret Scripture. He also criticized corruption among Church leaders and asked for the right for priests to marry. Based in Zurich and with the support of a council of elders, Zwingli came to rule both Church and state in Switzerland. Switzerland became a **theocracy** in which Church and state were united. More specifically, in a theocracy the religious leaders make the rules governing all aspects of society because they are seen as divinely guided.

Reformed Christianity
Protestant Churches emerging in Europe from the Reformation and following primarily the teachings of Zwingli and John Calvin

In Switzerland, Zwingli decided what beliefs were acceptable and what beliefs were not. His rejection of traditional Catholic teachings went beyond Luther. For instance, in 1529 he and Luther met to discuss their theologies. Zwingli suggested that the Eucharistic words, "This is my body," should be interpreted spiritually. Luther pointed out that the biblical text states clearly and precisely that Jesus said, "This is my body." Luther believed that the meaning of this phrase should not be spiritualized. Although he understood it somewhat differently than Catholicism did, Luther held to a belief in the Real Presence of Christ in the Eucharist. Thus, Zwingli and others took the Protestant movement further away from Catholicism than Luther intended or wanted. Their more radical expression of Protestantism came to be known as **Reformed Christianity.**

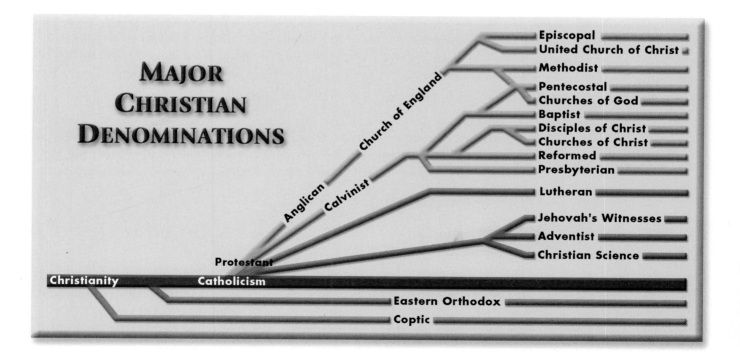

MAJOR CHRISTIAN DENOMINATIONS

The leader of the Reformed movement who had the greatest impact on Protestantism was John Calvin (1509–1564). French by birth but drawn to the Reformed expression of Christianity in Switzerland, Calvin made his way to Geneva where his writings served as a model for governance of the city. A group of elders, or presbyters, decided all matters, both religious and secular. This **Presbyterian** form of Church leadership continues to be followed by many Protestant communities today. Calvin based all laws on the Bible. However, people were not to interpret the Bible for themselves, but were required to accept what the clergy and the ruling presbyters decreed the Bible to mean. Calvin and his successors in Geneva focused on discipline as a mark of the Presbyterian Church.

One belief that Calvin held was **predestination.** That is, people are destined by God for either eternal salvation or eternal damnation. Only a select few are saved. We can't know whether or not we're counted among the saved, but good indications are that we live a morally upright life and are industrious members of society. Calvin's message appealed to the growing middle class of northern Europe. John Knox introduced Presbyterianism to Scotland, where it became the dominant version of Christianity.

Discussion

Choose one of the following questions to debate with someone who has a different viewpoint.

1. If you believed that you were predestined either for heaven or for hell and that you could do nothing about it, what effect do you think this belief would have on how you lived your life?

2. Does Catholicism advocate predestination? Explain.

3. Concerning people who find themselves poor, Calvin wrote: "And so he [God] urges the poor to patience; because those who are not content with their own lot try to shake off the burden laid upon them by God" (*Institutes of the Christian Religion,* chapter XVI, number 6). What does Calvin mean? Describe the pros and cons of this statement.

Activity

1. Calvin viewed God primarily as a judge. Draw or write a report on your image of God when you were younger and your image now.

2. Write a report on one of the following groups who emerged during or shortly after the Reformation period:

   Anabaptists   Quakers
   Methodists   Presbyterians

Heroes of the Reformation

During any time of crisis, heroes emerge. They can be people who hold to their principles in the face of personal risk or who seek common ground among conflicting parties. Depending on your point of view, many leaders who held a variety of positions on the debates of the time would qualify as heroes. Here are three prominent figures from the time who deserve consideration.

Erasmus—The Great Humanist. Erasmus was a Dutch monk who was the greatest humanist thinker of his time. Erasmus remained a faithful Catholic while constantly calling for reform. He wanted a reformation without violence and debate without animosity. He constantly called upon people to conduct themselves toward others as Christ would want them to do: How can you say "Our" Father if you plunge steel into the guts of your brother?

Thomas More—Martyr of Conscience. Catholic layman and a friend of Erasmus, Thomas More was appointed chancellor of England in the midst of King Henry VIII's battle with the pope over seeking to have his first marriage annulled. After Henry declared himself head of the Church in England, he called upon significant English subjects to sign a statement to that effect. After a trial in which he was falsely accused, More was sentenced to be beheaded. Once he was condemned, More explained that a temporal ruler had no right to declare himself head of the Church. For remaining true to his beliefs, More was beheaded. His dying words were, "I die as the king's true servant, but God's first." Thomas More is a saint of the Church and patron of lawyers.

Philip Melancthon—Scholar and Conciliator. Melancthon (1497–1560), friend and associate of Luther, was a scholar who tried to present Lutheran teachings in ways that made them compatible with Catholic teachings. He continued to hold out hope that a reunited Church would emerge from the turmoil of the Reformation. He felt compelled to address the many theological controversies swirling around him at the time. Although he did much to shape Lutheran theology, Melancthon never viewed his beliefs as a rejection of true Catholicism.

Review

1. What type of governance did Ulrich Zwingli institute in Switzerland?

2. What term came to be applied to those people who went beyond Luther in their rejection of Catholic beliefs and practices?

3. What is a Presbyterian form of leadership?

4. What is predestination?

5. Who was John Knox?

CAUSES OF THE REFORMATION

The break with Catholicism that began with Luther and was carried along by other reformers was not inevitable. Specific decisions by people on all sides of the issues created the impasse that led to division within the Christian Church and to Protestantism. We can identify a number of factors that created an atmosphere conducive to hard feelings, divisions, and the call for and resistance to change within the Church. Many of these problems were brewing for some time and were discussed in earlier chapters. Here are some of the conditions that existed in Europe and Christianity at the beginning of the sixteenth century; conditions that led to the Reformation.

Regal clothing and furnishings often hampered the spiritual work of Church leaders.

The Extravagant Lifestyle of Church Leaders. Prior to and during the Reformation, Church leaders were secular rulers as well. That is, bishops who were "princes of the Church" were typically princes in the real sense. Therefore, they lived like any other prince would live. The pope himself was both head of the Church and ruler of the Papal States. Sometimes he would place concern for his secular power over concern for the spiritual welfare of the Church. For example, one Reformation-era pope spent a good deal of money on extravagant weddings for his children and his grandchildren, just as a king would do. In 1463—about fifty years before the start of the Reformation—Pope Pius II described the state of affairs at the papal court of his day in these words:

> People say that we live for pleasure, accumulate wealth, bear ourselves arrogantly, ride on fat mules, trail the fringes of our cloaks after us, and show round plump faces beneath the red hat and white hood, keep hounds for the chase, spend much on actors and parasites, and nothing in defense of the Faith. And there is some truth in their words: many among the Cardinals and other officials of our court do lead this kind of life. If the truth be confessed, the luxury and pomp at our court is too great. And this is why we are so detested by the people that they will not listen to us, even when we say what is just and reasonable.
>
> quoted in Anthony E. Gilles, *The People of Anguish* (Cincinnati, Ohio: St. Anthony Messenger Press, 1987), 29–30.

Chapter Seven

Buying and Selling of Church Offices. The medieval practice of buying the position of bishop or abbot of a monastery continued up to the time of the Reformation. Often wealthy families would see to it that their second or third son would receive the title of bishop, sometimes at a very early age. Many Church leaders, therefore, had no training in or sensitivity for the spiritual life.

Poorly Trained and Uneducated Lower Clergy. In the last chapter, we mentioned the devastating effect that the plague had on the clergy. Even without the disruption caused by the plague, priests received no formal training before the Reformation. While bishops were associated with the nobles, priests were members of the lower classes serving the needs of their communities as best they could. Often they had little theological education. Many priests merely read the Latin words of the Mass and went through the motions, which was essentially all they could do. For sermons, people relied on visiting preachers from the various universities. Many priests kept unofficial families. Popular religion was often tinged with superstition, and fear of the devil was a big concern at the time. Getting priests to celebrate Mass so that one's time in purgatory would be cut short was also a popular practice. Having Masses said was considered more important and more beneficial than actually attending or participating in the Mass.

Spirituality of Laypeople. Before the late Middle Ages, spiritual renewal in the Church usually meant a new type of religious order or monks returning to a strict regimen of monastic life. Just prior to the Reformation, however, religious communities for **laypeople** and spiritual practices directed toward laypeople became popular. In addition to certain theological positions that it held counter to traditional Catholicism, Protestantism was also a movement away from the clerical system in place at the time and toward Christianity centered around living the lay life.

laypeople
members of the Church who are not ordained clergy or members of a religious order

The Spirit of the Renaissance. As mentioned in the last chapter, the Renaissance emphasized the capacity of humans to create and discover truth on their own. On the one hand, Luther and other Protestant leaders tapped into this spirit, rebelling against Church and secular authority and appealing to the authority of their own beliefs. However, Protestants also mounted an attack against many aspects of the Renaissance. They criticized the pope and other Church leaders for investing so much money and energy in the paintings, sculpture, and churches popular during the Renaissance. They also questioned the use of the classical Greek and Roman sources of knowledge. Instead, they looked to the Bible as the fountain of all truth. Lastly, they emphasized the glory of God and downplayed human potential apart from God. Unlike Renaissance humanism and traditional Catholicism, Protestant leaders considered humans, of themselves, to be worthless and powerless sinners. Any hope that humans have lies totally in the hands of God and his grace.

"Departure from Lisbon for Brazil, the East Indies and America" by Theodore de Bry (1528–1598).

Nationalism. Europeans of the time increasingly identified with their particular nation or locale. Although the Holy Roman Empire continued to exist and encompassed much of Western Europe, in fact, local princes, bishops, or abbots ruled their territory independently. The emperor had to concern himself with many matters, such as the ongoing threat of the Turks in the East, so that he couldn't enforce any lasting power over local rulers. These rulers saw themselves as responsible for overseeing both secular and Church affairs. They often used the religious conflicts occurring at the time to serve their own interests. Because of fragmentation in Europe during the 1500s, the Reformation was able to spread to one locality or one nation at a time.

Discovery of New Lands. European discovery of the Americas in 1492 preceded the Reformation by a few decades. During this age of discovery, Europeans were beginning to realize how vast the earth is. Europe became less of a closed society and more open to new worlds and new ideas.

Invention of the Printing Press. The printing press doesn't seem to belong in the same category as other factors leading up to the Reformation. However, without this marvelous technological breakthrough, the Reformation might not have happened. In 1455 the first book printed by Johannes Gutenberg, the inventor of the printing press, was the Bible. Within decades, printing presses were established in most major cities, especially in Germany. The Protestant reformers' call to rely on Scripture as the sole source of truth would have been meaningless if there hadn't been Bibles readily available at the time—thanks to printing presses and the newly developed process for making cheap paper. When Luther appeared before the Diet of Worms, he was presented with a pile of books and pamphlets that he was told to renounce. Those books have since been printed a thousand times over. Although in 1500 few people could read (perhaps as few as four percent of the German population), nonetheless, Luther's ideas were taught and preached about by those who *could* read. Without the printing press the revolutionary ideas of Luther and the other reformers might have remained local controversies. Only a handful of scholars would actually have been able to read and discuss them.

The success of the Protestant reformers was due in part to the invention of the printing press.

Rise of the Middle Class and Social Unrest. At the time of the Reformation, Germany was a nation of towns. The towns were dominated by a rising middle class composed of merchants and artisans. To this group and to the rural peasants, the Church represented the old order in which nobles and Church leaders exacted money from them. Peasants and townspeople saw their tax money supporting the extravagance of the large landowners. The lower classes harbored a great deal of resentment against the Church, mainly for financial reasons. One of the teachings of Luther was that everyone is equal in the sight of God; thus Christians are priests by virtue of their Baptism. Therefore, a separate clerical group is no longer needed. German peasants took this teaching as a theological justification for overthrowing their harsh landlords, some of whom were also bishops. The failure of the Peasants' Revolt of 1525–26 and Luther's turning against them caused peasants for the most part to reject Lutheranism. However, many people in the German middle class found a home in Lutheranism.

Activity

Using the explanations given in your text, rank the causes of the Reformation from most important to least important. Explain your ranking.

Review

1. Give an example of the extravagant lifestyle of Church leaders at the time of the Reformation.

2. Why did many Church leaders have no training in or sensitivity for spiritual matters?

3. What was the state of popular religion at the time of the Reformation?

4. On the one hand, Protestant reformers embraced the spirit of the Renaissance; on the other hand, they reacted against it. Explain.

5. What impact did nationalism, the discovery of new lands, and the printing press have on the Reformation?

6. What Lutheran teaching did the German middle class embrace?

DIFFERENCES IN TEACHINGS

Political and economic factors contributed to the Reformation. The Reformation was also a protest against the rampant corruption exhibited by many Church leaders. However, Protestantism did foster certain theological positions that ran counter to Catholic positions at the time. Neither Protestantism nor Catholicism has remained unchanged since the time of the Reformation, and there continue to be differences in emphasis between the two traditions even today. Three of the principal theological differences between Protestantism and Catholicism are addressed in the following sections.

Scripture Alone or Scripture and Tradition?

The person at the ball game who holds up a sign citing a particular passage from the Bible is probably a Protestant. The Bible in the motel room drawer was almost certainly placed there by a Protestant organization. The church with the sign out front advertising that Sunday's sermon will be on a particular Scripture passage is quite likely a Protestant church. How can we make such claims? Don't Catholics also believe in the Bible?

sola scriptura
Protestant belief that the Bible is the sole source of religious truth

One of the fundamental principles advocated by Luther that carried through the entire Reformation was *sola scriptura*—Scripture alone is the source of divine revelation and truth. Church leaders, being human, could not be trusted to know or speak divine revelation and truth. Church leaders of the past, whether popes or councils, were merely humans and prone to mistakes. The Bible alone is the infallible, divinely inspired source of truth. To be true to Christ, the Church must be true to the gospel of Christ. Christians must always return to Scripture for guidance in the spiritual life. Scripture alone, and not Church tradition, is the authority for the Christian life.

Many Protestant denominations are known as "Bible Churches."

When starting to read the Bible, you might want to begin with the psalms or the short stories, such as Ruth or Tobit. History buffs might like some of the historical books, such as Samuel or Kings. If starting with the New Testament, Mark's Gospel or Acts would be a good choice. Remember that in reading the Bible, you gain knowledge of and reflect on our wonderful and awesome God who challenges, consoles, strengthens, encourages, and transforms us. So begin today to read the greatest love story ever written.

Discussion

1. Name three activities that are part of the tradition of your family or community. How important are these traditions to you? Explain. What are some ways that traditions can be misused? Explain.

2. What are some ways Tradition helps us understand Scripture better?

3. Medieval theologians used Greek philosophical concepts to explain Christian beliefs such as the Real Presence of Christ in the Eucharist. Protestants questioned using non-biblical sources to explain biblical realities. What are some ideas from today's culture that might help us better appreciate Christian teachings?

However, as our study has indicated, the Christian community has always faced conflicts, and Church leaders have always made decisions in response to those conflicts. The Church has never existed apart from historical realities within it and around it. Recall that as early as twenty years after the death of Jesus, Church leaders hotly debated whether or not to accept non-Jews into the Christian community. Had Peter and the apostles decided differently, it would have had a great impact on how the Church developed. Recall also that Church leaders even determined what was to be accepted as Scripture and what was not. In other words, the very instrument that Protestants look to as source of truth and divine revelation—Scripture—cannot be separated from the historical reality of the Church.

Instead of *sola scriptura*, the Catholic position is that *Scripture and Tradition together are unified channels of revelation and are the basis for truth*. Both Scripture and Tradition find their source in God, thus becoming one sacred deposit coming from and pointing toward the same God. Both are to be accepted and honored with equal sentiments of devotion and reverence. In other words, the Holy Spirit did not abandon the Christian community after Pentecost. Catholicism recognizes that the Bible plays a central role in determining truth for Christians—it is the inspired word of God. However, the Catholic viewpoint holds that it is also important to see how the Church has interpreted and applied God's word in the ever-changing historical circumstances in which the Church has found itself. This is known as the *apostolic Tradition*. Our belief in the Trinity, in Mary as the Virgin Mother of God, and in the Real Presence of Christ in the Eucharist are all examples of scriptural apostolic Tradition.

Faith Alone or Faith and Good Works?

Medieval Christians seemed to do things the aim of which was to gain favor with God: going on pilgrimages, collecting relics, and treating sacraments and sacred objects as if they had magical powers. The Renaissance ushered in a spirit of humanism, placing great trust in human abilities. Luther saw both of these perspectives on the human condition as an affront to God. For Luther, God gives, and humans receive. On their own, humans can do nothing to bring about their salvation. Being saved is a totally free gift from God, merited by Jesus Christ's sacrifice on the cross. If humans could do anything to merit this gift, it would no longer be a gift. Therefore, humans can do nothing but have faith in God. Even faith itself is a gift. This complete trust that God takes sinful humans and makes them righteous, or just, in God's eyes is known as **justification by faith.** According to Luther, the justified Christian then engages in good works not for reward but to express his or her faith and to serve.

The traditional Catholic perspective on justification is that humans are not passive recipients of God's grace but instead participate in the action of salvation. Also, faith is not just a matter between an individual and God. Rather, humans stand before God as members of a community. Therefore, Church and sacraments play a vital role in the faith life of Catholics. However, the Lutheran and Catholic positions on justification are not really so different. In part, Luther was reacting to some legalistic and mechanistic interpretations of the doctrine, such as the way some preachers were explaining the purchase of indulgences. Recently, Lutheran and Catholic scholars presented their findings that no real conflict exists between the two groups in their understanding of justification.

justification by faith
God's gracious act of rendering a sinful human to be holy and endowed with grace (in Catholic and Orthodox doctrines) or as acceptable to God (Lutheran)

Some pilgrimage processions include relics. The gold and silver reliquary on the right is now part of the sacred art exhibition at the Vatican.

Activity

1. Draw a set of scales. On one side of the scales, write "The suffering and death of Christ on the cross." On the other side of the scales, write "All the wrongdoing and sinfulness that exist in the world." Which side carries more weight? If you believe that Christ's sacrifice outweighs any evil that exists, then you are a Christian and believe in justification by faith.

2. How would you describe the relationship between faith and good works?

Chapter Seven

Saint Margaret Clitherow

During the Reformation, debates about religion became so heated that people representing every expression of Christianity died for their beliefs. For instance, in 1570 the pope declared that Queen Elizabeth, who sided with Protestantism, was not the rightful ruler of England and excommunicated her. Fearing a Catholic uprising in response to this proclamation, Elizabeth called for persecution of Catholics. Priests especially were hunted down and killed. The city of York had a particularly strong Catholic population. One woman, a butcher's wife named Margaret Clitherow, became a Catholic in 1574. Even though her husband attended the established Anglican Church, the couple built a "priest hole" in their home to hide priests who came to celebrate Mass in secret. The couple also sent their son to France to learn Catholicism in the English Catholic community in exile there.

In 1585 Margaret's husband, John, was questioned about the Catholic activities of his wife and son. The sheriff of York raided the home and discovered the secret room and Mass vestments and sacred vessels hidden there. Margaret was arrested, and the court decided to make an example of her. Margaret refused to enter a plea, saying, "Having made no offense, I need no trial." By her silence she kept secret any information she had about the members of the Catholic community in York. The judge tried to convince her to think of her husband and children. He warned her that her death would be slow and painful. Margaret remained silent. The judge ordered her to be "pressed to death." That is, a board was to be placed upon her and weights would be added over a period of three days after which a sharp stone would be placed behind her until the weight would cause the stone to pierce her heart. When Margaret still would make no plea, the judge decided to put the sharp stone under her on the first day and had an eight hundred-pound weight placed upon her. Margaret died within fifteen minutes. She was declared a saint and martyr in 1970.

The Priesthood of All Believers or a Separate Priesthood?

Catholicism is a sacramental religion. That is, it sees material realities as capable of manifesting God. Traditionally, Catholic churches would be more likely to have statues and paintings, candles and vigil lights, bells and incense, priests in vestments, and elaborate rituals. During the sixteenth century, Protestants took over churches and vastly simplified the décor inside them. They often destroyed statues and replaced elaborate altars with simple wooden tables. In fact, altars became less significant and pulpits became much more significant. Protestantism emphasized "word" to a degree that Catholicism never has. The written word (the Bible), the spoken word (the sermon), and the sung word (hymn singing) play a prominent role in most Protestant services. Most Protestant denominations celebrate only the two sacraments which they see as having clear Gospel mandates—Baptism and Eucharist. Even after the invention of the printing press, Catholicism continued to emphasize symbols and rituals in its services. To the ordinary Catholic, the words of the sacraments, recited in Latin until about fifty years ago, were less important than the actions and the elements—the bread, wine, water, oil.

One external held onto by Catholics but either dropped or downplayed by Protestants was the ordained priesthood. Luther, who was a priest, eventually married and had a number of children. He praised the Christian family as the ideal and spoke out against having a separate clerical caste. According to Luther, all Christians are priests by virtue of their faith in Christ. In Catholicism, ordained priests serve an important function within the sacramental system and, like all sacraments, represent Christ to the people and the people before God. Especially since the Second Vatican Council, held in the 1960s, the Catholic Church also recognizes that each believer, through his or her baptism, belongs to the priesthood of Christ as priest, prophet, and king. However, the Church sees men ordained as bishops, priests, or deacons as being necessary for apostolic ministry in the life of the Church.

Activity

1. List the priests who have been part of the sacramental celebrations of your life. Find their addresses through a diocesan directory and send them a thank you note for representing Christ to you through the sacraments.

2. Have you ever experienced yourself as engaging in the priesthood of Christ as priest, prophet, or king? If so, depict this experience in some way. If not, write about some way that you might live out that priesthood.

Review

1. What does the Protestant principle *sola scriptura* mean? What is the traditional Catholic position on this principle?

2. Explain what justification by faith means in Catholicism. In Lutheranism.

3. What is the difference between the Catholic and the Lutheran position on priesthood?

THE CATHOLIC REFORMATION

Council of Trent
post-Reformation meeting of the world's Catholic bishops to reform the Church and clarify Catholic teaching

The second half of the sixteenth century was a period for reform within the Catholic Church itself. The event most closely associated with Catholic reform is the **Council of Trent,** which lasted off and on from 1545 to 1563. Over the course of these eighteen years, Church leaders addressed abuses among their members and also clarified Catholic theological positions. In addition to the council, a second expression of Catholic reform was manifest through new religious orders and renewed spiritual life among Catholics.

The Council of Trent

Emperor Charles V proposed that a council be held on German soil in response to the Protestant Reformation. At the end of 1545, Pope Paul III convened a council in Trent, just over the Italian border in German territory, at which thirty Church leaders participated. The poor attendance indicates that Church leaders were not exactly sure how to go about reforming the Church. Some wanted to address abuses; others wanted to clarify Catholic Church teaching to meet the Protestant challenges. By the time the council finally ended, both goals would be met, making the split with the Protestants irrevocable.

One of the major reforms brought about by the council was the revitalization of the life of priests on all levels. The council instructed the pope to be careful and thoughtful in selecting cardinals. During the time of Trent, a number of cardinals were appointed who took active roles in Church reform. Bishops were instructed to reside in their diocese, to meet with their clergy regularly, and to visit the parishes in their diocese. Although this change did not occur immediately, over time Catholic bishops came to view their role as being pastors of the people in their particular diocese. Finally, the council reaffirmed celibacy for priests in the West and notified priests not living a celibate life that they would lose their positions. Priests were also to wear distinctive garb so that they could be distinguished from laypeople. Seminaries were to be instituted for the education and training of priests. If possible, candidates for priesthood were to begin seminary training at a very early age.

Regarding Church teaching, the council did not take innovative stands. Rather, it restated and clarified what had been longstanding Catholic teachings on all major doctrines. However, clarifying authentic teachings in this way was itself a reforming step. As pointed out earlier, problems often arose because beliefs were misunderstood or misrepresented. For instance, Luther found that some people viewed grace as something they gained as a result of actions they performed rather than as a gift from God. The idea of "gaining grace" is a misinterpretation of traditional teaching on the subject. Similarly, Christ's Real Presence in the Eucharist had always been a matter of Church teaching. As mentioned earlier, medieval theologians used concepts borrowed from Greek philosophy to explain this teaching. In doing so, some popular preachers described Christ's presence in the Eucharist in ways that were inaccurate, which led to reactions in opposite directions by other preachers.

Eighteenth century print of the Council of Trent.

To correct misinterpretation of Catholic teachings from the Middle Ages and to counteract positions advocated by Protestants, the Council of Trent often stated Catholic Church teachings in legalistic terms. For instance, since Protestants rejected private confession of sins, the Council of Trent specified rules for confession to a degree that had not been necessary previously. As recommended by the council, a catechism stating fundamental Catholic beliefs in precise terms was published in 1566. It was called the *Catechism of the Council of Trent.* It served as the official catechism of the Catholic Church until a new catechism replaced it in the 1990s. In 1570 an official Roman Missal was published. A missal contains the words to be said and the gestures to be followed by the priest at Mass. Eventually, words to be said by the priest were written in black while directions for actions to be taken during Mass were printed in red and thus came to be known as *rubrics,* from the Latin word for red.

The council stated teachings in terms that were critical of Protestant positions and condemned those who held such positions. For instance, most Protestants accepted only two sacraments, Baptism and Eucharist, as having a firm basis in Scripture. By way of contrast the council said:

If anyone says that the sacraments of the new law were not all instituted by Jesus Christ, or that there are more or less than seven, or that any of the seven is not truly and strictly speaking a sacrament, let them be anathema [cursed, banned].

Quoted in Jean Comby and Diarmaid MacCulloch, *How to Read Church History, Vol. 2* (New York: Crossroad, 1989), 27.

Activity

Hold a debate on the following statements:

- Religious brothers, nuns, and priests should always wear distinctive clothing.
- Boys who express an interest in becoming priests should enter a seminary program as early as ninth grade.
- People who attend Mass should have a missalette in hand in order to follow along with the words and actions of the liturgy.
- Catholic schools should base their religious education exclusively on a catechism stating core Catholic beliefs.

Saint Charles Borromeo—
Applying the Council of Trent

Charles Borromeo was in his early twenties and not even a priest when his uncle, Pope Pius IV, made him a cardinal of the Church. Borromeo served his uncle as Secretary of State at the Vatican, was ordained a priest, and then spearheaded the call for reform during the last sessions of the Council of Trent—all while still in his twenties. During this time Borromeo was wounded by an assassin who was angry at his reform proposals. After the council, as bishop of Milan, Borromeo worked diligently to transform his diocese into the ideal that the council wanted the Church to be. When a famine struck the city, he oversaw the feeding of thousands of people every day. An outbreak of the plague also took place in Milan during his time as its bishop. He personally cared for plague victims and instructed all priests and religious of the region to do likewise.

Four hundred years later, during Vatican Council II, Pope Paul VI gave all the participating bishops a copy of the life of Charles Borromeo. Paul VI hoped that after Vatican II each bishop would return to his diocese to put into practice on a local level the vision of the council, just as Borromeo had done after Trent.

Review

1. What were the two main goals of the Council of Trent?

2. What three things were bishops instructed to do by the Council of Trent?

3. How was priestly life to change after the Council of Trent?

4. The Council of Trent clarified Catholic teachings. Why was this a reforming step?

5. What does it mean to say that the spirit of the teachings at the Council of Trent was legalistic and critical?

6. What role did Saint Charles Borromeo play in relation to the Council of Trent?

CATHOLIC SPIRITUALITY

Even as Christianity was being torn apart by the Reformation, Catholicism was actually enjoying a golden age of spirituality. There were the Jesuits, and there were the mystics.

The Society of Jesus

In 1521, while Luther was gaining followers in Germany, a young soldier from the Basque region of Spain lay recuperating in a castle after a cannonball had shattered his leg. He spent over a year in the castle. His constant companions were two books—a life of Christ and a book on the lives of the saints. As a soldier, he was impressed with the courage and dedication of the saints that he read about. He decided that if and when he recovered, he would live the life of a saint himself.

Thus began the journey of a man, and a group of men, who would help prevent the further expansion of Protestantism in Europe, introduce Catholicism to people in distant lands, educate many of the best minds in Europe and eventually around the world, and greatly renew the spiritual life of Catholics on all levels. Ignatius Loyola left his castle and began to live a life of extreme poverty and self-denial. During this time he devised a system of **spiritual exercises** designed to help people overcome self-centeredness, encounter Christ on a personal level, and discern God's will for them. After this period of spiritual cleansing, Ignatius believed that his task was to go to the Holy Land and seek the conversion of Muslims to Christianity. After an initial trip to Jerusalem, he realized that he needed more education to accomplish his goal.

spiritual exercises
a thirty-day program of spiritual practices developed by Saint Ignatius Loyola

Jesuit universities are known as centers for learning of the highest order. They are also centers for Ignatian spirituality.

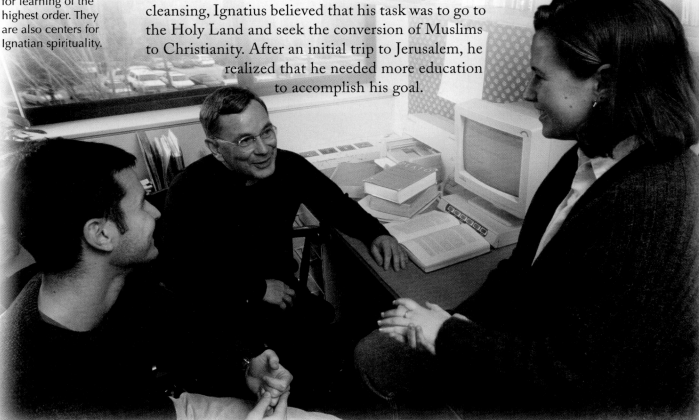

Ignatius spent the next eleven years in various universities. A group of young men gathered around him. Together they journeyed to Rome, intending to travel again to Muslim territory to seek converts. Once in Rome they realized that missionary work in the Holy Land was impossible. Therefore, Ignatius presented himself and his companions to the pope, intending to do whatever menial tasks the pope would choose for them. They presumed that the pope would want them to work among those who were poor and care for those who were sick in Rome, which they immediately began to do. However, the pope saw a different potential in this group who would dedicate themselves to carrying out his directives. He saw the group as an antidote to the Protestants, who were going about rejecting the pope and Church leadership at every turn. In 1540 the pope designated Ignatius's group to be not just another religious order but a new society—the Society of Jesus, or Jesuits.

Ignatius founded the Gregorian University in Rome and a German college designed to train priests to combat Protestantism. Within twenty-five years, over a thousand Jesuits ran one hundred colleges in Europe and the New World. Their rigorous program of study, coupled with the Ignatian program of spiritual exercises, created an educated group of Catholics who could challenge the best Protestant minds and thus hold in check extensive Protestant expansion to other parts of Europe. Zeal for the faith among Jesuits led to many of them making their way to other continents where they spread the Christian message. Jesuits soon became outlawed in a number of countries, but they carried on their work in secret and continued to grow in numbers. The Jesuits played a major role in the Catholic Reformation and in making Catholicism a dynamic faith as it entered the modern world.

JESUIT SPIRITUALITY BASED ON THE SPIRITUAL EXERCISES

Christ centered—an ever-deepening relationship with Jesus in all parts of life

Apostolic—service in collaboration with God for the well-being of others

Discerning—individual and communal experiences which aid in choosing options that support and collaborate with God's action in the world

Generous—offering fairness and charity in response to others

Fraternal—companionship in service

Spiritual integration—finding God in all things

Richard P. McBrien, ed., *Encyclopedia of Catholicism* (N.Y.: HarperCollins,1995), 694.

Activity

1. Read one of the following Gospel passages and imagine yourself actually present at the event. Describe the event in your own words and suggest possible questions or meanings that the passage presents to you. (This activity is in the spirit of Jesuit meditation.)

   John 3:1–21
   John 9:1–41
   Luke 4:14–21
   Matthew 15:21–26

   Matthew 26:26–30
   Luke 23:39–43
   John 13:1–15

2. Write a report on one of the following early Jesuits:

   Francis Xavier
   Peter Faber
   Peter Canisius

   Francis Borgia
   Edmund Campion
   Aloysius Gonzaga

Two Catholic Visionaries

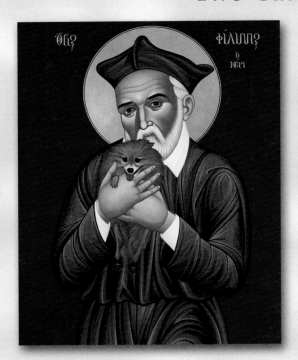

Saint Philip Neri—The "Second Apostle of Rome."
Talk of the corruption that existed in Church circles during the Reformation can give the impression that such problems represented the entire life of the Church at the time. In fact, quite a few models of saintliness lived an active spiritual life apart from the abuses and apart from the Protestant-Catholic conflicts. Someone who exemplified a unique expression of spirituality was Philip Neri (1515–1595). In his late teens Philip left his uncle's business and went to Rome to dedicate himself to God's service. He formed a community of young men who met to discuss religious matters and to care for those who were sick or on pilgrimage to the city.

When people sought this famous holy man out, Philip would often respond in very playful ways. Once he greeted a group of guests while wearing a hat that was many sizes too small for his head. Another time he shaved off half of his beard. On one occasion he was hearing confessions when a man came to him and confessed a long list of minor offenses. Philip said to the man that he was taking himself much too seriously and told him for his penance that he should walk around Rome for the day with a live chicken on his head. Philip's spirituality of playfulness and his celebration of God who delights in people, even in their foibles, make a pleasant contrast to the seriousness of the conflicts going on throughout the Christian world of the time.

Saint Angela Merici. Up until this time, religious life for women meant entering a cloistered convent and living the monastic life. Angela Merici (c. 1470–1540) had the vision to create a whole new way for women to live the Christian life. In her northern Italian city, she saw many poor girls in need of help. She decided that she was called to care for them and educate them. As often happens when good work is being done, other women joined Angela in her endeavors. Although they took the name "Ursulines," Angela didn't see her group as a new religious order. They didn't wear distinctive clothing, take vows, or live in convents. They were simply a group of women doing God's work. Many people questioned this new way for women to live. However, Angela received approval for her community from the pope. Today, we are familiar with many religious communities of women and men who dedicate their lives to education, health care, and social work. It is important to remember that these communities exist because people like Angela Merici had the foresight to respond in creative ways to the needs of people they saw around them.

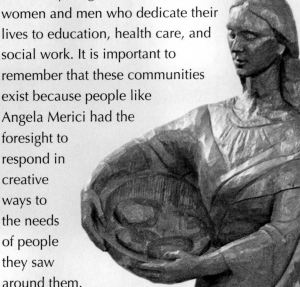

The Mystics

The Catholic mystical tradition flourished during the Reformation period. Indeed, two of the greatest Catholic mystics of all time were the Spaniards Teresa of Ávila (1515–1582) and John of the Cross (1542–1591).

Teresa entered a bustling convent, only to find that the sisters there were not working diligently at pursuing spiritual development. She decided to found another convent where a simpler life and a more rigid expression of spiritual discipline would be the rule. To distinguish her group from a religious order known as the Carmelites she named them *discalced* Carmelites (meaning "without shoes"). Many women joined Teresa, and she traveled about founding many convents. She attained such a depth of spiritual experience that she was called before the Inquisition to explain her "visions." To answer their questions, Teresa wrote about her experiences. Her writings on the levels of spiritual development continue to inspire people today, and she is numbered among the Doctors of the Church for her contribution to explaining the Christian life. Like Philip Neri, Teresa also exhibited a lighter side to her spirituality. One day, when the sisters were gathered for their community recreation, she entered the room dancing and playing castanets. She remarked, "God deliver us from sullen saints."

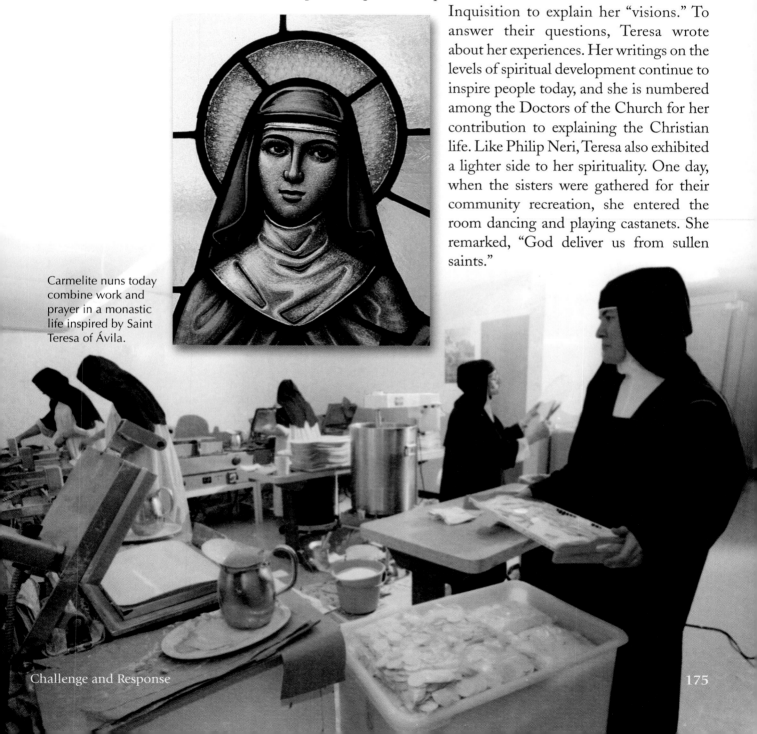

Carmelite nuns today combine work and prayer in a monastic life inspired by Saint Teresa of Ávila.

Under the guidance of Teresa, John of the Cross led the reform of the Carmelite order for men. His attempts at reforming the order met with such resistance that one group of monks locked him in a cell for months. His friend Teresa appealed to the king to have him released. Eventually, John managed to escape. Like Teresa, John reached the heights of mystical experience. Although no words can capture what a mystical experience is like, John wrote with such inspiration about his experiences that his Spanish poems are recognized as some of the best ever written. John used sensual imagery to describe the relationship that occurs between the mystic and God. For example, in the passage below to explain his experience of God, he uses the image of a bride and groom united in marriage. For his exceptional writings John of the Cross is also recognized as a Doctor of the Church.

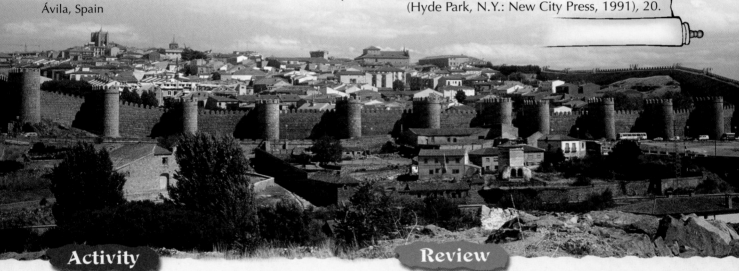

Oh, how sweet Your presence will be to me. You Who are the supreme good! I must draw near You in silence and uncover my feet before You that You may be pleased to unite me to You in marriage (Ruth 3:7), and I will not rest until I rejoice in Your arms.

Alphonse Ruiz OCD, ed., *The Prayers of John of the Cross*, (Hyde Park, N.Y.: New City Press, 1991), 20.

Ávila, Spain

Activity

Slowly and meditatively read the following poem written by John of the Cross:

How gently and lovingly
You wake in my heart,
Where in secret You dwell alone;
And by Your sweet breathing,
Filled with good and glory,
How tenderly You swell my heart with love!

The Prayers of John of the Cross, 38.

Think about or imagine experiencing God's presence in your life. Write a poem or song that expresses that experience.

Review

1. What incident led to Saint Ignatius Loyola's spiritual quest?

2. Name four contributions that Ignatius and the Society of Jesus made to Catholicism.

3. What was unique about the spirituality of Saint Philip Neri?

4. What innovation did Saint Angela Merici make to women's ways of living the Christian life?

5. Name two groups who helped foster Catholic spirituality during the Reformation period.

6. What two Spanish Carmelite saints became Doctors of the Church for their writings on mysticism?

Conclusion

Even though in 1500 the Church in Europe clearly needed major reform, no one would have predicted the extent of change that was to take place over the next one hundred years. The intensity of the ill feelings among various factions would color Christianity for the next four hundred years. Over time, Protestantism rejected more and more of Catholic teachings from the medieval period. The Catholic Church itself reformed and redefined itself over against the Protestants, who no longer saw themselves as a part of Catholicism. However, Christians—both Catholic and Protestant—found new ways to live out their relationship with Christ. Unfortunately, as we will see, both Catholics and Protestants suffered because of their battles with each other. After the period of the Reformation, many people in Europe would decide that they no longer needed any religion to guide their lives or to give their lives meaning. In other words, once again the Christian Church would find itself seeking to remain faithful to Christ on a new battleground.

Jesus, Lord and Savior of the world, may we respond to the call to spread the good news, sharing the gifts with which you have blessed us. Guide us as we seek to make good use of all things new. Keep us open to change but always faithful to you. Amen.

1600–1870

1615
Roman Inquisition condemns Galileo

1618
Thirty Years War begins

1648
Peace of Westphalia ends Thirty Years War

1650
Death of Descartes

1682
King Louis XIV issues Gallican Articles

1773
Suppression of the Jesuits

1789
French Revolution

1793
Reign of Terror begins

SACRED OR SECULAR?

*Rationalism Confronts
the Catholic Church*

CHAPTER OVERVIEW

- The Enlightenment presents new challenges for the Catholic Church.

- Political changes in Europe affect the way the Catholic Church views its role.

- Dedicated Catholics give themselves to new ways of living the Christian life.

1804		1846	1869–1870
Reign of Napoleon begins		Election of Pope Pius IX	Vatican Council I

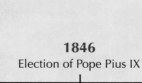

1814	1833	1858	1870
Congress of Vienna	Oxford Movement in England	Bernadette of Lourdes	End of the Papal States

If, on the evening news you heard that a new galaxy had been discovered or that a cure had been found for a deadly disease, would you be surprised? Probably not. You were born during a century when over three-quarters of the machines now in use were invented. You accept that new discoveries are part of life. You also accept that things go out of fashion and become obsolete quickly. Change is the one constant.

However, for seventeenth-century people, their world did not change much. What was true yesterday was true today. They accepted the structures and beliefs passed on to them by previous generations. Then, during the Reformation time-honored truths were challenged and fought over. Generally speaking, Protestantism stood for change; Catholicism stood for things as they were.

During this period of European history, the Christian worldview itself would be challenged. A transformation known as the Enlightenment would lead to questioning Church, religion, and, indeed, the existence of God. As you might expect, leaders of the Catholic Church took a defensive posture toward the Enlightenment and its glorification of the rational mind over all other sources of truth. For the first time since before Constantine, the Catholic Church found itself on the outside of major political conflicts and intellectual developments. Nonetheless, great numbers of people stayed with the Church or joined it as their life-giving link to Christ.

Before We Begin . . .

Imagine that your school is sponsoring a panel discussion of Church leaders and renowned scientists who will address the following questions:

■ **What can science offer the Catholic Church?**

■ **What can the Catholic Church offer science?**

1. **If you were the moderator of the panel, what questions would you ask of the various panel members?**

2. **If you were one of the scientists, what points about the topic would you want to make?**

3. **If you were a Catholic Church leader, what points about the topic would you want to make?**

THE CHURCH AND SCIENCE

Galileo, Science, and the Catholic Church

Science and technology are precious resources when placed at the service of man and promote his integral development for the benefit of all. By themselves however they cannot disclose the meaning of existence and of human progress.

Catechism of the Catholic Church, #2293.

heliocentric
belief that the earth and other planets revolve around the sun

geocentric
belief that the sun revolves around the earth

The Italian scientist Galileo Galilei (1564–1642) wanted to test longstanding notions by using direct observation. For instance, most scholars of the time believed that two objects of different weights would fall at different speeds. Galileo, a native of Pisa, climbed its famous tower and demonstrated that this viewpoint was false. His findings contradicted what the Greek philosopher Aristotle had said on the matter. Therefore, many Aristotelians, who believed their master to be the final word on scientific truth, rejected Galileo's results. Galileo had to leave town but was offered teaching positions in mathematics, first at Padua and then at Florence.

Later, Galileo heard about a Dutch optician who produced an instrument that magnified distant objects. Galileo immediately understood the theory behind this discovery and worked through the night to create his own such instrument, the telescope. Galileo used his telescope to support a theory that had previously been proposed by the Polish astronomer Copernicus—namely, that the earth and other planets revolve around the sun. When Galileo published his opinions proposing a **heliocentric** system as opposed to a **geocentric** system, he was again going against commonly held beliefs. Much controversy followed.

Galileo's use of the telescope opened the door to a new way of looking at the world. What event or invention has done that for you?

Joshua prayed to the Lord,
   and said in the presence of Israel:
Stand still, O sun, at Gibeon,
   O moon, in the valley of Aijalon!
And the sun stood still,
   and the moon stayed,
   while the nation took vengeance
      on its foes.
            —Joshua 10:12–13

It would be wrong to say that Catholic Church leaders were against Galileo or against science. (After all, Copernicus had proposed a heliocentric solar system almost seventy-five years before Galileo did. Copernicus received support from a local cardinal and a bishop, and even dedicated his work to the pope of the time.) However, because a number of people denounced his ideas as heresy, Galileo went to Rome in 1615 and appeared before the court of the Inquisition. Essentially the court raised three objections against Galileo's heliocentric theory:

1. Galileo offered no firm proof for it.
2. It appeared to contradict certain statements in the Bible. (See the above caption for an example.)
3. It could present a danger to the faith of the common people if it circulated beyond the scientific community itself.

Galileo left the Inquisition promising not to speak or write about this particular topic. Nonetheless, when he returned to Florence he upheld his heliocentric teachings and taught about them on many occasions. Galileo again appeared before the Inquisition and denied his belief in the Copernican system. This time, however, the judges did not accept his denial, and Galileo spent the rest of his life officially under arrest—but living comfortably with various friends in and around Rome.

The time of Galileo marks another transition period in the history of the world. As it has always had to do, the Catholic Church had to meet the challenges posed by new ideas and new perspectives. The worldview that emerged after the Reformation period had intellectual, moral, and political implications. Galileo's story points out a number of issues the Catholic Church faced as it entered into the dramatically changed world of the seventeenth and eighteenth centuries.

First, since the time of the great medieval thinkers, Catholicism had sided with scholastic philosophy as its window into the truths of the natural world. **Scholasticism,** based primarily on the ancient Greek philosopher Aristotle and "Christianized" by Thomas Aquinas and other medieval scholars, used human reason in a particular way to determine truth. Essentially, scholasticism used deductive reasoning in its approach. (Deductive reasoning poses general principles, raises questions about those principles, and then uses logic to draw conclusions "deduced" from the principles. Recall that Aquinas deduced the existence of God using this approach.) Galileo was using an inductive approach in the search for truth. (Inductive reasoning draws a generalized conclusion from particular instances.) Over the next few centuries, Christianity, both Catholic and Protestant, would face challenges posed by a developing modern science. Until well into the twentieth century, most Catholic thinkers continued to rely on scholasticism as their primary approach to truth seeking. Some Protestant groups came to be reconciled with modern scientific thought as early as the nineteenth century.

Second, at the time many people considered the Bible to be literally true. For instance, the Book of Joshua reports that during a battle the sun stood still for an entire day (Joshua 10:12–13). If the earth revolves around the sun, how could that passage from the Bible be true? Catholics today are comfortable saying that the Bible teaches us "how to go to heaven, not how the heavens go." That is, we misread the Bible if we treat it only as a scientific text. However, determining the correct relationship between the Bible and science would remain a challenge for centuries. Some Protestant communities still hold that we must choose between literal biblical truths and scientific truths and that the two are irreconcilable.

Third, Galileo's story represents a shift in the role Catholic Church authorities would play in the pursuit of truth. For centuries the most learned people in the Christian world were Church people. Universities were viewed as extensions of the teaching mission of the Church. As already mentioned, in the mid-1500s Copernicus received sponsorship from Church leaders; and at the beginning of the 1600s Galileo subjected his theories to investigation by Church courts. After this time, science and religion would for the most part go their separate ways. Most scientists would no longer view their work as a function of the Church searching for truth or as one piece of a total, interrelated system of truth. In fact, many scientists would consider the Church and religion itself to be an obstacle to authentic truth seeking. The medieval synthesis of the sacred and the secular was unraveling.

Activity

1. Discuss how science and technology can enhance or inhibit the mission of the Church.

2. The motto of the Crusades was "God wills it!" and a red cross was its symbol. Design a web page, create an electronic slide presentation, or draw a symbol that would represent the relationship between Christianity and science. Include a motto in your drawing.

Rene Descartes   Francis Bacon   Immanuel Kant

Characteristics of the New Age of Science

An early proponent of the new age of science was the French mathematician and philosopher Rene Descartes (1596–1650). Take note of his fundamental point of view, and imagine how it might have been received by Christian thinkers of the time. Descartes believed that nothing should be accepted unquestioningly. In fact, it is our very ability to question that proves our existence. You are probably familiar with his famous maxim, "I think; therefore, I am." Descartes could have substituted the words "I doubt" or "I question; therefore, I am." In effect, Descartes believed that reason was the key source of human truth. Leading thinkers during and after the time of Descartes posed new challenges for the Catholic Church. For instance, Francis Bacon (1561–1626) proposed that nothing should be accepted solely on the basis of authority. Tradition was an obstacle to truth. The scholastic approach to truth-seeking was too abstract. Inductive reasoning, beginning with observable phenomena, was for Bacon far superior to deductive reasoning. That is, knowledge comes from using the senses to observe the natural world.

Enlightenment
the seventeenth-
and eighteenth-
century movement
in Europe during
which reason and
science held a
privileged position
as sources of truth

This period, during which science was elevated to being the exclusive source of truth, is known as the **Enlightenment.** When asked, "What is the Enlightenment?" philosopher Immanuel Kant replied that it meant "Courage to use the mind without the guidance of another. Dare to know! Have the courage to use your own understanding!" (Quoted in Jaroslav Pelikan, *The Melody of Theology* [Cambridge, Mass.: Harvard University Press, 1988], 69.) Although the Enlightenment encouraged innovations in science and technology and promoted charitable standards of tolerance, equality, and freedom in social reforms, the challenges of the Enlightenment struck at the heart of the Catholic Church even more than the Reformation did. The Reformation split Western Christianity. The Enlightenment undermined Christianity itself.

rationalism

a theory that nothing is true unless founded on scientifically demonstrable proofs based solely on reason and the five senses; condemned by the First Vatican Council

deism

belief that God created the world and then left it to run according to natural laws

Discussion

Might people who know you consider you to be a deist? Why or why not?

Actually, most Enlightenment thinkers did not reject Christianity. Instead, they found Christianity to be in agreement with reason. In fact, for Enlightenment thinkers belief in reason was the one true religion. In their view humans are basically good and powerful. People should concentrate on this world and not on the next. The natural world holds out the possibility of things being known and controlled; the supernatural should be left in God's hands. The more people live and act according to reason, the better the world will be. Superstitions, prejudices, and preconceived notions hold people back. Once these are let go, humans will have created a paradise on earth. (Most Enlightenment thinkers did not distinguish between what was superstitious in religion and what was authentic religious practice.) The belief in unbounded human progress achievable through ever-increasing knowledge of the natural world has been called **rationalism.** Rationalist thinkers stood in opposition to any religious tradition based on mystery or revealed truth.

Another view of God and religion that rejected revealed truth also surfaced during this period—**deism.** This view looks at God and religion as being about the past; deism's focus is the future. God was neither a positive nor a negative force. The God of the deists is a passive, uninvolved God. God created the world but no longer interferes in its workings. God is like a watchmaker. God made the world and sent it off into history with all its inner workings in place that keep it running on its own. Humans—using reason, experimenting with science, and observing the natural world—can come to know the inner workings of nature without needing to refer to divine revelation. Deists held that

- God exists.
- God created the world.
- Once it was created, God left the world alone.
- The world operates by definite natural laws.
- Humans can discover these laws through the use of reason.
- Human reason should be used to scrutinize all truth claims.
- Human reason should guide all human endeavors.

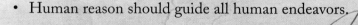

"The Creation of Adam" by Michelangelo in the Sistine Chapel, the Vatican.

Activity

Make a list of activities or practices that are being debated in various scientific fields today. Next to each item, state what the Catholic Church has said, if anything, about this issue.

Sacred or Secular?

The Catholic Response to Rationalism and Deism

> Reason and human science often lead you into error because they are too weak and limited to penetrate to the knowledge of the things of God, which are infinite and incomprehensible.
>
> Saint John Eudes as quoted in Jill Haak Adels, *The Wisdom of the Saints* (New York: Oxford University Press, 1987), 176.

Inspired by the Holy Spirit at Pentecost, from its very beginning the Church understood that it was to engage the world. A Spirit-inspired Church was not to stand still but was to grow and develop as it encountered the various cultures in which its representatives found themselves. Early on, Christianity was able to explain itself to proponents of reason, the great philosophical thinkers of the classical world, in their own terms. Saint Paul himself made a case for the reasonableness of Christianity to the people of Athens. Christianity was such a vibrant movement partially because it was able to synthesize Jewish thought with the insights of classical philosophy.

The French scientist, Jollivet Castelot, at work in his laboratory, late nineteenth century.

The seventeenth and eighteenth centuries brought new intellectual challenges to the Catholic Church. By making reason their universal starting point, Descartes and Bacon attempted to start fresh in making sense of the world. They believed that as Europe had recently discovered new lands across the seas, so European minds could discover new truths. Enlightenment thinkers came to believe in unbounded human progress gained through the use of human reason. The free and unfettered investigation of nature and the application of the principles of nature to human problems would improve the common lot of humanity. Just as Catholicism in the Reformation held onto its essential beliefs from the time of the early Church and many practices carried over from the Middle Ages, so it rejected the basic tenets of rationalism and deism that seemed to contradict those beliefs and practices. For centuries, the Catholic Church stood firm against both, even while the world was embracing them.

What was the nature of the Catholic Church's response to rationalism and deism? Essentially, there were three levels of response.

Entrenchment of Scholasticism. For one, Catholic scholars held onto scholasticism as their principal method for seeking truth. Often the scholastic approach as it was taught in seminaries and Catholic universities was rigid. Students would learn the formulas of Aquinas—in Latin. These formulas were presented as inarguable truths. Most Catholic teachers feared steering off course and ending up in the dangerous waters of rationalism. In the nineteenth century a group of German Catholics called themselves "Enlightenment Catholics." Their movement was suppressed. As we will see later, toward the end of the century, popes condemned rationalism. Not until Vatican Council II would many Catholic leaders and scholars truly be open to dialogue with the intellectual currents coming out of the Enlightenment.

Popular Devotions. A second level of response to rationalism took place among the Catholic faithful. Whereas deism painted the picture of a distant, removed, impersonal God, popular Catholic piety offered many personal images of God, Jesus, Mary, and the saints. For instance, in the seventeenth century, devotion to the Sacred Heart of Jesus became very popular. This image of Jesus, with his heart externally visible, offered a feeling of warmth, care, compassion, and love that the God of deism seemed not to offer. Catholics also developed a great devotion to the Blessed Sacrament. (For many people the church building became the place that housed the Blessed Sacrament, rather than the place where the Christian community gathered for worship.)

This is a typical image of the Immaculate Heart of Mary that was part of the popular devotion to Mary.

A similar image of the Immaculate Heart of Mary became popular at the same time. In addition, Catholics found the rosary, with its powerful images of sorrowful, joyful, and glorious mysteries, to be spiritually enriching.

Other events that generated popular piety were the apparitions of Mary. In 1858 a young teenaged French girl named Bernadette Soubirous claimed to have had a vision of the Virgin Mary in a cave near Lourdes. Although authorities tried to suppress her claims, the spot became one of the most frequented pilgrimage sites in Europe. A spring emerged from the cave soon after Bernadette's vision. The spring continues to produce water on a regular basis, and many people have found the water to have miraculous healing powers.

Activity

Research one of the following European saints. Make a collage of images that reflect the life or message of the saint. Include a description or key words of one lesson that we today can learn from this person's life. Also note the date on which he or she is honored.

- Camillus de Lellis
- John Vianney
- Jane de Chantal
- Alphonsus Liguori
- Carmelite Nuns of Compiègne
- Clement Maria Hofbauer

- Benedict the Moor
- Dominic Savio
- John Bosco
- Edmund Ignatius Rice
- Gerard Majella
- John Baptist de Rossi

- Maria Francesca Gallo
- Josaphat
- Joseph Pignatelli
- Mary Margaret Alacoque
- John Berchmans
- Jornet Ibars

The Moral and Spiritual Authority of the Pope. A third reaction to rationalism was the strengthening of the role of the pope as a moral and spiritual leader. Some popes of the Middle Ages and the Reformation saw themselves as the secular ruler of the Papal States first and the spiritual head of Christianity second. As the secular power of the popes declined, they tended to speak out more forcefully on moral and spiritual matters. The strongest pronouncement of papal power in the area of faith and morals came at the First Vatican Council, in 1870. The bishops gathered in Rome declared the pope to be **infallible** when making an official definitive statement about faith or morals.

infallible
incapable of error in defining doctrines involving faith or morals

[W]e teach and declare as a divinely revealed dogma that when the Roman pontiff speaks **ex cathedra,** that is, when, in the exercise of his office as shepherd and teacher of all Christians, in virtue of his supreme apostolic teaching, he defines a doctrine concerning faith or morals to be held by the whole Church, he possesses, by the divine assistance promised to him in blessed Peter, that infallibility which the divine Redeemer willed his Church to enjoy in defining doctrine concerning faith or morals.

Vatican Council I as quoted in Alfred McBride O.P.raem., *The Story of the Church* (Cincinnati, Ohio: St. Anthony Messenger Press, 1996), 153.

A society of atheists would practice civil and moral actions just as well as other societies, provided that it saw that crimes were severely punished and that it attached honor and infamy to certain things. . . . the ideas of honesty which prevail among Christians do not come from the religion which they profess.

Pierre Bayle as quoted in Jean Comby with Diarmaid MacCulloch, *How to Read Church History, Vol. 2* (New York: Crossroad, 1996), 103–104.

fyi!

A pronouncement made *ex cathedra*— "from the chair" of Peter—identified a papal statement as infallible. In 1950 Pope Pius XII declared *ex cathedra* that the Virgin Mary was bodily assumed into heaven. Therefore, Mary's assumption is an infallible Catholic doctrine.

Activity

If you were a Catholic theologian, how would you respond to the following statement?

I believe in God, though I get on very well with atheists. It is very important not to mistake hemlock for parsley; but it does not matter whether one does or does not believe in God.

Diderot to Voltaire, 1749

Review

1. What instrument did Galileo create that helped him in his astronomy investigations?

2. What is the difference between a geocentric and a heliocentric system?

3. What three reasons did the Inquisition give for condemning Galileo's position?

4. What three issues facing the Church does Galileo's story illustrate?

5. What perspective on truth seeking did Descartes and Bacon advocate?

6. According to Kant, what was the spirit of the Enlightenment?

7. What position on Christianity did most Enlightenment thinkers hold?

8. What is rationalism?

9. How do deists perceive God?

10. In what three ways did the Catholic Church respond to rationalism and deism?

AN AGE OF NATION-STATES

Besides its emphasis on science, the post-Reformation period in Europe was characterized by the formation of clearly distinct nation-states. Europe had kings before this time, but during feudalism they functioned as the first among equals. Also, the emperor at least theoretically held authority over all local rulers. In the

Discussion

Discuss whether the following emphasize or de-emphasize separate nation-states: business, religion, television, the Internet, the military, terrorism, natural resources.

Based on your discussion, is the world moving away from emphasizing separate nation-states? Explain.

monarch
head of a nation-state who claims to have complete authority in its governance

Thirty Years War
war over religious, dynastic, and territorial issues which involved most European nations but was fought mainly in Germany

seventeenth century the concept of a **monarch,** someone who was the one and only ruler of a nation, began to develop. People saw themselves not as Bavarians or Normans (people who spoke a particular dialect and lived in a specific section of a country) but as German or French. While we take for granted that the world is divided into separate and distinct nation-states, this concept is a relatively recent one. Monarchs who saw themselves as possessing absolute power were the embodiment of unified nations. On the one hand, monarchs lessened the power of nobles under them. On the other hand, they also greatly diminished the power of transnational entities, such as the emperor and the pope.

At the Battle of Lech. April 1632, Swedish troops overwhelmed the allied forces of the Catholic League and the Holy Roman Empire.

The event that did much to establish in Europe a system of nation-states ruled by monarchs was the **Thirty Years War.** The war lasted from 1618 to 1648, leaving Germany in ruins and the Holy Roman Empire politically doomed. The war began with the rebellion of the Bohemians against King Ferdinand II. When the Peace of Westphalia ended the conflict, three outcomes strengthened the modern nation-state system of Europe. First, the Holy Roman Empire was reduced to being one nation among many. The emperor ruled Germany as its monarch but could no longer lay claim to exercising power over other European countries. Germany became simply one more nation-state of Europe. Second, the pope complained about anti-Catholic wording in the treaty, but his complaints went unheeded. From this time forward, the pope would become a minor voice in European politics. Third, religious lines were sharply drawn in Europe. The Lutherans were mainly located in Scandinavia, Prussia, and parts of southern Germany; most Calvinists lived in Switzerland, much of Holland, and Scotland; England had its own Church; and all the rest of Europe was predominantly Catholic. Therefore, in future political conflicts, religion became less important than national identity.

Christina, Queen of Sweden

At the battle of Lutzen in 1632 during the Thirty Years War, King Gustavus Adolphus Wasa of Sweden was killed. His daughter and heir Christina was only six years old at the time, so a council of regents ran the country until she became an adult. When she turned eighteen in 1644, Christina took the throne and used her influence to end the war and bring about the Treaty of Westphalia. According to the terms of the treaty, every nation would take the religion of its ruler. Christina was a Protestant, as was Sweden. However, she was drawn to Catholicism and considered converting. Her advisers attempted to arrange a marriage for her with a number of Protestant rulers, but she declined their offers. Ten years after assuming the throne, Christina decided to begin instructions in the Catholic faith. She abdicated to her cousin, joined the Catholic Church in 1655, and moved to Rome. Although she twice attempted to regain her throne, she instead lived out her life in Rome doing acts of charity for those who were poor. She died in 1689 and is buried in St. Peter's Basilica, the only woman accorded this privilege.

National Churches Versus the Universal Church

France is the best example of a nation-state that was ruled by a powerful monarch following the Thirty Years War. Its greatest king, Louis XIV, attempted to wrestle control of the Catholic Church in France away from Rome. He advocated what came to be known as **Gallicanism**—control of Church affairs by the nation and not by the pope. King Louis XIV issued the *Four Gallican Articles* in 1682 and called upon all French clergy to agree to them. The articles stated that:

Gallicanism
a movement originating among the French Catholic clergy based on national rulers having authority for Church governance in their country

- Neither the pope nor the Church has power over temporal and civil matters.
- The power of Church councils is greater than that of the pope.
- The pope's power is limited by the customs and privileges of national churches.
- The pope's decisions require the consent of the Church.

The king insisted that the Gallican Articles be taught in French seminaries, and he recommended as bishops only those priests who agreed to the articles. However, Pope Innocent XI rejected the articles and refused to assign bishops to French dioceses when they became vacant. Finally, after thirty dioceses were without bishops, the pope agreed to appoint as bishops the priests chosen by the king but only if they renounced the articles. However, the bishops in France were more loyal to the state than they were to the Catholic Church, even though they had renounced the articles. A similar conflict between papal control and national control of the Catholic Church emerged in Germany and Austria.

Many European monarchs applied Enlightenment concepts to themselves and thought of themselves as "enlightened despots." That is, they saw themselves as being the correct person to be in their position at that particular time. Curbing the power of the papacy over the Church in their country was part of their attempt to exercise complete control over the nation. In order to ensure that the pope was weak, monarchs influenced their bishops to elect popes who were not strong leaders. For a period of time, the men chosen to be pope were old and sickly. Between 1585 and 1605, six popes were elected—an average of about one every three years.

Control of the papacy by secular rulers also led to the suppression of the Jesuits in 1773. Suppression of the Jesuits meant that at a time when the Church needed educated Catholics, many of the best colleges and universities worldwide were closed. (At the time, the Jesuits ran 266 colleges and 103 seminaries.) Interestingly, one of the few places that welcomed Jesuits was Russia, where Czarina Catherine the Great appreciated their contributions to knowledge.

fyi!

The word *Gallicanism* comes from the ancient Roman name for French territory, *Gaul*.

THE PAPACY FROM 1585 TO 1605	
Sixtus V	April 24, 1585–August 27, 1590
Urban VII	September 15–27, 1590
Gregory XIV	December 5, 1590–October 16, 1591
Innocent IX	October 29–December 30, 1591
Clement VIII	January 30, 1592–March 5, 1605
Leo XI	April 1–17, 1605

Activity

To put the idea of a new pope about every three years into perspective, look up the length of time each twentieth-century pope reigned.

- Who was pope for the longest time?
- Who had the shortest reign?
- Discounting the shortest, what was the average number of years a twentieth-century pope reigned?

The violence of the French Revolution set the Catholic Church against many of the principles of the movement for decades after the Reign of Terror.

The Impact of the French Revolution

The French Revolution was actually a series of events that happened over a period of time in the latter part of the eighteenth century. The Enlightenment serves as an important backdrop to the revolution because, as mentioned earlier, Enlightenment thinkers called into question all the institutions that had been held up as the pillars of society. On May 5, 1789, King Louis XVI called together the Estates General, the French parliament, because his treasury was depleted due to the cost of fighting recent wars. This body, which had not met since 1614, was made up of representatives from the three estates: clergy, nobility, and common people. Almost from the beginning the third estate (representing the common people), many clergy, and some nobles tried to steer the meeting into a movement demanding changes in the government. On June 17 many members of the Estates General gathered in a tennis court and proclaimed themselves a National Assembly, vowing not to leave until a constitution was approved.

On July 14, 1789, citizens of Paris attacked the Bastille prison and set its prisoners free. Because this act marked the beginning of the involvement of the common people in the process, this date is celebrated as the official beginning of the French Revolution. Over the next few years, stability in France deteriorated rapidly. In 1793 the king and his family were executed. During the next two years, tens of thousands of people were executed during the **Reign of Terror.** Church leaders, most of whom came from the noble class and sided with the nobility, went to the guillotine, as did many priests. In 1795 a group of leaders known as the Directory used the army to restore order. Then, in 1799 the most popular of the French generals, Napoleon Bonaparte, declared himself leader of France.

To understand the impact of the French Revolution on the Catholic Church, it is important to recall that France became Christian in 496 under King Clovis and, therefore, saw itself as "the eldest daughter of the Church." Although the faith was strong on the eve of the revolution, and although local clergy generally identified with the common people, the Church was identified with the nobility and held much property in this time when food and other resources were scarce. During the

Reign of Terror
period during the French Revolution when nobility and many clergy were executed by French revolutionary leaders

revolutionary period, monasteries were overtaken, and communities of monks and nuns were disbanded. Instead of the pope appointing bishops, the people voted for their bishops and priests. All members of the clergy had to swear allegiance to the state rather than to the pope. As part of the revolutionary agenda, French leaders during the Reign of Terror tried to eliminate all reminders of the way things used to be run. They even proposed a ten-day week so that there would no longer be a sabbath day for worship. In effect, the French Revolution was not simply anti-nobility; it was also anti-Church. For decades following the revolution, Church leaders were fearful of ideas and movements that reflected a revolutionary spirit.

concordat
an agreement between the pope and a head of state identifying the role that each would play in Church governance in that country

Napoleon and the Concordat with the Pope

Before Napoleon gained power, French armies had invaded Italy and deported the pope to France. The college of cardinals was disbanded, and many people thought that the papacy had come to an end. However, when Napoleon came to power, he realized that the majority of the common people throughout Europe clung to their Catholic faith. If he were to create the empire that he wanted, his task would be easier *with* Catholicism rather than against it. Napoleon, therefore, signed a **concordat** with the new pope, Pius VII. According to the concordat, Napoleon would appoint bishops, but the pope would approve the appointments. By making this agreement directly with the pope, Napoleon validated the pope as the spiritual head of the Church, even in France.

This acceptance of the pope's authority signaled a move away from Gallicanism to **Ultramontanism.** (*Ultramontanism,* Latin phrase meaning "beyond the mountains," meant that control of the French Church was in the hands of the pope, who resided beyond the mountains rather than in France.) As European Catholics soured of the revolution and Napoleon, more and more of them looked to the pope as a symbol of an alternate system. Generally, Ultramontanists sided with those forces who wanted to restore the prerevolutionary order of things, often in an exaggerated way. Thus, the fate of the Catholic Church in France during most of the nineteenth century rose or fell in conjunction with the fortunes of the nobility.

"Napolean on Horseback at the St. Bernard Pass" by Jacques-Louis David.

Ultramontanism
belief, often in an exaggerated form, that the pope alone has ultimate authority for Church governance in all countries

Since the time of Emperor Constantine, there had been a history of involvement in Church affairs by secular rulers. After Napoleon, popes found it necessary and beneficial to make concordats with many of the European countries ruled by Catholic monarchs. These concordats aimed at a balance of power between pope and ruler. As the nineteenth century progressed and democratically elected leaders governed European nations, concordats were either dismissed or ignored. By the time of Pius IX, who was pope from 1846 to 1878, the pope had little political power, but there was no question that the pope was the supreme and sole head of the Catholic Church.

Cardinal Ercole Consalvi

The Church had a talented diplomat in Cardinal Ercole Consalvi (1757–1824), son of a noble family from Pisa, Italy. Cardinal Consalvi served as Vatican Secretary of State during the difficult years of Napoleon's rule. Consalvi brought a number of laypeople into the government of the Papal States and advised the pope to insist on making a concordat with Napoleon so that Church interests would be protected. In 1809 Consalvi and twelve other cardinals refused to recognize Napoleon's marriage to Marie Louise of Austria. Napoleon first ordered them to be shot but then instead ordered that they were to be deprived of their property and forbidden to wear any sign that they were cardinals. These thirteen cardinals came to be known as the *black cardinals* since they couldn't wear the red robes that other cardinals did. When Napoleon was defeated, Consalvi was reinstated as Vatican Secretary of State and negotiated restoration of the Papal States at the Congress of Vienna in 1814–1815.

Pope Pius IX—The First Modern Pope

Giovanni Maria Mastai Ferretti, Pope Pius IX, 1792–1878, pope from 1846.

After the chaos of the Napoleonic era, the leaders of Europe came together at the Congress of Vienna in 1814–1815. During this gathering they redrew the map of Europe. Through the efforts of its main architect, Prince Metternich of Austria, all royal monarchs were restored to their thrones. Metternich took particular pains to prevent any one country from becoming a "super nation" dominating all others. Metternich totally opposed democracy and predicted that the "American experiment" would never see a second generation. He also restored the Papal States to the pope. Metternich's reactionary views so dominated Europe until 1858 that this period is often called "the age of Metternich."

Church leaders of the time felt as most of Europe did—that it was time to return to the stability of the pre-Napoleonic days. The three popes elected during this period, while they were good persons and encouraged much good work, expressed the conservative views toward politics common among the European monarchs of the time. The Papal States restored a feudal system. Jews were restricted to living apart from Christians, in ghettos. One pope considered trains to be the work of the devil and resisted installation of street lights. Most citizens of the Papal States viewed these popes as tyrants.

Discussion

Some Catholic thinkers of the time believed that the themes of the French Revolution—freedom, equality, fraternity—actually reflected the spirit of the early Church. Debate the following statement: Even though the French Revolution went in directions that were clearly un-Christian, its original spirit embodied true Christian ideals.

fyi!

The Second Vatican Council, in the 1960s, clarified the Church's teaching on infallibility, explaining that the college of bishops in union with the pope, could also teach infallibly.

infallibility
the gift of the Holy Spirit to the Church whereby either the pope or bishops in union with him can definitively proclaim a doctrine of faith or morals for the belief of the faithful

In 1846 the cardinals chose as pope someone identified with a more liberal viewpoint. He took the name Pope Pius IX and led the Church for thirty-two years, the longest reigning pope in history. The new pope began by taking steps that pleased the liberals of Europe. He offered amnesty to all political prisoners in the Papal States, instituted a representative form of government, and did away with censorship of ideas.

However, when, in 1848, a revolution forced Pius IX to flee to Naples and a republic was established in Rome, he quickly turned against liberalism and democracy. With the help of French troops, he regained control of the Papal States. However, republican forces continued to take control of more and more portions of papal territory. Then, in 1870, French troops withdrew to participate in a war in which France was engaged at the time. This allowed the Italian general Garibaldi to storm Rome. He declared Rome capital of a united Italy under King Victor Emmanuel.

Pope Pius IX refused to accept any terms under which he would give up his claims to the Papal States. He would not even sign a document that said he could "continue to enjoy the area of the Vatican and the papal apartments." He said that "enjoy" meant that he was there as a courtesy from the Italian government and could be told to vacate it if his "landlord" wanted it for other purposes. The pope announced instead that he would continue to live there as "the prisoner of the Vatican."

As he was losing temporal power, Pope Pius IX started to take more seriously his role as pastor of the universal Church. For instance, in 1854 he proclaimed the dogma of the Immaculate Conception. (Most earlier statements of official Church teachings came from Church councils.) He also issued the Syllabus of Errors, a list of eighty errors that he regarded as being incompatible with Catholicism. In 1869 Pius IX called for an ecumenical council, Vatican Council I, which proclaimed the doctrine of papal **infallibility.** Interestingly, as the council was voting on this teaching, Italian forces were overtaking Rome. Vatican Council I, along with the end of the Papal States, signaled a change in the role of the pope. From now on, popes would be spiritual and moral leaders, not secular rulers. Thus, Pius IX was the first of the modern popes.

Review

1. What is the difference between a feudal king and a monarch?

2. What three outcomes of the Peace of Westphalia strengthened the modern nation-state system in Europe?

3. What is Gallicanism?

4. What did European monarchs do to maintain a weakened papacy?

5. What impact did the suppression of the Jesuits have on Catholic education?

6. What event is celebrated as the official beginning of the French Revolution?

7. What effect did the French Revolution have on the Catholic Church?

8. Why did Napoleon's concordat with the pope support Ultramontanism?

9. When was the "age of Metternich"? Why is it so called?

10. What event occurred in 1870 that led Pope Pius IX to declare himself to be "the the prisoner of the Vatican"? What was he protesting by taking this title?

11. Why is Pope Pius IX considered the first modern pope?

12. When was the First Vatican Council? What doctrine did it proclaim?

ENGLAND AND IRELAND

As mentioned in the last chapter, after King Henry VIII, England adopted a state-controlled religion that tended to be Catholic in theology and practice but that was not aligned with the universal Church centered in Rome. For over a century after Henry, the Church of England contended with Catholics on the one hand and, on the other, with groups who wanted a reformed expression of Protestantism. Under Henry's daughter, Queen Elizabeth I, England enacted many anti-Catholic laws and moved closer to the Protestant camp. However, over the course of the eighteenth century, anti-Catholic laws came to be ignored. England perceived itself as an enlightened, tolerant nation that didn't need to resort to old-fashioned persecution of religious dissenters to maintain stability. Finally, in 1829 England officially eliminated its anti-Catholic laws. During the period of the French Revolution, many French clergy made their way to England to avoid persecution at the hands of the revolutionary forces in France.

One of the colleges at Oxford University, Oxford, England.

In the 1830s a number of Anglican priests and bishops wanted the Church of England to become more Catholic. Some of the brightest churchmen in England joined this movement, called the *Oxford Movement* since a number of its members were associated with Oxford University. One of these Anglican priests, John Henry Newman, studied the early Church and concluded that the true Church should be centered around the bishop of Rome. Newman joined the Catholic Church in 1845. After Newman a number of other influential English people joined the Catholic Church. These English Catholics advocated strong, centralized authority of the pope in spiritual matters.

Ireland never entertained Protestantism. When Henry VIII broke with Catholicism, the Irish in large measure remained staunchly Catholic. Protestantism gained a foothold in Ireland only when Scottish Presbyterians and some English Protestants settled in a section of Northern Ireland. In 1688 the English forced the reigning king, James II, out of England. (James leaned toward Catholicism.) In what the English call the *Glorious Revolution,* William and Mary were given the English throne. The ousted James II attempted to regain control of England, using Ireland as a base. However, his forces were defeated by those of the new king, William of Orange. To this day Protestants in Northern Ireland are known as *Orangemen,* and Catholicism in Ireland and Northern Ireland is linked to anti-English resistance.

Three Leaders of the Church in England

Three men played an important role in the resurgence of Catholicism in England during the nineteenth century. Nicholas Wiseman was actually born in Spain in 1802 but moved to Ireland as a child. He studied in Rome and was ordained a bishop. In 1840 Wiseman moved to England. He spent ten years traveling throughout the British Isles, getting a sense of the needs of the Catholic people, preaching, and developing contacts with all segments of English society. The pope appointed him Archbishop of Westminster in 1850. Because of the strong anti-Catholic reaction to this appointment, Wiseman wrote a pastoral letter called "Appeal to Reason and Good Feeling of the English People on the Subject of the Catholic Hierarchy." His eloquence and bold public appearances quieted antipapal activities in England. Wiseman became England's first cardinal since the time of Queen Elizabeth and supported the Oxford Movement that made Catholicism an intellectual force in the country.

Henry Edward Manning was born into a wealthy and distinguished English family in 1808. He chose to become a college professor and a deacon in the Anglican Church. Manning became involved in the Oxford Movement where he became friends with John Henry Newman. In 1851 he was ordained a Catholic priest and went to study in Rome. When Cardinal Wiseman died in 1865, Manning was named the second Archbishop of Westminster and later a cardinal. He participated in Vatican Council I and was a leading proponent of the Church's support for working class people, becoming especially involved in the London dock strike of 1889.

John Henry Newman was born in 1801 in London. He received a classical education, coming into contact with Enlightenment thinkers such as Voltaire and Hume, whereupon he announced that he was an atheist. Convinced by a teacher to read the works of John Calvin, Newman converted to Anglicanism and was ordained a priest. He served as vicar at St. Mary's in Oxford and led the Oxford Movement. Initially, he attempted to show that Anglicanism was a middle ground between Romanism (centered on papal authority) and Protestantism (centered on individual judgment). Members of the Oxford Movement began to enter the Catholic Church, but Newman hoped for reconciliation between his religion and his questions. He articulated his search in a hymn called "Lead, Kindly Light." Finally Newman traveled to Rome and joined the Catholic Church. Two years later he was ordained and received permission from the pope to join the Oratory, a religious community founded by Saint Philip Neri. He continued to be a great influence on the scholarly communities of the Church and was named a cardinal in 1877.

Activity

1. Research the conflict happening in Ireland today. What part has religion played in the conflict?

2. Write a report on an aspect of English-Irish relations. As part of your report, agree or disagree with the following statement: The conflict between England and Ireland was political and economic rather than religious.

Review

1. What was the Oxford Movement?

2. John Henry Newman concluded that the true Church should be centered upon what institution?

3. What effect did the Glorious Revolution have on English-Irish relations?

4. Why are Protestants in Northern Ireland known as *Orangemen*?

A CHANGING WORLD

The Age of Enlightenment certainly did not bring about a world that was free of strife and guided by rational principles as promised. Common people suffered and often looked to the Catholic Church for comfort and meaning. While the leaders of Church and state argued over control of the Church at its higher levels, at the lower levels of society, in response to their Christian faith, heroic men and women gave their lives helping people in need. Also, as doors opened to lands where people had never encountered Christianity, other Catholics set out to spread the good news of Christ to the people who lived there. In other words, the Christian message flourished even in the midst of the great changes taking place worldwide. Here are some of the major expressions of how the gospel was lived out during the age of Enlightenment.

The Baroque in Art and Worship

baroque
a style of art, architecture, and spirituality that emphasizes feelings and sentimentality

In French *baroque* means "odd." **Baroque** art, architecture, music, style of worship, and even theological reflection were very popular in Catholic communities following the Reformation and throughout the Enlightenment period. The baroque style certainly was unusual, given the currents associated with Protestantism and the Enlightenment. While Reformed Protestants were dismantling churches of statues and simplifying their services, baroque churches were very ornate, and worship services were like grand theatrical productions. Baroque religious expression appealed to the senses. Religious expression was emotional, with joyful and exuberant art and music.

Although the baroque style appears to emphasize sensual and surface expressions of religion rather than depth, it certainly had its appeal, especially among ordinary Catholics. The Jesuit mother church in Rome, known as the *Gesu*, represents the baroque style of architecture. The baroque emphasized the humanity of Jesus and the tender, motherly qualities of Mary. Devotions to the Blessed Mother and adoration of the Blessed Sacrament appealed to the common people, offering them emotional, joyous religious experiences in contrast to their otherwise drab lives.

Gesu church in Rome is an example of baroque art and architecture. This is the main Jesuit church in Rome.

Varieties of Spiritual Life

Service to People Who Are Poor. The seventeenth and eighteenth centuries offered a vast array of ways that people found to live the spiritual life. Two saints who deserve special mention are Vincent de Paul (1581–1660) and Louise de Marillac (1591–1660). Vincent was born into a peasant family but pursued the priesthood as a way to escape the poverty of his family. He used his charm to become a chaplain to the wealthiest families of Paris, including the queen herself. One day his father, who was dressed in shabby farmer's clothes, came to visit Vincent, and Vincent refused to acknowledge him. Vincent had a dramatic change of heart when a peasant on the estate of a wealthy family was near death and asked Vincent to hear his confession. After the confession the man thanked Vincent and remarked that if it were not for him, he might have died without benefit of confessing his sins.

Saint Vincent de Paul icon by Robert Lentz.

This experience led Vincent to realize what a wonderful gift his priesthood was and that he should use it to be of service to those in need. The first thing he did was to train and organize priests for work in the French countryside, where the clergy were notoriously unprepared. Then he used his contacts among the wealthy to fund a variety of charitable projects. Vincent even convinced a number of wealthy women to dedicate part of their time to working among people who were poor and destitute. One woman, Louise de Marillac, realized that part-time workers were not sufficient to meet the needs of those suffering in and around Paris. Under Vincent's guidance, Louise founded the Daughters of Charity. The women chose not to live in convents or dress as nuns. Instead they lived among people who were poor and served their needs. This was a radical idea. People who were poor were not to be brought to the convent; rather, the convent was to go out to them. Vincent admonished his workers to treat those who were poor as if they were dealing with their own child, or rather with God, since God is present in those who are poor.

Youth News

Saint Vincent de Paul gave his life to helping people who were poor. In our world today there are many agencies whose main mission is to provide direct aid to those who are poor. One such organization is Catholic Relief Services. Founded by the Catholic bishops of the United States in 1943, CRS helps people who are poor to realize their potential and encourages them to develop their God-given skills and talents. Additionally, CRS educates the people of the United States to fulfill their moral responsibilities toward their brothers and sisters around the world by helping those who are poor, working to remove the causes of poverty, and promoting social justice. Visit **www.catholicrelief.org** for more information on CRS. What have you done lately to fulfill your moral responsibility to help those who are poor? Does your school or church community sponsor a service trip you can participate in? Can you help at a soup kitchen or food bank? Find out what opportunities are available to you for helping people in need and get involved.

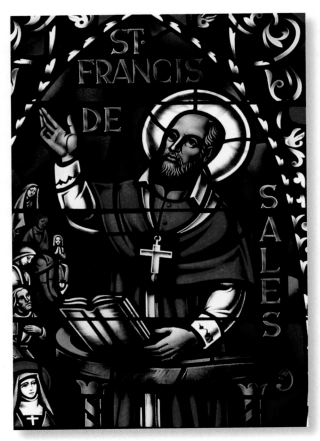

Vincent de Paul and Louise de Marillac succeeded in creating organizations that we today might label forms of social work. They also stretched the understanding of the kinds of work that women could undertake. Vincent is the patron saint of charitable societies. In 1960 Pope John XXIII proclaimed Louise de Marillac patron of all Christian social work.

Everyday Spirituality. Because of his outstanding writings on the spiritual life, Saint Francis de Sales (1567–1622) is patron of writers and the press. However, his message about how to live the spiritual life has something for everyone. After becoming a lawyer, Francis decided to pursue his dream of becoming a priest and he worked in Geneva, Switzerland. If you recall from the last chapter, Geneva was at the time a hotbed of Calvinism. Francis was taking his life in his hands by speaking out for Catholicism there. However, his holiness impressed so many that a number of Calvinists brought their families back to Catholicism. In his spiritual writings, Francis suggested that people should not concentrate on practices of self-mortification but on love. He also pointed out that the spiritual life is different, depending on a person's vocation in life. A student can practice devotion as much as a teacher or a priest can; the experience will simply be different because of the difference in circumstances. For Francis a key was for people to develop good habits in their everyday lives, habits that lead them to be aware of God and to act out of love of God.

The Holy Vagabond. Does the idea of traveling around and living off of the land or on the streets have any appeal to you? A young Frenchman named Benedict Joseph Labre (1748–1783) attempted to enter a number of religious orders but was always turned down. He decided that his vocation was to live in the world as simply as he could, visiting shrines and praying as he traveled. He eventually arrived in Rome where he lived on the streets and never bathed or changed his clothes. Needless to say, people kept their distance from him. He did frequent the various churches of the city, however, and some people began to think that perhaps he wasn't just a homeless derelict but indeed a holy man. At the age of thirty-five, he collapsed on the steps of a church and died. Children began calling out, "The saint is dead, the saint is dead!" From there his reputation as a holy man grew, and he was canonized one hundred years later.

Visit **www. employees. csbsju.edu/ roliver/orders. html# orders** to research a religious order that exists in the Catholic Church today. Describe the circumstances surrounding its beginning, the type of work it originally set out to do, and the types of ministry its members currently perform.

Teaching Children Who Are Poor. In the seventeenth century, schooling was almost exclusively a privilege of the rich who could afford tutors for their children. The Frenchman, John Baptist de la Salle (1651–1719), patron saint of teachers, felt that men should be trained specifically to teach boys who were poor, in order to help them out of poverty. La Salle introduced a number of innovations that have since become standard practice in teaching. Subjects were taught in the language of the students rather than in Latin. Teaching took place in groups rather than one-on-one. Also, subjects were taught according to a set schedule. La Salle did not want priests for this work but men dedicated exclusively to teaching. To that end he founded a community of religious brothers called the Brothers of the Christian Schools or simply the Christian Brothers. Today, members of the order he founded administer many educational institutions, and all teachers owe a debt to him.

A number of women also began communities dedicated to teaching and service to those who were poor. For instance, the French woman Julie Billiart (1751–1816) helped found a community of women known as the Institute of Notre Dame de Namur. When aristocrats and clergy were losing their heads to the guillotine in Paris, Julie risked her own life to hide priests who were being pursued by revolutionary forces. Even though she suffered from physical ailments for most of her life, Julie managed to establish many convents and to expand the work of her community.

Right: John Baptist de la Salle
Below: Julie Billiart

Activity

1. List three habits that you personally could develop that would help you in your spiritual life. Explain why these habits would be particularly beneficial for you.

2. As you go about your business over the next two days, think to yourself that every person you meet is made in the image of God and is called to be a saint. Write about the experience.

Sacred or Secular?

The Santa Maria may have been only 75 feet long. Sailing the ocean in ships this size and smaller was the first challenge for missionaries.

Catholic Missionaries to Foreign Lands

The Gospels clearly state that the followers of Jesus are to spread his message to every nation. The period of the Reformation was also an age of exploration for European adventurers. Sailors, particularly under the flags of Portugal and Spain, made their way to parts of the world that only a few Europeans had previously visited. While their primary motives were trade and conquest, the sponsors of these sea voyages also saw an opportunity to introduce the gospel message to new populations. Since Portugal and Spain were Catholic countries, the missionaries who traveled to these new lands were also Catholic, mostly Franciscans and Jesuits.

As happened in earlier periods in Church history when Christians introduced the faith to new cultures, martyrdom usually followed. The missionaries who went to far-away lands knew that their lives were in danger, and yet many priests eagerly joined the missionary effort. Similarly, the first converts in these lands also were likely to suffer, either the strain of rejection from their countrymen or torture and death at the hands of those who felt threatened by a new religion and culture.

We will hold off discussion of missionary activity in the Americas until the next chapter. Northern Africa had a Christian population from the beginning period of Christianity, and, in a later chapter, we will examine more recent trends in African Catholicism. The story of Catholicism in Australia is linked to the story of Catholic, mostly Irish, prisoners sent there in exile. However, the story of Christianity's encounter with the highly developed cultures of Southeast Asia and India demonstrates the appeal of the faith and its flexibility.

Christianity in China and its Neighbors

China possessed an ancient and highly developed culture before it encountered Christianity. The first known presence of Christianity in China is traced to the year 635. A group of Christians called Nestorians traveled east from Persia and settled in China, but their descendants did not survive into the modern period. After 1500, European missionaries in the Far East used two approaches to win converts to Christianity. Missionaries from the mendicant orders (Franciscans and Dominicans) worked among the common people and tried to make inroads there. Jesuits, on the other hand, engaged the most educated members of society and tried to make a case for Christianity in terms of the most exalted ideas of the native culture. Jesuits were more open to **accommodation** than the mendicant missionaries were. For instance, in China Jesuits determined that Confucius was revered as a great sage and not a god and that therefore the Chinese did not need to reject his teachings to be Christian. Also, the Jesuit missionaries concluded that the great respect Chinese had for their ancestors was also compatible with Christianity.

accommodation
the practice of incorporating beliefs and practices from local cultures into Christianity

The most famous advocate of an accommodationist approach to missionary activity in China was the Jesuit Matteo Ricci (1521–1610). Ricci mastered the Chinese language and literature. He made a case for Christianity in terms of ancient Chinese writings. Ricci also tried to convince Chinese scholars that Europeans were not uncultured people. To do this he adopted upper-class Chinese manners in dress, eating habits, and behavior. Some missionaries working among the poorer classes criticized this accommodationist approach and asked the pope to rule on the matter. In 1715 Pope Clement XI pronounced that accommodation to local cultures as the Jesuits were doing was unacceptable. As a result, Christianity was presented strictly in European terms and came to be perceived as foreign and as a threat to Chinese and Japanese culture. Persecution of Christians set in. The struggle regarding inculturation in the Asian church continues to this day.

Two countries in Southeast Asia where Christianity made strong inroads were the Philippines and Vietnam. Korea encountered Christianity later than other countries, but Christianity—both Catholicism and Protestantism—has developed a strong presence there.

The Catholic faith remains strong in countries such as Vietnam, pictured here, and the Philippines.

Saint Paul Miki and Companions

Saint Francis Xavier first introduced Christianity to Japan in 1549. By the end of the century, tens of thousands of Japanese had joined the Christian community. Paul Miki not only became Christian, he also joined the Jesuits and was renowned for his preaching. Japanese rulers began to fear the influence of this religion from a European culture and forbade Christian missionary activity. When some Christians violated this law, the Japanese emperor decided to execute a group of known Christians. In 1597 he condemned twenty-six Christians to death by crucifixion. Soon after the death of Paul Miki and his companions, Japanese authorities began an active campaign to ferret out all Christians and put them to death. Many Christians were crucified. To identify Christians, Japanese authorities would place images of Christ or Mary on the ground and require everyone to stamp on them. Punishment for those who refused was death—for themselves and their families.

After such stringent persecution, Christianity apparently died out in Japan until 1854 when Japan's isolation from the West ended. A French priest arrived in 1860 to serve the French Catholic community in Nagasaki. In 1865 a group of Japanese citizens approached the priest and cautiously told him that they were Christians. Even after two hundred years without a priest or contact from other Christians, thousands of Japanese had continued to practice their Catholicism in secret and had handed the faith down to their children.

India—Missionaries Discover an Ancient Christian Community

Portuguese missionaries first arrived in India in 1498. When they arrived they discovered an unexpected phenomenon—a small community of Christians already living there! These Christians claimed to be descendants of a Christian community founded by the apostle Thomas in the very first century. They had the equivalent of bishops and priests, practiced Christian rites, and possessed Christian writings including a composite of the Gospels.

At first these **Christians of Saint Thomas** welcomed the Portuguese as fellow Christians, and the missionaries were glad to see a Christian presence already in India. However, in time the two groups ran into conflict. For instance, the Saint

Christians of Saint Thomas
Indian Christians who trace their origins to the first century

Thomas Christians did not use images in their places of worship, their priests married, and they used both water and oil in Baptism. (The Hindus of India had many sacred images. Therefore, to distinguish themselves from their Hindu neighbors, Saint Thomas Christians didn't use images.) The Saint Thomas Christians were disturbed by certain Portuguese practices such as their use of images, their meat-eating habits, and their referring to Mary as Mother of God instead of Mother of Christ. Appeals to the pope from both sides attempted to resolve the conflict between the two groups. However, the two groups still remain in India today: Catholics who trace their lineage to the Portuguese missionaries, and a number of Christian groups who see themselves as descendants of Thomas and first-century Indian Christians.

Portuguese missionaries did manage to gain converts among a portion of the population of India that was not already Christian. The first group to convert to Christianity were lower-caste fishermen living along the seacoast. Entire clans of fishermen accepted Christianity, along with their wives and children. When the Spanish Jesuit Francis Xavier (1506–1552) arrived in India in 1542, he realized that these converts knew very little about Christian beliefs. Therefore, he wrote basic prayers and the creed in simple rhymes that were easy to remember and recite. Indian children would follow him around and recite the Lord's Prayer and other prayers with him. Through Francis Xavier, Catholicism gained a firm foothold in India. Pope Pius X declared Francis Xavier patron saint of Christian missions. He is also known as "the Apostle to India" and as "the Apostle to Japan," since he at a later time also traveled to that country.

Missionaries of Charity pray at the tomb of their founder, Mother Teresa, in Calcutta, India.

Above: Roberto de Nobili.

Right: A Brahmin priest prepares for a special ritual in Bali, Indonesia.

Brahmins
in the traditional Indian caste system, members of the priestly caste

The Italian Jesuit Roberto de Nobili added an entirely different dimension when he arrived in India in 1606. He realized that the religious scholars and holy men of the country were the **Brahmins.** In the Indian caste system, Brahmins dressed differently from others and would not eat or socialize with lower-caste persons. De Nobili decided that he would learn the ways of the Brahmins. He mastered their beliefs, joined in their austere practices, and even began to dress like them. He also disassociated himself from the crude, meat-eating Portuguese Christians whom the Brahmins disdained. De Nobili concluded that he could become a Brahmin without denouncing Christianity and that Brahmins could become Christian without giving up their social caste, their distinctive dress, or their learning. Within three years he converted fifty Brahmins to the faith. He also was accused of heresy by the Portuguese Christians. Nonetheless, de Nobili lived in India as the "Roman Brahmin" for fifty years and added to the Christian tradition there.

Activity

Debate the following statements. Explain your answers.

1. Missionaries who want to introduce people to the faith should spend their time with the leaders of a country rather than with the common folk.

2. People should respect other people's religions. Therefore, there is no place for seeking converts in today's world.

3. Christians who want to work among people of other faiths should spend their time helping people in need rather than in directly trying to convert people.

4. Christianity is not the same as European culture; it should be expressed in terms of the culture in which it finds itself.

5. All Catholics who take their faith seriously should do what they can to bring others to the faith.

6. The Catholic Church today does not do enough to bring people into the Church.

Review

1. Describe a baroque style of spirituality.

2. What experience led Vincent de Paul to become involved in service to people who were poor?

3. What group was founded by Louise de Marillac?

4. What did Francis de Sales emphasize in his spirituality?

5. Why was Benedict Joseph Labre considered a saint?

6. What changes did John Baptist de La Salle introduce into education?

7. Who was Matteo Ricci, and what is an accommodationist approach to missionary work?

8. Who were the Christians of Saint Thomas?

9. How did Francis Xavier help Indian converts to Christianity remember the basic prayers and creeds of the faith?

10. What approach did Roberto de Nobili use in his missionary work?

Conclusion

The Catholic Church underwent a major transformation during the period of the Enlightenment, the age of discovery, and that time of intense political change in Europe. Catholics made major contributions to what would become the modern world. Men and women we now recognize as saints instituted modern approaches to social work, hospital care, and education. Catholic missionaries spread out across the globe and made Catholicism a religion that now has a home in practically every country and culture. The papacy itself underwent many painful changes during this era of transformation. The sixteenth century had ended with a divided Christianity in the West. Following this jarring experience, the papacy had to deal with scholars who looked to radically new sources of truth and rejected teachings that had been handed down. By the middle of the nineteenth century, the pope no longer served as both a head of state and the spiritual leader of the Church. Flowing from these difficult transformations, both the pope and the Church emerged in the modern world as a sacred presence in an increasingly secularized world.

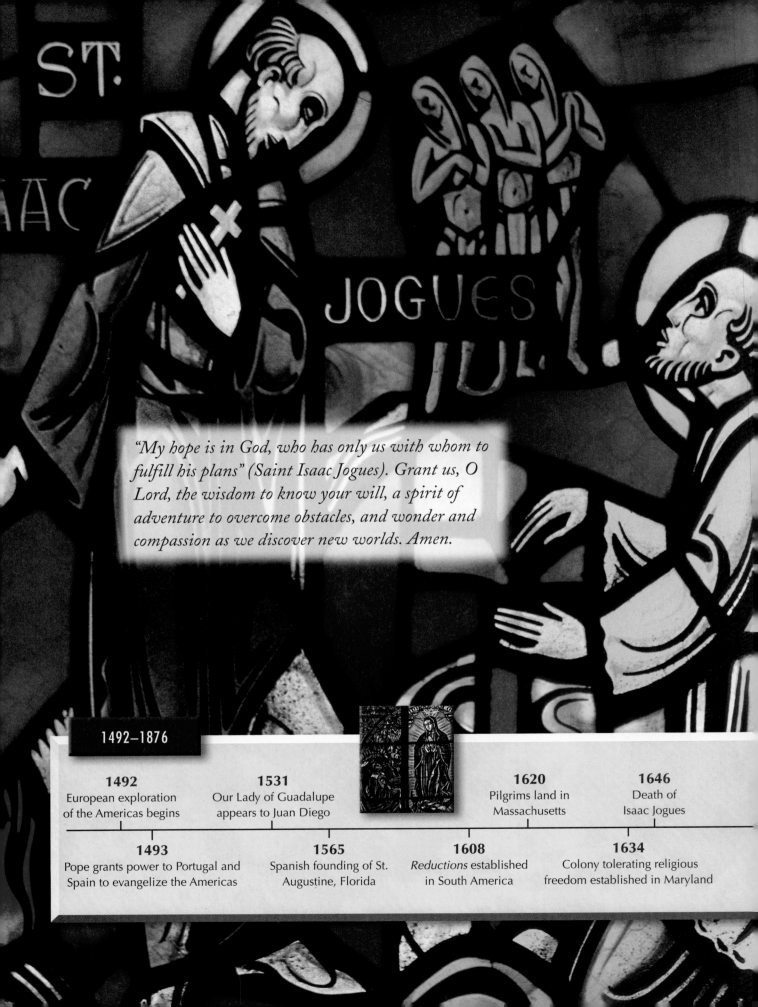

"My hope is in God, who has only us with whom to fulfill his plans" (Saint Isaac Jogues). Grant us, O Lord, the wisdom to know your will, a spirit of adventure to overcome obstacles, and wonder and compassion as we discover new worlds. Amen.

1492–1876

1492
European exploration of the Americas begins

1493
Pope grants power to Portugal and Spain to evangelize the Americas

1531
Our Lady of Guadalupe appears to Juan Diego

1565
Spanish founding of St. Augustine, Florida

1608
Reductions established in South America

1620
Pilgrims land in Massachusetts

1634
Colony tolerating religious freedom established in Maryland

1646
Death of Isaac Jogues

MOSAIC OF UNITY AND DIVERSITY

The Church in the Americas

CHAPTER OVERVIEW

- Spanish explorers, missionaries, and settlers create a Catholic New Spain extending from southern South America to Northern California.

- French missionaries introduce northern Native Americans to Catholicism.

- Catholics in the English colonies and during the first century of the United States attempt to express their Catholicism in a predominantly Protestant society and in a new kind of political environment.

1769
Junipero Serra founds
California missions

1787
United States Constitution
declares separation of
Church and state

1809
Mother Seton
establishes a
Catholic school

1844
Nativist riots in
Philadelphia

1680
Death of Kateri
Tekakwitha

1767
Closing of the
Paraguay *reduction*

1776
Declaration of
Independence

1788
John Carroll elected
first United States
Catholic bishop

1875
James Healy becomes
first mixed-race
U.S. Catholic bishop

If you had to move to another country, would you try to hold onto your old ways or decide to blend into the ways of your new culture? Can you imagine ever feeling "at home" some place else? Today, "being Catholic" and "being American" do not seem contradictory in any way. Indeed, over twenty-six percent of the population of the United States is Catholic. However, that has not always been the case. Catholicism first came to the New World along with the conquering Spanish, Portuguese, and French explorers and traders. The English colonies were less hospitable to Catholics. One of the great tests of the freedom of religion clause in the United States Constitution came when waves of immigrants greatly increased the nation's Catholic population.

The story of Catholicism in the Americas began in 1492 with the arrival of Europeans. Since then, Catholicism has added greatly to the identity of the American continents, both North and South. While tensions between North and South American standards and the values of the Catholic Church have always existed, the Americas have done much to reshape Catholicism. Eventually, the success of the American experiment helped the Catholic Church become less fearful of and more open to the modern world.

Before We Begin...

The American Catholic Church is a "mosaic of unity and diversity." Find statistics about the makeup of the Catholic Church in the Americas. Create a visual or audio representation of the Catholic Church of the Americas.

A COLLISION OF CULTURES

Catholicism in Spanish America

conquistadores
Spanish word for "conquerors"; the Spanish soldiers who first came to the Americas especially in search of wealth

In 1492 Christopher Columbus reached an island of the Americas, believing that he had landed on the eastern side of Asia. Although an Italian, Columbus sailed for the country of Spain, the most powerful European country of the fifteenth century and one that had avoided the turmoil of the Reformation. In 1493 the pope granted Spain and Portugal total responsibility for evangelizing—that is, spreading the gospel message—to all the new lands discovered by these two countries. Thus, European involvement in the Americas was from the beginning intimately connected with the religious situation in Europe. For the first decade or so, "America" meant the islands of the Caribbean. The Spanish established a capital city on Hispaniola and called it Santo Domingo. In 1504, just twelve years after the arrival of the first Spaniards, the Spanish Church established the diocese of Santo Domingo. In 1515 **conquistadores** took control of Cuba. Then, in 1519 they invaded the North American mainland, and New Spain began.

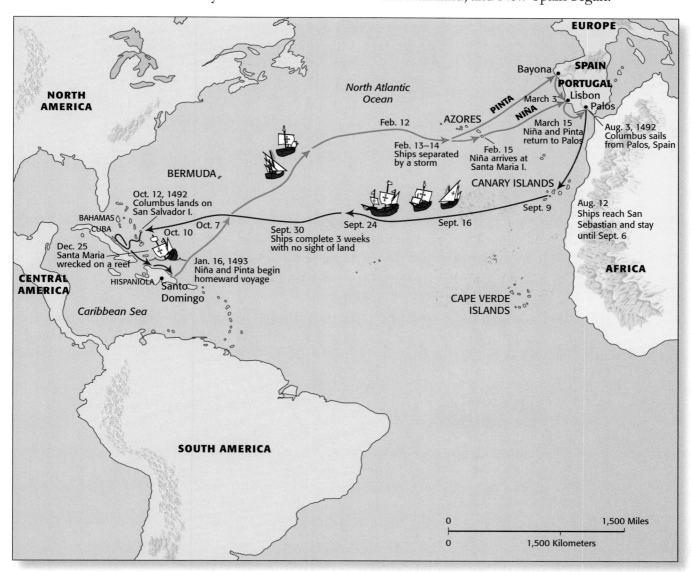

Mistreatment of the Native Americans

Use the keywords "Native American Navigator" to find a host of websites on Native American history or current news about Native Americans.

Everyone familiar with the story of Europe's conquest of the Americas knows that the native populations were devastated by it. Within forty years, no "Indians," as the Spanish called the native people, were living on Hispaniola. Columbus had reported a thriving population on the island when he first arrived there. Diseases introduced by the Spanish, destruction of the Native American social systems, and direct killing combined to decrease the native population on the mainland as well. Estimates are that less than twenty-five percent of the Native American people survived. This genocide was not intended by the Spanish government and certainly was fought against by most representatives of the Catholic Church. Catholic Church leaders saw converts in these new lands as a sign of the health and well-being of Catholicism at a time when the reformers were questioning Catholicism.

In 1511 a Dominican priest who had recently arrived in Hispaniola denounced the Spanish from the pulpit for their mistreatment of the Native Americans:

> "Are they not men? . . . You are all in a state of mortal sin . . . because of the cruelty and the tyranny you are inflicting on these innocent victims."
>
> Quoted in Adrian Hastings,
> *A World History of Christianity*
> (Grand Rapids, MI.: Eerdmans, 1999), 332.

Another Dominican, Antonio Valdivieso, went back to Spain to complain to King Charles V personally about the terrible treatment Native Americans were receiving. The king appointed Valdivieso bishop of Nicaragua. When he returned to Central America, Valdivieso realized that local Spanish leaders did not want to hear his message of justice for the natives and that his life was in danger if he continued preaching it. Nonetheless, Valdivieso made his way to the capital of Nicaragua and used the pulpit of the cathedral to defend the Native Americans. In 1550 the governor's son and several accomplices stabbed to death Valdivieso and two other Dominicans.

Activity

Research and give a written or oral report or electronic slide presentation on one of the more than fifty Native American tribes of the Americas. Include in your report a description of religous beliefs or practices of the tribe.

This painting by Diego Rivera is titled "The Conquest of Mexico: Invaders attack with cannon and firearms." It hangs in the National Palace in Mexico City.

The Conquistadores and the Search for Gold

Finding new sources of wealth, opening new trade routes to the East, and spreading the Christian message to new lands were the three reasons for Spain's active involvement in the conquest of the Americas. The conquistadores reduced these goals to one—finding wealth. The two major civilizations of Latin America were centered in Mexico and in Peru. The capital cities of the Aztecs (in Mexico) and Incas (in Peru) did in fact possess signs of splendor and wealth. However, the conquistadores found little silver and gold in the territory they initially conquered. They therefore looked to another source of wealth—enslavement of the native people.

Even though the rulers of Spain had forbidden making slaves of any people under their rule, the conquistadores and later Spanish settlers used forced Native American labor in mines and fields. The rulers of Spain faced a dilemma regarding slavery. On the one hand, they were against it. On the other hand, they were becoming increasingly dependent on the wealth coming from the Americas—wealth gained from slave labor. The Native Americans, suffering from diseases and the total disruption of their social life, proved to be very unproductive as slaves. Most of those subjected to slavery died. In 1542 the Spanish crown ordered that all Native American slaves be freed. The crown further ordered the institution of reforms aimed at improving conditions for the native people. However, much damage had already been done; besides, the settlers in New Spain did not always follow the orders coming from Spain.

The only voices speaking out for the Native Americans were the missionaries. Surprisingly, Mexicans (the Aztecs) adopted Catholicism with much enthusiasm. One perspective on this phenomenon is that when their social and political world collapsed, so did their religious world. This collapse left a vacuum. The king of Spain replaced their ruler Montezuma, and Catholicism replaced the worship of the sun. Mexicans built many churches and participated with particular fervor in the penitential processions of Good Friday. The first archbishop of Mexico established a college, hoping to educate some of the Mexicans for the priesthood. However, no priestly vocations came of this enterprise, perhaps because celibacy was totally foreign to the Native American culture. The Native Americans of Peru (the Incas) accepted Catholicism more slowly than the Mexicans did, and with less enthusiasm. Missionary Church leaders allowed Peruvian Native Americans only the Sacraments of Baptism, Penance, and Marriage. They didn't permit natives to receive Communion since they felt that they were incapable of understanding it.

Native American Catholicism

fyi!

Members of a third order are laypeople associated with a religious community such as the Franciscans or Dominicans. Some groups of third-order members have bonded together in active orders of men and women religious.

However, one reality facing critics of the social dislocation, suffering, and death caused by European conquest of the Americas was that a European presence there could not be reversed. Church and government leaders, European settlers, and Native Americans lived in either a Spanish- or Portuguese-controlled land, and a growing number of people with mixed blood had to deal with the tremendous transformation that had so rapidly taken place in the Americas. Once again, certain people and groups stepped forward, guided by the Holy Spirit, to aid the people in the adjustments.

Saint Rose of Lima

One saint who lived all of her life in the New World but who exhibited a spirituality of an earlier European era was Rose of Lima (1586–1617). Rose was the daughter of Spanish settlers in Peru who were not making ends meet in the mines that were the family business. Her parents hoped that Rose, who was stunningly beautiful, would marry someone who could help the family financially. However, Rose felt called to the religious life, specifically to a life of prayer and self-sacrifice. She purposely disfigured her face so that she would be less attractive and then joined the Third Order of the Dominicans. Rose helped her family, gardening and working on various crafts, while living alone in a hut near her house. Eventually, she also worked in Lima among those who were poor, especially the Native Americans and slaves. During her life, Rose experienced much physical and spiritual suffering, which led to her death at the age of thirty-one. Canonized in 1671, Rose is the first American declared a saint. She is the patron saint of South America.

Our Lady of Guadalupe

On December 9, 1531, barely ten years after the Spanish conquest of Mexico, a native named Juan Diego was making his way to Mass in Mexico City. On the way he passed a hill that had been the site of a shrine to a Native American goddess. Juan Diego heard a woman call his name, and looking up he saw a woman speaking to him. The woman told Juan Diego that she was the Mother of God. She spoke to him of love, compassion, and hospitality. She instructed Juan Diego to tell the bishop to build on the hill a chapel in her honor. Juan Diego did as he was told. Not surprisingly, the bishop ignored him.

Two more times Juan Diego encountered the woman. The third time Mary appeared to him was in December. In spite of the cold, roses were growing at her feet. She instructed Juan Diego to gather the roses in his cape and present himself to the bishop. When Juan Diego opened his cape before the bishop, the picture of the Virgin Mary was imprinted on it. The bishop built the chapel and placed Juan Diego's cape on display within it. **Our Lady of Guadalupe** has been the object of great devotion ever since.

The story of Our Lady of Guadalupe is remarkable for a number of reasons. So much about it would have been unacceptable to the Spanish coming to power in Mexico, and yet devotion to Our Lady of Guadalupe has gained universal recognition in the Church. The event took place at a time when Franciscan missionaries were destroying temples dedicated to the Aztec gods upon whom Mexican religion centered. Mary appeared on the spot where a temple to a Native American goddess had stood. She appeared not to one of the Spanish settlers, but to a Native American. She left not words, as she typically did in Europe, but a visible image of herself. She identified not with the oppressors, but with those who were poor and oppressed.

The image of Our Lady of Guadalupe is neither of a Native American goddess nor a European Madonna. Her dress is European but with Native American decorations. Her face is **mestizo.** Devotion to Our Lady of Guadalupe has sustained and given hope to Latin American and Native American people for over four hundred years. As one author states:

This stained glass window of Our Lady of Guadalupe is in Vienna, Austria.

Our Lady of Guadalupe
patronof the Americas

mestizo
a person of mixed European and Native American ancestry

> The image of Guadalupe continues to hold a special meaning for the humble and oppressed peoples of the Americas. For others she is a potent symbol of the church of the future—a church that celebrates diversity, empowers the poor, and speaks with the voice of compassion. Where such a church lives, roses bloom in December.
>
> Robert Ellsberg, *All Saints* (New York: Crossroad, 1997), 538.

Activity

Name specific ways that the message of Our Lady of Guadalupe can be applied to the world today.

Bartolome de Las Casas

Not every missionary spoke out against the horrible conditions imposed on the Native Americans. A few tried to make the fact-based case that Native American religious practices before the introduction of Christianity were non-Christian and inhumane, with their temples to the sun and human sacrifices. The good or end was a just one. In other words they proposed that despite the disruption and destruction the European invasion caused the Native Americans, introducing them to Christianity and providing them with Baptism justified the harsh measures. The missionaries built churches and provided for the religious needs of the Native Americans without addressing issues of justice. This means their goal and its narrowness must be criticized.

However, some missionaries attempted to improve conditions for Native Americans. The greatest defender of the Native Americans was Bartolome de Las Casas (1484–1566). Las Casas left Spain for the New World in 1502 at the age of eighteen. His father and uncle had sailed with Columbus on his second voyage, and Las Casas had heard about their adventures. He lived as a settler in the New World for a number of years and then was ordained a priest. Las Casas joined the conquistadores who invaded Cuba. There, he acquired Native American slaves, whom he put to work in a mine. In 1514 Dominican priests convinced Las Casas that his use of slave labor was wrong. Las Casas freed his slaves, joined the Dominicans, and returned to Spain where, for the rest of his fifty-one years, he became the leading advocate for the Native Americans,

doing everything possible to have the Spanish government pass laws in their favor.

The devastation of Native American people and their civilization was not without evil and sin by the conquerors. The "discovery" of the Americas was, in truth, the European takeover of the territory of Native Americans and the people themselves. For these people, this meant the undermining of their civilization and way of life; for many, it meant death. For potential victims of human sacrifice to pagan gods, it meant life. For possible victims of war between Native American tribes and nations, it meant the end of those wars. For people oppressed by Native American rulers, it meant freedom from them. For all, it meant the offer of salvation in Christ.

Native American groups in North America, especially within the boundaries of the present United States.

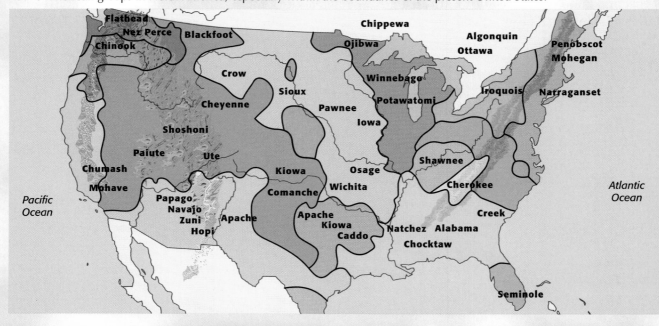

The Reductions of Paraguay

together tribes who previously did not speak to one another. These communities were known as *reductions*. All indications are that they did function well, blending together European and native cultures. They faced two problems, however. For one, Native Americans in the *reductions* faced attacks from Portuguese slave traders. (The Jesuits in Paraguay received permission to train some of the Native Americans in the use of firearms so that they could serve as a police force protecting the community from harm.) Second, leadership in these communities remained in the hands of the Jesuits. This became a problem when the Jesuits were being suppressed in the area. Even though some priests continued the *reductions* as best they could, the lack of native priests and native leaders led eventually to the disintegration of this system.

In working with the Native Americans, Jesuit missionaries tended to follow a strategy different from that of the Dominicans and Franciscans. Rather than concentrating on the two highly developed Aztec and Inca peoples, Jesuits went out into the frontiers and worked with the many Native American groups clustered in small villages apart from other tribes. Following an approach advocated by Las Casas, the Jesuits introduced Christianity and European farming methods and craft work to the Native Americans. They transformed groups of Native Americans into self-sufficient farming communities who celebrated the Catholic feasts with much singing and ritual flare. Often the Jesuits would bring

Spanish Catholicism Moves North

We tend to think of the history of the Church in North America in terms of the thirteen English colonies. In fact, Christianity first entered what was to become the United States by way of Spanish explorers and missionaries, and later the French. Both Spain and Portugal considered the spread of Catholicism to be their God-given responsibility. A map of Mexico, or New Spain, from the seventeenth and eighteenth centuries reveals that it included a large portion of what later was the United States. In fact, only a small portion of North America was English.

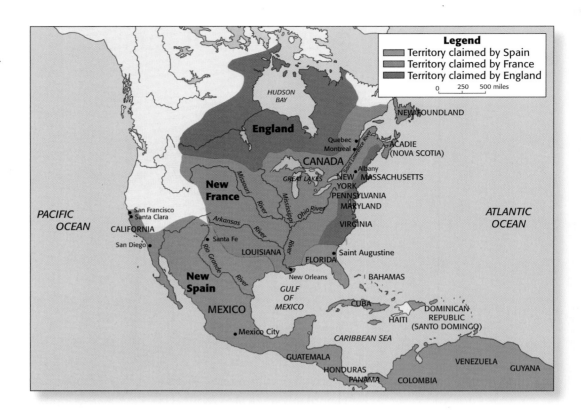

The Americas of the seventeenth and eighteenth centuries.

In 1513 Ponce de Leon, searching for a "fountain of youth" that was spoken of in legends, arrived on the east coast of the North American mainland and called the area Florida. The Spanish established a permanent settlement in 1565 at a place they called St. Augustine. Missionaries built a church and mission there called *Nombre de Dios*. The mission still exists and claims to be the oldest parish in continual use in the United States. In 1598 a statue of Our Lady of La Leche, depicting Mary feeding the baby Jesus at her breast, was brought to the mission. Devotion to Our Lady under this title still exists at the mission today. At different times Florida passed between Spanish and English control.

Spanish explorers arrived in California as early as 1542. By 1772 missions for Native Americans dotted the California coast from the San Diego mission to the mission of San Francisco. Missionaries also served Spanish communities in other parts of the Southwest. By 1630 mission records document that over five thousand Baptisms of native people took place in the area that is now New Mexico.

Juan de Padilla

Many brave men and women brought the message of Christ to the native peoples who lived in what is now the United States. Many of them lost their lives for their efforts. The Franciscan friar Juan de Padilla came to Mexico in 1528. He learned the language of the Native Americans and worked on their behalf. When Francisco de Coronado announced his intention to lead an expedition into what is today New Mexico, Juan asked to join him. Over the next two years, de Padilla visited the pueblos of the Hopi and other groups. In 1542 Coronado decided to return to New Spain, since he had not achieved his intended goal of finding the legendary cities of gold. De Padilla stayed behind in New Mexico and continued his missionary journeys. With the help of some members of the Wichita nation, he traveled into and began a mission in what is now Kansas. In time, de Padilla decided to visit another Native American group, one that was the enemy of the people among whom he was then working. To prevent him from making this journey, one of the men in the band in which he was living killed him. Thus, Juan de Padilla became the first Christian martyr in what was to become the United States.

Eusebio Francisco Kino

fyi!

The state of Arizona chose a statue of Father Kino as one of their two statues adorning the Capitol of the United States in Washington, D.C.

Another early missionary to what is now the U.S. Southwest was Eusebio Francisco Kino. The only son of German noble parents living in Italy, Kino joined the Jesuits in gratitude to God after recovering from a serious illness. He was ordained in 1678 and requested to go to the Philippines, hoping eventually to enter China. Instead, his Jesuit superiors sent him to New Spain. From there Kino went to work in California, learning the Piman language, which he always spoke with a German accent. As he traveled around northwest Mexico, including present-day Arizona, Kino used his knowledge of science to develop maps of the area.

Because he was a personal friend of King Carlos II of Spain, Kino secured a decree dispensing all Native Americans who converted to Christianity from working in the mines for twenty years. This made him a hated man among mine owners. They requested that another Jesuit be sent to investigate Kino's work, hoping that Kino would be removed. Instead, his fellow Jesuit who examined his efforts with the Native Americans found Kino's work to be worthy of high praise. Kino went on to discover the overland route to California and to open missions there without the assistance of the military. To make this possible he received financial support from generous benefactors. Using his missions as a base, Kino explored and mapped out most of the northwestern Mexican territory, which included portions of what is now the U.S. Southwest. He wrote a thesis demonstrating that Baja, or lower, California was a peninsula, not an island as previously thought.

Junipero Serra and the California Missions

Born on the island of Majorca in 1713, Miguel Jose Serra joined the Franciscans at the age of sixteen and took the name Junipero. An excellent student, Serra was assigned to teach at the university but longed to go to the missions. In 1750 he was released from his teaching responsibilities and permitted to go to New Spain. Once he arrived in Mexico City, he was again assigned to teaching and was only occasionally sent to do mission work.

Mosaic of Unity and Diversity

When the pope suppressed the Jesuits, they had to abandon their California missions. Serra quickly volunteered to go to California to take up the work the Jesuits had begun there. Serra devised a plan to establish a series of missions along the coast. He eventually founded twenty-one missions, each one a day's walk from the previous mission. On July 1, 1784, Father Junipero Serra reported on life at the Mission of San Carlos de Monterey:

> The Christians living at the mission pray twice daily with the priest in the church. More than one hundred twenty of them confess in Spanish and many who have died used to do it as well. The others confess as best they can. They work at all kinds of mission labor, such as farm hands, herdsmen, cowboys, shepherds, milkers, diggers, gardeners, carpenters, farmers, irrigators, reapers, blacksmiths, sacristans, and they do everything else that comes along for their corporal and spiritual welfare.
>
> Quoted in *Documents of American Catholic History,* edited by John Tracy Ellis (Milwaukee: Bruce Publishing Company, 1962), 44.

Serra mastered the Otomi language so that he could effectively communicate with the Pames. He was an advocate for the natives against the brutality of many obstinate white leaders. Serra made sure that Native Americans at the missions were taught agricultural and academic subjects. By the time of Junipero Serra's death in 1784, over 6,700 Baptisms were recorded and over 4,600 Christian Native Americans were living in the missions.

Activity

List six cities in the western or southwestern United States whose names in Spanish have religious significance. Translate the names into English. For one of these cities, write a prayer based on its religious name.

Review

1. What responsibility did the pope give the governments of Spain and Portugal in 1493?

2. Who were the conquistadores?

3. What three factors led to the decrease of the Native American populations who had contact with the Spanish?

4. How did local Spanish leaders respond to Antonio Valdivieso's criticism of their treatment of Native American people?

5. What were the two most powerful Native American groups during the time of the Spanish conquest of the Americas?

6. Who were the voices speaking out for Native American people during the time of the Spanish conquest?

7. Who was the greatest defender of Native Americans among the Spanish?

8. Who is the first American declared a saint?

9. How was Juan Diego's bishop convinced to build a chapel in honor of Mary?

10. Where was the oldest parish in the present-day United States founded?

11. Who was the first martyr in what is today the United States?

12. Who was the German Jesuit who began missions in southern Arizona and California?

13. What Franciscan founded a series of missions along the California coast?

THE FRENCH PRESENCE

Northwest Passage
a non-existent waterway through the northern part of the Americas that explorers hoped would lead from the Atlantic Ocean to the Pacific Ocean

French intentions upon arriving in Canada in 1534 were less grandiose than those of Spain. French explorers set out to find a **Northwest Passage** to the Far East and to search for silver and gold. Not until seven years later, in 1541, did the French attempt to establish a settlement in the New World, near Quebec. When they found no precious metals in the region, they abandoned this settlement. In time, the French did find wealth in the area, but it came in the form of fish off the Grand Banks of Newfoundland, and then in furs gained from trading with Native Americans or from trapping. Finally, in 1608, Samuel de Champlain tried to make Canada more than a trading post. Even his attempts were modest in comparison to those of the Spanish colonization.

Jesuit Work among Northern Native Americans

During his short life Saint Isaac Jogues (1607–1646) worked in difficult circumstances to bring the Christian message to Native Americans. Art by Robert Lentz.

The real impetus for colonizing New France came from the Jesuits. Beginning in 1632, Church leaders in France saw the French presence in the New World as an opportunity to engage in missionary activity. (Remember that this was a period of great religious fervor in France, when Louise de Marillac, Vincent de Paul, and many others worked among those who were poor.) The Jesuits in particular took on this missionary task. They believed, at least initially, that the Native Americans would need to adopt a European lifestyle if conversion to Christianity was to be truly effective. A number of French men and women, both religious and lay people, caught the missionary spirit. Mademoiselle Jeanne Mance founded the Hospital of Saint Joseph in Montreal, and a noblewoman named Madame de la Peltrie convinced the Ursuline nuns to establish a school for Native American girls. Other schools and hospitals followed.

Saint Isaac Jogues

Black Robes
northern Native American term given to the Jesuits because of their distinctive garb

One of the first Jesuits to take on the task of working among the Native Americans of North America was Isaac Jogues. He arrived in New France in 1636. The Hurons were the first tribe friendly to the **Black Robes,** as they called the Jesuits. Jogues and the other Jesuits quickly discovered that the Native Americans had a deep spirituality centered around the Great Spirit, Mother Earth, and nature.

A problem with which the Jesuits had to deal was that the various Native American tribes were constantly at war with one another. Identifying with one tribe invariably meant animosity from another. Thus while living with the Hurons, Jogues and his companions witnessed the torture of several Iroquois prisoners. In 1642, Mohawks—part of the Iroquois Confederation—captured Jogues and a few of his companions. Although Jogues underwent extreme torture, including having his thumb and some of his fingers chewed off, he was kept alive as a slave for a Mohawk woman.

Jogues, now a worn-down skeleton of a man, managed to escape. He returned to France. However, Jogues felt his work with the Native Americans was not

finished, so he returned to New France and took part in negotiations aimed at bringing peace among warring tribes. In 1646 at the age of 39, Jogues was killed by an Iroquois warrior who superstitiously thought Jogues was the cause of an outbreak of illness and crop failure. Jogues and seven companions were canonized in 1930 and were proclaimed patron saints of Canada in 1940.

Blessed Kateri Tekakwitha, Lily of the Mohawks

Kateri Tekakwitha (1656–1680) was born of a Mohawk chief and an Algonquin Christian woman in the very village where Isaac Jogues was martyred. Kateri's parents died from smallpox, and she herself became partially blind and had a disfigured face from the illness. Nonetheless, Kateri continued to be raised as a princess. When a priest visited the village, Kateri asked for Baptism, which she received. Her conversion to Christianity and her refusal to marry led the other members of her tribe to mock her.

In this icon, Kateri Tekakwitha holds the Christian cross in one hand and her culture's tree of peace in the other. The tree rests on a turtle, representing the giant turtle on which the earth rests, according to Iroquois tradition.

Kateri fled her village and made her way to a Christian Native American community near Montreal. There, she received her first Holy Communion and took a vow dedicating herself to Christ. Soon after, both French and Native Americans in the area noticed that she seemed to possess mystical powers. The people around her began to treat her with great reverence. When she died, her face was cleared of the blemishes and disfigurement that she had had since a child. Even after her death, a number of priests and Native Americans reported that Kateri appeared to them, and miracles were reported through her intercession. Kateri's feast day is April 17.

Activity

1. One aspect of Native American spirituality that has become important to some people of the United States is the Native American's respect for the earth. Create and celebrate a class prayer service using passages and themes from the Christian and Native American traditions.

2. Research various other beliefs of Native Americans. Discuss how the missionaries could have used these beliefs to help Native Americans understand similar Christian beliefs.

Chapter Nine

Pere Jacques Marquette

Jacques Marquette was born in France in 1637, was educated by Jesuits in Rheims, and was ordained in 1666. He went to Montreal and studied the Algonquian dialects for two years. He then joined a mission near present-day Sault Sainte Marie, Michigan—1,500 miles west of Montreal. From there he moved even farther west along Lake Superior. Eventually, he founded the mission of Saint Ignace on Mackinac Island in northern Michigan. Around this time, he met Louis Jolliet, who was trading with Native Americans in the same area. In 1672 Jolliet was named leader of an expedition that would explore the northern part of the Mississippi River the following year. Jolliet asked Father Marquette to be the chaplain of this group. The two, along with five other men, set out by canoe along the northern shore of Lake Michigan. They traveled the Fox River, Wisconsin River, and Mississippi River. Jolliet kept journals and created maps, which provided much information for later explorers.

The first Native Americans the group encountered were the friendly Illinois. Father Marquette promised to return to work with the people. In 1675 he traveled back to live among the Illinois, establishing the Kaskaskia Mission among them. Recognizing that his health was failing, Marquette decided to return to a mission in the north, but he died before reaching his destination.

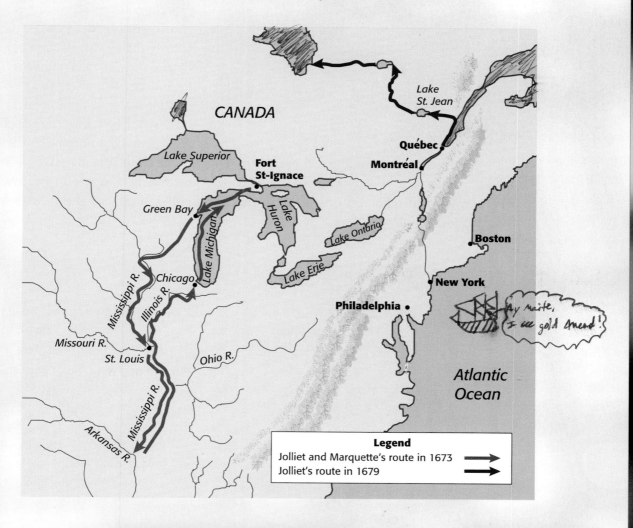

The North American martyrs.

How Successful Were the Missionaries?

Despite the stories of heroic efforts on the part of French missionaries, the Native Americans of the northern regions of America did not become Catholic in the numbers like those of the Native Americans among the Spanish. One difference between New France and New Spain was that, compared to the Spanish, few French people wanted to immigrate to the New World. While the French presence was certainly strong, Canada did not become a "New France" to the degree that Mexico became a "New Spain." Second, when the Jesuits were disbanded they were hard to replace in the mission fields. The fading spiritual fervor of the post-Reformation era in France meant fewer people were willing to undergo the sufferings of the earlier missionaries. One French missionary reported baptizing numerous Native Americans but noted that these Native Americans would return to their old ways "at the drop of a hatchet." The French Catholic presence in Canada survived the takeover of the region by the English, but Catholicism did not become the dominant religion of the North American Native Americans.

Activity

Research a French missionary to Canada or the United States and tell the story in poetry, drama, or a video presentation.

Review

1. What two reasons led French explorers to go to Canada? What two sources of wealth did the French find there?

2. Why did the Jesuits want the French colonization of North America?

3. What obstacle did the Jesuits face in their attempts to convert the Native Americans they encountered?

4. What was the cause of the death of Saint Isaac Jogues?

5. Why did the people around Montreal treat Kateri Tekakwitha with great reverence?

6. Among what group of Native Americans did Father Marquette work?

7. Why were the French missions less successful in bringing about conversions among the Native Americans than the Spanish missions were?

CATHOLICISM IN THE COLONIES

The tenor of the Catholic experience in the English colonies was very different from that in New Spain and in New France. The colonies were Protestant territory. Even in Maryland—chartered to the Catholic Calvert family—Catholicism was the Church of the governing elite, where it was not the Church of all the colonists. Also, Maryland was surrounded by colonies where the great majority of people were Protestants and suspicious of Catholics. In 1633 Cecil Calvert, the second Lord Baltimore, said to his fellow Catholics making their way to Maryland:

> No scandal nor offence [is] to be given to any of the Protestants . . . all Acts of Romane Catholique Religion [are] to be done as privately as may be. And . . . all the Romane Catholiques [are] to be silent upon all occasions of discourse concerning matters of Religion.
>
> Quoted in *Documents of American Catholic History,* 98.

Maryland—A Safe Haven for Catholics

People from England founded all thirteen colonies along the eastern coast of North America. Members of the established Church of England governed in Virginia, the original English colony. However, religious dissidents of one sort or another founded most of the other colonies. They came to North America seeking the freedom to practice their religion without interference. Puritans settled in Massachusetts. Roger Williams, who broke with the Puritans, founded Rhode Island. Much later, in 1681, William Penn began his "holy experiment" in Pennsylvania. He envisioned a place where Quakers could practice their religion but, in a rare gesture for the time, he also welcomed members of other faiths to live together in peace and harmony.

Maryland began as a safe haven for Catholics, but it was not founded as a Catholic colony. In 1624 George Calvert, a member of Parliament and the first Lord Baltimore, became a Catholic. Because he was a favorite of King James I, Calvert's joining the Catholic Church did not negatively affect his position in society. He asked permission to begin a colony in the New World and tried Newfoundland, but the harsh weather discouraged him. He considered Virginia but soon realized that Catholics would not be welcome there. He therefore sought a charter to establish a colony north of Virginia. When Calvert died, his son Cecil received the charter and he arranged for two ships to carry settlers to the new colony. Calvert's second son Leonard became Maryland's first governor. In 1649 the colonial government passed the **Act of Toleration.** Unfortunately, in time Puritans took over the colony and deprived Catholics of the right to vote, to worship publicly, or to run schools. This situation remained in force until just before the American (U.S.) Revolution.

Act of Toleration decree by the government of Maryland granting freedom of religion for the colony

Only about twenty of the two hundred people who originally set sail for Maryland were Catholic. One of those was a Jesuit priest, Father Andrew White. Father White had been banished to Belgium for serving the Catholic community in England during persecution there. When the two ships, the Ark and the Dove, sailed up Chesapeake Bay and landed on an island, Father White celebrated Mass on what settlers later named St. Clement. As the settlers cleared land, Father White built a mission he named St. Inigoes in honor of Ignatius Loyola, founder of the Jesuits. Father White moved among the Native Americans in the area and learned their language. He wrote a dictionary, a grammar book, and a catechism in the Algonquian language.

When the town of St. Mary's was established as the capital of Maryland, Father White built a church there. Lord Baltimore had insisted that religious toleration should be extended to all Christians in the colony. This system worked until 1645, when a Puritan ship stole into St. Mary's harbor and the crew overthrew Lord Baltimore's officials, destroyed all Catholic chapels, and arrested Father White and another Jesuit. The two priests were sent back to England in chains where they remained in prison for three years until they were acquitted, but again banished. Father White moved to southern England, where under an assumed name, he ministered to Catholics in the area until his death in 1656. He is known as the "Apostle of Maryland."

John Carroll of Maryland, the Nation's First Bishop

The predominant figure in colonial Catholicism was clearly John Carroll. Born in Maryland in 1735, John and his cousin Charles left for Europe to study at a Jesuit school in Saint Omer, France. Upon graduation, Charles returned home to Maryland. John went on to become ordained a Jesuit priest and taught in Europe. He traveled throughout the continent as a tutor, getting a sense of the many countries of Europe. In 1773, when the Jesuits were suppressed by the pope, Father Carroll returned to his mother's home in Rock Creek, Maryland. From there he served the spiritual needs of people in the surrounding area.

In 1776 John Carroll joined his cousin Charles and the great American diplomat Benjamin Franklin in seeking Canadian support for the colonies' rebellion against England. French Canadians in particular were suspicious of anti-Catholic attitudes in the colonies, and the delegation failed to gain the support of Canada for the rebellion. Nonetheless, Franklin and Father Carroll developed a close friendship that endured through the years.

In 1782 there were twenty-one former Jesuits in what was by then called the United States. Father Carroll organized the men and wrote the pope a letter requesting that one of their number, Father John Lewis, be appointed superior of all United States clergy. They begged the pope not to appoint a bishop at that time, since they feared that U.S. Protestants would view a Catholic bishop as an extension of bad experiences they had had with Catholic Church leaders in Europe. They especially did not want a bishop appointed from Europe, for fear that he would not understand the new U.S. experiment of separation of Church and state.

The pope agreed to appoint one of the former Jesuits as their superior. The pope discussed the appointment with various clergymen and ambassadors, among them the United States ambassador to France at the time, Benjamin Franklin. All agreed that Father Carroll should be the superior of the U.S. clergy and the official contact between the United States Church and Rome. Six years later Father Carroll requested that the priests be allowed to elect their first bishop. Again, the pope heard their request. The U.S. clergy met in 1789 and elected John Carroll the first Catholic bishop of the United States.

Bishop Carroll was appointed bishop of Baltimore, but his diocese included all the thirteen colonies. In 1791, with the help of Sulpician priests from France, he established Saint Mary's in Baltimore as the first U.S. seminary for the training of priests. In 1808 the Sulpicians opened Mount St. Mary's College in Emmitsburg, Maryland. Bishop Carroll also helped develop Georgetown College, now Georgetown University in Washington, D.C. In 1803, when President Thomas Jefferson purchased the Louisiana Territory, Bishop Carroll's diocese doubled in size. He therefore arranged for four new dioceses to be created. John Carroll died in 1815.

By the time of the signing of the Declaration of Independence, Catholics numbered 30,000—one percent of the United States population. By 1815 there were 200,000 Catholics in the United States. Catholics gained acceptance in the early days of the republic for two primary reasons. First, their numbers were so small that they were not perceived as a threat. Second, Bishop Carroll demonstrated such support for and sensitivity toward the new system of government that he convinced others that members of the Church could be both Catholic and American.

fyi!

John Carroll was the only United States Catholic bishop ever to be elected by the clergy, rather than being appointed by the pope.

This statue of John Carroll sits near Healy Hall at Georgetown University in Washington D.C.

Religious Freedom

fyi!

In 1733 the Catholic community of Philadelphia built St. Joseph's Church. In 1763 another church, St. Mary's, was built nearby. These two churches survived periods of strong anti-Catholic activity and today continue to serve thriving Catholic communities particularly in the old colonial section of Philadelphia.

One of the reasons Maryland granted religious freedom to its colonists probably was that, although Catholics from the beginning governed the colony, they were a distinct minority. On the other hand, William Penn, the founder of Pennsylvania, granted religious toleration on more strictly religious grounds. Penn was a member of the Religious Society of Friends, or Quakers, a religious group that had emerged in England late in the Reformation period. The Quakers in England had experienced firsthand persecution for their beliefs. Because of Pennsylvania's policy of religious toleration, a number of Catholics—mostly of German descent—settled there. By the time of independence, most U.S. Catholics lived in either Maryland or Pennsylvania.

"The Quakers' Meeting" was captured by Egbert Ivan Heemsbeck and Carclus Allard.

Activity

Write a report on a Catholic in the United States or Canada from colonial or post-colonial times. Some possibilities are: Charles Carroll, Daniel Carroll, Thomas Fitzsimmons, Thomas Dongan, and John Barry.

Review

1. In what sense was the Catholic experience in the English colonies different from that in Spanish and French colonies?

2. What advice did Lord Baltimore give to the Catholics traveling to Maryland?

3. What was the Act of Toleration?

4. Who is the Apostle of Maryland?

5. Why did Catholics initially not want Rome to appoint a bishop for the United States?

6. Who was the first U.S. Catholic bishop? How was he chosen?

7. What religious group controlled colonial Pennsylvania? What policy did they espouse toward other religions?

THE AMERICAN SYSTEM

After independence from England, U.S. Catholics lived in a new kind of political system. Recall that in Europe the first half of the nineteenth century was the "age of Metternich," when the rulers of Europe, including the pope, returned with great determination to the old order of absolute monarchs. In the United States, on the other hand, people elected their own leaders. At least in theory, religion was to be completely separate from politics. People were free to practice the religion of their choice, and they had the right of free speech. No wonder that Metternich saw no future in the American system. It represented something novel and untried, and it certainly did not reflect the commonly accepted view of governance sweeping Europe at the time.

lay trusteeism
control of parish funds and resources by an elected body of laypeople

Should the American system carry over into the area of Church governance? For many U.S. Catholics in the beginning of the nineteenth century, the answer was yes. For some, electing governing bodies on the parish level was both the American way and also the way of the early Church. This system was known as **lay trusteeism.** Theoretically, this elected body could also choose the parish priest, since it controlled parish finances.

Bishop Carroll recognized that lay trustees posed a problem. If members of a parish could hire or fire their priests, what would prevent them from choosing priests who did and said what they wanted rather than what was faithful to universal Catholicism? What about the pope's authority to shepherd his flock? Also, canon law, the official law of the Catholic Church, stated that only bishops could assign responsibility for a parish church to a priest. Nonetheless, Bishop Carroll allowed the trustee system to continue. Keep in mind that no one at the time was entirely sure how to blend together being Catholic and being American in the U.S. sense. The system was as new for Catholics as it was for other religious groups. In addition, since priests had been scarce during the colonial period, Catholic laypeople were accustomed to running their own religious affairs.

Parish lay participation today differs greatly from the lay trusteeism of the past.

Discussion

Among the parishes to which members of your class belong, describe the types of activities in which laypeople are involved. Explain the importance of laypeople for active parish life.

Trusteeism was an internal affair not supported by all Catholics in the United States. Conflicts between ethnic groups added to the controversy. Often a parish would find itself with a pastor of a different nationality and with a different understanding of Church from that of the majority of the parishioners. For instance, the U.S. Catholic population was becoming more and more Irish, while most bishops were French or German. When some Irish American Catholics complained, the pope appointed a young Irish priest as bishop of the small, newly established diocese of Charleston, South Carolina. Bishop John England was only thirty-two at the time, but he was recognized as one of the brightest churchmen in Ireland. When he came to the U.S., he took a strong leadership role in the Church. He also spoke regularly to non-Catholic groups, explaining to them that being Catholic and being American were not inconsistent. He even addressed the United States Congress on the matter. In his own diocese Bishop England wrote up a constitution, whereby representatives of clergy and laypeople would meet annually to look over Church affairs of the diocese and recommend changes. The constitution worked well but didn't survive after the death of Bishop England.

On the national level, the United States Catholic bishops held a series of councils during which they addressed common concerns. The 1837 Provincial Council, at which Bishop England played an important role, tried to relay to the country that no one has anything to fear from Catholics. They pointed out that:

The Basilica of the National Shrine of the Assumption of the Blessed Virgin Mary in Baltimore, Maryland, was the site of the Third Provincial Council of Baltimore.

We are indeed comparatively few amongst the millions of our fellow-citizens; the greater portion of our flocks are in the humble, laborious, but useful occupations of life; we do not aspire to power, we do not calculate by what process we should be able, at some future day, to control the councils of the republic. . . . We do not detract from the allegiance to which the temporal governments are plainly entitled, and which we cheerfully give; nor do we acknowledge any civil or political supremacy, or power over us in any foreign potentate or power, though that potentate might be the chief pastor of our church.

(Pastoral Letter of the Third Provincial Council of Baltimore, #7).

In other words, the bishops were stating that Catholics owed spiritual fidelity to the pope but that this fidelity in no way interfered with their ability to participate freely in the political system of the United States.

Democracy in America

In 1835 a Frenchman named Alexis de Tocqueville published a book about what he observed while traveling about the United States. His *Democracy in America* offered an insightful report about the state of U.S. social and political life at the time. De Tocqueville made the following startling observations about U.S. Catholics:

These Catholics are faithful to the observances of their religion; they are fervent and zealous in the belief of their doctrines. Yet they constitute the most republican and the most democratic class in the United States. This fact may surprise the observer at first, but the cause of it may easily be discovered upon reflection.

> Catholicism . . . confounds all the distinctions of society at the foot of the same altar.
>
> —Alexus de Tocqueville

I think that the Catholic religion has erroneously been regarded as the natural enemy of democracy. Among the various sects of Christians, Catholicism seems to be, on the contrary, . . . one of the most favorable to equality of condition among men. In the Catholic Church the religious community is composed of only two elements, the priest and the people. The priest alone rises above the rank of his flock, and all below him are equal.

On doctrinal points the Catholic faith places all human capacities upon the same level; it subjects the wise and ignorant, the man of genius and the vulgar crowd, to the details of the same creed; it imposes the same observances upon the rich and the needy; it inflicts the same austerities upon the strong and the weak; it listens to no compromise with mortal man, but reducing all the human race to the same standard, it confounds all the distinctions of society at the foot of the same altar.

Quoted in *Documents of American Catholic History,* 233–34.

Discussion

1. Upon what basis did Alexis de Tocqueville claim that Catholicism lends itself to democracy? Do you agree or disagree with his assessment? Explain.

2. Do you think that being Catholic today supports democratic attitudes? Why or why not?

Review

1. Define lay trusteeism.

2. Who was John England?

3. What position on being Catholic and being American did the United States Catholic bishops state in 1837?

THE IMMIGRANT CHURCH

The main characteristic of the Catholic Church in the United States from early in the nineteenth to around the middle of the twentieth century was the sheer volume of Catholic immigrants entering the country. The first major wave of immigrants were the Irish, who tended to cluster together in the major cities on the East Coast. Later, German Catholics arrived in large numbers and typically made their way to the Midwest, where they took up farming and related occupations. Still later, Italians and people from Eastern Europe entered the country. Estimates are that between 1790 and 1850 over a million Catholics immigrated to the United States, causing Catholicism to become the largest single religious denomination in the United States. A steady stream of Catholic immigrants continued until 1924, when the government enacted immigration laws, at least partially intended to reduce the influx of Catholics into the country.

This long period of immigration caused a strong negative reaction against Catholic immigrants from many native-born, white, Anglo-Saxon Protestants. This group began a movement known as **Nativism.** In 1834 nativists burned down a convent in Massachusetts. In 1844 rioters burned down two Catholic churches in Philadelphia. During the riots thirteen people were killed and over fifty people were wounded. Nativism even at times expressed itself in specific political parties, such as the **Know Nothing Party.**

Nativism
anti-Catholic and anti-immigrant movement

Know Nothing Party
anti-foreign, anti-Catholic political organization that flourished in the United States between 1852 and 1856

Discussion

Using the reasons listed on the *Causes for Nativism* chart, discuss possible parallels that exist in the United States today.

CAUSES FOR NATIVISM

- Bias a prejudice against Catholics and the Catholic faith
- Fear of foreigners and their languages
- Racist stereotypes, for example, about the Irish, the Italians, or East Europeans
- Fear of a Catholic takeover of the Protestant-dominated land
- Fear of a return to the medieval world of superstitions and absolute monarchs
- Large numbers of Catholic immigrants perceived to be a threat to the social landscape of the new nation
- Irish and German immigrants willingly working for less money, thus supplanting the position of native-born workers

Chapter Nine

Bishop John Hughes of New York

Irish-born John Joseph Hughes (1797–1864) immigrated to the United States at the age of twenty and found work constructing bridges and roads in Pennsylvania and Maryland. While working on the farm at Mount St. Mary's Seminary in Emmitsburg, Maryland, he requested acceptance into priesthood. The rector in charge thought that Hughes was too headstrong to make a good priest and put him off. Hughes sought help from a woman named Mother Elizabeth Seton who ran a school nearby. With her recommendation, the rector accepted Hughes into the seminary program. He was a fine student and exhibited great powers of persuasion with his speaking skills.

Upon ordination Hughes was sent to Philadelphia where he successfully defended the Catholic Church's position against lay trusteeism. He also faced the anti-Catholic propaganda that was leading to acts of violence against Catholics and Catholic Church property. In 1838 Father Hughes was named the bishop of New York and became the leading spokesman for the Catholic Church in the U.S.

In New York, Bishop Hughes continued to take on Nativism and he also defended immigrants. When New York Nativists threatened to imitate the violence that took place in Philadelphia, Bishop Hughes took a strong stand against them, and no major anti-Catholic incidents occurred in his city. To make a lasting public statement that Catholicism was here to stay, Bishop Hughes announced the building of a cathedral in Manhattan that would be dedicated to Saint Patrick. Today, St. Patrick's Cathedral is one of the best-known landmarks in New York City.

Sisters of Our Lady of Mercy

One way that Catholicism gained respect among the rest of the U.S. population was through the good works performed by women religious. For instance, during the yellow fever epidemics that hit Charleston, South Carolina, in the 1850s, the Sisters of Our Lady of Mercy set aside their teaching duties and cared for those who were sick, regardless of their religious background. One of the sisters wrote the following account of their work:

During these years the Sisters had no hospital, but went about from street to street, through lanes and alleys, wherever the sick might be found, carrying baskets filled with the necessities of life and medicine, as these were needed. They worked heroically, all through the periods of disease, and all classes of citizens recognized the debt of gratitude due to these noble women. . . . When the troubles were over, our Sisters quickly returned to their schoolrooms and seemed to have forgotten what no one who had seen them could ever forget, that they had but a short time before been active amid the dark scenes of death from yellow fever haunting the entire community.

Quoted in *In Our Own Voices*, edited by Rosemary Radford Reuther and Rosemary Skinner Keller (HarperSanFrancisco, 1995), 41.

Preserving the Catholic Faith of Immigrants

Until the mid-1800s most Catholic children, if they attended school, went to a public school in their town. Almost exclusively, Protestants sat on school boards. In keeping with the legal interpretation at that time of the relation between Church and state, public schools were Protestant-biased institutions. For instance, all students studied the *King James Bible,* which was a Protestant version, and they were required to recite Protestant prayers or attend Protestant services. Texts would often show white, Anglo-Saxon Protestants as hard-working, productive members of society. On the other hand texts portrayed immigrants, such as Italian and Irish Catholics, in a negative light—for instance, as lazy and as users of alcohol who often failed to show up for work.

Catholic schools eased the passage of immigrants into U.S. society.

In 1844 a number of bishops attempted to get public schools to become more Catholic-friendly institutions. Bishop Kenrick's appeal to the school board of Philadelphia set off the anti-Catholic riots in that city. The bishops feared that Catholic children, especially of newly arrived immigrants, were in danger of losing their faith in a school atmosphere hostile to Catholicism. Even though it would entail great expense, the bishops called for the creation of Catholic schools to accompany all parishes throughout the country. Catholic schools were so successful that the Council of Baltimore, held in 1884, ruled that within two years every parish had to have a Catholic grade school.

At this same council the bishops commissioned a priest to write in simple question-and-answer form a catechism that could be used with Catholic school children. The result, called the *Baltimore Catechism,* served as the standard text in religious education until the 1960s.

fyi!

When John McCloskey was born in 1810, the diocese of New York was two years old and had two churches and six priests. At his death in 1885, the New York diocese had 139 parishes and 279 priests. The growth that took place in Catholicism in New York City mirrors the growth that occurred throughout the Catholic Church in the United States. In 1875 the pope named John McCloskey a cardinal, the first U.S. priest so honored.

Activity

Debate the following statement: Today public schools are no longer Protestant-biased. Therefore, Catholic schools are an unnecessary expense and should be discontinued.

Saint Elizabeth Ann Seton— Pioneer of Catholic Schools

Elizabeth Ann Bayley was born into a prominent New York Episcopalian family in 1774. Elizabeth received a fine education and eventually married William Seton, whose family ran a successful shipping company. However, in 1797, the shipping business went bankrupt. William's health suffered, and a doctor suggested a sea voyage to restore his health. Elizabeth sold the last of their possessions so that she and their five children could accompany her husband on the journey. Together, they sailed to Italy but while there, William died and was buried.

While Elizabeth made arrangements to return the family home, she began to attend a Catholic Church where she discovered that she was particularly drawn to the belief in the Real Presence of Christ in the Eucharist. She returned the family home to New York, and in 1805, she became Catholic.

In 1809 Bishop Carroll gave Elizabeth some property in Emmitsburg, Maryland, on which she opened a school. Elizabeth, her daughters, and her sisters-in-law began the U.S. foundation of the Sisters of Charity. Although the order experienced long periods of near poverty and much illness that took the lives of three of the original sisters, the community survived and finally prospered. Mother Seton, as she came to be known, died in 1821. In 1975 she was named the first native-born United States saint.

African American Catholics

African American Catholics are often overlooked in the history of American Catholicism. Actually, some Africans living in the area of the Congo converted to Catholicism in the fifteenth century, and some of these Catholics entered the New World as slaves. Other slaves in Spanish territories became Catholic, as did slaves who worked for Jesuits in Maryland and Louisiana. There are also isolated stories of African Americans who were not slaves and who held onto their Catholicism despite discrimination from white Catholics.

One interesting family stands out as unusual for the time. An Irish immigrant named Michael Healy living in Macon, Georgia, had ten children with his slave wife. One of their sons, James Augustine Healy, wanted to become a priest. Because of his African American ancestry he had to attend seminary in Montreal and Paris. He was ordained in 1854 for the Boston archdiocese and served as rector of the cathedral and then as chancellor of the diocese. In 1875 he was named bishop of Portland, Maine. He died in 1900. Two of Bishop Healy's brothers became priests and two of his sisters entered religious life. His brother Patrick, a Jesuit, served as president of Georgetown University.

Go to **www.usccb.org/encuentro 2000** under Media Resources, Frequently Asked Questions to find statistics describing the current ethnic makeup of Catholics in the United States.

The first full-blooded African American priest was Augustus Tolton. He was born to Catholic slaves in Missouri in 1854. During the Civil War he and his mother escaped to Quincy, Illinois, where he attended the Catholic school. He inquired about becoming a priest, and since no U.S. seminary accepted black students at the time, he was sent to Rome to study. After his ordination in 1886, Father Tolton became a popular pastor in Quincy. Some other priests and his bishop did not support him when some people made racial comments about him. Discouraged, Father Tolton received permission to transfer to Chicago where he built St. Monica's church in what became a thriving Catholic parish.

American Catholics and Slavery

In 1839 Pope Gregory XVI condemned the slave trade. However, this pronouncement did not identify slavery as an evil in itself. In the earliest days of the English colonies, there were both black and white slaves; however, slavery soon came to be restricted exclusively to people of African descent. Slaves were viewed as the property of their owners. Many Catholics owned slaves, including the Jesuits in southern Maryland and the Ursuline sisters in Louisiana.

Theological speculation seemed to suggest that as long as slaves had an opportunity to practice their religion, then Catholic teaching had no basis on which to condemn the institution of slavery itself. To complicate matters, many of those calling for the abolition of slavery also spoke out against immigration. Some Irish immigrants complained that while blacks were slaves in the South, the Irish of the North were "wage slaves," living in conditions not much better than the conditions black slaves experienced.

During the Civil War Catholics fought on both sides. General Beauregard of Louisiana was a Catholic and a renowned Southern leader. On the Union side, General Sherman, who burned Atlanta to the ground, was Catholic. Though Catholic leaders generally tried to remain neutral and work for reconciliation, one Southern bishop wrote a widely circulated sermon that called for secession from the Union and urged Catholics to fight for the South. He also reminded slave owners that they had an obligation to treat their slaves justly. Bishop Hughes of New York flew the U.S. flag over the cathedral and recruited troops for the Union side. Midwestern bishops tended to support the war so that Nativists would not doubt Catholic patriotism, among other reasons.

Average Catholics followed the beliefs of their neighbors. With no official Catholic policy on slavery, most people based decisions on what was economically best for their families. Especially in the South, devastation from the war was great. Heroic actions by Catholic chaplains and women religious convinced many people of the virtue and loyalty of Catholics.

Activity

Find out in the history of the Catholic Church how many African Americans have served as bishops in the U.S. Catholic Church and how many men from the continent of Africa have served as popes.

Review

1. What is Nativism, and why it did flourish?

2. Why did the United States Catholic bishops call for the creation of Catholic schools?

3. Who were James Augustine Healy and Augustus Tolton?

4. What position did the average Catholic in general take toward the Civil War?

Conclusion

Because of the historical routes that each took, Canada, Mexico, Central and South America, and the United States entered the twentieth century very differently. Colonialism lasted a long time in the Southern Hemisphere and the development of democracy came late to many countries there. Unfortunately, as in Europe, the Catholic Church was identified with the repressive status quo, and it was not accepted as an impartial contributor to society. Canada continues to have a significant Catholic population especially in the province of Quebec, in spite of the simultaneous development of two societies, one English and Protestant, and one French and Catholic.

In the United States, however, the "American way," with its religious toleration, its separation of Church and state, and its democratic principles, was something new for the Catholic Church. The pope was accustomed to consulting with the heads of state before appointing bishops. The U.S. president would have no part of this! Through its experience in North and South America, the Church discovered that it could not only survive but thrive in the new world of democratic republics. By the end of the nineteenth century, the U.S. Catholic Church had grown into one of the most vibrant centers of Catholicism in the entire world. At the same time, the United States gained much from Catholicism. North America became the most culturally diverse continent in the world. Much of that diversity stems from northern European, southern European, Slavic, Hispanic, Asian, and African Catholics bringing their rich cultural heritages to the New World. The mosaic of unity and diversity that is the United States owes much to its Catholic population and the Catholic Church.

Let us pray.
"Is not this the fast that I choose:
to loose the bonds of injustice,
to undo the thongs of the yoke,
to let the oppressed go free,
and to break every yoke?
Is it not to share your bread with the hungry,
and bring the homeless poor into your house;
when you see the naked, to cover them,
and not to hide yourself from your own kin? . . .
If you offer your food to the hungry
and satisfy the needs of the afflicted,
then your light shall rise in the darkness,
and your gloom be like the noonday." Amen.

Isaiah 58:6–7, 10

1870–1950

1871
Kulturkampf in
Germany

1891
Rerum Novarum
written

1903
Pope Pius X elected

1907
Modernism
condemned

1878
Pope Leo XIII elected

1897
Catholic University of
America begins

1905
France breaks with
the Catholic Church

1908
U.S. ceases to be a
mission country

A SPIRITUAL AND MORAL PRESENCE

The Church in the Modern World

CHAPTER OVERVIEW

- Pope Leo XIII begins modern Catholic social teaching, making the Church a leading voice for justice.

- The Church addresses ongoing political conflicts associated with the modern world.

- Catholics create a variety of ways to live the spiritual life in the modern world.

- Church leaders seek ways to promote peace in an era of world wars.

| 1910 Maryknoll founded | 1917 Apparitions of Our Lady of Fatima | 1919 U.S. Catholic bishops publish "Bishops' Program of Social Reconstruction" | 1937 Pope Pius XI issues *Mit brennender Sorge* condemning Nazism |

| 1909 Mother Cabrini becomes an American citizen | 1914 World War I begins | 1917 Russian Revolution | 1919 Treaty of Versailles ending World War I | 1939–1945 World War II |

To whom do you turn when you are seeking guidance? The world is more complex than the one your parents, guardians, or even older sisters and brothers grew up in. That leaves you facing problems that no one, except your peers, have had to deal with. Is there nowhere to turn for answers and wisdom? In times of change, the Catholic Church has stepped forth to offer both.

Over one hundred years ago, the Catholic Church entered the modern world, carrying with it the life and teachings of Christ, which it offered people struggling to make sense of modern industry, modern warfare, and modern life. Stripped of its earthly kingdom in 1870, the Church was freed to become universally a spiritual and moral presence in the increasingly secularized world. The Church offered the wisdom it received from Christ, such as: Remember that you are made in the image and likeness of God; always respect the dignity of others; treat even people whom you don't like with loving concern; be particularly attentive to the needs of those who are poor and suffering; and war is not glorious but tragic. This chapter will examine how the Church attempted to stay the course as the world continued to identify itself less and less with ancient sources of wisdom such as that offered by the Church. During this period while an intense drama played itself out between the Church and the modern world, the Church offered invaluable resources that the world desperately needed, then as now.

Before We Begin . . .

In "The Truman Show", the main character unknowingly becomes the lead actor in his soap-opera life, which is televised for the world to see. Truman is lied to, cheated, deprived of his ability to make choices, controlled, and manipulated by everyone.

■ What does this plot have to say about the challenges the modern world presents to people trying to live a life of faith?

■ What role would you like the Church to have in the modern world?

■ How can the Church counteract modern tendencies that can make life seem like "The Truman Show"?

THE INDUSTRIAL REVOLUTION

Responses to the Industrial Revolution

In the nineteenth century, Europe underwent a revolution that was every bit as jarring as the French Revolution. What the French Revolution did to European politics, the Industrial Revolution did to European social and economic life. Factories manufactured a staggering array of new products, making them available to more and more people. However, the factory system also transformed the relationship between workers and the products they made. As workers converted from being craftsmen to production line members, the whole mentality of being a worker changed. Rather than working to make a product, men and women now worked to make money.

Prior to the Industrial Revolution, a person learning a skill served first as an apprentice, then as a journeyman working for someone else, and finally as a master craftsperson. After the Industrial Revolution most factory workers were reduced to serving as lifelong apprentices, performing unskilled labor for someone else's profit. Workers came to be viewed as parts of a huge machine. They had no say in their working conditions, the amount of time they were required to work, the pay they would receive for their work, or how long they would have a job.

Two positions surfaced as the way to respond to the increased industrialization sweeping the continent. One position was **laissez-faire capitalism;** the other was **socialism.** Capitalism advocated a "hands-off" approach by the government and workers (the French term *laissez faire* means "allow to do"). Invisible, unwritten laws of the marketplace would ensure that the entire capitalist system worked for the benefit of all. For example, if a factory is not run efficiently or products are not of high quality, then someone else will do better and force the original factory to close. Outside interference in the system, such as government regulations, only creates problems.

laissez-faire capitalism
economic system that advocates that people with money (capital) can use their money as they wish without restrictions from governments or other sources

socialism
economic system that advocates government control of all instruments of production, such as farms and factories

Early nineteenth century factory workers often included children.

A Spiritual and Moral Presence

Capitalism: Private ownership of the means of production
en of means of prod - capital, raw materials, labor, resources, plant + equip

241

Socialism, on the other hand, called for a great deal of regulation of industry. In fact, Karl Marx—the leading advocate of socialism—wanted to do away with individual owners altogether. He felt that if workers owned and ran the factories themselves through the government, then the benefits of industry would be evenly distributed. Everyone would share in responsibility, work, material rewards, and leisure time. Governments should be instruments of, for, and by workers. Therefore, while the *laissez-faire* approach advocated keeping government out of industry, socialism insisted on government-controlled industry.

Catholic leaders addressed the problems created by the Industrial Revolution by steering a middle-of-the-road course between these positions. They criticized capitalist thinkers who proposed that private property was an absolute right allowing them to do whatever they wanted with what they owned. This mindset had led to ruthless individualism among many early capitalists and to workers being treated like mere commodities. Church leaders also criticized socialism for rejecting the right of private property.

The Church has rejected the totalitarian and atheistic ideologies associated in modern times with "communism" or "socialism." She has likewise refused to accept, in the practice of "capitalism," individualism and the absolute primacy of the law of the marketplace over human labor [Cf. CA 10;13;44].

Catechism of the Catholic Church, #2425

In addition to entering into theoretical debates about what an industrialized society should be like, Church leaders offered specific recommendations about how to make the factory system more humane. For instance, near the end of 1869, Archbishop Ketteler of Germany, a leading Catholic voice for improving conditions for workers, asked his fellow German bishops to work for the entactment of the following laws:

1. "The prohibition of child labor in factories;
2. the limitation of working hours for factory workers;
3. the separation of the sexes in the workshops;
4. the closing of unsanitary workshops;
5. Sunday rest;
6. the obligation to care for workers who are temporarily or permanently disabled;
7. the appointment by the state of factory inspectors."

*Marvin L. Krier Mich, Catholic Social Teaching and Movements
(Mystic, Conn.: Twenty-Third Publications, 1998), 7.*

Looking at the list, we get a sense of conditions associated with factory work at the time.

Catholics have been a major force in the unionizing of workers.

"On the Condition of the Working Classes"

Pope Leo XIII, elected pope after Pius IX in 1878, was most responsible for formulating a Catholic position on problems associated with industrialization. Pope Leo was not blind to the horrible conditions that existed for many workers both in Europe and in the United States. He believed that the Church could and should provide moral guidance in this important area. He also knew that in Europe many workers were turning to socialism and the atheistic perspective of Marx. (Marx condemned religion for encouraging workers to accept their sufferings, arguing that religion's focus was on life after death and not on this life.) Pope Leo feared that workers were thus cutting themselves off from the graces available through the Church. Finally, Pope Leo did not want the Church to be untouched by and uninvolved in the plight of workers. Catholic workers were children of the Church; as the head of the Church he felt it necessary to address their needs.

In addition to a growing number of European Catholic leaders concerned about the plight of workers, the U.S. Church also petitioned the pope to speak out on this issue. In the United States, the vast majority of factory workers were Catholic. Many bishops and priests typically came from working families.

So, in 1891, Pope Leo issued an encyclical called *Rerum Novarum* (its title literally means "of new things"). It is commonly referred to as "On the Condition of the Working Classes," which was the relatively new thing that the pope wanted to address. Many of those who spearheaded the movement for unionizing workers were Catholics who were motivated by their Church's call for justice in this document.

RERUM NOVARUM

1. served notice to wealthy industrialists that they could not abuse workers for their own gain

2. urged governments to step in when problems arose within industry

3. declared that workers have a right to a living wage, thus ensuring basic rights for all citizens

4. taught that workers have a right to form unions

A Spiritual and Moral Presence

Rerum Novarum was a groundbreaking document. That the pope would take on such a controversial issue that did not directly affect the political life of the Church was unusual. Pope Leo addressed the issue of workers' rights from a strictly moral standpoint. Until this time people generally perceived the Church to be on the side of the old order and against the liberties advocated since the French Revolution. With his encyclical, Pope Leo announced to the world that the Church would engage in issues related to the problems and the freedoms associated with the modern world. Finally, *Rerum Novarum* added to the legitimacy of the union movement. We may take it for granted that workers have unions and that management and workers together agree on contracts between them. However, in the late 1800s unions still represented a radical movement. Unions were seen by many as an affront to charity and to private property. That is, owners were supposed to take care of their workers, but workers were not to *demand* anything of the owners. To do so took away an owner's opportunity to be charitable to workers. If workers required a factory to be shut down on Sundays, it violated an owner's private property rights. Now with Pope Leo's encyclical, workers could appeal to a document of the Catholic Church and demand their right to unionize.

The Lasting Impact of *Rerum Novarum*

Rerum Novarum began on the official level what became an ongoing examination of issues of justice by Church leaders and members of the Church. A series of encyclicals written by popes over the last one hundred years have offered Catholics a source of guidance as they seek to live their faith in the midst of the changes that have marked the modern world. The encyclicals are a voice for people suffering from injustice throughout the world. As a matter of fact, modern Catholic social teaching has put forth the principle that "those who are oppressed by poverty are the object of a *preferential love* on the part of the Church" (*Catechism of the Catholic Church,* #2448).

Beginning with *Rerum Novarum,* Pope Leo offered a process by which the Church could be involved in the modern world. In the words of the *Catechism of the Catholic Church:* "The Church's social teaching proposes principles for reflection; it provides criteria for judgment; it gives guidelines for action" (#2423).

Discussion

"On Human Work," an encyclical written by Pope John Paul II in 1981, contains comments about technological, economic, and political developments that influence the world of work. Describe changes that have taken place since 1981 which affect the world of work. What messages would you like the Church to offer the world today regarding the world of work?

Activity

Catholic social teaching says that private property is not an "absolute right." What does this mean? Give three examples to illustrate this teaching.

United States Contributions to Catholic Social Teaching

Leaders of the Catholic Church in the United States came to be actively involved in the labor movement for a very practical reason—that's where the vast majority of the country's Catholic people were. One of the first labor unions in the United States was the Knights of Labor, which functioned as a secret society to protect itself from outside interference. The majority of its leaders and members were Catholics.

In 1884, at the request of the Archbishop of Quebec, Pope Leo XIII condemned the Knights of Labor in Canada. In Europe, people typically joined secret societies as an alternative to the Church. Cardinal Gibbons of Baltimore knew that the Knights of Labor was not a secret society like the ones in Europe. He also knew that the Knights of Labor provided a valuable service to U.S. workers. Gibbons therefore traveled to Rome in 1887 to make the case that it would be a grave mistake for the pope to condemn the Knights of Labor in the United States.

Pope Leo XIII

He appealed to the pope that since "the great questions of the future are not those of war, of commerce or finance, but the social questions, the questions which concern the improvement of the condition of the great masses of people, and especially of the working people, it is evidently of supreme importance that the Church should always be found on the side of humanity, of justice toward the multitudes who compose the body of the human family" (John Ellis, ed., *Documents of American Catholic History* [Collegeville, MN.: The Liturgical Press, 1987], 448). The pope did not condemn the Knights of Labor in the United States. A few years later he wrote *Rerum Novarum*.

Following World War I, many people in the United States saw the end of the war as an opportunity to establish a new economic and social agenda. Father John A. Ryan, who taught at Catholic University of America, wrote *The Living Wage*—his vision of a social agenda for postwar United States. When the United States Catholic bishops adopted his plan and published it in 1919 as the "Bishops' Program of Social Reconstruction," many people accused the bishops of advocating socialism. Nevertheless, many proposals they made have become accepted policies in the United States.

BISHOPS' ECONOMIC AGENDA PROPOSALS

- initiate a minimum wage

- create and maintain high rates of wages

- originate a government-mandated social security insurance for all workers

- advocate worker participation in the management of industry

Documents of American Catholic History, 601.

The year 1919 was neither the first nor the last time that American bishops were labeled socialists because of their strong stand on behalf of workers. In 1894 an interviewer asked Bishop John Ireland how he responded to those who called him "the Socialist Bishop." Bishop Ireland answered in a way similar to how many Church leaders since then have answered that accusation:

If by Socialists you understand those who are preoccupied by social necessities and miseries, who desire to improve the state of society, and who ask, in view of this improvement, not only action of individuals and influence of voluntary associations, but also a reasonable intervention of the civil power, yes, I am a Socialist. But if by "Socialist" you understand those who share the theories of Marx, of Benoit Malon, of Greef, and others—theories which consist in denying the rightfulness of private property in land and in instruments of labor—no, I am not a Socialist.

Documents of American Church History, 486–87.

Mother Jones—American Labor Leader

One of the most outspoken members of the United States labor movement was Mary Harris Jones, who was known throughout most of her life as "Mother Jones." Born into a Catholic family, Mary taught in a convent school. She married, but her husband and four children died in the yellow fever epidemic in Memphis in 1867. She moved to Chicago and became a seamstress. One evening she wandered into a meeting of the Knights of Labor, one of the few labor organizations of the time to accept women equally with men. At the age of fifty, she immersed herself in the labor movement. Her outlook on religion was fairly simple: "Pray for the dead and fight like hell for the living."

For the next fifty years, Mother Jones appeared wherever workers were fighting for better conditions. She especially deplored child labor. In Mother Jones' autobiography, she catalogued some of the ways that life for workers improved over her lifetime, most of which she herself helped to bring about: "In spite of oppressors, in spite of false leaders, in spite of labor's own lack of understanding of its needs, the cause of the worker continues onward. Slowly his hours are shortened, giving him leisure to read and to think. Slowly his standard of living rises to include some of the good and beautiful things of this world. Slowly the cause of his children becomes the cause of all. His boy is taken from the breaker, his girl from the mill. Slowly those who create the wealth of the world are permitted to share it."

Quoted in Marvin L. Krier Mich, *Catholic Social Teaching and Movements* (Mystic, Conn.: Twenty-Third Publications, 1998), 39.

Mother Jones died in 1930, seven months after her one-hundredth birthday. Many dignitaries attended her funeral Mass at St. Gabriel's Church in Washington. Another funeral service followed in Illinois where a choir made up of miners sang the parts of the Mass.

One expression of Catholicism addressing the problems of workers in the United States was the Catholic Worker Movement, founded by Peter Maurin and Dorothy Day. Research the movement and write a report, poem, or play on it—its principles, its founders, and its work today.

Review

1. What is the difference between *laissez-faire* capitalism and socialism?

2. What position did Catholic Church leaders take toward capitalism and socialism?

3. What contribution did Pope Leo XIII make to Catholic social teaching in 1891?

4. What four principles did Pope Leo XIII propose that helped workers?

5. How did publication of *Rerum Novarum* help make the Church a spiritual and moral presence in the modern world?

6. What was the Knights of Labor? What position did Cardinal Gibbons take toward the Knights of Labor?

7. What four proposals did the U.S. Catholic bishops make in 1919?

POLITICAL CONTROVERSIES

The Catholic Church transcends all nations. During the last decades of the nineteenth century, however, the countries of Europe continued the march toward increasing their power as separate nations. This created tensions with the Catholic Church. In Germany, for instance, the powerful Prussian prime minister, Otto von Bismarck, waged a *Kulturkampf* ("culture war") against the Catholic Church. Beginning in 1873, Bismarck wanted to strengthen German identity by removing Catholicism from the daily life of the German people. He expelled religious communities and placed the schools they ran under the control of the state. He arrested members of the clergy, including cardinals, who resisted his decrees.

Some German citizens were enraged at this persecution of the Catholic Church. Many of those who opposed Bismarck's *Kulturkampf* policies formed a political party called the *Centrum*. When the party became a threat to Bismarck's plans, he sought a way to back down from his anti-Catholic stand without losing face. With the election of a new pope, Leo XIII, in 1878, Bismarck used the occasion to push for a concordat with the Church. The concordat restored the Church to its traditional place in German society.

France began a Third Republic in 1875. When Leo XIII became pope, he attempted to improve the relationship between the French leaders of the republic and Catholic Church leaders. Intellectuals in the French government, however, still perceived Catholicism as being opposed to liberty. In 1905 the French government suppressed all forms of the Catholic religion, closed over 13,000 schools, and expelled or secularized all religious communities.

In England, the Catholic Church restored its leadership in 1859 when Cardinal Wiseman was named Archbishop of Canterbury. After centuries of tension between Catholicism and Anglicanism, the Oxford Movement and the restoration of the hierarchy gave English Catholics hope that a rebirth of the Church in England would follow. However, the Church and the state merely settled into a peaceful coexistence. This condition lasted until 1896 when Pope Leo announced that Anglican orders were not valid. In other words, he declared that Anglican priests and bishops since about the time of Queen Elizabeth were not validly ordained and did not possess orders in line with apostolic succession. This papal proclamation was perceived as an insult to the members of the Church of England and led to a resurgence of anti-Catholic feelings in the country.

Activity

Name three symbols or practices traditionally associated with Catholicism. Choose one of these and with a story, a poem, a painting, a play, or another medium, illustrate for people who are not Catholic why the symbol or practice is important for Catholics.

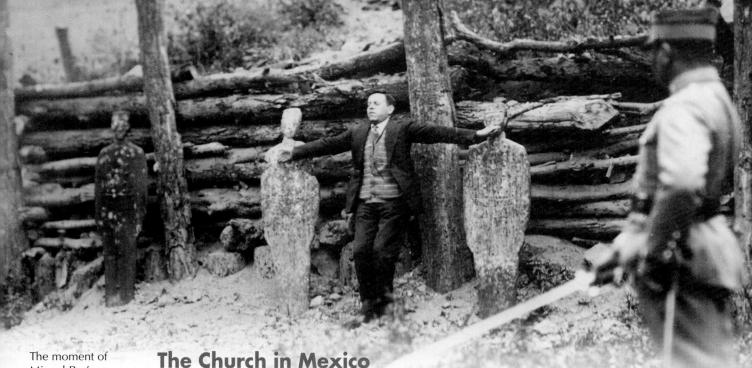

The moment of Miguel Pro's execution was captured on film.

The Church in Mexico

Mexico has had a confusing relationship with the Church. At times, priests actually ran the government there. At other times, Mexican rulers excluded Church leaders from participation in the government. The constitution of 1917 was particularly anti-Catholic. It declared that:

1. there could be no criticism of the government
2. only Mexicans could be clergy
3. the Church could not own property
4. privileges of the Church were revoked and the papal ambassador was expelled from the country

During this period the head of the Mexican government launched a wave of persecutions against Catholics. A Mexican young man named Miguel Pro went to Europe where he was ordained a Jesuit priest. He returned to Mexico and used a variety of disguises and accents to visit the underground Catholic community. One day he posed as a garbage man, another as a college professor. He celebrated the sacraments for people as often as possible at a time when performing even one Baptism would have earned him the death penalty.

A group of Mexicans, supposedly including some of Miguel Pro's brothers, attempted to assassinate the president. When the coup failed, police gathered all the Catholic leaders they could find. They captured Miguel and his bother Humberto and, although they found no evidence that they were involved in the plot, kept them in a dungeon without a trial. In 1927, at the age of thirty-six, Miguel was taken before a police firing squad where reporters were invited to witness the death of this "traitor." Miguel held out his arms in the form of a cross and proclaimed, "Viva Cristo Rey!"—a Spanish phrase for "Long live Christ the King." A photograph of Miguel Pro with arms extended became a holy card seen throughout the world. "Viva Cristo Rey!" became the motto of the underground Church in Mexico. On September 25, 1988, Father Pro was beatified by Pope John Paul II.

The Americanist Controversy

In the United States, tension between identifying with one's nation and identifying with one's faith expressed itself within the Catholic community. Key to the problem was the question of **assimilation.** For instance, should German Catholics and Italian Catholics become absorbed into the great melting pot of U.S. culture, or should they hold onto their differences? Some immigrant Catholics wanted to establish separate schools and maintain as much as possible a separate identity as Catholics and as members of their ethnic group. Other Catholics wanted to assimilate into the mainstream of U.S. life. They felt that there existed no fundamental conflict between Catholicism and U.S. culture. They wanted Catholics and the Catholic Church to exhibit an easy blending of Catholic faith and American culture. In the late 1800s, Archbishop Corrigan of New York represented the position that Catholics should remain separate. Archbishop Ireland of St. Paul, Minnesota, led those advocating an assimilationist position.

These Italian immigrants arrived at Ellis Island ready to begin a new life.

assimilation
members of minority groups adopting the values and characteristics of the dominant culture in which they live

ecumenism
actions aimed at dialogue and the restoration of unity among Christians

fyi!
Pope Leo XIII was the first pope to call non-Catholic Christians "separated brethren."

The controversy over Catholicism and U.S. culture became an international one when a short biography of a U.S. priest named Isaac Hecker was translated from English into French. Hecker, who had been active in New England intellectual circles, became a Catholic as an adult. In 1858 he received permission from Pope Pius IX to begin a new order of priests, called the Paulists, dedicated to bringing Protestants into the Catholic Church. He proposed to accomplish this by preaching in ways that would appeal to Protestants and by meeting intellectual challenges on their own ground. In a sense, Hecker wanted to "Catholicize" the United States by "Americanizing" Catholicism. That is, he believed that only a truly American Church would succeed in making the U.S. more Catholic. To him, the separation of Church and state created an ideal environment for the unhindered spreading of the Catholic message. Hecker attracted a number of well-educated men to Catholicism and to the Paulists. Paulists even preached in Protestant churches during an era when merely entering a Protestant church was frowned upon for Catholics. These priests engaged in what later would be called **ecumenism**—joining together with members of other religions for discussion and shared prayer.

A Paulist priest published in 1891 a biography of Isaac Hecker that included a preface by Archbishop Ireland. A French priest translated the biography in 1897 and then went about hailing Hecker as a model for spreading the Catholic faith everywhere. He praised Hecker's democratic spirit and his openness to modern culture. Some members of the French Church, who held onto traditional French Catholicism, challenged certain ideas that they associated with Hecker, such as the separation of Church and state, and asked Pope Leo XIII to address their concerns. They referred to the ideas to which they objected as *Americanism,* implying that the liberalism that had swept across Europe and had earlier been condemned by Pope Pius IX now found a home in the Catholicism of the United States.

fyi!

In a twenty-year period, from 1880 to 1900, nearly two and one-half million Catholics immigrated to the United States from twenty or more countries. In 1908 the United States ceased to be listed by the Church as mission territory. In time the U.S. Church would send thousands of missionaries to other countries.

In 1899 Pope Leo sent a letter to Cardinal Gibbons, Archbishop of Baltimore, condemning "what some have called Americanism." The pope carefully did not accuse any U.S. bishops or other members of the Church with holding these ideas, but he warned U.S. Catholics that such ideas were erroneous. (For instance, one belief condemned as Americanism was exalting the natural over the supernatural order.) Both liberal and conservative U.S. Catholic bishops felt affirmed by the pope's letter, since no one knew any Catholics who held positions condemned in it. Nonetheless, it caused American theologians to be cautious when offering theological opinions for fear that they would slip into positions that would fall under the category of Americanism.

A few years later, in 1902, the U.S. bishops sent Pope Leo a letter congratulating him on his twenty-fifth anniversary as pope. In his response to their letter, the pope revealed his feelings toward the great progress that U.S. Catholicism had made:

> While the changes and tendencies of nearly all the nations which were Catholic for many centuries give cause for sorrow, the state of your churches, in their flourishing youthfulness, cheers Our heart and fills it with delight.
>
> Pope Leo XIII's *"Congratulations to the Church of the United States,"* April 15, 1902, in John Tracy Ellis, Documents of American Catholic History, 544.

Immigrants leaving Ellis Island wait for a ferry to take them to New York City.

Activity

Debate the issue of assimilation. Do you believe that assimilation is an issue for any groups in the United States today? If so, who are those groups? If you know any immigrants or children of immigrants, how do they approach the issue of assimilation? What advice would you give children of immigrants regarding assimilation?

James Cardinal Gibbons

At the turn of the nineteenth century, the U.S. Church was blessed by the leadership of James Cardinal Gibbons. He was the leader of the Church in the United States who most forcefully took on the causes of workers and of Catholic assimilation into U.S. culture.

Born in Baltimore in 1834, Gibbons was baptized in its cathedral, where he would later serve as archbishop. As a child he returned to Ireland with his family until 1853. He and his family then moved to New Orleans where he decided to enter the seminary in Baltimore. In 1861 he was ordained. In 1872 he was appointed bishop of Richmond and became the youngest bishop to attend Vatican Council I. In 1877 he was named archbishop of Baltimore and served in that capacity until his death in 1921.

During his years as archbishop, Gibbons served as the leading spokesman for U.S. Catholicism. The pope chose him to preside over the Third Plenary Council of Baltimore held in 1884. This council did much to set the direction for U.S. Catholicism far into the twentieth century. It mandated parish schools and called for the writing of the *Baltimore Catechism*. It proposed establishing the Catholic University of America, which opened in Washington, D.C., in 1887. Until his death at the age of eighty-seven, Gibbons took on the many difficult issues facing U.S. Catholics. He particularly addressed the concerns of workers, calling for strict regulation of sweatshops, where many Catholics worked. He took the controversial stand of supporting the entrance of the United States into World War I. Finally, he helped to organize all United States bishops into a national conference, which provided a forum by which the U.S. Church has addressed important issues ever since.

The Modernist Controversy

Over the course of the nineteenth century, the Catholic Church felt that its position in the world was being diminished. In the eyes of Church leaders, without Christ and his Church to lead the way, the modern world was heading into treacherous waters. Certain viewpoints that seemed to go against traditional Catholicism came to be lumped together and were labeled *modernism*. By the end of the nineteenth century, it appeared that even Catholic priests and perhaps some bishops were advocating some dangerous teachings.

Modernism was not a specifically identifiable school of thought. Church leaders who condemned it associated modernism with denying that people could arrive at the existence of God through the use of reason as Saint Thomas Aquinas had done. They also identified modernism as proposing that the Church and Church practices developed over time in response to human need, as opposed to being divinely instituted by Christ. In 1907 Pope Pius X, who followed Pope Leo XIII, decided to address what he considered the errors of modernism in an encyclical, *Pascendi Dominici Gregis*, which means "Feeding the Lord's Flock." A number of priests were excommunicated for teaching modernism, and in 1910 the pope required all priests to take an oath against modernism. Although the next pope, Benedict XV, took immediate steps to ease tensions among Catholics who held different positions, the oath against modernism was not rescinded as a requirement for priesthood until 1967.

One of the unfortunate side effects of the campaign against modernism was that it stifled Catholic intellectual life for some time. Similar to the impact that the Church's condemnation of Americanism had, its condemnation of modernism left Catholic scholars hesitant to explore areas of research that might lead them to inadvertently teach modernist ideas. It would be decades before Catholic scholars felt comfortable that the modernism condemned by the Church did not rule out all modern approaches to studying Scripture and other areas of theology. Eventually scholars reasserted a more traditional Catholic position on the intellectual life held from the time of the Church fathers, namely, that Catholicism finds the use of reason and intellectual inquiry to be totally compatible with the life of faith.

The Church's stand against modernism faded during the twentieth century, and Catholics took their place in all areas of intellectual inquiry.

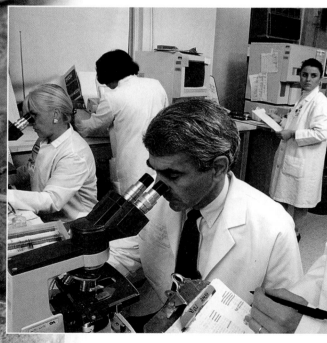

Activity

Three men who greatly influenced the modern world were Karl Marx, Charles Darwin, and Sigmund Freud. Describe the basic teachings of each one and explain the impact that each might have had on religion. Provide a Catholic response to each of the main teachings.

Pope Pius X

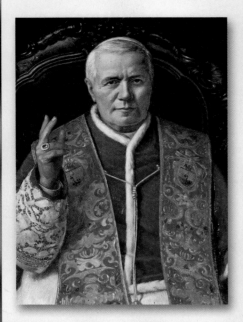

The man who became Pius X, Giuseppe Sarto, came from humble beginnings in northern Italy. Father Sarto was a parish priest for twenty years before being chosen to be spiritual director and rector of a seminary. Later, he became bishop of Mantua, a diocese that had been part of the Papal States but was then in disrepair. As the people grew to love their new pastor, Bishop Sarto revitalized the Church in the area. In recognition of his work, the pope named him a cardinal in 1894 and appointed him patriarch of Venice.

When Pope Leo XIII died, Cardinal Sarto bought a round-trip train ticket for Rome, sure that he would never be considered for pope. Once the conclave began, however, an old privilege that the Church had extended to a secular ruler came into play. The Holy Roman Emperor vetoed the election of a certain cardinal who appeared to be the front runner for the papacy. A number of cardinals then began to look to Cardinal Sarto as a worthy candidate because of his reputation for holiness and pastoral care. He reluctantly accepted the papacy, taking the name Pius X.

Pope Pius made his mark particularly in the area of liturgical reform. He encouraged daily reception of Communion and lowered to seven the age at which children could first receive Communion, allowing them to receive the Eucharist before Confirmation. He also supported the Catholic Action movement, which was an attempt to get laypeople more involved in the Church. Pope Pius served as pope during the period just before the outbreak of World War I. He spoke out strongly against building up armies and about the uselessness of war. He died within weeks of the start of the war, some said of a broken heart. Pope Pius was proclaimed a saint just forty years after his death, the first pope in over three hundred years to be so honored.

Review

1. Why did Otto von Bismarck initiate his *Kulturkampf?*

2. How did many French intellectuals at the end of the 1800s view Catholicism?

3. What action by Pope Leo XIII added to anti-Catholic feelings among Anglicans?

4. Who was Miguel Pro?

5. What is assimilation? What two positions did U.S. Catholic leaders take toward assimiliation?

6. What effect did Pope Leo XIII's condemnation of Americanism have on American theologians?

7. In his 1902 response to the U.S. bishops, how did Pope Leo XIII view the U.S. Church?

8. Name two positions associated with modernism.

9. What effect did condemnation of modernism have on Catholic intellectual activity? What more traditional understanding of Catholic scholarship eventually replaced this viewpoint?

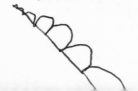

CATHOLIC SPIRITUAL LIFE

The modern era was characterized by increased secularization. That is, it focused more on the concerns of this world rather than on those of the next. It focused on material progress to a greater degree than interior, spiritual progress. Against the backdrop of increased secularization, Catholics found a variety of ways to live their spiritual life. One of the principal expressions of spirituality during this period can be characterized as **devotional Catholicism**. Devotional Catholicism refers to practicing popular devotions similar to those from the baroque period, such as devotion to the Sacred Heart. For instance, recitation of the rosary was a popular Catholic devotion throughout the modern period. Also, in 1830 a French nun in her mid-twenties, Catherine Laboure, reported to her confessor that she had received a vision of the Blessed Mother who asked to have a medal made to honor her Immaculate Conception.

devotional Catholicism
practices of religious piety among Catholics

From that time on, many Catholics worldwide wore what came to be known as the Miraculous Medal. A number of preachers, and eventually the pope, encouraged more frequent reception of Penance and Communion.

A series of apparitions of Mary took place in towns throughout Europe. At first Church leaders discouraged devotions related to these apparitions, but eventually they accepted and even encouraged a number of them. Besides Our Lady of Lourdes mentioned earlier, one of the most famous apparitions took place in Fatima, Portugal, in 1917, when three young children claimed to see the Blessed Mother.

While devotional practices sustained many Catholics during the modern period, Catholic leaders were often involved in theological disputes and in trying to resolve various political crises. However, as has always been true, there were also people living out the gospel message in saintly, heroic ways. Their stories tell of a Catholic faith that continued to inspire good works and compassion for others.

Devotion to Mary took new forms after apparitions such as that at Lourdes, France.

Father Damien stands with patients outside the church on Molokai.

Saint Damien— The Leper Priest

As a youth in Belgium, Joseph de Veuster was muscular but soft-spoken. He wanted to become a priest, but many people thought that he was not intellectually up to the challenge. His older brother, himself a priest, tutored him until he was accepted by the Sacred Heart Fathers, where he took the name Damien. The Sacred Heart Fathers sent Damien to their mission in Hawaii to serve a parish covering 2,000 square miles.

Damien loved his work. However, he discovered that leprosy was rampant on the islands. As soon as anyone contracted leprosy, by law he or she had to report to the authorities who would send the person to the island of Molokai. Molokai had no visitors and no laws. Children with the disease were sent to Molokai just like anyone else, to survive as best they could.

In 1873 the local bishop asked if any priest would volunteer to go to Molokai to serve the people there for a short time. Damien volunteered but insisted that he be sent there permanently. He was thirty-three at the time. When the bishop arrived with Damien on Molokai, he told the people, "I have brought you someone who will be a father to you." His words turned out to be true. Father Damien immediately began his work. He needed his physical strength to build chapels and houses on the island. Unfortunately, he also had to build coffins—over 2,000 in the first few months he was there. Before his arrival, death was so commonplace that there was no attempt at proper burials. Damien made sure that every person who died was buried with dignity. He introduced hygienic practices as best he could, but in his work Damien couldn't avoid contact with deteriorating flesh. At Mass one day in 1885 he began his sermon with the words, "We lepers. . . ." His people knew then that he, too, had contracted the disease.

Damien was able to continue his work for a few more years and died peacefully in 1889. He was pleased to be buried in the "garden of the dead" on Molokai, which he had managed to transform into a place where the dead would be viewed with respect. However, in 1936 the Belgian government returned his body to his native land so that the people of Belgium could honor their "Damien of Molokai."

Saint Thérèse of Lisieux—"The Little Flower"

Seven years after Damien's death, a young Carmelite nun died in a convent in Lisieux, France. Despite the fact that her only claim to fame was doing little things well and that she died when she was only twenty-four, this young woman, born Thérèse Martin, became one of the most popular saints of all time. Her appeal with so many people actually stems from what she herself would call her "littleness."

Brittany *and* **Brandon M. Backes**

As a child, Thérèse wanted to join her two older sisters who were nuns in the Carmelite monastery. When she was fourteen, she and her father, along with a group of pilgrims, had an opportunity to meet the pope. Everyone was told not to say anything when introduced to the pope, but Thérèse daringly said: "Holy Father, in honor of your anniversary, please allow me to enter Carmel although I am not of the age required." Touched by her faith, Pope Leo XIII assured her that if God wanted it, she would be in Carmel soon. The next year, her bishop allowed Thérèse to enter the convent.

When it was discovered that she was seriously ill with tuberculosis, her superior asked Thérèse to write her life story, which was published after her death as *The Story of a Soul*. In it she describes her approach to spirituality, "Do little things well, recognizing that our most insignificant actions are a response to the love of Jesus." After her death in 1897, Thérèse's life and spirituality sparked interest worldwide. She became known as "the Saint of the Little Way." Most people are not destined to achieve great accomplishments. Saint Thérèse's life reminds us that saintliness involves doing ordinary things with the right spirit—saying hello to a stranger in a supermarket, being nice to someone we don't like, cleaning dishes after a meal, or changing a child's diapers. Even though she never left her hometown except for her one trip to Rome, Thérèse (along with Francis Xavier), was declared a patroness of foreign missions. Her feast day is October 1.

Pius representations of Thérèse of Lisieux do not do justice to her strength of character. In 1997 she was named a doctor of the Church.

Mother Cabrini is the first U.S. citizen to be declared a saint. Her feast day is November 13.

Frances Cabrini and Katharine Drexel

Two women who did much for the U.S. Church are Frances Cabrini and Katharine Drexel. The thirteenth child of an Italian farm family, Cabrini became a nun and worked with orphans. Pope Leo XIII asked her to go to the United States to continue her work. She asked for advice and support from the Italian community in New York, and an orphanage was built. Mother Cabrini returned to Italy to bring to the U.S. more sisters to expand the work. She founded Columbus Hospital in New York and eventually opened fifty institutions in eight countries. She became a U.S. citizen in 1909.

Katharine Drexel was born into a wealthy Philadelphia Catholic family in 1858. The Drexels taught their children that wealth was a responsibility. When Katharine and her sister inherited the family fortune in 1885, Katharine decided that her share should be used to assist Native Americans and African Americans. She asked the pope to send missionaries to the United States for this work, but the pope instead challenged Katharine to become a missionary herself.

Mother Katharine Drexel died in 1955 and was declared a saint in 2000. Her feast day is March 3.

Katharine accepted the pope's challenge and formed a religious order known as the Sisters of the Blessed Sacrament for Indians and Colored People. She founded many educational institutions, including Xavier University in New Orleans, the only Catholic university dedicated to the education of African Americans.

Missionaries and Monasteries in the U.S. Church

In recent decades the Church in the United States has sent many missionaries to other lands. Surprisingly, in 1906 less than one hundred U.S. missionary sisters, priests, and brothers served the Church outside the country. Then, in 1911 two diocesan priests, Father James Walsh and Father Thomas F. Price, founded the Catholic Foreign Mission Society of America. They set up headquarters near Ossining, New York, and called it Maryknoll. Today, Maryknoll encompasses men and women religious and lay volunteers who perform missionary work throughout the world.

The contemplative life, which involved living apart from the world in monasteries as monks or as **cloistered** nuns, traditionally did not draw many U.S. Catholics. However, in 1790 some Carmelites began a monastery in Port Tobacco, Maryland. The cool reception they received led them to move to Baltimore in the early 1800s. In 1848 Trappist monks founded the Abbey of Gethsemani in Kentucky, and in 1849 other Trappists settled near Dubuque, Iowa. Both monasteries thrived and continue to exist today.

Thomas Merton is the most famous U.S. monk. Merton's parents died when he was young, leaving him a trust fund. Merton traveled around the world, experiencing and enjoying life. He finally entered Columbia University in New York to seek a serious career.

Through his studies and extensive reading, Merton found himself drawn to Catholicism. He joined the Church in 1938 and three years later entered Gethsemani monastery, where he lived the rest of his life.

Merton's abbot recognized the writing talent that the new monk possessed. He asked him to write the story of his spiritual journey. When it was published in 1948, *The Seven Storey Mountain* was the year's best-selling book. Even though Merton lived his life in his Kentucky monastery, he actively followed the critical issues facing the world and wrote about many of them. In 1968 on one of the rare occasions when he left Gethsemani, Merton died—the result of an accident while attending a conference on monasticism in Thailand.

cloistered
literally, "behind walls"; women and men religious who choose to live within monasteries

fyi!
The Maryknoll name is derived from the hill, or knoll, on the property in New York State where the first Maryknoll headquarters were established.

Activity

Research Brother Roger's Taizé community in France, Jean Vanier's international l'Arche communities, and Catherine de Hueck Doherty's Friendship and Madonna Houses in the United States and Canada. Which community would suit you? If none of these appeal to you, what kind of community might you form to live out your Christian witness to the world?

Review

1. Give two examples of Catholic devotional practices.

2. How did Father Damien try to restore a sense of dignity to the people of Molokai?

3. Describe Saint Thérèse of Lisieux's approach to the spiritual life.

4. Who was the first United States citizen to be declared a saint?

5. With what groups did Katharine Drexel's sisters work?

6. What type of work do members of Maryknoll perform?

AN AGE OF WORLD WARS

Called "the Great War" because it involved all of the world's great powers, World War I resulted in unparalleled devastation and loss of life. Catholics fought on both sides in the war. The papacy put its energy into trying to bring about an end to hostilities. Failing that, it used its resources to provide aid to the injured and support to people displaced by the conflict.

Politically, Pope Benedict XV remained neutral during the war. Both sides, therefore, accused him of favoring the enemy. The Germans called him "the French pope"; the Allies called him "the German pope." When the war ended, Pope Benedict encouraged the victors to avoid retaliation against those who were defeated and to restore order as much as possible.

At his election as pope, Pius XI stated his desired to resolve the relationship between the Vatican and the country of Italy. In 1922 Mussolini became dictator of Italy. His Fascist party was in complete control. He sought the complete support of the people and realized that he needed to settle the "Roman Question," as the status of the Vatican was called. In a 1929 agreement called the *Lateran Treaty,* the pope gave up all claims to the former Papal States. The pope accepted a financial settlement for the lost properties and was given complete control and ownership of Vatican City and certain other properties in and around Rome. There was also a concordat between the Vatican and the Italian government that dealt with religious practices and rights. However, Mussolini failed to live up to the concordat, and in 1931, the pope issued "On Catholic Action in Italy," an encyclical against Fascism.

Finding himself in a similar situation in 1937, Pope Pius XI wrote an encyclical condemning Hitler after he violated a concordat between the Vatican and the Nazi government. To avoid having it suppressed by Mussolini, Hitler's ally, the pope had the encyclical smuggled out of Rome in the suitcase of a young U.S. priest—the future cardinal archbishop of New York, Francis Cardinal Spellman.

These World War I marines in training in France wore gas masks to protect themselves from toxic gases.

fyi!

In 1984, the concordat between the Vatican and Italian government was renegotiated. Catholic instruction was no longer mandatory in government schools, and the clergy were no longer paid salaries by the government.

Developments Between the Wars

Catholic–Protestant Relations

Catholics and Protestants fought on both sides during World War I. Immediately following the war, Catholic and Protestant organizations worked together to aid the victims of the war. Therefore, much of the fear and distrust that had marked the relationship between the two groups disappeared. Scholars from both traditions tried working together on common projects, especially in the area of Scripture study. From 1921 to 1925, Catholics, with Vatican approval, and Anglicans held informal talks between themselves. Positive relations among various Christian groups in the 1920s and '30s paved the way for the spirit of ecumenism and for the intensive interreligious dialogue that took place following Vatican Council II.

Native Clergy

As French and German forces took over opposing territories, they expelled in large numbers missionaries from enemy nations. Because there were few native clergy in mission lands, this left many Catholics without the sacraments. The popes who served after World War I regretted that the Church had not done more to foster vocations in the mission lands. In 1923 Pope Pius XI appointed an Indian Jesuit as a bishop in India. In 1926 the pope personally ordained six native Chinese bishops. He later appointed a Japanese bishop for Nagasaki, a Vietnamese bishop, and in 1939 the first black African bishop. By the Second World War there were native bishops in forty-eight former mission countries. After the war, Pope Pius XII named many new cardinals, a number from non-European countries. Before native clergy achieved leadership positions in these countries, Catholicism was perceived as a foreign entity. Over the course of the twentieth century, the Catholic Church took on a truly universal character.

The expansion of native clergy was a priority of the Catholic Church in the twentieth century.

Lay Involvement

Since Vatican Council II, Catholics recognize that all members of the Church share a "universal call to holiness." This concept became popular early in the twentieth century under Pope Pius X. The pope called upon laypeople to get involved in what he called **Catholic Action**—small groups of Catholics meeting with a priest and trying to become more informed about the faith.

In the United States, one organization that took the pope's message to heart was the Extension Society. This group of lay Catholics dedicated themselves to building churches, rectories, and schools in isolated areas of the country. Pope Pius was so pleased with the work of Extension that he named it a pontifical institute, placing it under the direct supervision of the Vatican. In 1921 in Holland, the Grail movement promoted Christian values among women employed in social work, in medical fields, or in religious formation. The Catholic Students Mission Crusade involved young people in supporting the work of the missions. A number of groups formed for married couples to provide mutual support. Under Pope Pius XII groups of laypeople formed a variety of institutes engaged in ministries from running soup kitchens to houses of prayer.

Liturgical Renewal

Though lay Catholics were expected to take an active role in spreading the faith, the Mass as most people experienced it did not foster such a role. Someone unfamiliar with the liturgy of the time might have perceived it to be a private affair engaged in by the priest while people in the assembly were passive observers of the priest's actions. Some Catholics called for liturgical renewal. They wanted a clearer, more direct connection between the Mass and the Christian life. If that was to happen, the assembly needed to be more than passive observers of the liturgy. A Benedictine monk at St. John's Abbey in Minnesota, Virgil Michel (1890–1938), was an early advocate of liturgical renewal. He pointed out that "the entire life of the true Christian must be a reflection and a further expression of his life at the altar of God. If he is predominantly a passive Christian there, can we expect him to be an active Christian in his daily life out in the world?" (Quoted in Robert Ellsberg, *All Saints* [Maryknoll, N.Y.: Orbis Books, 1997], 276).

After World War II, Pope Pius XII made a number of changes in the rules concerning the liturgy. In 1953 he issued an apostolic constitution which allows evening Masses and reduced the amount of time required for fasting before receiving Communion. Following Vatican Council II in the 1960s, liturgical renewal would become one of the most apparent changes that took place in the Church.

The Church and Communism

The communist takeover of Russia was a great blow to the Church. Communism was stridently antireligious, and it proposed taking over the world. When Joseph Stalin succeeded Lenin in 1924, he began a series of persecutions against Lutherans, Baptists, and Catholics. Thousands of men and women religious were either imprisoned or killed. In the 1930s Pope Pius XI condemned communism and asked for worldwide prayers for Russian Christians.

From World War II to the Cold War

Eugenio Pacelli became Pope Pius XII in 1939, as the world was entering another devastating war. Pius XII was a good choice to lead the Church during this difficult time. He came from Roman nobility, served in the Vatican diplomatic corps—including a period as the pope's ambassador to the Nazi government in Germany—and traveled extensively while he was Vatican Secretary of State.

During World War II Pius XII was placed in an intolerable position. Surrounded by Italy, one of the axis powers, whatever the pope did might well have failed. In his first address, he pleaded for peace, and his first encyclical called upon all humanity to restore God to his rightful place in society. A number of people have questioned whether the pope might have done more to confront Hitler and a prevailing anti-Semitism; others believe he did all he could without endangering the lives of many Catholics in Germany and elsewhere. In 1939 he wrote what could only be interpreted as a condemnation of the Hitler regime, but he feared that continued confrontation with Hitler would actually lead to loss of more innocent lives. Around six million Jews died in the Holocaust. Millions of Catholics, including priests and nuns, also died in the war. Pope Pius XII and many Catholics in Europe did what they could to alleviate suffering. He arranged that churches, convents, and other Church properties should offer security and safety to Jewish refugees. Over fifteen thousand Jews were hidden in the papal summer residence, Castel Gandolfo.

In 1943 Nazis ordered Roman Jews to pay a large ransom or be shipped to a concentration camp. The pope ordered that sacred vessels should be melted down to help pay the ransom. He also instructed members of the Vatican diplomatic corps to use their resources to aid the safe passage of Jews from areas of danger. In Bulgaria his representative filled out five thousand fake baptismal certificates for Jewish children to save them from deportation. The pope believed that Hitler might kidnap him and take him to Germany. He therefore wrote a letter of resignation that would go into effect the moment he crossed the border of the Vatican. The cardinals would then be free to elect a new pope.

The 1999 Columbine school shootings shocked the world and changed the lives of the students who attended the Colorado high school.

Youth News

Violence today comes in many forms—from shootings in schools, to war situations, to deaths caused by abortion and capital punishment. There is physical and emotional abuse happening in relationships and there is exploitation of workers in sweatshops. What can you do about these situations? You can write letters to your representatives in Congress. You can also create an atmosphere of respect and dignity among those with whom you live, work, and worship.

When peace was finally restored in 1945, Pius XII addressed himself to the needs of refugees. Vatican resources helped in the search for over eleven million displaced persons. Another of the pope's major political concerns in the postwar era, however, was Communism. Communist governments controlled the Soviet Union and most of Eastern Europe and later spread to China. In 1949 the pope declared that any Catholic who joined the Communist party was excommunicated from the Church.

Activity

Three Christian witnesses who died during World War II were Maximilian Kolbe, Edith Stein, and Franz Jagerstatter. Research one of these people's lives or that of another Christian who died during the Holocaust, and present a written, oral, or electronic slide presentation based on your research.

Review

1. What political position did Pope Benedict XV take during World War I?

2. What effect did World War I and postwar activities have on Catholic–Protestant relations?

3. What steps did Pope Pius XI take to strengthen the Church in former mission countries?

4. What is Catholic Action? Give two examples of organizations that promoted Catholic Action.

5. What problem did Virgil Michel see in the way liturgy was typically experienced during his time?

6. What position did communism take toward religion?

7. Why did Pope Pius XII hesitate to confront Nazism too strongly?

8. Give an example of how Pope Pius XII assisted Jews during World War II.

9. What was Pope Pius XII's major political concern following World War II?

Conclusion

Major challenges faced the Church as it entered the modern world. The concept that civil governments should be totally separate from the Church went against longstanding Catholic practice, even though it seemed to be working in the United States. People in Europe and America had adopted new ways of making a living. Industrialization held out promise of improving lives, but it was causing a great deal of suffering in the process. Thus the Church was called upon to address social and economic issues. Finally, the first half of the twentieth century saw unparalleled devastation due to war and hatred. After tremendous transformations, and after two world wars, the Church remained strong and vital. In the late 1940s Church leaders decided that it would be a good time to take stock of the Church and of its place in this modern world. It would take a new pope, John XXIII, and another decade before the Church would call a council that would usher in changes rivaling those taking place in the world around it.

May Christ's message of salvation, love, and peace delivered to the world at Vatican Council II continue to inspire all members of his Church. May we work for justice and peace wherever we find them lacking, and through our efforts may the light of Christ shine more brightly throughout the world. Amen.

1950–1977

1958
Election of Pope John XXIII

1960
Election of John Kennedy, first Catholic United States president

1959
Pope John XXIII announces that there will be a council

1962
Beginning of Vatican Council II

THE CHURCH OF VATICAN COUNCIL II

CHAPTER OVERVIEW

- Pope John XXIII calls for a council to renew and update the Catholic Church.

- Pope Paul VI continues the council and implements changes following Vatican II.

1963
Death of Pope John XXIII; election of Pope Paul VI

1968
Latin American bishops meet and set agenda for the work of justice

1965
Vatican Council II ends; Pope Paul VI addresses the United Nations

Did you ever feel as though you needed to step back and take stock of yourself? Perhaps you began high school with grand plans, but somewhere along the way you became sidetracked. At such times, looking back and looking forward are important. The ancient philosophers were right: The unexamined life is not worth living.

The Catholic Church decided to take stock of itself in the early 1960s. It did so at a three-year event known as Vatican Council II. The immediate impetus for the council was the election of a new pope, John XXIII—a kindly, unassuming Italian who had worked in many of the world's trouble spots during his career as a diplomat and a bishop. His call for a council was by itself an omen that change was in the air. People debate how much the Catholic Church changed as a result of the council. Some say that the Church's teaching and practice changed little; others see radical change following the council. This chapter will look closely at the council and then at the post-Vatican II Church to see how the Church sees itself after this landmark event.

Before We Begin . . .

Imagine that you have been invited to Rome to participate in a meeting to bring about renewal of the Catholic Church today—Vatican Council III. In preparation for the meeting, write up the following: the strengths and weaknesses of the Church today, major principles and goals that should guide the meeting, and specific changes that you would hope to see occur.

THE CHURCH IS TRANSFORMED

A Spiritual and Moral World Crisis

Discussion

Defend or refute the following statement: Destruction is usually portrayed as being caused by people who are deranged or who are purposely and knowingly sadistic. However, the greatest evils and destruction of the twentieth century took place at the hands of supposedly rational, intelligent men.

During the first half of the twentieth century, two world wars devastated Europe. Besides the deaths and physical destruction, they also left a spiritual and moral vacuum. For instance, during World War II a group of well-educated, at least formerly Christian German men decided that the most efficient way to address the "Jewish problem" was to annihilate all Jews. How could men who had a Christian upbringing decide that children, women, and men should be killed indiscriminately simply because they were identified as belonging to a different religion or a different ethnic group? How could the physical remains of millions of people, burned in the ovens of concentration camps, be used for fertilizer after gold teeth were extracted and women's hair cut off to make rope? When word reached the press outside of Germany that the Nazi government was systematically killing all those who were Jewish, the announcement did not even make the front page of the *New York Times*. The Holocaust and circumstances surrounding it indicated that the world faced a serious spiritual and moral crisis.

One organization that showed signs of health after the war was the Catholic Church. It had a strong European base, but it was growing in other parts of the world as well. Before there was a United Nations, the Church was an international body made up of people from every nationality and ethnic group. The Church also had established itself as a voice for spiritual and moral concern. Although some people have accused Church leaders of being overly timid in helping the victims of the war, the case could also be made that the Church did more to protect victims than any non-governmental organization did. Church leaders realized that in this difficult post-war era the Church had much to offer the world. However, if the Church was to use the gifts of her founder and provide direction and hope to a despairing world, it would have to enter into serious dialogue with people from the world's many nations and religions. It would need to address expressions of contemporary culture, not simply condemn it from afar. It was time once again for the Church to follow the guidance of the Holy Spirit in its mission of bringing Christ to the world.

Pictured here are liberated survivors of two Nazi concentration camps, Ebensee in Austria (above) and Belsen in Germany (right).

The Post-War World and the Pre-Vatican II Church

Nuclear Weapons

In addition to the senseless destruction of World War II and the morally bankrupt murder of Holocaust victims, other events signaled the need for a re-examination of purpose by all factions of the world community. Toward the end of the war, the United States unleashed a weapon of unprecedented destructive capacity. The atomic bomb annihilated two Japanese cities—Hiroshima and Nagasaki, the center of Japanese Catholicism. The atomic bomb loomed as a specter overshadowing everything else in the post-war world. Nuclear weapons demanded that people learn how to live together peacefully or else die together. The term "nuclear holocaust" frightened the world community from the late nineteen forties into the nineteen eighties. When the bishops met at Vatican Council II, they recognized that peacemaking had to silence the guns of war: "All these considerations compel us to undertake an evaluation of war with an entirely new attitude" (*The Documents of Vatican II*, "The Church in the Modern World," #80).

Communism

The war ended Fascism in Italy and Germany. However, the atheistic Communism adopted by the Soviet Union earlier in the twentieth century now had spread into Asia and controlled most of Eastern Europe. Advocates of Communism seemed to be everywhere. Communism was not simply an alternative form of government; it proposed absolute control of all aspects of life. The Church and Communism were not compatible.

Pope Pius XII staunchly opposed Communism and spoke out against it often during the 1940s and '50s. At Vatican Council II, Church leaders called for establishment of a world order based on principles of justice and cooperation in order to avoid the destructiveness to the human spirit accompanying Communism. At the same time, the popes of the council attempted to open Communication with communist leaders.

The atomic bombing of Hiroshima, Japan, took place on August 6, 1945. Five square miles of the city were destroyed. It is estimated that between 70,000 and 100,000 people died in the blast. Thousands more died later as the result of atomic radiation.

Global Community

During the council Pope John XXIII took time to write an encyclical called *Peace on Earth*. In it he pointed out that "in the modern world human society has taken on an entirely new appearance in the field of social and political life. For since all nations have either achieved or are on the way to achieving independence, there will soon no longer exist a world divided into nations that rule others and nations that are subject to others" (#42). In other words, the pope was praising the end of **colonialism.** In the aftermath of World War II, creation of the United Nations indicated that the people of the world wanted to establish a mechanism that would help prevent wars in the future. The United Nations also embodied the hope for a global community. In 1965 Pope Paul VI endorsed the United Nations and its efforts by stating:

> Our message is meant to be first of all a solemn moral ratification of this lofty Institution, and it comes from Our experience of history. It is as an "expert on mankind" that We bring this Organization the support and approval of Our recent predecessors, that of the Catholic hierarchy and Our own, convinced as We are that this Organization represents the path that has to be taken for modern civilization and for world peace.

> Pope Paul VI, *"Address to the United Nations General Assembly,"* October 4, 1965, as quoted in Phyllis Zagano, Twentieth-Century Apostles (Collegeville, Minn.: The Liturgical Press, 1999), 35.

colonialism
the rule of one country by another

In the mid-nineteen fifties, the terms *first world, second world,* and *third world* began to be used to distinguish among Western industrialized countries, the communist bloc of countries, and the economically undeveloped countries of the world. Today the term *developing countries* is often used.

Liberation Movements

World War II was primarily a conflict among industrialized nations and the middle-class people who dominated them. Beginning in the nineteen fifties, new conflicts began to emerge on the world scene. Besides the "first world" of Western democracies and the "second world" of communist nations, there was also a "third world" of nations and peoples not aligned with either group. These nations and groups of people were crying out for recognition and equality. In response to inequalities and injustice, various groups formed liberation movements that would flourish, especially in the later 1960s. In Europe and the United States, university students in particular started calling for radical changes in the way power and economic prosperity were divided in the world. Even before the term "women's liberation movement" became popular, Pope John XXIII observed in 1963: "Since women are becoming ever more conscious of their human dignity, they will not tolerate being treated as mere material instruments, but demand rights befitting a human person both in domestic and in public life" (*Peace on Earth*, #41). Another liberation movement that had a significant effect on the Church was the one initiated by people who are poor in Latin America.

Activity

Research and report on the effect that the women's liberation movement had and continues to have on women's rights in the workplace and in society.

Pope John XXIII

Pope John XXIII

General Charles de Gaulle

Angelo Roncalli was born in 1881 to a family of peasant farmers in northern Italy, the third of thirteen children. Although he entered the seminary at age twelve and was ordained when he was twenty-three, Roncalli never lost touch with his peasant background. He studied at Rome, taught Church history, and published books on the subject. During World War I, Roncalli served as a chaplain in the army medical corps. After the war he was named an archbishop and represented the pope in Bulgaria, Greece, and Turkey. In these assignments he spent time with members of the Eastern Churches, other religions, and minority groups. Through these assignments he grew comfortable interacting with people of different faiths and ethnic backgrounds and learned more about the suffering of others. When World War II began, he managed to use his international contacts to secure safe passage for thousands of Jews fleeing Europe.

When the war ended, Archbishop Roncalli expected to settle into a less stressful position. However, the war had created a problem for the Catholic Church in France. During the war, a pro-German government had controlled France. After the war, General Charles de Gaulle led France in identifying those who had collaborated with the Nazis. De Gaulle insisted that thirty-three bishops had to be removed for collaborating with the Nazi regime during the war. The pope needed Roncalli's skill as a diplomat and his personal charm to help resolve the problem. Roncalli was able to convince General de Gaulle to allow all but three of the bishops to remain in their positions. He also averted other crises in France during his time there. When the pope named Roncalli a cardinal in 1953, the president of France claimed an old privilege. In Paris, de Gaulle personally presented Roncalli with the cardinal's hat and also invested him in the French Legion of Honor.

Once again, Roncalli expected that he would return to Rome and work in the Vatican offices. Instead, the pope named him Patriarch of Venice. For five years Roncalli served the people of Venice, who quickly came to love him. His kindly demeanor, coupled with his rotund shape, reminded many of his people of a favorite great-uncle or a grandfather.

In October 1958, Pope Pius XII died. Cardinal Roncalli, seventy-six at the time, left Venice for Rome, expecting to return shortly. However, Pope Pius had suffered through a lengthy illness and consequently had let the number of cardinals dwindle. Only fifty-one cardinals came to the conclave to elect a new pope and nineteen of them were over seventy-eight years old. After three days, no one person emerged as a favorite. The cardinals looked for a compromise candidate, perhaps someone who would serve as pope for a short time. Then additional cardinals could be named so that a clearer choice for a longer reigning pope could be made later. On the fourth day of the conclave, the cardinals elected Roncalli. Even he referred to himself as *papa de passagio*—a transitional pope.

A Pope *from* and *of* the People

Upon becoming pope, John XXIII surprised many people when he quickly named twenty-three new cardinals. This broke a longstanding tradition that there be no more than seventy cardinals at any given time. For the first time, cardinals were named from the Philippines, Japan, Mexico, and Africa. Pope John's personal style and pastoral spirit were also a big surprise to those used to the previous formality of the Vatican structure. During the first few months of his pontificate, the pope visited orphanages and hospitals. He discontinued the tradition of the pope dining alone, often inviting one or more people to join him for meals. He dropped in on Vatican offices to meet the staff, learn their names, and talk with them. His greatest surprise, however, came on January 25, 1959, when he announced to a few cardinals that there was soon to be an ecumenical council of the Church.

Pope John XXIII was famous for his visits to orphanages, hospitals, and prisons. On September 3, 2000, John was beatified and given the title "Blessed."

Review

1. What event associated with World War II led Church leaders to realize that the world faced a moral and spiritual vacuum?

2. What change in perspective did the Church need to make if it was to address the problems facing the world following World War II?

3. What four developments in the post-war world led the Church to examine its role in the world?

4. Name two assignments served by Pope John XXIII that helped prepare him for the papacy during a time of change. Explain.

5. What does it mean to say Pope John XXIII was initially thought to be a *papa de passagio?*

The Church of Vatican Council II

VATICAN II—CHRIST'S PRESENCE

A pivotal event in the history of the Church took place around the year A.D. 50 when members of the Christian community were struggling with the question of what to do about non-Jews who wanted to join them. Recalling the words of Jesus that "where two or three are gathered together in my name, there I am in the midst of them" (Matthew 18:20), the Church held its first council. That gathering at Jerusalem represented the beginning of a pattern that developed more formally later on when every so often Church leaders came together to deal with issues.

The first session of the Second Vatican Council took place in late 1962. The bishops gathered in St. Peter's Basilica.

However, in the five hundred years before Vatican II there had been only two councils. The Council of Trent (1545–1563) followed on the heels of the Protestant Reformation. Vatican Council I (1869–1870), which defined papal infallibility, ended abruptly because of the overthrow of the Papal States. Since Trent, the Vatican had become an intricate bureaucracy. Vatican offices were in place to run the Church and to decide on important matters. Under Pope Pius XII, many non-Europeans worked in Vatican offices as representatives from throughout the world.

When John XXIII announced that he wanted to hold a council, he received an unexpected response. Many officials in the Vatican opposed it. They felt that after the First Vatican Council the Church no longer needed councils since Vatican I had greatly strengthened the position of the pope and the Vatican. The pope, with the help of his staff, could settle any issue without the messy, wide-ranging consultation that a council entails. However, Pope John with his outgoing personality, courage, and foresight saw things differently. Pope John said that the Church is not a museum. Rather, she is a loving mother who has much to share with her children. He desired to throw open the windows of the Vatican to allow fresh air into its corridors. Since historically a council was the instrument the Church had used to bring about thoughtful change, Pope John XXIII took the risk of calling for a council. He set a date for the opening session and told those responsible to get materials together in time.

The council began on October 11, 1962, when 2,500 bishops from all over the world processed for two hours through Saint Peter's piazza into the largest church in the world. Their faces represented all the colors and continents of the world. Among the bishops were over 500 from South America, 118 from Africa, and 126 from Asia. This diversity was a monumental change from Vatican Council I, where, of the eight hundred participants, only fifty-five were non-Europeans, with no Africans or Asians among them. At the end of the procession Pope John was carried aloft for all to see. Tears accompanied his smiles, as he was overjoyed that his council had finally begun.

During his sermon at the liturgy beginning the council, the pope first warned against the "prophets of doom" who could see only the "darkness burdening the face of the earth." John XXIII said that such people were acting as if they had learned nothing from history, the great teacher of life. He then went on to set out his intentions for the council. It was not to define new doctrines or dogmas. Instead, the Church needed to "bring herself up to date where required." He desired ***aggiornamento*** in the Church, an Italian word meaning to make things ready for today—today's needs, today's times, today's people. He wished the council fathers to express the substance of ancient doctrine in new ways. As part of its agenda, he wanted the council to condemn no one, saying that: "Nowadays . . . the Spouse of Christ [the Church] prefers to make use of the medicine of mercy rather than that of severity." After his opening remarks, the pope left the council fathers alone to their own deliberations and did not return until the closing ceremony of the first session two months later.

As the council was getting underway, Pope John's doctors informed him that he had stomach cancer. He felt certain that Cardinal Montini, the first man he named a cardinal, would succeed him as pope and that the council would be in good hands.

aggiornamento
the spirit of updating the Church that Pope John XXIII wanted to underlie Vatican Council II

Pope John XXIII intended the Council to be both the occasion and the means for renewing the Church. He spoke of the paradoxes by which the Church is "always living and always young." She "feels the rhythm of the times" and, therefore, in a marvelous manner "radiates new light, achieves new conquests, while remaining identical with herself, faithful to the divine image impressed on her countenance by her Spouse, Who loves her and protects her, Christ Jesus" (*Bull of Convocation: December 25, 1961*).

U.S. Catholic Bishops, *The Church in Our Day* (1967), #11.

Pope John Sets the Tone for the Council

fyi!

Sister Mary Luke Tobin was one of the women who attended the council. At the Shrine of the Immaculate Conception in Washington, D.C., on the right side of the main altar there is a mosaic of some of those who attended Vatican Council II. Sister Mary Luke is in the mosaic standing next to Pope John XXIII.

www.

Visit **www. national shrineinteractive.com** to go on a virtual tour of the Shrine of the Immaculate Conception.

Many people thought that the council would make few changes. They imagined that the world's bishops would simply enjoy meeting their friends from seminary days and would quickly ratify the documents prepared by various commissions before the council began. As it turned out, the bishops overwhelmingly rejected such a scenario. In fact, the very first meeting ended after fifteen minutes because two cardinals asked for time to consult with other bishops about membership on the commissions. When presented with opportunities to vote on prepared documents, the vast majority of bishops voted against the documents presented to them. As a result, everyone involved went scrambling to study matters anew. Bishops themselves attended evening gatherings at which leading theologians explained recent developments in liturgical studies, biblical studies, and theologies in the Church.

By staying away from the council, the pope assured the bishops that the process would be a more democratic one. Watching the proceedings on close-circuit television, Pope John enjoyed seeing the free exchange of ideas that was taking place and the way bishops were now working together and even challenging one another. Although only Catholic bishops could speak during the formal sessions, representatives from other denominations and religions attended the council as observers. Some bishops noted that, at the council, exchanges during coffee breaks were often more fruitful than the formal presentations.

Fifteen women were originally chosen to be official *auditors* (listeners) at the council. The women auditors received some of the best seats at the council. One woman auditor later reported that while she was to be a listener at formal sessions, she was encouraged to be an active participant in commissions and other working groups of the council. By the third session of the council, the women auditors were placed on committees working on the documents. Through this committee work, their views were included in the vision of the Church that came out of the council.

Bishop Peter Cule of Mostar

The following incident demonstrates how Pope John's style set the tone for the council. A month into the first session, Yugoslavian bishop, Bishop Peter Cule of Mostar, addressed the members about his belief that the name of Saint Joseph should be added to the canon of the Mass. All speeches were to be delivered in Latin and limited to a certain amount of time. The Yugoslavian bishop spoke haltingly and in a nervous manner, continuing on past his allotted time. He was hard to understand, and the bishops were losing patience with his ramblings. The president of the council finally interrupted him and said, "Complete your holy and eloquent speech. We all love Saint Joseph." Soon after, the president turned off the microphone, and Bishop Cule returned to his seat with his speech unfinished. Pope John, who was watching these proceedings, knew the bishop personally. He knew that the bishop's speech problem resulted from four years spent in a concentration camp and from his torture at the hands of Communists. One time the bishop had even been put on a train that

Discussion

Name three characteristics of today's world that the Church would benefit from adopting and three characteristics that the Church should criticize. Give reasons.

was deliberately crashed, with the intention of killing everyone on board. The bishop survived with two broken hips. Although he was in poor health, he had come to the council specifically to make his plea on behalf of Saint Joseph. Three days after Bishop Cule's speech, Pope John announced to the world that he had made a decision. Effective December 8, 1962, the name of Saint Joseph was to be inserted in the canon of the Mass.

The Death of Pope John XXIII

When the first session of the council ended, some people pronounced it a failure, since the bishops had agreed on no decrees. Pope John, however, gave a closing address in which he expressed how pleased he was at the work accomplished. He pointed out that starting slowly afforded the bishops an opportunity to get to know each other. Disagreements were an important step in the council's process. Meanwhile, the Church had to use all of its resources to bring Christ to the world. The council was to begin again in September of 1963. However, Pope John's health continued to deteriorate over the early part of the year. Surrounded by his family and friends, "good Pope John" died on June 3, 1963, at the age of eighty-one. Whether the council continued would be the decision of his successor.

At his death Pope John XXIII was deeply mourned by people near and far, by people of all faiths worldwide.

Review

1. What is the meaning of *aggiornamento*?

2. What type of direct involvement did Pope John XXIII make in deliberations of Vatican Council II? What effect did this have on council deliberations?

3. How did Pope John XXIII respond to the work of the first session?

THE IMPACT OF VATICAN II

Anyone born after 1960 grew up in the post-Vatican II Church. There are Catholics who remember when *the Church* meant priests and nuns, when the Mass was entirely in Latin, when a Catholic wouldn't dare set foot in the church of another religion, and when not eating meat on Fridays was a Catholic's most distinguishing characteristic. In hindsight, the seeds of change were planted before Vatican II, the council promoted the growth, and major developments have continued to take place in the Church up to the present time.

The Council Was More than Its Documents

While the council produced sixteen documents, the impact of the council cannot be reduced to its documents. The council carried with it a spirit of inquiry and self-reflection, an attitude of dialogue, and an openness to change that went beyond the walls of Saint Peter's Basilica where the bishops met. As word leaked out about discussions taking place within Saint Peter's, Catholics in many parts of the world were buzzing about topics related to their religion that they had taken for granted a few years earlier. Lively discussion and anticipation were the order of the day. It was an exciting time to be Catholic.

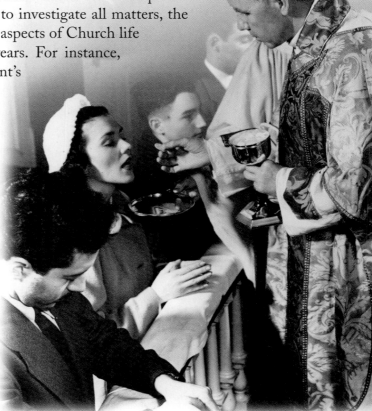

The way Communion is received was just one of numerous ritual changes that followed the council.

No one knew where the Holy Spirit would lead the Church. When the bishops voted on a particular statement or called for further debate on a controversial issue, they were never completely certain what all the consequences would be. Realizing that they did not have time to investigate all matters, the bishops designated commissions to study various aspects of Church life and to recommend changes over the coming years. For instance, commissions were formed to update each sacrament's theology and practice. The efforts of these commissions would bring about changes in the rites of the sacraments over the next ten years. For example, the new rite of the Sacrament of Penance, or Reconciliation, emphasized the communal nature and scriptural basis of the sacrament, which were barely noticeable in its previous form. As a result of changes to this sacrament, during the 1970s young Catholics learned about "celebrating the Sacrament of Reconciliation" while older Catholics talked about "going to confession." In other words, there was a different emphasis accompanying the newer experience of the sacrament compared to the former experience. The same can be said for each of the sacraments, as well as for many other Church practices.

Only St. Peter's Basilica could hold the large number of bishops and other participants and observers at the Second Vatican council.

The Documents

Near the entrance to Saint Peter's Basilica in Rome is a plaque naming the bishops who participated in Vatican Council II. They were proud of their work. The documents of the council deserve close attention. People seeking to understand Catholicism and to live as a Christian would find worth pondering passages such as the following from "The Pastoral Constitution on the Church in the Modern World."

The joy and hope, the grief and anguish of the men of our time, especially of those who are poor or afflicted in any way, are the joy and the hope, the grief and anguish of the followers of Christ as well. Nothing that is genuinely human fails to find an echo in their hearts (#1).

Yet it happens rather frequently, and legitimately so, that some of the faithful, with no less sincerity, will see the problem quite differently. . . . Let them, then, try to guide each other by sincere dialogue in a spirit of mutual charity and with anxious interest about all in the common good (#43).

Theological research, while it deepens knowledge of revealed truth, should not lose contact with its own times, so that experts in various fields may be led to a deeper knowledge of the faith (#62).

Austin Flannery, *Vatican Council II* (Collegeville, Minn.: Liturgical Press, 1977.

Review

1. In what sense was Vatican Council II greater than the documents it produced?

2. What changes continued to occur in the Church for years following the council?

3. How did younger Catholics view the Sacrament of Reconciliation compared to the way older Catholics were accustomed to viewing it?

Titles	Themes	Implications
Constitution on the Sacred Liturgy	• expresses principles for liturgical renewal that laid the groundwork for the many liturgical reforms that have followed the council *ex Most important*	• Liturgy becomes an impetus for ecumenism. • Revisions are made to the rituals of the Mass and the sacraments. • The language of the people replaces Latin in rites for the sacraments and liturgy. • Official liturgy and sacraments are emphasized over sacramentals. • Church art, architecture, and decorations focus on the liturgy.
Decree on the Means of Social Communication	• discusses the importance of communications for continuing human progress and the contribution that Catholics in particular might make	• Church leaders more clearly recognize the power of the media.
Dogmatic Constitution on the Church *(Lumen Gentium)*	• promotes an understanding of the Church that highlights mystery, ecumenism, shared authority, the laity, and the need for reform and renewal	• There is increased participation of laypeople in the Church. • There is an increased respect for those not of the Catholic faith.
Decree on the Catholic Eastern Churches	• praises the theological and liturgical heritage of those Churches in the East that have remained united with Rome	• There is greater recognition that "Catholicism" is more than just "Roman Catholicism."
Decree on Ecumenism	• acknowledges blame on all sides for the controversies underlying divisions among Christians; seeks dialogue and unity with "our separated brethren"	• Catholics on all levels engage more strongly in inter-religious dialogue.
Decree on the Pastoral Office of Bishops in the Church	• defines the authority and duties of bishops in their own dioceses, in their regional gatherings, and in the Church as a whole	• The collegial role of bishops receives greater clarification and is increased.
Decree on the Up-to-Date Renewal of Religious Life	• calls for reforms in institutional structures and regulations, but sees the key to renewal as the practice of the vows of poverty, chastity, and obedience	• Members of religious orders are encouraged to study original spirit of their founder.
Decree on the Training of Priests	• calls for sound formation of priests, including particular attention to high standards in academic, spiritual, and pastoral training	• The unity of priests and people is emphasized.
Declaration on Christian Education	• affirms the importance of Christian education in home, school, and church and calls for an updating of methods in line with the social sciences	• Greater numbers of laypeople and non-ordained religious receive professional theological training. • Parishes increase religious education opportunities for adults. • Religious education on all levels experiment with various techniques.

Titles	Themes	Implications
Declaration on the Relation of the Church to Non-Christian Religions	• calls for openness toward and cooperation with the major religions of the world	• Respect and dialogue replace fear of and hostility toward other religions.
Dogmatic Constitution on Divine Revelation	• defines how Scripture and Tradition function as the primary expressions of Christian revelation; notable for its acceptance of up-to-date methods in Scripture study and in theology	• There is deepened appreciation for nature and the non-human world as good. • There is recognition that all people can come to know God. • Scripture and Tradition are reaffirmed and understood. • Scientific analysis of Scripture is increased.
Decree on the Apostolate of Laypeople	• encourages the laity to live a spiritual life and to proclaim the gospel through family, work, and social action	• The role of the laity continues to expand in the Church.
Declaration of Religious Liberty	• argues that the basic dignity of human beings demands freedom from coercion in matters of religion. All people should be free to worship according to their own conscience.	• Human dignity, freedom, and primacy of conscience all become key themes in Catholicism. • Church teaching advocates freedom of religion.
Decree on the Church's Missionary Activity	• stresses the importance of the missionary outreach of the Church, particularly through the formation of community in local churches	• New styles of missionary activity that are more accepting of and respectful toward local cultures are developed.
Decree on the Ministry and Life of Priests	• clarifies the duties of priests and their relations with bishops and laypeople	• All priests reflect the priesthood of Jesus. • Priests should foster greater involvement of laypeople in the life of the Church.
Pastoral Constitution on the Church in the Modern World *(Gaudium et Spes)*	• portrays the Church as being in service to the world; presents in particular the Church's positions concerning family, culture, economics, politics, and peace	• Church leaders advocate balance between holding onto the past and openness to new ideas, symbols, and change. • The Church is recognized as a voice of challenge and hope. • The Church endorses certain characteristics associated with the modern world, such as freedom, tolerance, and the use of science. • Married life is emphasized as a fundamental form of spirituality. • The Church speaks out more forcefully about justice and peace.

Theme column information from Dennis M. Doyle, T*he Church Emerging from Vatican II* (Mystic, Conn: Twenty-Third Publications, 1992) 18–19.

POPE PAUL VI

As Pope John suspected, Giovanni Montini was the next cardinal elected pope. In June 1963, Paul VI immediately announced that he would continue the council and the direction that the Church had taken under Pope John. The council reconvened in September of 1963. In his opening address Pope Paul laid out his understanding of the council's four principal aims: First, the Church must impart to herself and to the world a new awareness of her inner nature; second, there must be a renewal and reform of the Church; third, the Church should work to bring about Christian unity; and finally, the Church should be in dialogue with today's world. These aims resonate through many of the council's documents and continue to resonate through the Church today.

An Advocate of Ecumenism

As Pope Paul announced the goal of Christian unity, he turned to face the area where observer-delegates from other Christian communities were seated. He said that their presence at the council stirred great hope in his heart, as well as a feeling of sadness at their separation. "If we are to blame in any way for that separation," he said to them, "we humbly beg God's forgiveness, and ask pardon, too, of our brethren who feel themselves to have been injured by us." His statement shocked those who insisted that the Church has no stain or blemish but was greeted by the majority of those listening with great joy. It was one of the more important moments of the council.

Pope Paul became the most traveled pope up to his time. Many of his journeys included meetings with leaders of other religions. In 1964 he traveled to the Holy Land where he met with the Orthodox Patriarch of Constantinople. It was at this historic meeting that the two leaders removed the mutual excommunications that had been in place since 1054, the year of the East–West Schism. In 1969 Pope Paul addressed the World Council of Churches, the largest body representing Christians in the world. He also continued to seek open exchanges with Communist leaders as Pope John had done before him. To improve relations between the Church and the Communist governments in Eastern Europe he took a more open stance toward them, called *ostpolitik*. In this way he hoped to gain some religious freedom for Christians living under Communism.

The Pope of Social Justice

Pope Paul VI's mother and father had been heavily involved in charitable work and in politics. His father was co-founder of the Italian Popular Party and was one of the first Catholics allowed to run for public office after the pope permitted Catholics to participate in Italian politics. Even as a child, therefore, Pope Paul heard about problems facing workers who were poor. When he became archbishop of Milan, he dedicated himself to the workers of the city, celebrating Mass with them in factories and holding meetings where the Church's teachings on social justice could receive a fair hearing.

Upon becoming pope, Paul VI composed a number of documents that contain some of the Church's hardest-hitting statements about justice and concern for those who are poor. In 1968 Pope Paul traveled to Bogota, Colombia, where he delivered his message about the needs of those who are poor. Later that same year, the bishops of Latin America met in Colombia to discuss how Vatican Council II could be applied to their area. They realized that the great gulf between the few who were extremely rich and the many who were extremely poor was the "sign of the times" that they needed to address throughout their countries.

These Latin American bishops realized that the gospel message could not be separated from the work of justice; the good news of Christ had to be good news for people who were poor in their specific social and economic circumstances. Second, people who are poor need to develop a sense of their own dignity and grow in power. This conclusion meant that Church leaders needed to begin working directly with those who are poor rather than trying to coerce rich people and government officials to offer charity to those who are poor. Some Church leaders who took this stance came to be viewed as enemies of the state or of wealthy landowners. Over the next few decades, Catholics involved with those who were poor were martyred for the work they were doing. The bishops also realized that poverty in Latin America was tied to a broad system that created wealth for some but that kept large numbers of people poor. Thus, the bishops started looking at economic systems and social structures. For example, North American companies owned large tracts of land in South America. These companies used cheap labor to produce coffee, sugar, and fruit to be shipped to North American markets. The bishops realized that any program for helping people who are poor needed to analyze how economic systems operated.

Youth News

Observe. Judge. Act. These steps can still help you as you examine social justice issues. In *Sharing Catholic Social Teaching,* the seven main themes presented are life and dignity of the human person; call to family, community, and participation; rights and responsibilities; option for the poor and vulnerable; the dignity of work and the rights of workers; solidarity; and care for God's creation. In which area(s) are you looking, judging, and doing something? If not you, who? If not now, when?

Activity

Read one of the following documents that reflect Pope Paul VI's vision of justice. Select one passage from the document and create a collage, a drawing, or a poem that would reflect its message.

- "On the Development of Peoples" *(Popularum Progessio)*
- "A Call to Action: Letter on the Eightieth Anniversary of *Rerum Novarum"*
- "Justice in the World"

Active participation of the assembly is a significant and blessed result of the liturgical changes inspired by Vatican II.

The Pope of Liturgical Reform

For most Catholics of the 1960s and '70s, liturgical renewal was the most evident sign that the Church was changing. The Mass and the sacraments were celebrated completely in the language of the people. The altar looked like and served the function of a table around which the community gathered, rather than being exclusively a place of sacrifice. Before Vatican II laypeople were expected to remain silent whenever they were in church, including during the liturgy. After Vatican II people could recite responses, offer intercessions, and greet one another during the sign of peace. Before Vatican II, choirs sang most of the music during the Masses. After Vatican II liturgies began to include more congregational singing led by choirs or a cantor.

One significant change in the liturgy that reflected a general change in emphasis within Catholicism was the emphasis placed on the Scripture readings. The Church switched from a one-year cycle of two readings to a three-year cycle of three Scripture readings—all proclaimed in the language of the people. Therefore, Catholics were exposed to the richness of the Scriptures as they never had been before.

Before Paul VI was pope the sanctuary of a church was exclusively the place of the priest along with the few altar boys who served him. Since the time of Paul VI, laypeople share the sacred space around the altar as lectors and Eucharistic ministers.

Pope Paul also restored the ministry of **permanent deacons** for Church service. Since early in Church history, being a deacon was a step toward being ordained as a priest. With the changes directed by Pope Paul, men—including married men—could be ordained as permanent deacons.

permanent deacons
men ordained to assist the bishop and priests in various pastoral duties and ministries of hospitality and charity

In 1992 the Vatican authorized the bishop of each diocese to decide whether girls would be allowed to be altar servers. In the United States, most dioceses now have altar servers of both genders.

Activity

Interview someone over sixty and ask the person to describe the Church and Church practices that existed before the changes brought about by Vatican Council II.

Review

1. What four aims for the council did Pope Paul VI identify?

2. What was Pope Paul VI's stance toward the Orthodox Patriarch of Constantinople and Communist governments of Eastern Europe?

3. What three conclusions did the Latin American bishops arrive at that reshaped Catholic social teaching?

4. Name three changes in the liturgy that occurred during the papacy of Pope Paul VI.

Conclusion

Inspired by the Holy Spirit, the bishops of Vatican Council II ushered in monumental changes for the Church. When calling for a council, Pope John XXIII trusted in God's grace and the guidance of the Holy Spirit. He believed that a council would produce great enlightenment and necessary renewal for the Church. Since the council, the Church has helped bring about positive change for itself and for the people of the world. Every pope since the council has dedicated himself to continuing and implementing the vision of Church identified at the council. While only a few thousand bishops directly participated in the council, every participating Catholic was involved in what can rightly be called the "Vatican II Church." The work of the Church following the council continues the work of the Church commissioned by Jesus two thousand years ago—to bring the light of Christ to the world.

> *Lord, who created manna in the desert and who caused to flow the living springs, who made disciples of fishermen and tax collectors, and a king of a shepherd boy, grant these Thy servants the gift of new enthusiasms, protect them from diseases of the spine, so that they may turn and bend to glimpse Your Hand at the fork of roads not taken, at the tunnel's end. Amen.*

Mary Gordon, "Prayers," in *The Best Spiritual Writing 2000*
Philip Zaleski, ed. (HarperSanFrancisco, 2000), 146.

1978–2002

1978
Election and death of Pope John Paul I; election of Pope John Paul II

1983
U.S. Catholic bishops publish *The Challenge of Peace*

1989
Fall of the Iron Curtain

1979
Mother Teresa of Calcutta receives Nobel Peace Prize

1986
U.S. Catholic bishops publish *Economic Justice for All*

THE GOSPEL OF LIFE

The Church in the Global Community

CHAPTER OVERVIEW

- Pope John Paul II guides the Church as it enters the twenty-first century.

- The Catholic Church in the United States seeks to define its role.

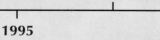

1992
Defeat of California physician-assisted death initiative

1997
Saint Thérèse of Lisieux declared a Doctor of the Church

1995
The Gospel of Life,
encyclical by John Paul II

2000
The worldwide Church celebrates the Great Jubilee Year

If you have an Internet service in your home, determine the greatest distance to which you have had instant access. Do you think of countries in other parts of the world as "distant lands" or as part of a "global village"? Fifty years ago, if you had left home on a trip to many parts of the world, you would have been out of touch with family and friends for weeks. Now you can travel almost anywhere and be in constant contact with people back home. As the clock turned from 1999 to 2000 around the world, you may have watched on television how people in every time zone celebrated the event.

The world of recent decades is a different place from what it was.

The Catholic Church has not stood frozen in time in response to recent changes. Our Church leaders pay close attention to current world developments. They continue to voice their concerns about matters of world interest. Political and religious leaders of all types meet to discuss and solve major and minor problems. The Church proclaims the gospel of life to a world community undergoing rapid change but still desperately in need of the counsel and consolation which comes from faith in Christ.

Before We Begin . . .

Select a section or a country of the world. Write a report describing the issues facing the Church in that area.

Controversial Pastoral Letters

conscientious objector
one who refuses in conscience to participate in all wars

selective conscientious objection
refusing in conscience to participate in one particular war that a person believes to be immoral

Protests against war and military excesses continue to this day among Catholic social justice activists.

As the world moved into the middle of the twentieth century, U.S. Catholics were moving into a new phase. Up until World War II, they belonged to what we described earlier as the immigrant Church. Even into the 1950s, many priests serving parishes in the United States were from Ireland. The event that most clearly demonstrated that Catholics had finally "made it" in the United States was the 1960 election of John Kennedy, the first—and to date, the only—Catholic president in the nation's history.

Remember that anti-Catholic and anti-immigrant prejudice had a strong history in the United States. Therefore, Catholic leaders hesitated to say anything negative about the way of life in the U.S. Beginning in the 1960s, the U.S. Catholic bishops became more vocal in criticizing some policies and values dominant in the culture of the United States. For instance, during the Vietnam War the United States bishops stated that young people protesting the war were often motivated by principles that were consistent with Catholic principles (1966 Pastoral Letter of the U.S. Catholic Bishops on "Peace and Vietnam," #9). They declared that a person had a right to register as a **conscientious objector** and also a right to **selective conscientious objection**. Selective conscientious objection was a controversial position at the time since many young people were opposed to the Vietnam War but not necessarily to all warfare.

Union Farm Workers leader, Cesar Chavez, led many boycotts and other nonviolent actions to better the pay and working conditions of migrant workers.

During World War II very few Catholic men registered for the military draft as conscientious objectors. With the voice of the Church supporting them, during the Vietnam War the number of young people registering as conscientious objectors increased. This number continued to expand during the period of the Gulf War when peace groups estimated that 2,500 military men and women sought conscientious objector status. Unfortunately the United States government discriminates against Catholics by refusing to allow for selective conscientious objection.

In the 1980s, the U.S. Catholic bishops produced two pastoral letters that proved to be highly controversial, one in 1983 on war and peace, focusing on war and nuclear weapons—*The Challenge of Peace: God's Promise and Our Response*—and one in 1986 on the United States economy which focused on fair distribution of wealth resources—*Economic Justice for All.* A number of Catholics felt as though the bishops had gone too far in their criticisms of the country in these two letters. However, these letters signaled that Catholic leaders were going to speak out against policies, practices, and values that they believed to be contrary to gospel values and harmful to people. The letters led to serious discussion within and outside the Church and influenced statements by other churches and political policies.

Beginning in the '60s, individual Catholics, often motivated by their religious beliefs, also took stands critical of United States policies. Besides those that chose conscientious objector status, many Catholics were active in the civil rights movement. In addition, large numbers of Catholics participated in the movement to unionize migrant farm workers. Cesar Chavez, who led the movement, was personally inspired by Catholic teachings on justice.

Activity

1. Some anti-war protestors during the Vietnam War era and afterward were Catholic. Write a report about one of these protestors.

2. Research and report on Cesar Chavez and the creation of the United Farm Workers Union.

3. Research and report on *Pax Christi*.

Pope John Paul I—The "Smiling Pope"

After the death of Pope Paul VI, on the very first ballot, the cardinals elected as pope Albino Luciani, Patriarch of Venice. To honor his recent predecessors, the new pope was the first in history to take two names—Pope John Paul I. The son of a migrant worker and sometimes socialist, John Paul I was the first pope born in the twentieth century. He immediately broke tradition by refusing to be crowned with the papal tiara. Instead, he chose to be installed as "the Universal Pastor of the Church."

Pope John Paul I died on September 28, 1978, after serving as pope for only thirty-three days. During his time as pope, he endeared people with his wonderful sense of humor and his gentleness of spirit. He gained the nickname "the smiling pope" because of his way of dealing with people. He often brought children up to his throne during official audiences and spoke with them directly. Earlier, when he was an archbishop, John Paul I wrote a series of letters to fictional characters or people from history explaining Catholic teaching in simple language. These letters were published a book entitled *Illustrissimi*. The following passage is characteristic of the compassionate spirit of John Paul I:

How wrong, dear Peguy, are those who do not have hope! . . . it is never too late. God is not merely called Father. He is the Father of the prodigal son, and sees us when we are still far off, and is moved and, running, comes to throw His arms around us and kiss us tenderly.

Letters from John Paul I
(Boston: Little, Brown and Company, 1978), 25.

Pope John Paul II: A New Pope for a New Time

Karol Wojtyla of Poland, Pope John Paul II, was the first non-Italian pope since the sixteenth century. He was fifty-eight when elected (young compared to other popes). He was from a Communist country, and he spoke many languages proficiently. He had been an actor, a poet, and a philosopher. For recreation he enjoyed mountain climbing. He soon became the most widely traveled pope in history. By 2001 he had made ninety-three international trips to one hundred and four countries. On numerous occasions he visited Asia and Africa where the Catholic Church was experiencing great growth. In 1998 he made history by visiting Cuba and meeting with its Communist leader, Fidel Castro. In March of 2000 he visited the Holy Land, stopping to pray at the Western Wall. In 2001 Pope John Paul II became the first pope in over a thousand years to visit Greece, taking an important step toward continuing dialogue with the Orthodox Churches. In the same year he became the first pope to enter a Muslim mosque.

Pope John Paul II published over thirteen encyclicals and many other writings. Under his direction, the Church adopted a new code of Canon Law, regulating Church practices. In 1985 bishops who were gathered in Rome decided that it was time to put together a new official catechism for the Catholic Church, as there had not been an official catechism since the one written immediately after the Council of Trent in the sixteenth century. Pope John Paul agreed to appoint a commission to write a new catechism. Originally written in French, an English translation of this catechism appeared in 1994 and it became an important reference book for Catholic religious education.

Pope John Paul II met with many ethnic groups at the Vatican and traveled worldwide to meet with Catholics, other Christians, and people of other faiths.

Besides his travels and his writings, another aspect of Church life in which Pope John Paul II made a great contribution was his naming of saints. He declared nearly one thousand people as "blessed" and over four hundred people "saints." Catholics from around the globe now have officially recognized saints from their own cultures.

Every pope since Vatican Council II has dedicated his papacy to continuing its work. In 2001 Pope John Paul II continued this tradition by stating:

> With the passing of the years, *the council documents have lost nothing of their value or brilliance* . . . Now that the Jubilee has ended, I feel more than ever in duty bound to point to *the Council as the great grace bestowed on the Church in the 20th century:* There we find a sure compass by which to take our bearings in the century now beginning.
>
> *"Apostolic Letter Novo Millenio Ineunte for the Closing of the Jubilee of the Year 2000,"* #57, italics added for emphasis.

Lech Walesa of Poland led the country in overthrowing Communism.

Pope John Paul II and the Fall of Communism

The contribution to the modern world for which Pope John Paul II received greatest recognition is also one of the most important events of the twentieth century—the end of Communism in the former Soviet Union and in Eastern Europe in the 1990s. Certainly, people in these countries rejected Communism for a variety of reasons: Workers felt violated and not treated with dignity; Communism proved to be economically inefficient; and because of its strident atheistic stance, Communism left a spiritual void. In the pope's native country of Poland, a peculiar state of affairs existed. While the government officially endorsed atheism, the people themselves were over ninety-five percent Catholic. Catholic leaders were the foremost proponents of an alternative to Communism in Poland. Pope John Paul II worked publicly and behind the scenes to bring about a loosening of control by Communist leaders. Eventually, Communism lost its hold on Poland, then on the rest of Eastern Europe and Russia.

Activity

Present a report, poem, video, or electronic slide presentation on the life of Pope John Paul II or describe key points made in one of his writings.

Review

1. How did the place of Catholics in U.S. society change from the late 1940s to the '60s?

2. Give three examples of how Catholic leaders, beginning in the late 1960s, became critical of U.S. society.

3. Name two protest movements in which individual Catholics participated, beginning in the '60s.

4. Name three characteristics that made Pope John Paul II unique among modern popes.

5. List four ways that Pope John Paul II contributed to the modern world.

A VOICE FOR LIFE

Oscar Romero continues to be honored in El Salvador. As the sign indicates, the people continue to follow his example.

From the beginning of his papacy, Pope John Paul II was aware that Christianity would soon be celebrating two thousand years of existence. He wanted to lead the Catholic Church into the new millennium as a vibrant community, one ever faithful to Christ. As he had led the Polish Church against Communism, so he intended to lead the universal Church to be a voice for life wherever there was what he called a "culture of death." In recent decades many people have worked within the Church and through the Church to proclaim life against the forces of death.

The Church in El Salvador

In recent decades, the Latin American Church has had more than its share of martyrs. Perhaps the continent's most well-known martyr was the archbishop of San Salvador, Oscar Romero, who died a martyr's death on March 24, 1980.

At the beginning of his ministry, Romero was not a likely candidate for martyrdom. As a priest, he believed that his role was to live a life of personal holiness. He condemned priests who became involved in social issues, calling such actions "the politicization of the priesthood." When named bishop of Santiago de Maria in 1972, Romero had Jesuits removed from the national seminary because they spoke out on economic and social issues. Thus, government officials saw him as docile and unthreatening. Romero was named archbishop of San Salvador, capital of El Salvador, in 1977. The very week that Romero was installed as archbishop, government troops began a series of massacres. Romero protested the killings, but meekly and respectfully. He urged charity on the part of the government and restraint on the part of the clergy.

Archbishop Romero's attitude changed radically when a priest friend, Father Rutilio Grande, was killed during one of the massacres and his body was dumped on top of the garbage heap where the government dumped their victims to warn others about the consequences of rebellion. Romero knew Father Grande was a good and committed priest who was always balanced and sensible in his work with those who were poor. After Father Grande's death, Archbishop Romero became an active voice for those who were poor and oppressed in El Salvador.

He personally went daily to the dump and gathered the bodies of those killed. He announced on the radio the names of the victims and begged the army to stop the killings. He suspended Mass everywhere in the archdiocese but in the cathedral so that people could assemble together. He preached regularly about the commitment of the Church to be with those who were oppressed.

His fellow bishops urged him to go slowly in his condemnation of violence and injustice, but he insisted that it was his duty as bishop to serve the people. He stopped attending government functions to express his rejection of its policies. Romero spent more and more time with the people, saying that, "With this people, it is not hard to be a good shepherd." He wrote the President of the United States to ask him to stop providing military assistance to the Salvadoran government. In his radio address on March 23, 1980, Romero directly addressed the soldiers in the army:

Archbishop
Oscar Romero

"We are your people. The peasants you kill are your own brothers and sisters. When you hear the voice of the man commanding you to kill, remember instead the voice of God. Thou Shalt not Kill. . . . In the name of God, in the name of our tormented people whose cries rise up to heaven, I beseech you, I beg you, I command you, *stop the repression.*"

The next day, while celebrating Mass in the chapel of the hospital where he lived, he was shot through the heart, dying within minutes. He was the first bishop to be killed at the altar since Saint Thomas Becket in the twelfth century. Romero had spoken of his death in an interview two weeks before the event: "I have frequently been threatened by death. I must tell you, as a Christian, I do not believe in death without resurrection. If I am killed, I shall arise in the Salvadoran people."

Story adapted from and quote taken from Robert Ellsberg, *All Saints* (Maryknoll, N.Y.: Orbis Books, 1997).

Activity

Debate the following statements.

1. The United States should give and sell military weapons to countries that are unstable politically.

2. The United States should train military leaders from other countries.

3. The United States should increase the amount of economic aid it provides countries where there are many people who are poor.

4. The Catholic Church in the United States should send priests, religious, and committed laypeople to work in less developed countries, such as in Latin America.

5. In countries where they believe oppression exists, Church leaders should publicly criticize oppressive government policies.

The Gospel of Life

Women Martyrs in El Salvador

Ita Ford MM

Jean Donovan

Maura
Clarke MM

Dorothy
Kazel OSU

Four women from the United States—Sister Ita Ford MM, Sister Dorothy Kazel OSU, Sister Maura Clarke, MM, and Jean Donovan—were so deeply touched by people of El Salvador who were caught up in the crossfire of political conflicts and economic hardships that they chose to live among them and help them in whatever way they could. The layperson in the group, Jean Donovan, grew up in Connecticut and learned courage and compassion from her brother, Michael, who suffered from Hodgkin's disease.

Jean moved to Cleveland for work and served as a volunteer in the diocesan youth ministry program. When she heard about a mission project in El Salvador sponsored by the diocese, she felt called to go there and to spend some time helping people whose lives were marked by so much suffering. She joined a group dedicated to helping refugees—people who had lost home and livelihood due to the violent exchanges that constantly occurred between government and rebel forces. Mainly, Jean cared for the children who were wounded or who had lost their families in the conflict. Because she used her natural sense of humor to lighten their lives, her co-workers called her "Saint Jean the Playful."

Jean steered clear of any involvement in political issues. Most of her time was spent with Sister Dorothy Kazel. They transported those who were sick and brought food and medical supplies to people in areas not otherwise easily accessed. Jean and Dorothy also trained catechists who taught others about the Christian faith. They helped prepare people for celebrating the sacraments. She wrote home that she often thought about returning to the U.S. but didn't want to leave the children whom she called "the poor bruised victims of adult lunacy."

The murder of Archbishop Romero in March 1980 did not deter Jean from continuing her work. She had personally witnessed the death of Salvadorans with whom she worked. These atrocities actually strengthened her resolve to stay with the people she had come to love. She assured her friends back home who feared for her safety that "they don't kill blond-haired, blue-eyed North Americans."

On December 2, 1980, Jean and Sister Dorothy drove off in their van to pick up Sisters Maura Clark and Ita Ford at the airport. From the airport the four women headed back to the mission. Members of the Salvadoran National Guard stopped their van at a roadblock and took the women to an isolated location where they were abused and shot. The soldiers buried their bodies in a shallow grave by the side of the road.

These brave and dedicated women knew the danger they were in because of their continuing work with people who sought safety and to have their basic needs met. Archbishop Romero had earlier said: "One who is committed to the poor must risk the same fate as the poor. And in El Salvador we know what the fate of the poor signifies: to disappear, to be tortured, to be captive, and to be found dead."

Story is adapted from and quotes taken from the following website:
www.rtfcam.org/martyrs/women/jean_donovan.htm

Activity

Research the story of one of the women martyred in El Salvador or research why the government of El Salvador found these four women to be a threat. In story, poem, song, or other medium of your choice, share your research with the class.

The Church in India

The last few decades of the twentieth century produced a number of saintly Christians who carried on the work of the Church throughout the world. None received greater international recognition than Agnes Bojaxhiu of Albania, known to the world as Mother Teresa. At seventeen she entered the Sisters of Loreto and set sail for Calcutta, India, where she taught in a school for wealthy girls. At the age of thirty-six, while traveling on a train through the Himalayan mountains, Sister Teresa received what she described as "a call within a call." She felt that God wanted more of her, namely, he wanted her "to be poor with the poor and to love him in the distressing disguise of the poorest of the poor."

Teresa asked permission to give up teaching and to devote herself to caring for the people of Calcutta who were poor. Instead of her religious habit, she wore a simple Indian-style sari. She went barefoot through the slums of the city tending those on the streets who were sick and dying. She also taught children who lived in these poor sections. By 1948 enough women joined her in her work that she sought permission to form a new religious community, the Missionaries of Charity. Mother Teresa and her sisters performed a simple act of charity: they took people dying in the gutters and cared for them, letting them know that someone loved them and valued them as children of God. The sisters found God in the face of the people who had nothing and were dying. As her work became better known, the Indian government awarded Mother Teresa the "Lord of the Lotus," an honor given to those who have aided the people of India. She received the first Pope John XXIII Peace Prize from the Vatican. In 1979 she was awarded the Nobel Peace Prize. She traveled throughout the world and spoke about the need to relieve both physical and spiritual poverty. By the time she died in 1999, viewed by many as a saint of our day, her sisters had missions in over thirty countries.

Youth News

Mother Teresa tried to help one person at a time. You, too, can make a difference in one person's life each day. Take time to talk to someone who always sits alone at lunch, smile and say hello to someone who seems to be feeling down. Want to act more globally? Give up one pop or soda each day and use the money to sponsor a child through Food for the Hungry. Your thoughtfulness and generosity will make a difference.

Activity

Obtain a book that contains the writings of Mother Teresa. Describe and explain how three of Mother Teresa's messages can be applied to your own life.

The Church in Canada

Canadian Jean Vanier was born in 1928 to a family of wealth and privilege. By his early twenties he was an officer in both the Canadian and British navies. His life changed in the 1960s after he visited a home for men with mental disabilities. Vanier was deeply moved by how each of the men seemed starved for simple friendship, attention, and affection. Vanier began visiting a series of such institutions, and in each one he found people who felt unwanted and unnecessary. He also discovered that when treated with kindness, these same people would beam with joy.

In August, 1964, Vanier founded L'Arche. In a farmhouse in France, people both with and without mental handicaps lived in community. For Vanier, Christian virtues such as mercy and loving-kindness remain abstractions except in a community context. He felt that regardless of class or state in life, no one should be left out of experiencing life in community. According to its charter, L'Arche intended to be a new type of family or community where the strong help the weak, and the weak help the strong. In time, L'Arche grew to over one hundred communities in twenty-six countries. There are also non-residential communities in which people meet to "share their sufferings, their joys, to celebrate together and to pray."

Jean Vanier

> Story adapted from and quotes taken from Phyllis Zagano,
> *Twentieth Century Apostles* Collegeville, Minn.:
> The Liturgical Press,) 1999.

Jean Vanier's message is particularly important today. We have made great advances in so many areas of life—technology, medicine, scientific knowledge. And yet so many people feel lonely; so many people continue to feel starved for basic community. Vanier decided that he would focus on persons with mental disabilities as the basis for forming community. However, true friendships and community can happen in any setting.

fyi!
The name of the L'Arche movement was derived from the house called Noah's Ark by members of the first community. *L'Arche* is French for "the ark."

Discussion

1. In what ways do you seek to meet the need for community relationships in your own life? Based on your experiences with friendships, do you believe that community is a basic human need? Explain. What qualities does a healthy community possess? What role does the Church play as the basis for community in your life?

2. The Church is, by definition, a community. Describe one historical circumstance when the community dimension of the Church was strongly manifested.

The Church in Africa

Pope John Paul II made numerous visits to the continent of Africa, where Catholics enthusiastically greeted the messages of Vatican II. In 1939 Masaka, Uganda, became the first Catholic diocese entirely staffed by African clergy under its bishop, Joseph Kiwanuka. African Catholics welcomed the "world Church" that Vatican II and Pope Paul had called for. The Africans didn't want "being Catholic" to mean "being European." Even before the council, elements of African culture had been introduced into the liturgy in Africa. The approval by the council of using the language of the people in the liturgy opened up new and exciting possibilities for African Catholicism. Africa is a pluralistic continent with tribal, language, and religious diversity. The spirit of Vatican II helped guide African Catholics in meeting the challenges of their diverse culture. Finally, the Vatican II Church took a stand against colonialism at the very time that many African nations were gaining independence from colonial rule. Vatican II's emphasis on social justice gave Africans, suffering oppression left over from their colonial past, a sense of hope that the world recognized their problems and wanted to help.

While Africa has experienced a great deal of turmoil, bloodshed, AIDS, and natural disasters such as droughts in recent decades, African Catholicism has continued to thrive since the time of the council. In recent years, however, Catholics have been both the perpetrators and the victims of violence between ethnic groups. For instance, over the last four decades of the twentieth century, over two hundred African priests were murdered. Sisters of religious orders have related tales of armed youths entering convents and killing everyone they can find. Unfortunately, sometimes those doing the killing have been Catholics themselves. The Church's teachings on peace, justice, acceptance of diversity, and faith in God are needed tools for helping Africans shape their future.

The Catholic Church in Africa experienced tremendous growth during the twentieth century.

Activity

Use the medium of your choice to report on one of the following:

- Catholicism in Africa
- Catholic martyrs in Africa
- One of Pope John Paul II's visits to Africa
- Problems confronting Catholicism in Africa

Sister Thea Bowman—A Dancing Prophet

In 1989 an African American woman from Mississippi who was a granddaughter of slaves was invited to address the United States Catholic bishops' conference on Black Catholics. Following her spirited presentation on what being black and Catholic meant in the Church of the '90s, she asked the bishops to stand and clap their hands and praise God with their voices and with their bodies. With gusto, they joined her in singing, "We Shall Overcome."

Who was this woman who could challenge the bishops to give blacks a greater voice in the modern Church, and who could coax the bishops to join her in singing and dancing? Her name was Bertha Bowman. Bertha was born in Yazoo City, Mississippi, in 1937. Although Baptist, she attended a Catholic school run by Franciscan sisters. Bertha decided that she wanted to become a Catholic and a nun. At the age of fifteen she left Mississippi for Wisconsin to finish her education and become a Franciscan sister— the only black woman in the entire order. She took Thea as her religious name in honor of her father. After college, Sister Thea attended Catholic University in Washington, D.C., where she encountered the African American style of Catholic worship that she missed while living in LaCrosse, Wisconsin. The gospel hymns, the spirituals, the dancing, and the testifying that made up black Church services reflected the message of deliverance from sin and slavery and entrance into freedom and life. This message spoke to the black experience in America.

After her studies at Catholic University, Sister Thea went on to help found the Institute of Black Catholic Studies at Xavier University in New Orleans. From this base, Sister Thea traveled throughout the country, combining musical performance, preaching, and storytelling. Her message was, "If we speak the word that is Christ in love and faith, with patience and prayer and perseverance, it will take root. It does have power to save us. Call one another! Testify! Teach! Act on the Word! Witness!" She would always have her audience on their feet, clapping their hands in songs of praise.

In her forties Sister Thea was diagnosed with breast cancer. The prayers and hymns that she offered for other people, she now needed to sustain herself. She prayed, "Lord, let me live until I die." She continued her work, sometimes giving presentations from a wheelchair and wrapping her almost bald head in a bright turban. Sister Thea died in 1990, having touched the hearts of thousands of U.S. Catholics through her spirited worship of our loving God.

Story is adapted and quotes taken from Phyllis Zagano, *Twentieth-Century Apostles* (Collegeville, Minn.: The Liturgical Press,) 1999.

The Church in Europe

After the great devastation of two world wars, Europe needed rebuilding—not only its physical structures and infrastructures, but its spirit as well. Following World War II, church attendance dropped off significantly, and a sharp decline in religious vocations occurred. Vatican II did much to reinvigorate religious fervor among Catholics, especially in its promotion of ecumenism.

Leading up to the 2000 Jubilee Year, during the 1990s the Catholic Church held six regional assemblies to address concerns and identify signs of hope for particular areas. There was one for Africa in 1994, for America in 1997, for Asia in the spring of 1998, and for Oceania in the fall of that year. The European Church held two regional assemblies, in 1991 and in 1999. At these European synods the bishops of the continent addressed the collapse of Communism in Eastern Europe and expressed hope for the newly developing democratic governments replacing Communist regimes there. They also raised concern about problems for family life and society that can accompany quick prosperity and issued a call for justice in the treatment of new immigrants. The 1999 synod specified ten signs of hope for European Catholicism and for all citizens of Europe. These signs of hope suggest that Christian values and Christians themselves will continue to play an important role in European life of the third millennium.

SIGNS OF HOPE FOR THE EUROPEAN CHURCH

1. the Christian martyrs of the twentieth century
2. the holiness exhibited by many Christians
3. the "rediscovered freedom" of Churches in Eastern Europe
4. the Catholic Church's increased focus on its mission to spread Christ's message
5. new religious movements and communities
6. renewed interest in traditional religious institutions and expressions of faith
7. increased awareness of the co-responsibility shared by all Christians
8. the growing involvement of women in the Church
9. the great progress experienced in the area of ecumenism, especially the Lutheran-Catholic "Joint Declaration on the Doctrine of Justification"
10. growing interaction between the Churches of the East and the Church of the West

Activity

Research and report on the areas of agreements that were reached between the Lutherans and Catholics in the "Joint Declaration on the Doctrine of Justification."

The Church in the United States

The Church has continued to be a meaningful part of the lives of United States Catholics. In Catholic parishes throughout the United States, teens and adults assist at liturgies in various ways and volunteer their time to run sports programs and tutor children. Parishes often coordinate clothing drives and food preparation for homeless shelters. In some parishes English, Spanish, Vietnamese, and other cultural elements are integrated in prayer services. Men and women come to parish centers early in the morning to participate in spirituality groups before heading off to work. Masses are offered daily, and parish renewal programs take place regularly. Baptisms, weddings, and funerals crowd parish schedules, offering people an opportunity to celebrate within a Church context their most important events. Parishes provide time and space for visits before the Blessed Sacrament and for quiet prayer. Bible groups meet to pray and study the Scriptures together, and a variety of Lenten services help Catholics make that season spiritually rich. Within the RCIA (Rite of Christian Initiation for Adults), people prepare for reception of the Sacraments of Initiation, guided by committed volunteers who serve as their catechists and sponsors.

Some surveys of U.S. Catholics, however, state that only about one third of Catholics are consistent, active members of the Church. Vocations to the priesthood and religious orders have fallen dramatically since the 1960s. Nonetheless, all Catholics depend on the Church to help them grow toward God and find meaning in life and death and in the rhythms of the liturgical year. The Church continues to provide the way for Catholics to encounter Christ.

WWW. Do you feel God might be calling you to the priesthood or religious life? Visit **www.visionguide. org/dir.htm** for a complete online directory of American men and women's religious communities.

Activity

Imagine that you are a doctor examining the Catholic Church in the United States for signs of health. List as many criteria as possible to determine the health and vitality of the Church. Based on your list, write a health report on the Catholic Church as you experience it. Then, write a prescription for improving the Church's health.

Review

1. How did Archbishop Oscar Romero's stance on political involvement change after the death of Father Rutilio Grande?

2. In what ways did Jean Donovan serve the people of El Salvador?

3. For what type of work is Mother Teresa noted?

4. What is the name of the religious order founded by Mother Teresa?

5. Name four reasons why African Catholics welcomed the changes encouraged by Vatican Council II.

6. Name two signs of hope for the European Church.

7. Give three examples of signs of life in the U.S. Catholic Church.

Conclusion

One day in 1999 two older priests watched as the church where they had served for many years was being torn down. One remarked to the other that their church would soon be gone. They both realized that "the church" to which they referred was not only a building. Rather, "the Church" they had known and in which they had grown up was now transformed into something quite different. Certainly, it still proclaimed Christ Jesus, the gospel, and Christ's presence in the historical and universal Church. Nonetheless, the Church of 2000 was in many ways a new and different entity from what they had known during their youth.

Pope John Paul II and other leaders have guided the Catholic Church into a new millennium. Many Catholics have demonstrated that Christ's presence in the Church continues through their lives of active participation in the Church, service, and prayer. As in the past, the Church of tomorrow will be the work of the Holy Spirit made visible through its people. The epilogue to this book, therefore, invites you to think about your role as Church leaders of the present and the future. How will your presence make a difference to the Church in the world?

Prayer of Saint Francis

Lord, make me an instrument of your peace.
Where there is hatred, let me sow love;
where there is injury, pardon;
where there is doubt, faith;
where there is despair, hope;
where there is darkness, light;
where there is sadness, joy.

O Divine Master, grant that I may not so much seek
to be consoled, as to console;
to be understood, as to understand;
to be loved, as to love.
For it is in giving that we receive;
it is in pardoning that we are pardoned;
and it is in dying that we are born to eternal life.

MAKING YOUR MARK

The New and Future Church

CHAPTER OVERVIEW

- The Church continues as a communion of saints, a communion of sinners.

- The Beatitudes provide guidance for living the Christian life and contributing to the life of the Church.

Do you feel as though you have something special to offer the world? What gifts, what talents, what personality traits do you share with others? How do you bring happiness to family, friends, acquaintances, and strangers? History is, by definition, about the past. The Church, however, is a living organism. It has a past, a present, and a future. God's presence in the world remains an abstract concept unless it is channeled through people.

Many people today have taken up the banner of being the Church in the world; saintly people are not just figures from the past. The people mentioned in this Epilogue are making history now. The part that you play in that history is up to you.

To provide some guidelines for determining what the present Church does and the future Church will look like, we will use the description of his followers that Jesus himself used—the Beatitudes. As is characteristic of the Christian life, the Beatitudes are mystifying and intriguing. This Epilogue will look at some examples of people who are living them. In the light of the Beatitudes, you are invited to think about your own contributions to the Church, now and in the future.

Before We Begin . . .

Read Matthew 5:1–12, or scan the pages of this chapter to find a list of the Beatitudes. For each Beatitude, identify one person whom you met during this study of Church history who exemplifies that Beatitude. Explain how he or she lived the Beatitude.

PRESENT AND FUTURE

Communion of Saints; Communion of Sinners

Everyone who breathes, high and low, educated and ignorant, young and old, man and woman, has a mission, has a work. We are not sent into this world for nothing; we are not born at random; we are not here, that we may go to bed at night, and get up in the morning, toil for bread, eat and drink, laugh and joke, sin when we have a mind, and reform when we are tired of sinning, rear a family and die. God sees every one of us; he creates every soul . . . for a purpose. He needs, he deigns to need, every one of us. He has an end for each of us; we are all equal in his sight, and we are placed in our different ranks and stations, not to get what we can out of them for ourselves, but to labor in them for him. As Christ has his work, we too have ours; as he rejoiced to do his work, we must rejoice in ours also.

John Henry Cardinal Newman, "God's Will the End of Life," from *Discourses Addressed to Mixed Congregations,* 1849, in Daniel M. O'Connell, *Favorite Newman Sermons* (New York: The America Press, 2nd ed., 1940), 177–178.

In some Catholic elementary schools, it is customary for each first grader to learn about a particular saint, memorize a few lines about his or her life, and dress up like that saint for a presentation to the rest of the school. Some high school students can still remember the speech they memorized about the saint many years earlier. The presentation often ends with one of the children reminding the audience, "We hope you have learned something about the saints and the good they did. Now it is our turn. You and I are the saints of the twenty-first century. We can model Jesus in our day just as these earlier saints did in their day."

Even at a young age, children can learn from the saints and seek their intercession.

In every age people of the Church have loved as Jesus did. Many are honored as saints.

Throughout this book the lives of saints of the Church have been presented. Too often saints are thought of as the exceptional ones, as people who couldn't possibly have lived normal lives. The saints mentioned in this text have sometimes been heroic witnesses to faith, and led active lives during which they initiated new groups or programs. Others have lived their lives in very ordinary, commonplace ways. However, there is one thing all saints have in common—all of them have experienced the wonder of God's presence in their lives. All Christians *believe* in God, but saints have a *love relationship* with God. You may come to recognize that the wonder of life is a gift from a loving God in which you will want to participate as much as you can— even though many forces may seem to be holding you back. Your attempts to live life to the fullest, a life that is not yours alone but is shared with everyone else on earth, is a call to holiness and sainthood.

However, the invitation is not without its struggles. The Church is a communion of sinners as well as a communion of saints. Our study of history has revealed that to us. Today we share our strengths and our weaknesses, just as people of the past did. However, we must not overlook the goodness that surrounds us simply because it is manifest in flesh and blood people rather than in characters described in a book. Families seek ways to live Christian values. In schools and hospitals, in parishes and houses of hospitality, people pray together, try to be kind to one another, and help one another out. They search for ways to be of service to people in need in their communities. They dedicate themselves to working for justice and peace, and they study Scripture and Church history in order to know God's will better. These people are the saints of today.

Activity

Write a short story or present a visual depiction describing how a fault or a weakness ends up being the means by which someone helps others.

THE BEATITUDES

The Beatitudes are challenges to our imagination. They are to be concretized in our lives so that they are not ideal truths but realized truths. They are not to be accepted or believed; they are to be done.

Michael J. Himes, *Doing the Truth in Love* (New York: Paulist Press, 1995), 143.

There's no simple one-way route for Christians to be the Church in the world. Some people find a quiet, solitary life appealing; for others, such a life would seem crazy. Some people are doers, while others are content just to be. For all of us, however, the Beatitudes are a "map" for the Christian life. By living the Beatitudes we witness to Christ in our world.

Poor in Spirit, Open to God

Blessed are the poor in spirit, for theirs is the kingdom of heaven.

Because God loves you, you never stand alone.

Because God loves you, you can go beyond yourself and forgive those who have hurt you, however deeply.

Because God loves you, you can ask forgiveness of those you have hurt.

Because God loves you, you can care for the weak, remove injustices, alleviate poverty, annihilate oppression, and restore righteousness in the world.

Because God loves you, you have the power to touch hearts with compassion, heal wounds in those around you, and act selflessly.

Summary points from the U.S. Catholic Bishops' Jubilee Year 2000 Message, *"Because God Loves You"* (from *Christopher News Notes*, no. 433, March 2001).

It is in community that we best live out the Beatitudes.

Being a member of the Church presupposes having a relationship with God and with a community; people are not Church by themselves. The first Beatitude, blessed are the poor in spirit, means emptying ourselves, setting aside our spirit of self-concern, so that the Holy Spirit who dwells within us can have room to breathe. (This is one of the great benefits of attending Sunday Mass. It forces us to be less self-absorbed and to think about the bigger world picture, the larger community to which we belong.) Jesus exemplifies what it means to be "poor in spirit" as he gave of himself totally and completely upon the cross.

Being poor in spirit means trusting in God. If we think we can make a difference in the world by ourselves, we will soon be disillusioned. However, if we realize that *God works through us,* then we trust that our actions are not isolated acts but are part of a whole. Every little act of kindness we do—to make life better for people who are hurting—has significance beyond itself. Trust in God, therefore, does not diminish the importance of our actions but actually magnifies them to an infinite degree. The Church—the community of people who trust in God in Christ Jesus—is a community of people who are poor in spirit.

Recently, a teenage boy in East Timor acted in a way that courageously demonstrated the first Beatitude. East Timor and Indonesia share a large island off the coast of Southeast Asia. Tensions between the two countries have been great ever since colonial times, enhanced by the fact that Indonesia is predominantly Muslim and East Timor predominantly Catholic. One day a gang of young men fighting for Indonesia attacked a group of people in the Catholic section of a small town. The people gathered in a plaza near the bishop's house. The gang of youth surrounded the people and set fire to the bishop's house. The people wanted to attack the gang members, but the bishop calmed them by saying, "It is just a building. Our response must be love."

Wanting the people to riot so that gang members would have an excuse to slaughter the defenseless people, the gang leader pushed his gun into the bishop's side. "Love?" he mocked. The crowd froze, but the bishop just continued looking at the fire. The gang leader cocked his gun, and still the bishop did not react. Then a young teenager quietly stepped out of the crowd and slowly walked toward the bishop and the man with the gun. He cautiously moved the bishop to the side and slid in between the bishop and the gun until the gun was touching *his* side, not the bishop's.

He, too, said nothing but simply stood there looking at the fire. Everyone, including gang members, waited in silence to see what would happen. Finally the gang leader uncocked his gun and said, "We're finished here. Let's go." As the gang withdrew, the young man melted back into the crowd.

The Poor in Spirit Closer to Home

Examples of such self-emptying are not confined to areas of the world torn by overt conflicts. For many years now, Catholic colleges and high schools have encouraged their students to participate in service activities. Some students spend their spring break or their summer vacation in Latin America working with homeless people to build homes or helping other people in need. One of the great benefits of programs such as these is that students are able to put a name and a face on people who are poor. Therefore, the students are making room within themselves for people whom they might otherwise have locked out of their consciousness and concern. Through such service activities, young people learn to be poor in spirit.

Looking beyond ourselves to address the needs of others is a requirement for those who call themselves Christian.

Activity

1. Are you:
   - Self-absorbed or self-emptying?
   - Self-centered or other-centered?
   - Aware of God or unaware of God?
   - An active participant or a bystander?
   - Involved in service or uninvolved in service?
   - Informed about problems in the world or uninformed?
   - Passionate about contributing to life or dispassionate?

   Give examples to support your answers. Choose one of the pairs and explain why you would want to be one way or the other.

2. Members of the Church have always struggled to live in relationship with God. Name one type of activity advocated by a member of the Church from history that you feel could help you in your own relationship with God. Explain how.

Those Who Mourn—Sharing the Gift of Tears

Blessed are those who mourn, for they will be comforted.

The word *compassion* is derived from the Latin words *pati* and *cum,* which together mean "to suffer with." Compassion asks us to go where it hurts, to enter into places of pain, to share in brokenness, fear, confusion, and anguish. Compassion challenges us to cry out with those in misery, to mourn with those who are lonely, to weep with those in tears. Compassion requires us to be weak with the weak, vulnerable with the vulnerable, and powerless with the powerless. Compassion means full immersion in the condition of being human.

Donald P. McNeil, Douglas A. Morrison, and Henri J. M. Nouwen,
Compassion (Garden City, N.Y.: Image Books, 1982), 4.

"Jesus wept" (John 11:35). These two words make up the shortest verse in the Bible, but they tell us a great deal about Jesus and about what it means to live the Christian life. They record the response that Jesus made upon hearing that his friend Lazarus had died. We may feel uncomfortable attending a funeral or visiting someone who is sick in a hospital. Part of our discomfort is that we don't know what to say, and part of it is we would like to make things better but we can't. However, the best gift we can give another at such times is to mourn with them, as Jesus did with the sisters of Lazarus.

Certainly we have much to cry about. Our world is not all that we would like it to be; we ourselves are not all that we want to be. As the fictional Zorba the Greek said, "Life is suffering; only death is not." The first step on the way to facing life's problems and working toward change is to cry, to be upset, to mourn. Crying reveals our humanness. Unless we're experienced actors, it happens uncontrollably; we cry because we have been deeply touched by another's pain or our own. For example, we may come to see our own failures and shortcomings. They may cause us to mourn and suffer deep within ourselves where no one else can see the pain, until by the grace of God we begin to take our suffering and transform it into something beautiful for God.

Chris was one such young man who tried to hide his suffering, then chose to transform his personal troubles into a gift for others. Chris began drinking in eighth grade. Within a year he was addicted. At first neither he nor his friends knew that he was an alcoholic. In tenth grade, Chris began to realize that he spent his entire school day thinking about how he might get a few drinks later that night. His many attempts to avoid drinking on his own lasted at best until a Friday night came along. Chris finally admitted that he needed help.

Chris knew about Alcoholics Anonymous. He even found that a group met on Thursday nights in the basement of a church near his house. Just before his junior year began, after a particularly difficult summer, Chris attended his first AA meeting. To Chris most of the people at the meeting looked pretty burned out. They seemed nervous and constantly in need of a cigarette. Chris thought that he definitely did not belong in this group. Then people began to talk about themselves and their struggles with alcohol. Some of the battles these older people were fighting actually sounded similar to his own battle with alcohol. After the meeting, one of the leaders of the group invited Chris to return and to tell his own story the next week.

However, Chris felt too ashamed to return the next week because he had done quite a bit of drinking on the weekend. But a month into the school year, Chris realized that he had to face his problem head-on. He attended the next Alcoholics Anonymous meeting and eventually, hesitantly, told his story. Chris became a regular at these meetings and also started going to Alateen meetings where most of those attending were younger people like himself. He became more vocal at meetings and found the courage to be supportive to other young people who were taking the first step toward recovery.

Toward the end of his junior year, Chris's school held a program on alcohol awareness. His fellow students didn't seem to be taking the message very seriously. Then during the discussion session that followed, Chris told something of his own struggles with alcohol. He explained how he was fighting his own battle with alcohol one day at a time. The other students listened with rapt attention. Over the next week or so, many students thanked him for speaking out. Some even asked him where AA meetings were being held. The school counselor approached Chris about speaking to freshman classes, and Chris agreed.

Chris would laugh if anyone suggested that he was a saint. He could tell you many stories that would confirm that he was indeed a sinner. However, for many people at his school and in his community, Chris performed saintly acts. He could be both comforting and challenging, as all saints tend to be. Chris—Christopher, which means "Christ bearer"—truly was living up to his name. As Chris's story demonstrates, to mourn is not a passive Beatitude. When we mourn, we are touched and we are changed. As we change, we may be moved to action. Jesus assures us that, in the end, through our mourning, we will be comforted.

Activity

1. Look through recent newspapers and news magazines. Make a collage of ways that people are hurting in our world today. Write a prayer to accompany your collage.

2. Name one Christian community in history that fits the description, "Blessed are those who mourn." Explain.

The Meek—Finding God in Our Littleness

Blessed are the meek, for they will inherit the earth.

The important thing is not to stop questioning. Curiosity has its own reason for existing.

One cannot help but be in awe when he contemplates the mysteries of eternity, of life, of the marvelous structure of reality. It is enough if one tries merely to comprehend a little of this mystery every day.

Albert Einstein as quoted in *The Hand of God, Michael Reagan,* ed. (Kansas City, Mo.: Andrews McMeel Publishing, 1999), 92.

A personal spirituality within the tradition of the Church is essential to living as Jesus did. This young man wears a reminder to ask himself: What would Jesus do?

"Now, Moses himself was by far the meekest man on the face of the earth" (NAB). We may think of someone who is meek as being weak, but who could ever call Moses weak? Moses faced down Pharaoh and led the Israelites through the wilderness for forty years. Moses weak? Hardly! The description of Moses as meek has to do with the way he saw things rather than with any personal limitations. Moses saw things as they were and then went about trying to change things—with God's guidance—into what they ought to be. If we try to follow the example of Moses, it will lead us into questioning the way things are. Such questioning requires strength—not weakness—because it may lead us to change the way we live. We must ponder whether the values and concerns that seem most important to us, or that our peer group advocates, are those that will truly bring us joy. To be meek means to be open to conversion. When Jesus said to the people of his day, "repent, and believe in the good news" (Mark 1:15), he was encouraging people to be meek. For instance, we have a tendency to believe that accumulating things will bring us happiness: the more we have—clothes, CDs, computer equipment—the better off we are. We may believe that if we could break into the popular clique at school, then we would have it made. To achieve this end, we may even treat "outsiders" at school with disdain. Meekness suggests that unless we find joy in God and ourselves, we will never truly be happy. Here is the story of someone who discovered this simple truth and faced the challenge of living it.

Javier attended the retreat because his buddy, Edgar, said that a lot of girls were going to be there. When Javier walked into the room where everyone was gathered, he thought he had made a big mistake. Some of the young people were singing religious songs. A couple of kids were looking through Bibles. Javier feared he was going to be spending the weekend with a bunch of religious fanatics.

What turned him around was the talk by Derek on what Jesus meant in his life. Derek was a senior, an athlete admired by everyone. On the way to the retreat, Derek missed the turn into the camp where the retreat was being held, so he made a U-turn to get back to the driveway. A police officer who pulled him over immediately called for back-up when he realized that Derek's car was filled with black and Latino teens. The police officer pulled out his gun and demanded that Derek get out of the car. During his talk at the retreat, Derek told everyone about his experience and about how frightened he was. He also told them that after the incident he was very angry but then began thinking about his talk on his relationship with Christ. He related that when he first made a retreat like this, he was asked to consider "What would Jesus do?" when faced with a crisis. He thought about that question after his experience with the police officer and determined that Jesus would forgive the officer. Derek tried to bring himself to react in the way he thought Jesus would, and he found that he actually felt better and freer about it.

At the end of the retreat, Javier and the others received a cross with the letters WWJD inscribed on the back. The letters stood for What Would Jesus Do? Javier decided that he would take the message seriously.

A month after the retreat, Javier was at a party with some of his friends. Some of them started to say nasty things about a couple of girls at the party. The girls were clearly angry and upset, but his friends wouldn't stop. Javier nervously played with the cross around his neck. The saying, "What would Jesus do?" flashed into Javier's consciousness. Javier made a joke, trying to get his friends to lighten up. Then he and the girls moved to another part of the room. His friends called after him, "What's the matter, Javier? Aren't you going to stay with your friends? You don't want to be seen with them!" Javier didn't turn around or acknowledge them. This time he wanted to do what Jesus would do, even if it cost him his friends.

Activity

1. Role-play some situations in which teens might find themselves facing a challenge. Show the different actions of the participants, based on whether or not they try to live by the question "What would Jesus do?"

2. In writing, name five problems that confront your community or the world today. For each one, describe what you think Jesus would have to say about it.

3. Using the medium of your choice, describe a situation in history when the message of Jesus was particularly needed. Explain why.

Our beliefs mus lead to action. Justice is more than a concept; it is a way of life.

Hunger and Thirst for Righteousness—Working for Justice

Blessed are those who hunger and thirst for righteousness, for they will be filled.

I know that you, like students all over the world, are troubled by the problems that weigh on society, around you and on the whole world. Look at those problems, explore them, study them and accept them as a challenge. But do so in the light of Christ.

Pope John Paul II, *You Are the Future, You Are My Hope*
(Boston, Mass.: St. Paul Editions, 1979), 285.

This particular Beatitude makes it clear that the Christian life is a life of action. Imagine a survey that asks people: How can you tell if someone is a member of the Catholic Church? Answers might range from "They share certain beliefs about Jesus" to "They participate in the sacraments, especially in the Eucharist." However, one of the fundamental responses to that question should be: "Members of the Catholic Church work for justice in the world." In this Beatitude Jesus is saying that working for justice is as essential for the Christian life as food and drink are.

The Christian stories presented in this book have already given us many examples of people whose lives were marked by a hunger and thirst for justice. Saint Lawrence knew that those who are poor and in need are the treasure of the Church. Saint John Chrysostom preached fiery sermons warning against those who overlook justice. Saint Elizabeth of Hungary depleted the wealth of her court in order to provide for those who were sick or suffering in her realm. The message of justice continues to ring throughout the Church on all levels.

Catholic high schools typically have clubs and activities for involving students in service projects. Theresa rose to a leadership position in the service organization at her school. She tutored children and helped collect food and toys at Thanksgiving and Christmas time. Then as part of a project for religion class, Theresa learned about some of the ways that people are mistreated by governments in the world today. She received most of her information from an organization called Amnesty International. As she read through the material, she thought that she would like to remain informed about the problem of ongoing violations of human rights and that she would like to do something for this particular cause. Her religion teacher encouraged her and even offered to serve as an Amnesty International school moderator if Theresa could get other students interested. Theresa hung posters, talked to her friends, and set a date for a meeting. Six students showed up; four of them were friends who just wanted to support Theresa. She recommended that they begin by becoming informed about one particular political prisoner that she had read about and begin a letter-writing campaign for that prisoner.

A few months later, Amnesty International announced that this particular prisoner had been set free. The small group at Theresa's school wanted to believe that their effort had helped but realized the main thing was that one less person in the world was being persecuted for being true to his conscience.

The world is truly a global village, and human rights abuses on the other side of the world are the concern of Christians right here.

Activity

1. Read through a recent Church document that addresses issues of justice. Choose one of the issues and report on what basic teachings on the issue are put forth in the document. How might young people today work toward achieving justice as described in the document?

2. Describe a time in history when the Church's message of social justice was particularly strong. Describe an expression of injustice present at the time and the way the Church or Church members addressed the injustice.

The Merciful—Finding God in Others

Blessed are the merciful, for they will receive mercy.

Often, today, Catholic education takes place in changing neighborhoods; it requires respect for cultural diversity, love for those of different ethnic backgrounds, service to those in need, without discrimination. . . . Help your students to see themselves as members of the universal Church and the world community. Help them to understand the implications of justice and mercy. Foster in your students a social *consciousness* which will move them to meet the needs of their neighbors, and to discern and seek to remove the sources of injustice in society. No human anxiety or sorrow should leave the disciples of Jesus Christ indifferent.

Pope John Paul II, *John Paul II in America* (Boston, Mass.: St. Paul Books & Media, 1987), *81.*

Mercy costs nothing, but we are enriched by it.

The Hebrew word for mercy also means tenderness, kindness, graciousness, and unconditional love. Are our relationships characterized by such qualities? Are we tender and kind, even to our family members and our closest friends? When we joke around with others, are we clear that we do so in a kind-hearted way? Do we give priority to being kind and considerate of the other person in our boy-girl relationships? Mercy also implies caring for those whom most other people overlook, caring for them despite their failings and faults. It also means forgiving when we are drawn to hatred and vengeance. Consider the forgiveness needed by the brother in the following story.

A young boy, found alone in a fast food restaurant, was chased and beaten by a gang of youth who were reportedly revenging the harassment of a member of their group. The young boy died on the steps of the neighborhood Catholic church where he had served as an altar boy.

The young people involved in the attack and murder went to trial and received relatively lenient sentences. Some people from the neighborhood were angry that the perpetrators of the crime had gotten off so easy. Immediately after the trial, reporters tried to elicit responses from family and friends. The brother of the boy who had been killed said to reporters, "My brother was a forgiving person. I'm sure he is looking down from heaven and is glad that the lives of these other young people are not further ruined."

Jesus proclaims that those who show mercy are truly blessed. Mercy requires that people bring kindness, gentleness, and concern into their everyday relationships. The family and friends of the boy senselessly killed were left to explore the meaning of mercy. For them, mercy was not an easy, comfortable Beatitude. Rather, it challenged them at the core of their being, where love for one of their own resides. Jesus leaves them and us the simple but profound message that, in the end, those who show mercy will receive mercy.

Each day brings new opportunities to be kind, gentle, and concerned with those around us.

Activity

1. Describe a situation when forgiving another was a difficult challenge for you or someone you know or about whom you have heard.

2. In your study of history, name a time when forgiveness—either giving or receiving it—was an important concern for members of the Church.

Pure in Heart—Looking More Deeply

Blessed are the pure in heart, for they will see God.

For the truth to have an impact, for it really to set us free, it must become *our* truth. It must be operative *within us*. It must penetrate and ignite our hearts.

Anthony Cardinal Bevilacqua, *"A Pastoral Letter on Healing Racism through Faith and Truth"* (1998).

The meaning of this Beatitude is two-fold. Not only will the pure of heart see God, but they will see things as God sees them. We encounter many forces that attempt to direct our gaze—just think of the many commercials that we see on television and in popular magazines. Ads can and do attract our attention. Purity of heart, however, means seeing instead from the depth of our being, symbolized by the word "heart." From this place, the core of our being, our gaze is on God and is that of God.

When a parish advertised that it would hold a program for teenagers interested in strengthening their relationship with Christ, six hundred teens showed up. The program featured song, talks, and discussion sessions. The event focused on the "three Rs" for teens: real friends, right relationships, and radical trust.

The messages the teens heard that night were not ones that they heard from their peers at school or from popular media. The teens stated that they really felt the need for God in their lives and wished that they took more time to pray. The teens also said they wanted relationships that were healthy, but they felt compelled to live up to expectations placed upon them by peers or the media, even if they knew some of these expectations were harmful. A ninth-grade boy, Tim, remarked that the popular kids at school often bragged of sexual exploits, talked about parties, and clustered in their own group. A senior told Tim, "Sometimes to be true to yourself, you may have to give up the idea of being popular. Two years ago I came to the realization that I couldn't live with myself if I went against my beliefs just to fit in. I don't always succeed at that, but at least I try."

The adults involved in the program were amazed by the depth of spirituality exhibited by the teens assembled. They were witnessing teens who were seeing with the eyes of God.

Activity

1. If you were to design a program for teens in your area that would address their concerns, what three themes would you propose for the program? Why these themes?

2. Choose a conflict that the Church faced sometime in its history. Describe how looking at it more deeply could help you understand it better.

Peacemakers—Clinging to the Dream

Blessed are the peacemakers, for they will be called children of God.

Peace is not the product of terror or fear.
Peace is not the silence of cemeteries.
Peace is not the silent result of violent repression.
Peace is the generous, tranquil contribution of all to the good of all.
Peace is dynamism. Peace is generosity.
It is right and it is duty.

Archbishop Oscar Romero, quoted in *Peace Prayers*
(HarperSanFrancisco: 1992), 130.

This Beatitude advocates peacemaking, not peace. That is, peacemakers struggle, meet with people they may not like, and challenge themselves and others. Jesus himself, known as the Prince of Peace, often seemed to disturb the peace rather than uphold a false sense of peace. Jesus knew that there exists an important difference between avoiding conflict and true peace. Here is the story of a group of women who worked for peace by tackling a conflict that had existed for centuries.

A young girl from Uisneach, not far from Londonderry in Northern Ireland, was spending the summer in Connecticut. She was taking part in a program called "Project Children," which brought together Catholic and Protestant children from Northern Ireland. The children spent time away from the troubles of their home country while learning to live in peace and harmony with children who would have been considered the "enemy" at home in Ireland. At one of the gatherings, Mariead, a Catholic, recognized a Protestant boy named Shamus. Both young people had reason to hate the other as both had lost relatives in the fighting that took place sporadically between IRA soldiers and British troops.

Mariead didn't care much for "Orangies," as her family called Protestants. Shamus thought of Catholics as troublemakers. However, they both enjoyed the chance to be in the beautiful and peaceful setting of Connecticut. With the guidance of some local families, as the summer progressed Mariead and Shamus talked and socialized with the other children in the program. In time, they didn't notice whether their playmates were Catholics or Protestants. They were all just children having fun. As part of the program, however, the children spoke of the problems back home. Tensions resurfaced as the young people talked about their experiences and how they stereotyped each other. Sometimes they became angry; sometimes they laughed at the distorted views expressed. They realized that either they could learn to get along back home as they were doing in Connecticut or else they would continue to live a life of tension and hate.

Who created this simple but effective program? It started after an IRA attack on a British patrol led to the death of three children. Following the incident, two women organized a "Women for Peace" march in violence-ridden Northern Ireland. By their third march, over thirty thousand people participated—Catholics and Protestants marching side-by-side. Knowing that bad feelings between the two groups began at an early age, the women also began Project Children. For their peacemaking efforts, the women won the 1976 Nobel Peace Prize. One of the women said the following in her acceptance speech:

> We must take seriously the words of Carl Sandburg: "Someday there will be a war, and no one will come." Wouldn't that be beautiful? And of course, if no one comes there will be no war. And we don't have to go, we don't have to have war, but it seems to take more courage to say no to war than to say yes, and perhaps we women have for too long encouraged the idea that it is brave and manly to go to war, often to "defend" women and children. Let women everywhere from this day on encourage men to have the courage not to turn up for war, not to work for a militarized world but a world of peace, a nonviolent world.

Betty Williams (left) and Mairead Corrigan (right) lead a rally for peace in Northern Ireland.

Activity

1. What groups of young people in the United States could benefit from a program where children from different cultures or backgrounds would come together to help them better get along?

2. Name three ways that you personally could live the Beatitude of being a peacemaker.

3. Describe how the following groups from Church history either were or might have been agents of peace:
   - Nuns and monks who lived apart from the rest of society or in monasteries
   - Missionaries to non-Christian lands
   - Social workers, teachers, and health-care workers dedicated to Christian service
   - Laborers who organized workers based on Christian principles
   - Catholics during the wars of the twentieth century
   - Young people who seek to live the Christian life today

Persecuted—Taking on the Challenge

Blessed are those who are persecuted for righteousness' sake, for theirs is the kingdom of heaven.

The main symbol of Christianity is not the star of Bethlehem or the empty tomb but the cross. For the ancient Romans it could hardly be imagined that the cross might one day become a religious symbol. The cross in the Roman Empire was what the electric chair, guillotine, and hangman's noose are in our world, except the cross was an especially slow, painful, and humiliating form of capital punishment.

Jim Forest, *The Ladder of the Beatitudes*
(Maryknoll, N.Y.: Orbis Books, 1999), 136.

We would like to live in a world where goodness is rewarded and wrongdoers get what they deserve. The last Beatitude points to a different experience of the world. As this book has shown, during the early centuries of the Church, being persecuted became one of the hallmarks of the Christian life. Since people are still hurting in our world—often because of some form of injustice—anyone who attempts to alleviate suffering or stands up to injustice may encounter persecution.

In March, 2001, a fifteen-year-old student from a Massachusetts Catholic high school spoke at the United Nations in New York for twenty-five minutes. What circumstances led to the unlikely situation of someone so young addressing representatives from the nations of the world? Actually, it began in the young girl's history class in junior high. She and her classmates were studying labor problems in the nineteenth century. Her teacher invited a twelve-year-old Pakistani boy to speak to the history class. The young boy's story illustrated courage and the power of the human spirit.

At the age of four, Iqbal Masih was sold into forced labor by his parents for the equivalent of twelve dollars. He was chained to a loom where he and other Pakistani children helped to make rugs. At the age of ten, Iqbal and some of the other enslaved children stole away and attended a rally sponsored by an organization that works against forced labor of children. At the gathering, Iqbal was moved to give an impromptu speech that was printed in the local newspaper. He refused to return to his owner and, on his own initiative, sought out a lawyer who helped him obtain a letter of freedom.

Iqbal continued speaking out eloquently about the horrors of child bondage. On Easter Sunday, 1995, he was shot and killed while riding his bike. Although never proven, it was believed that people involved with child labor in his country had him killed.

State your agreement or disagreement with the following statement:

- People who tend to be picked on or persecuted in any way at my school would find support from me.

The students of the Massachusetts middle school who had met Iqbal wanted to do something in his memory. They launched a program to raise money to build a school where Pakistani children like Iqbal could receive an education and avoid the forced labor that so many of the poorest children in the country experienced. They invited students from other schools to contribute twelve dollars—the price Iqbal's parents received for his enslavement and also his age when he died. They hoped to raise $10,000. Instead, they raised $150,000. The money helped to construct a school in Iqbal's hometown. Some money was also donated to parents interested in buying back their children. Though the students from the middle school in Massachusetts have since moved on to high school, many of them continue to work for the cause of child labor around the globe. The young woman who spoke at the UN said about the problem, "I know it's real, and it's not just something that happens in another country where I can't do something about it. I've also realized the power kids have to make a difference."

Quoted in "Child's Death Stirs Another's Crusade," by Sandy Coleman,
The Boston Globe (March 2, 2001).

At 13, Craig Kielburger read about the murder of Iqbal Masih, and founded "Kids Can Free the Children," to fight forced child labor. Here, at center, Craig works with other volunteers to build a school in India.

Iqbal Masih

Activity

1. Write a report on child labor abuses and on what people and organizations are doing to address this problem.

2. Give an example from history when the experience of persecution proved to be lifegiving.

THE BEATITUDE FOR YOU!

Blessed are you when people revile you and persecute you and utter all kinds of evil against you falsely on my account. Rejoice and be glad, for your reward is great in heaven, for in the same way they persecuted the prophets who were before you.

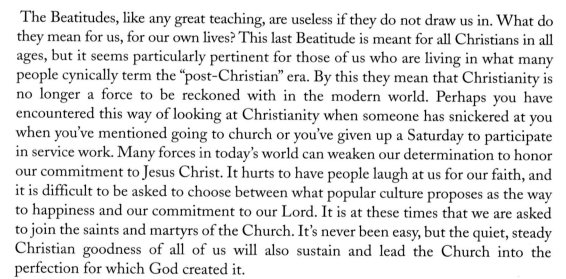

Awaiting you are tasks and goals which can appear out of proportion to human strengths. Do not be discouraged! Being Christian has never been easy, nor is it today. Following Christ requires the courage to make radical decisions, often against the current.

Pope John Paul II, (Jubilee Mass Dedicated to the Laity, November 26, 2000).

The Beatitudes, like any great teaching, are useless if they do not draw us in. What do they mean for us, for our own lives? This last Beatitude is meant for all Christians in all ages, but it seems particularly pertinent for those of us who are living in what many people cynically term the "post-Christian" era. By this they mean that Christianity is no longer a force to be reckoned with in the modern world. Perhaps you have encountered this way of looking at Christianity when someone has snickered at you when you've mentioned going to church or you've given up a Saturday to participate in service work. Many forces in today's world can weaken our determination to honor our commitment to Jesus Christ. It hurts to have people laugh at us for our faith, and it is difficult to be asked to choose between what popular culture proposes as the way to happiness and our commitment to our Lord. It is at these times that we are asked to join the saints and martyrs of the Church. It's never been easy, but the quiet, steady Christian goodness of all of us will also sustain and lead the Church into the perfection for which God created it.

Hopefully, your study of Church history has introduced you to a community attempting to be faithful to God, worthy of the sacrifices that are being asked to be made, and grateful for the blessings received.

Activity

1. Have you ever felt scorn and contempt about the Church and your Christian identity? What form did this take? How did you cope with the situation?

2. How might Christians strengthen you to live the Beatitudes? How would you be willing to help others live a Christian life?

3. Based on your study of history, how would you describe your hope for the Church of the future?

4. Based on your study of Church history, write a conclusion to this book and your course.

GLOSSARY

accommodation—the practice of incorporating beliefs and practices from local cultures into Christianity

Act of Toleration—decree by the government of Maryland granting freedom of religion for the colony

Acts of the Apostles—the book of the New Testament that depicts the actions of the early Church community

Aggiornamento—the spirit of updating the Church that Pope John XXIII wanted to underlie Vatican Council II

Albigensianism—heresy that believes the physical to be evil and only the spiritual to be good, similar to the beliefs of Manicheism

apologist—a Christian thinker who defended and explained Christian beliefs

Apostolic See—a term used for the papacy, identifying papal power with that of the apostles; also called the "Holy See"

Arianism—a heresy denying that Jesus is truly God

ascension—the full entry of Jesus' humanity into divine glory in God's heavenly domain, forty days after his resurrection

assimilation—members of minority groups adopting the values and characteristics of the dominant culture in which they live

atheism—the denial that God exists

Babylonian Captivity—period from 587–539 B.C. when the Jewish nation did not exist and Jewish leaders were exiled to Babylon

Babylonian Captivity of the Papacy—period during which the pope resided in Avignon, (France), in the kingdom of Naples

bapistry—the place where Baptisms are celebrated; originally a separate building and now typically a section of a church

baroque—a style of art, architecture, and spirituality that emphasizes feelings and sentimentality

basilica—a Greek word meaning "king's hall"; currently the term is used to designate a certain church of historical significance that continues to play an important part in the religious life of a particular region

bishop—means "overseer"; in the Catholic faith the word refers to one who has received the fullness of the Sacrament of Holy Orders; the shepherd of a particular church entrusted to him

Black Death—popular name for the bubonic plague, so named because body parts turned black from lack of blood

Black Robes—northern Native American term given to the Jesuits because of their distinctive garb

Brahmins—in the traditional Indian caste system, members of the priestly caste

canon—the authentic list of books which makes up the Old and New Testament; chosen through apostolic Tradition

catechumens—an unbaptized person preparing for membership in the Church

Catholic—a word that means "universal" or "everywhere"

Catholic Action—the movement calling for active involvement of laypeople in the Church

celibacy—the state or condition of those who have chosen to remain unmarried for the sake of the kingdom of heaven in order to give themselves entirely to God and to the service of his people

Charlemagne—King of the Franks who was crowned Roman Emperor by the pope in 800

Christendom—the Christian world as dominated by Christianity; used during the Middle Ages to denote Western Europe

Christians of Saint Thomas—Indian Christians who trace their origins to the first century

cloistered—literally, "behind walls," women and men religious who choose to live within monasteries

colonialism—the rule of one country by another

conciliarism—belief that Church councils have greater authority than the pope

conclave—a meeting of cardinals to elect a pope

concordat—an agreement between the pope and a head of state identifying the role that each would play in Church governance in that country

conquistadores—Spanish word for "conquerors"; the Spanish soldiers who first came to the Americas especially in search of wealth

conscientious objector—one who refuses in conscience to participate in all wars

convent—the residence of religious women who are bound together by vows to a religious life

conversion—a radical reorientation of the whole life away from sin and evil and toward God

conversos—Jews and Muslims who converted to Christianity, either willingly or unwillingly, following the Christian takeover of Spain

Council of Jerusalem—the first Church council which was called to resolve the growing controversy over whether or not Gentile Christians would have to observe Jewish law

Council of Nicaea—meeting of bishops in 325 that condemned Arianism and formulated the Nicene Creed

Council of Trent—post-Reformation meeting of the world's Catholic bishops to reform the Church and clarify Catholic teaching

deacon—third degree of the Sacrament of Holy Orders; an assistant to a bishop or a priest; in the early Church, someone appointed to serve those who were poor or otherwise needy in the community

deism—belief that God created the world and then left it to run according to natural laws

Desert Fathers—Christian men who lived alone in desert territories of northern Africa and the Middle East in order to sacrifice their lives to Christ

devotional Catholicism—practices of religious piety among Catholics

diaspora—scattering of the Israelites, Jewish people from their homeland

Diet of Worms—meeting of the leadership of the Holy Roman Empire during which Luther refused to recant his beliefs

Donation of Pepin—King Pepin's designation of the central part of Italy to be governed by the pope

Eastern Rite Catholic Churches—Christian Churches whose origins were in the Eastern Roman Empire that are in union with the Church centered in Rome

Eastern Orthodox Churches—Christian Churches with origins in the Eastern Roman Empire that are not in union with the Church centered in Rome

East–West Schism—The official separation of the Eastern (Orthodox) Church from the Western Church; sometimes referred to as the Great Schism

ecumenical council—a meeting to which all bishops of the world are invited in the exercise of their collegial authority for the purpose of addressing common concerns facing the worldwide Church

ecumenism—actions aimed at dialogue and the restoration of unity among Christians

Edict of Milan—declaration allowing religious freedom in the Roman Empire

Edict of Nantes—document granting some rights to Huguenots

Enlightenment—the seventeenth- and eighteenth-century movement in Europe during which reason and science held a privileged position as sources of truth

excommunication—a severe ecclesiastical penalty which excludes the offender from taking part in the Eucharist or other sacraments

Exodus—God's saving intervention in history, as narrated in the Book of Exodus, by which he liberated the Hebrew people from slavery in Egypt, made a covenant with them, and brought them into the Promised Land

Exsurge Domine and ***Decet Romanum Pontificem***—papal decrees excommunicating Martin Luther

Fathers of the Church—a designation for Church leaders during the early centuries of Christianity whose teachings collectively formulated Christian doctrine and practices

feudalism—a social form of interlocking relationships based on the use of land in payment for military services

filioque—Latin term meaning "and from the Son"

Friars Minor—the community of "little brothers" founded by Saint Francis of Assisi

Gallicanism—movement originating among the French Catholic clergy based on national rulers having authority for Church governance in their country

Gentile—a person of non-Jewish faith or origin

geocentric—belief that the sun revolves around the earth

God fearers—Gentiles attracted to Judaism who maintained some association with local Jewish communities without becoming Jews

Gothic—a style of architecture developed in northern France that allowed for higher walls and expanded space for windows

grace—participation in the life of God and the free and undeserved gift that God gives us to respond to our vocation to become his adopted children

Great Chain of Being—perception of reality as a pyramid from God at the top to inanimate objects at the bottom

Great Western Schism—the period from 1378 to 1417 during which two and then three rival people claimed papal authority

Gregorian Chant—song in which one vocal part predominates and no instruments are used; mainly uses chords D, E, F, and G

Gregorian Reforms—a series of reforms under Pope Gregory VII that addressed major problems in the Church

Hagia Sophia—Church of the Holy Wisdom built in Constantinople and currently serving as a museum in Istanbul, Turkey

heliocentric—belief that the earth and other planets revolve around the sun

heresy—a position on an article of faith that conflicts with officially defined teachings

heretic—one who holds a position on an article of faith that conflicts with officially defined teachings

hijrah—the flight of Muslims from Mecca to Medina in 622; event marks the beginning of the Muslim calendar

Huguenots—members of the French Reformed community

humanism—during the Renaissance, an emphasis on the human in intellectual and artistic activity

Huns—a tribe originating in China; one of the last barbarian groups to invade Western Europe

icon—a highly stylized painting venerated in Eastern Christianity

iconoclast controversy—disagreement caused by the Eastern emperor's decision to condemn the use of icons in worship

idolatry—worship of false gods or of an image of God

incarnation—the fact that the Son of God assumed human nature and became man in order to accomplish our salvation

indulgences—the remission before God of the temporal punishment due to sin the guilt of which has already been forgiven

infallible—incapable of error in defining doctrines involving faith or morals

infallibility—the gift of the Holy Spirit to the Church whereby either the pope or bishops in union with him can definitively proclaim a doctrine of faith or morals for the belief of the faithful

Inquisition—Church trials established to help curb the spread of heretical doctrines

interdict—prohibition against celebrating sacraments in a particular area

Islam—a religion based on submission to God's will as it was revealed to Muhammad

jubilee year—a special year of prayer and pilgrimage in the Catholic Church that takes place every fifty years; also called a holy year

justification by faith—God's gracious act of rendering a sinful human to be holy and endowed with grace (in Catholic and Orthodox doctrines) or as acceptable to God (Lutheran)

Know Nothing Party—anti-foreign, anti-Catholic political organization that flourished in the United States between 1852 and 1856

La Pietà—Michelangelo's statue of Mary holding the crucified Jesus

laissez-faire **capitalism**—economic system that advocates that people with money (capital) can use their money as they wish without restrictions from governments or other sources

lay investiture—the practice of lay persons (such as kings) appointing bishops, priests, abbots, and abbesses

lay trusteeism—control of parish funds and resources by an elected body of laypeople

laypeople—members of the Church who are not ordained clergy or members of a religious order

legend—a story regarded as historical although not verifiable

liturgical calendar—division of the year to mark events in the life of Christ

Magyars—nomadic people from the Eastern frontier

Manicheism—a religious movement that viewed reality as a constant struggle between the forces of spiritual good and physical evil

marks of the Church—four characteristics mentioned in the Nicene-Constantinopolitan creed that are associated with the true Church of Christ: one, holy, Catholic, and apostolic

martyr—a witness to the truth of the faith, in which the martyr endures even death to be faithful to Christ

medieval—pertaining to the Middle Ages

mendicant—religious communities whose members live among people and rely on the charity of others or work at the lowest-paying jobs available

Messiah—In traditional Jewish belief, someone who will become king and restore Israel to peace and prosperity; Jesus radically challenged this definition with his divine mission of priest, prophet, and king.

mestizo—a person of mixed European and Native American ancestry

missionaries—people who spread the Christian message to other people, specifically in other lands

monarch—head of a nation-state who claims to have complete authority in its governance

monastic movement—living alone or in community apart from the rest of society in order to experience God's presence, especially through regular prayer and self-denial, marked by the profession of religious vows

monk—a person who lives the monastic life

Monophysitism—belief that Jesus has only a divine nature, instead of the traditional Christian teaching that Jesus has two natures—human and divine

Muhammad (560–632)—founder of the Islamic religion

Muslim—a member of the religion of Islam

mysticism—the highest expression of Christian prayer—communion with God

Nativism—anti-Catholic and anti-immigrant movement

negative theology—belief that God can never be known by the intellect

Nicene Creed—summary of essential Christian beliefs written and approved at the Councils of Nicaea (324) and Constantinople (381)

ninety-five theses—Martin Luther's statement of principles regarding penance and the abuse of indulgences

Northwest Passage—a non-existent waterway through the northern part of the Americas that explorers hoped would lead from the Atlantic Ocean to the Pacific Ocean

Order of Preachers—the religious community founded by Saint Dominic

orthodoxy—correct teachings about basic Christian beliefs

Our Lady of Guadalupe—patron of the Americas

papal bull—a formal decree by a pope sealed with a round leaden seal (in Latin, *bulla*)

Papal States—section of Italy ruled by the pope until 1870

Paschal mystery—Christ's work of redemption accomplished principally by his passion, death, resurrection, and glorious ascension

Passover—Jewish feast commemorating the deliverance of the Jewish people from death by the blood of the lamb sprinkled on the doorposts in Egypt, which the angel of death saw and "passed over"

patriarch—leader of the Christian community in major cities of the Roman Empire

Pax Romana—literally "Roman peace"; the time of stability and order afforded people who lived in the Roman Empire during the height of its power

Peace of Augsburg—allowed each prince to decide the religion of his subjects

Peasants' Revolt—a series of uprisings by German peasants against their landowners

Pentecost—for Christians, the day the Holy Spirit was manifested, given, and communicated as a divine Person to the Church, fulfilling the paschal mystery of Christ according to his promise

permanent deacons—men ordained to assist the bishop and priests in various pastoral duties and ministries of hospitality and charity

Pontifex Maximus—the term means "the greatest bridge builder"; title for emperors and eventually, the pope

predestination—belief that God has selected some people for hell and others for heaven regardless of any personal actions or merit

presbyter—another name for elder or priest; in the early Church presbyters served in leadership positions in some faith communities; one who has received the second order in Holy Orders

Presbyterianism—a Protestant Christian religion characterized by governance by a group of elders and traditionally Calvinistic in doctrine

rationalism—a theory that nothing is true unless founded on scientifically demonstrable proofs based solely on reason and the five senses; condemned by the First Vatican Council

Reformation—political and religious event beginning in the sixteenth century that resulted in the division of Western Christianity into Catholic and Protestant faiths

Reformed Christianity—Protestant Churches emerging in Europe from the Reformation and following primarily the teachings of Zwingli and John Calvin

reign of God—also known as the kingdom of God; righteousness, peace, and joy in the Holy Spirit present in the Person of Jesus; remains in our midst through the people of God and the Eucharist, and will be fully realized in heaven

Reign of Terror—period during the French Revolution when nobility and many clergy were executed by French revolutionary leaders

Rogation Days—three days of prayer and penance before the Solemnity of the Ascension to ask God's blessing on the harvest

Romanesque—style of architecture developed in Italy characterized by decorative use of arcades and profuse ornamentation

Sacrament of Reconciliation—one of the Sacraments of Healing in which one is forgiven and healed of sin and reunited with God and the Christian community

sacrament—an efficacious sign of grace, instituted by Christ and entrusted to the Church, by which divine life is dispensed to us through the work of the Holy Spirit

Sanhedrin—in Jesus' time, a group of seventy-one men made up of the chief priest, scribes, and elders who made decisions regarding actions of the people of the Jewish community

Saracens—nomadic Muslim people who raided Mediterranean coastal areas, especially around southern Italy

scholasticism—a method of intellectual inquiry dominant in western Christian civilization from the ninth until the seventeenth century, and into the twentieth century among Catholic scholars

selective conscientious objection—refusing in conscience to participate in one particular war that a person believes to be immoral

serf—one who tilled soil in the feudal system and was bound to the will of the landowner

showing—Julian of Norwich's term for her mystical encounters with Christ

simony—the payment of money to be appointed to a Church office

socialism—economic system that advocates government control of all instruments of production, such as farms and factories

sola scriptura—Protestant belief that the Bible is the sole source of religious truth

Spanish Inquisition—the process in Spain for identifying and punishing non-Christians and those said to be heretics

spiritual exercises—a thirty-day program of spiritual practices developed by Saint Ignatius Loyola

Summa Theologica—Saint Thomas Aquinas's comprehensive systematic examination of Christian theology

Synod of Whitby—A meeting of Roman and Celtic Christians to determine which style of Christianity would be followed in England

theocracy—form of government in which religious leaders are the secular leaders as well

Thirty Years War—war over religious, dynastic, and territorial issues which involved most European nations but was fought mainly in Germany

Tradition—the deposit of faith as found in the preaching of the apostles, handed on through the apostolic succession in the Church

Truce of God—a rule enacted by the medieval Church forbidding warfare during certain holy days of the year

Ultramontanism—belief, often in an exaggerated form, that the pope alone has ultimate authority for Church governance in all countries

Union of Florence—a short-lived agreement between leaders of Eastern and Western Christianity on certain doctrines of faith

Vandals—one of the most destructive nomadic tribes; adopted Arianism when they converted to Christianity

vassal—in the feudal system, someone who is subject to and under the protection of another person

Vikings—a seafaring people who originated in Denmark

Visigoths—a Germanic tribe who settled primarily in Spain; the first such group to lay siege to Rome

Vulgate—Saint Jerome's Latin translation of the Bible; the word *vulgate* is derived from the same Latin root as *vulgar*, which originally simply meant "of the common people"

INDEX

C

and Crusades, 117–118
and images, 108
and monotheism, 9
and Spanish Inquisition, 140–141
Islamic calendar, 75
Isle of Saints, 82; *see also* Ireland
Israel, 10
Israel Jews, 10–12; *see also* Jews
Italy, and Renaissance, 142–144

J

James II, 196
Jesuits, 172–173
   and Gregorian University, 173
   and Northern Native Americans,
     221–223
   and Protestant expansion, 173
   spiritual exercises, 173
   suppression of, 191
Jesus
   human and divine, 53
   Jewishness of, 8
   as Messiah, 15
   as Son of God, 15
Jewish roots, and Christian Church, 8
Jews
   and Babylonian Captivity, 10
   and Baptism, 22–23
   and Black Death, 135
   brief history of, 10–12
   and Christian, 18
   and *conversos*, 141
   and Crusades, 117–118
   and Greek culture influence,
     11–12
   Hellenistic, 10–12
   and Hellenistic periods, 10–12
   Israel, 10–12
   Israel versus Hellenistic, 10–12
   Roman periods, 10–12
   and Spanish Inquisition, 140–141
Joan of Arc, story of, 138
John 11:35, 310
John, and Sanhedrin, 17
John of the Cross, 175–176
John Paul II in America, 316
John XXIII; *see* Great Western Schism
Jones, Mary Harris, story of, 247
Joshua 10:12–13, 183
Joyful Mysteries, 19
jubilee year, 127
Judaism; *see also* Jews
   and Abraham, 9
   belief in God, 34
   and Christian relations, 88
   and Christianity, 8, 18, 88

and Crusades, 117–118
of the diaspora, 12
and images, 108
and monotheism, 9
Palestine practice, 12
and Spanish Inquisition, 140–141
and Roman Empire, 88
separation from Christianity,
   22–23
and the Torah, 34
Judea, 10
Julian of Norwich, and mysticism, 137
justification by faith, 166

K

Kant, Immanuel, 184
Keller, Rosemary Skinner, 233
Kennedy, John, 287
King Clovis, and Europe conversion,
   85–86
King Ferdinand, 140
Kino, Eusebio Francisco, 219
Kiwanuka, Joseph, and Uganda, 297
Klein, Rev. Peter, 77
knight, 116
Knights of Labor, 245
   and Cardinal Gibbons, 245–246
Know Nothing Party, 232
Knox, John, and Presbyterianism, 158
Korea, Catholicism and Protestantism,
   203
Krier, Marvin L., 242
Kulturkampf, 248

L

La Pietà, 142, 143
Laboure, Catherine, 255
Labre, Benedict Joseph, 200
Ladder of the Beatitudes, The, 321
laissez-faire capitalism, 241
languages, difficulties with Churches,
   73
lapsi, 35
   and Baptisms, 36
   and Cornelius, 35
   and Cyprian, 35
   and Novatian, 35
Lateran Treaty, 259
Latin Church, 73; *see also* Western
   Church
Lawyers, patron saint of, 159
lay investiture, 100
lay trusteeism, 229
laypeople, 161
Leo the Isaurian, and icon, 108

Leper Priest, The, 256; *see also* Saint
   Damien
Lewis, Father John, 226–228
liberation movements, 269
Life of Saint Anthony, 65
Lily of the Mohawks, 222; *see also*
   Tekakwitha, Kateri
Little Flower, The, and modern
   spiritual life, 256–257; *see also* Saint
   Thérèse of Lisieux
liturgical calendar, 77
liturgical reform, 282
liturgical renewal, 261
Living Wage, The, 246
Louis XIV, 190–191
Louis XVI, and French Revolution,
   192–193
Luciani, Albino; *see* Pope John Paul I
Luke 10:1–3, 81
Luke 24:51, 5
Luke 24:6, 5
Luther: A Reformer for the Churches, 153
Luther, Martin
   breaking with Catholicism, 153
   excommunication of, 153
   and indulgences, 151
   and ninety-five theses, 149–152
   and pilgrimage, 112

M

MacCulloch, Diarmaid, 170, 188
Macedonia, 11
Magyars, 97
Maid of Orleans; *see* Joan of Arc
Manicheism, 61
Manning, Henry Edward, 197
Margaret of Scotland, story of, 105
Mark 1:15, 312
Mark 8:31, 5
marks of the Church, 72
Marquette, Pere Jacques, story of, 223
Martel, Charles, 86
*Martin Luther: Selections from His
   Writings*, 151
Martos, Joseph, 60
Martyr, 27
   Deacon Laurence, 30
   as heroes, 32
   Justin, 35
   Romero, Oscar, 292–293
   Perpetua and Felicity, 30
   Stephen, 27
Martyr of Conscience, 159; *see also*
   More, Thomas
Martyrs, 27–32
Marx, Karl, 242

Price, Father Thomas F., 258
priest, and Council of Trent, 169
Prince Metternich, 194
printing press, and Reformation era,
    162–163
Pro, Miguel, 249
Promised Land, 10
Protestant Reformation, 36, 149–154
    and Peasants' Revolt, 154
    Council of Trent, 169–170
    spread of, 155–156
Protestantism
    differences with Catholicism,
        164–168
    emphasis on word, 168
    and Jesuits, 173
    literal and Biblical truth, 183
    and modern science, 183
    and Northern Ireland, 196
    and priesthood, 168
    and *sola scriptura*, 164
Protestants, meaning of, 154
Provincial Council, 230
Puritans, 156
    and Maryland, 225
    and Massachusetts, 225

Q

Quakers, 225, 228
Queen Isabella, 140
Quigley, James F., 111

R

rationalism, 185
    and Catholicism, 186–188
RCIA; *see* Rite of Christian Initiation
Readings in Western Religious Thought,
    137
reductions, 217
Reformation, 149; *see also* Reformation
    era
Reformation era, 112, 149–176
    buying and selling of church
        offices, 161
    and Catholic mystical tradition,
        175–176
    Catholicism, 169–176
    causes of, 160–163
    church leaders, 160
    Church of England, 156
    Diet of Speyer, 154
    heroes of, 159
    and indulgences, 149–152
    and King Henry VIII, 156
    and Martin Luther, 149–152

middle class, 163–164
    and nationalism, 162
    new land discovery, 162
    Peace of Augsburg, 154
    Peasants' Revolt, 154
    poorly trained clergy, 161
    and Presbyterianism, 158
    printing press, 162–163
    Protestantism and Catholicism,
        164–168
    Queen Elizabeth I, 156
    and Reformed Christianity,
        157–158
    and Renaissance, 162
    spirituality of laypeople, 161
    and spread of Protestantism,
        155–156
    and Switzerland, 157
    and theocracy, 157–158
regional assemblies, 299
    Africa, 299
    America, 299
    Asia, 299
    European Church, 299
    and signs of hope, 299
Reid, Patrick V., 137
reign of God, 13–14
    and Apostles, 15
    coming of, 15
Reign of Terror, 192
Renaissance, 142–144
    problems during, 144
    and Reformation era, 162
Rerum Novarum, 243–244
    impact of, 244
Reuther, Rosemary Radford, 233
Rhode Island, and Roger Williams,
    225
Richard the Lionhearted of England,
    and crusades, 118
Rite of Christian Initiation (RCIA),
    41, 300
Rogation Days, 77–78
Roger of Geneva, and Great Western
    Schism, 129
Roman Empire; *see also* Eastern
    Church; Western Church
    and Arianism, 52
    and bishop of Rome, 57
    and Charlemagne, 95
    and Christian centers, 73–74
    and Constantine, 31, 49, 50
    East and West, 31, 95, 107–110
    Easter controversy, 36
    and Edict of Milan, 31, 49
    fall of Western, 55–58
    influence on Christianity, 78

    and Jewish people, 88
    and persecution, 31
    and Thirty Years War, 189
Roman gods, 29
Romanesque, 113
Romans 12:4–5, 42
Romans 16:1–7, 44
Romero, Oscar, 292–293, 319
Roncalli, Angelo, 270; *see also* Pope
    John XXIII
Rose of Lima, 214
rubrics, 170
Ruiz, Alphonese, 176
Russia
    conversion to Christianity, 106
    Orthodox Church of, 139
Russian Orthodox Church, 139; *see
    also* Russia
Ryan, Father John A., and social
    reconstruction, 246

S

Sacrament of Penance, and Vatican II,
    276
Sacrament of Reconciliation, 80
    and indulgences, 152
    and Saint Columban, 80
    and Vatican II, 276
sacraments, 36, 39
    Baptism, 40
    beginnings of, 39–41
    Church initiation, 41
    and Church practice, 79–80
    development of, 79–80
    Eucharist, 39
    pre-Christian origins, 39
sacramentum, 39, 40
Saint Ambrose, bishop of Milan, 59,
    60–61
    and Arians, 61
    and Saint Augustine, 61
Saint Angela Merici, story of, 174
Saint Anselm, 114
Saint Anthony of Egypt, 64
    story of, 65
Saint Athanasius, archbishop of
    Alexandria, 59
Saint Augustine, bishop of Hippo, 59,
    61
    and Jewish people, 88
    and Western Church, 77
Saint Basil, archbishop of Caesarea,
    59
    and monasticism, 66
Saint Bernard of Clairvaux, and
    crusades, 118

tradition, 38
    Protestantism and Catholicism,
        164–165
Tradition of the Church, 38
    and knowledge of Jesus, 13–14
trains, 194
Trappists, 258
Trinity, 51
    and Council of Nicaea, 52
    and Eastern Orthodox, 52
    and Western Church, 52
Truce of God, 101

U

U.S. Catholic Bishops' Jubilee Year
    2000, summary points, 307
Ukraine
    and Vladimir of Rus, 106
    conversion to Christianity, 106
Ultramontanism, 193
Unam Sanctam, 127
Union of Florence, 139
United Nations, 269
United States, and Church, 300
Ur, 9; *see also* Iraq

V

Valdivieso, Antonio, Native American
    mistreatment, 212
Vandals, 55
    and Arianism, 55
Vanier, Jean, 296
vassal, 98
Vatican Council I, 188, 195, 272
Vatican Council II, 187, 268, 272–279
    as advocate of ecumenism, 280
    documents, 277–279
    impact of, 276–279
    Jesus' presence, 272–275
    liturgical reform, 282
    social justice, 280–281
    themes and implications, 278–279
    tone of, 274–275
Vatican Hill, 7
Venerable Bede, 83
Vietnam, and Christianity, 203
Vikings, 97
    and monasteries, 97
Visigoths, 55
Vladimir of Rus, 106
Vulgate, 62

W

Walsh, Father James, 258
Walton, Robert C., 54, 115

Western Christianity; *see* Christianity;
    Church; Eastern Church; Western
    Church
Western Church
    and celibacy, 80
    and Christian centers, 73–74
    development of, 71–72
    differences with Eastern, 74, 95
    and Gothic, 113
    and icons, 108
    language difficulties, 73
    and Latin language, 73
    and mystery, 74
    and patriarch, 73
    and Saint Augustine, bishop of
        Hippo, 77
    and Sicily, 109
    and split from Eastern Churches,
        73, 107–110
    and Trinity, 52
    uniformity through Charlemagne,
        96
    Union of Florence, 139
    union with Western Europe, 95
Western Europe; *see also* Christianity;
    Church; Eastern Church; Roman
    Empire; Western Church
    chaos of, 97
    and Charlemagne, 94–97
    and feudalism, 98
    and Magyars, 97
    and Saracens, 97
    and Vikings, 97
White, Andrew, 226
William and Mary, 196
William of Orange, 196
Williams, Roger, and Rhode Island,
    225
Wiseman, Nicholas, 197
Wojtyla, Karol; *see* Pope John Paul II
women
    auditors at Vatican II, 274
    Billiart, Julie, 201
    Bowman, Sister Thea, 298
    Cabrini, Frances, 257
    Christina, Queen of Sweden, 190
    Clarke, Sister Maura, 294
    and convent, 66
    Donovan, Jean, 294
    Drexel, Katharine, 257
    and early Church, 43–44
    Ford, Sister Ita, 294
    and influence of Catholic Church,
        65
    Ireland, 84
    Jones, Mary Harris, 247
    Laboure, Catherine, 255

    Margaret of Scotland, 105
    martyrs in El Salvador, 294
    and monasteries, 66
    and monasticism, 66
    Mother Theresa, 296
    and Pope John Paul II, 44
    Romans 16:1–7, 44
    Rose of Lima, 214
    Saint Angela Merici, 174
    and Saint Jerome, 62
    Sisters of Our Lady of Mercy, 233
    teaching and living the faith, 65
    Tekakwitha, Kateri, 222
women's liberation movement, 269
World Wars
    Catholic Students Mission
        Crusade, 261
    Catholic–Protestant Relations,
        260
    and Catholicism, 259–262
    Church and communism, 261
    II to the Cold War, 262
    lay involvement, 261
    liturgical renewal, 261
    and Native Clergy, 260
World Youth Day, 5
written Gospel, 37
www.adherent.com, 50
www.catholic-extension.org
www.discovery.com/stories/history/
    blackdeath/blackdeath.html, 133
www.employees.csbsju.edu/roliver/orde
    rs.
    html, 201
www.jesus2000.com, 112
www.maryknoll.org/mmaf, 81
www.nationalshrineinteractive.com,
    274
www.rtfcam.org/martyrs/women/
    jean_donovan.htm, 294
www.salesianmission.org/salesians/who
    /lay.htm, 81
www.visionguide.org/dir.htm., 300
Wyclif, John, 144

X

Xavier, Francis, 205

Y

You Are the Future, You Are My
    Hope, 314

Z

Zwingli, Ulrich, 157

PHOTO LIST

AP/Wide World Photos —270, 284; Marco Ravagli: 5; Jim Cole: 96; Eric Herter: 111; Massimo Sambucetti: 122, 290; Toby Talbot: 175; Richard Vogel: 203; Bikas Das: 205; Mosconi: 289; Eddie Adams: 295; Barry Sweet: 288; Luis Romero: 292; Bunnar Ask: 322; **Archive Photos/Getty**—2, 3, 267, 287; **Art Resource**—Scala: 20, 57, 78, 83, 95, 101, 114, 152; Giraudon: 83, 113, 162; Foto Marburg: 101; Schalkwijk: 213; **Bridge Building Images, Inc.**—19, 21, 121, 132; Robert Lenz: 24, 174, 199, 221, 222; **Catholic News Service**—54, 280; Sisters of the Blessed Sacrament: 257; Autro Mari: 290; Dianne Towalski, St. Cloud Visitor: 296; Martin Lueders: 297; Nancy Wiechec: 312; **College of the Holy Cross**—209; **Corbis**—150, 228, 233, 252, 256; Bettmann: ix, 25, 69, 97, 102, 109, 128, 140, 144, 163, 175, 181, 190, 217, 228, 241, 243, 247, 251, 257, 259, 264, 267, 268, 271, 320; Kelly-Mooney Photography: x; Francis G. Mayer: 24, 119; Araldo de Luca: 59, 78, 142; Archivo Iconografico, S.A.: 51, 86, 158, 159, 160, 170, 184, 193, 206, 245; Elio Ciol: 59, 69, 89; Adam Woolfitt: 71, 115; Richard T. Nowitz—227; Reuters NewMedia Inc.: 76, 260; Galen Rowell: 82; Elio Ciol: 89; Historical Picture Archive: 93, 105; AFP: 106, 315; Gianni Dagli Orti: 134; Mimmo Jodice: 130; Philip James Corwin: 143; Gustavo Tomsich: 156; Bohemian Nomad Picturemakers: 165; Charles & Josette Lenars: 166; David Lees: 166, 272, 275; James Marshall: 172; Francesc Muntada: 176; Arte & Immagini srl: 190; Hulton-Deutsch Collection: 186, 270; Andrea Jemolo: 187; Edifice: 196; John Heseltine: 198; Lindsay Hebberd: 206, 239; Underwood & Underwood: 249; Mark L. Stephenson: 277; Wally McNamee: 287; Vittoriano Rastelli: 290; **Editorial Development Assoc.**—41, 67; **David E. Griffin**—63; **Michael R. Hoyt/The Catholic Standard**—298; **Hulton Archive/Getty Images**—189, 194, 245, 267, 276, 285, 291; Reuters/David Brauchli: 284; **The Image Works**—262; **Marc Kielburger**—321; **The Maryland Historical Society, Baltimore, Maryland**—230; **James M. Mejuto**—164; **North Wind**—3, 7, 28, 55, 89, 140, 155, 184, 192, 202, 219; **O.D.M., St. Jovite, QC, Canada**—224; **Photo Researchers, Inc.**—Mehmet Biber: 76; George Holton: 116; **PhotoEdit**—42; A. Ramey: 14; Michael Newman: 14; David Kelly Cros: 36; Myrleen Ferguson Cate: 66, 317; Rhoda Sidney: 120; Spencer Grant: 138; Tony Freeman: 316, 317; Mary Conner: 253; Tom McCarthy: 253; Mark Richards: 309; Mary Kate Denny: 311; David Young-Wolff: 314; **Gene Plaisted/The Crosiers**—2, 24, 25, 38, 41, 46, 58, 62, 64, 65, 68, 69, 84, 85, 105, 124, 146, 150, 159, 167, 171, 179, 182, 204, 208, 215, 229, 231, 235, 238, 255, 257, 264, 284, 302, 308; **John Rudy Photography**—110; **James L. Shaffer**—33, 44, 74, 105, 161, 234, 255, 282, 305; **Skjold Photographs**—31; **SuperStock**—3, 8, 13, 22, 34, 40, 49, 56, 57, 60, 90, 254, 264, 268; Jewish Museum, New York: 9; The Brancacci Chapel, Santa Maria del Carmine, Florence, Italy/Canali Photobank Milan: 18; Christie's Images: 32; Galleria degli Uffizi, Florence: 61; Sistine Chapel, Vatican, Rome/Canali Photobank Milan: 185; **Ursuline Sisters of Mount Merici Convent**—174; **Jim Whitmer Photography**—81